The Decline of Serfdom
in Late Medieval England

T0327462

The Decline of Serfdom in Late Medieval England

From Bondage to Freedom

Mark Bailey

THE BOYDELL PRESS

First published 2014
The Boydell Press, Woodbridge
Paperback edition 2016

ISBN 978 1 84383 890 6 hardback
ISBN 978 1 78327 128 3 paperback

The Boydell Press is an imprint of Boydell & Brewer Ltd
PO Box 9, Woodbridge, Suffolk IP12 3DF, UK
and of Boydell & Brewer Inc.
668 Mt Hope Avenue, Rochester, NY 14620–2731, USA
website: www.boydellandbrewer.com

The publisher has no responsibility for the continued existence or accuracy
of URLs for external or third-party internet websites referred to in this book,
and does not guarantee that any content on such websites is,
or will remain, accurate or appropriate

A CIP catalogue record for this book is available
from the British Library

This publication is printed on acid-free paper

Printed and bound by CPI Group (UK) Ltd, Croydon, CR0 4YY

Contents

Maps

Graphs

Tables

.

Acknowledgements

The preparation of this book has taken many years and incurred many debts. Staff of various record offices have ferried hundreds of documents, often more than once, from strong room to reading room, notably at the Suffolk Record Office (Bury St Edmunds and Ipswich), the Norfolk Record Office, Cambridge University Library, and The National Archives, Kew. Jennifer Thorp and Julian Reid were welcoming and attentive archivists at New College, Oxford, and Merton College, Oxford, respectively. The late Ray Lock and the late Audrey McLaughlin introduced me to the Walsham material, and generously shared their transcripts of certain documents and their local knowledge. Geoff and Barbara Leake likewise introduced me to the Beeston and Runton documents. Cath D'Alton drew the maps. The staff at Boydell have been friendly and efficient.

I was able to reflect upon the progress of the research, and to extend it in new directions, through a Visiting Fellowship at All Souls College, Oxford, in the Trinity Term, 2010. This, in turn, was only made possible through the provision of a sabbatical term by my then employers, the Governing Body of The Grammar School at Leeds. In Oxford I benefited from discussing specific ideas with Rowena Archer, Paul Brand, Stephen Gunn, Pamela Nightingale and Chris Wickham. A subsequent appointment to the Chair of Late Medieval History at the University of East Anglia enabled the book to approach completion, and my colleagues there, especially Nick Vincent, Tom Williamson and Andy Wood, contributed more than they might realise through numerous, sometimes snatched, conversations.

Various versions of chapters within the book, at various stages of maturity, have been presented as seminar papers at the Universities of Oxford and Cambridge, and at the annual conference of the British Agricultural History Society in 2011, where the comments and questions helped to sharpen some of the arguments and ideas. Richard Smith has been very perceptive and encouraging. Paul Harvey, Richard Hoyle and David Stone have each read early versions of at least one chapter, and their observations were highly beneficial: Richard, in particular, has discussed complex tenurial issues generously and willingly. Richard Britnell first introduced me to serfdom when I was an undergraduate at the University of Durham, and his shrewd comments on the first draft of the book for Boydell helped to tighten and clarify its arguments. Steve Rigby provided very direct, extraordinarily detailed, and highly perceptive criticisms of early drafts of all of the chapters. If the final version of the book is accessible to the non-specialist, then it is largely due to the influence, care and admonition of Duncan Bythell. John Hatcher has stimulated, debated and challenged my emerging views on English serfdom for as long as I can remember. None of them are responsible for what follows.

Abbreviations

AgHEW, III	Miller, E., ed., *The Agrarian History of England and Wales, volume III: 1348 – 1500* (Cambridge, 1991)
BL	British Library
CIM	*Calendar of Inquisitions Miscellaneous* (HMSO, London)
CUL	Cambridge University Library
NRO	Norfolk Record Office
SROB	Suffolk Record Office, Bury St Edmunds branch
SROI	Suffolk Record Office, Ipswich branch
TNA	The National Archives, Kew
VCH	*The Victoria County History*

Part I

The Decline of Serfdom: Questions and Approaches

1

The Decline of Serfdom
and its Historical Significance

The vast majority of people in medieval England were rural dwellers who eked a living as peasant smallholders, landless labourers and petty traders. In c.1300 around one half of these people were 'servile', 'villeins', or 'unfree'. These terms were used to describe peasants who were 'bonded in some fashion to a lord or a particular piece of land. This tie was hereditary rather than merely contractual or temporary, and it placed the serf under the jurisdiction (and sometimes the arbitrary power) of the lords.'[1] This general condition, known as serfdom, was found throughout medieval Europe. Serfdom constrained the freedom of time and action of individuals by imposing legal restrictions upon their movement, and by placing inescapable economic burdens and rents of various sorts. These restrictions and burdens were widely regarded as degrading, and, according to leading historians such as Hilton, they enabled lords to extract from peasant families all the labour and landed produce which was surplus to their subsistence and to their basic operating needs.[2] Serfdom is therefore regarded as an inherently exploitative relationship, skewed heavily to the benefit of landlords.

Serfdom was not present in every part of medieval Europe and, where it existed, its specific characteristics varied so much that 'serfdom' in one place could be very different from that in another.[3] 'It is such an elastic concept as to lead some historians to doubt whether the term has any analytical value … its precise form must be established empirically for each particular time and place.'[4] Within the specific context of late medieval England, serfs were

[1] P. Freedman and M. Bourin, 'Introduction', in P. Freedman and M. Bourin, eds., *Forms of servitude in northern and central Europe. Decline, resistance and expansion* (Turnhout, 2005), p. 1.

[2] R.H. Hilton, 'Feudalism and the origins of capitalism', in Hilton, *Class conflict and the crisis of feudalism. Essays in medieval social history* (second edition, London, 1990), p. 209.

[3] P. Freedman, 'Rural society', in M. Jones, ed., *The new Cambridge medieval history* (Cambridge, 2000), p. 86; Hilton, 'Feudalism and the origins of capitalism', pp. 209–21; P. Freedman, *The origins of peasant servitude in medieval Catalonia* (Cambridge, 1991), pp. 3–7.

[4] S.H. Rigby, 'Serfdom', in *The Oxford Encyclopaedia of Economic History*, volume 4 (2003), p. 463.

hereditary through the male line; they were legally subordinated to the will of their manorial lord; their freedom of movement was restricted in various ways; and servile tenants were denied access to any court other than that of their own lord in the key issue of property rights.[5] Serfdom in England is also known as 'villeinage', which in strict technical terms was a narrower and more legalistic form of servitude that emerged during the course of the twelfth century as a by-product of the development of the common law.[6] Consequently, the two words 'serfdom' and 'villeinage' are used interchangeably throughout this book to refer to the general conditions of personal and tenurial servility in late medieval England.

English serfdom peaked in the thirteenth century but then declined over the course of the next three centuries. In c.1300 perhaps two million of the five million people living in England, comprising half the rural population, were serfs (also known as 'villeins', 'neifs', 'bondmen' and 'churls').[7] In c.1400 there were fewer than 1 million, and, a century later, just a few thousand.[8] In 1536 the House of Lords rejected a proposal to abolish serfdom formally, although towards the end of the sixteenth century the few hundred serfs who remained obtained their legal freedom through purchase, a process known as manumission.[9] Similarly, in c.1300 villein (also known as 'unfree', 'customary'

---

[5] P. Vinogradoff, *Villeinage in England* (Oxford, 1892) remains an invaluable starting point. For accessible modern summaries, see E. Miller and J. Hatcher, *Medieval England: rural society and economic change* (London, 1978), pp. 111–33; R. Faith, *The English peasantry and the growth of lordship* (Leicester, 1997), pp. 245–65; S.H. Rigby, *English society in the late Middle Ages. Class, status and gender* (Basingstoke, 1995), pp. 25–33; R.M. Smith, 'The English peasantry 1250–1600', in T. Scott, ed., *The peasantries of Europe from the fourteenth to the eighteenth centuries* (London, 1998), pp. 341–7; Rigby, 'Serfdom', p. 463.

[6] J. Hatcher, 'English serfdom and villeinage: towards a reassessment', *Past and Present*, 90 (1981), pp. 3–4; C. Dyer, *Lords and peasants in a changing society. The estates of the Bishopric of Worcester 680 to 1540* (Cambridge, 1980), pp. 104–5.

[7] This figure is based upon the following, cautious, assumptions: a total English population of 5 million people in c.1300, of whom 20% lived in towns, and of whom 50% of the rural population were villeins. Some historians would prefer a higher proportion of villeins, such as the 60% proposed by E. King, *England 1175–1425* (London, 1979), p. 50, but most would regard this proportion as the ceiling, see Hatcher, 'English serfdom', pp. 6–7. Population estimates are discussed in Rigby, *English society*, pp. 69–82. The percentage of urban dwellers is from R.H. Britnell, *The commercialisation of English society, 1000–1500* (Cambridge, 1993), p. 115.

[8] The 1400 figure is based on Chris Dyer's estimates of 200,000 serf families, out of a population of 2.8 million, and of a few hundred serf families in 1500, C. Dyer, 'Villeins, bondsmen, neifs and serfs: new serfdom in England, c.1200–c.1600', in Freedman and Bourin, eds., *Forms of servitude*, p. 433.

[9] A. Savine, 'Bondmen under the Tudors', *Transactions of the Royal Historical Society*, XVII (1903), pp. 241–89.

and 'bond') land comprised nearly one half of all peasant land.[10] Yet, over the next two centuries, unfree tenures gradually evolved into contractual tenancies, such as copyhold and leasehold, whose rent packages were dominated by cash renders rather than by compulsory services and demeaning incidents, so that by c.1500 villein tenure had effectively disappeared from England.

Serfdom was never formally abolished in England. Between c.1350 and c.1500 it simply withered away. A succession of nineteenth-century historians regarded 'the end of villeinage as an event of central importance' in the history of medieval England.[11] Modern historians concur. Britnell regards 'the collapse of serfdom [as] the most important thing that happened between 1330 and 1500'; Pollard states 'the most important social transformation in the later Middle Ages was the collapse of serfdom'; and Harriss suggests that this 'momentous change' transformed the social, legal and economic position of the English people.[12] Thus the decline of serfdom can be regarded as the single most important cross-disciplinary theme of the fourteenth and fifteenth centuries, bringing together political, legal, social and economic history, and encompassing the power of lords, legal process, social aspirations of peasants, and economic and demographic change.

This alone provides sufficient justification for studying serfdom in England. Another reason is that its sheer scale in c.1300 meant that it shaped both everyday social relations and the productive capacity of the economy. Until recently, many historians had assumed that the impact of such a restrictive and coercive social structure was negative, because of the way in which it enabled landlords to coerce their villeins into paying rent above the prevailing economic level.[13] Marxist historians argue that this seigniorial exploitation deprived villeins of the resources and capital necessary to raise agricultural productivity during the thirteenth century, when the population rose and landed resources became scarce. Meanwhile, the landlords themselves frittered away their expanding share of the national income on conspicuous consumption and wasteful martial pursuits. The result was

---

[10]   E.A. Kosminsky, *Studies in the agrarian history of England in the thirteenth century* (Oxford, 1956), pp. 95–108, 270–8; B.M.S. Campbell, 'The agrarian problem in the early fourteenth century', *Past and Present*, 188 (2005), p. 36.

[11]   N. Hybell, *Crisis and change. The concept of crisis in the light of agrarian structural reorganisation in late-medieval England* (Aarhus, 1989), p. 49.

[12]   Britnell, *Commercialization of English society*, p. 223; A.J. Pollard, *Late medieval England 1399–1509* (Harlow, 2005), p. 183; G. Harriss, *Shaping the Nation. England 1360 to 1461* (Oxford, 2005), p. 234.

[13]   This viewpoint is expertly summarized in Rigby, *English society*, pp. 25–34.

a severe crisis of productivity in the decades around 1300 throughout the whole economy.[14]

Thus serfdom has been depicted as the source of deteriorating relations in thirteenth-century society, and as the key influence upon the fortunes and subsequent direction of the English economy. Yet in recent years this compelling interpretation has been subject to mounting challenge from historians who emphasize the sizeable gap that existed between the legal theory of villeinage and its practice on the ground. They contend that, despite the extensive theoretical inefficiencies of villeinage and its inherently exploitative nature, the nature and the dynamic of the relationship between lords and villeins was regulated in practice by local custom, whose action provided some protection to the latter. Custom thus constrained the ability of the lord to act arbitrarily or ruthlessly, even to the extent of ossifying villein rents at a level below the real value of land during the thirteenth century, and of providing some security of tenure and inheritance. Villeinage, it is argued, weighed less heavily in practice than in theory, and its impositions were fewer and lighter, and less vulnerable to seigniorial manipulation, than strict legal theory might indicate. If this interpretation is correct, then around c.1300 the social relations created by serfdom were less exploitative than often portrayed, and the problems of the English economy require a different explanation.[15]

Another, and perhaps the most important, reason for studying serfdom is because its disappearance was the necessary prerequisite for the emergence of agrarian capitalism, and, by extension, the transition from the pre-industrial to the modern world. The end of serfdom meant the removal of personal restrictions upon movement, releasing people to participate in a free and competitive labour market, which Marx identified as one of the key characteristics of capitalism.[16] Yet there was nothing inevitable about the 'destruction' of serfdom, which survived long after the Middle Ages across many areas of Europe.[17] So how and why did serfdom disappear from late medieval

---

[14] For an introduction to, and survey of, these arguments, see J. Hatcher and M. Bailey, *Modelling the Middle Ages. The theory and practice of England's economic development* (Oxford, 2000), pp. 71–84.

[15] Hatcher, 'English serfdom', pp. 3–39; J. Kanaza, 'Villein rents in thirteenth-century England: an analysis of the Hundred Rolls of 1279–80', *Economic History Review*, 55 (2002), pp. 593–618; Campbell, 'Agrarian problem', pp. 24–44; M. Bailey, 'Villeinage in England: a regional case study c.1250-c.1349', *Economic History Review*, 62 (2009), pp. 430–57.

[16] J. Whittle, *The development of agrarian capitalism. Land and labour in Norfolk 1440–1580* (Oxford, 2000), p. 9.

[17] R. Brenner, 'Agrarian class structure and economic development in pre-industrial Europe', in T.H. Aston and C.H.E. Philpin, eds., *The Brenner Debate* (Cambridge, 1985), p. 30.

England, and what was distinctive about the process? Do the social structures and property rights that emerged from its wreckage after the fifteenth century explain the subsequent development of capitalism, or was the latter dependent upon further structural changes during the course of the early modern period? The transformation of English society, and its formative role as one of the first in Europe to shed serfdom and to emerge as Europe's first modern market economy, had profound consequences far beyond England.

The disappearance of personal restrictions upon serfs, and the dissolution of burdensome villein tenures, in the late fourteenth and fifteenth centuries substantially released the markets for land and labour, and therefore constituted a fundamental rationalization and reconfiguration of the two main factors of production.[18] Most historical attention has been focused upon the nature and the importance of changes to the villein land market. For example, Robert Brenner has explored the ways in which different forms of proprietary rights in fifteenth- and sixteenth-century Europe resulted in different trajectories of regional economic development. Although the transformation of villein tenure into copyholds released English peasants from the shackles of serfdom, he speculated that they had still not obtained a secure legal title to their property, which enabled fifteenth- and sixteenth-century landlords to exploit this weakness and wrest control of vast areas of former villein land. This land was consolidated into larger farms and repackaged on commercial rents, which in turn forced tenants to adopt 'modern' agricultural practices. Brenner thus offered an explanation as to why agrarian capitalism first emerged in early modern England, but not in other parts of western Europe where the peasantry enjoyed greater security of tenure and were therefore less vulnerable to seigniorial manipulation of the land market.[19]

For all the cogency of Brenner's broadly Marxist thesis, and for all its success in drawing scholastic attention to the 'Transition Debate' in the 1980s and 1990s, its detail has not withstood critical scrutiny.[20] Tenants of customary land – including sixteenth-century copyholders – actually enjoyed a good deal of security, which the courts of common law increasingly recognized: they had acquired the ability to grant and sell land to heirs or assignees with little interference, despite the vulnerability of their position

---

[18]   B.M.S. Campbell, 'The Land', in R. Horrox and W.M. Ormrod, *A social history of England 1200–1500* (Cambridge, 2006), p. 237.

[19]   Brenner, 'Agrarian class structure', pp. 10–63; and 'The agrarian roots of European capitalism', in Aston and Philpin, eds., *The Brenner Debate*, pp. 213–327.

[20]   For recent, general, assessments of the historical validity of Brenner's claims see Rigby, *English society*, pp. 127–42; Whittle, *Agrarian capitalism*, pp. 21–6, 306–8; Hatcher and Bailey, *Modelling the Middle Ages*, pp. 106–20; H.R. French and R.W. Hoyle, *The character of English rural society. Earls Colne, 1550–1750* (Manchester, 2007), pp. 4–12.

in legal theory, and they even possessed a range of options for disposing of their land securely through the private manorial courts of their landlords.[21] Consequently, English landlords were not able to consolidate peasant holdings, or to introduce new commercial rents, with anything like the ease or on anything like the scale that Brenner advocated, and therefore the emergence of agrarian capitalism in England requires a different explanation.[22]

The participation of historians in the 'Transition Debate' has forced social theorists – with their abstract ideas about the transition from feudalism to capitalism – to confront the uncomfortable contradictions of historical evidence and reality.[23] The resultant exchange of ideas has also stimulated medieval and early modern historians to seek a better understanding of the complex relationship between variations in property rights and observed patterns of economic development. Places where tenures were insecure, and carried variable rents and fines, favoured the landlord, because they offered opportunities for seigniorial consolidation and engrossment of landholdings, and therefore for radical changes to farm structure and rents. Places where tenures were secure, with relatively low and fixed rents, favoured the tenant, and therefore offered greater protection against commercial forces and seigniorial intervention in the land market.[24] There is no doubt that the dissolution of villein tenure was a significant and beneficial contributor to economic development, because conditions in late sixteenth-century England were much better suited to the accumulation of wealth among the peasantry than they had been in the late thirteenth century. So the real interest in the decay of villein tenures in late medieval England lies in *what* they became, and how they varied regionally. As Whittle observes, 'forms of land tenure were the most significant legacy of the [medieval] manorial system to the sixteenth century and beyond'.[25] Thus did the transition from bondage to freedom determine the pathway to capitalism.

Given the overriding importance of the decline of serfdom for the history of England between 1200 and 1800, and for its transition from a bonded to a free society, it is astonishing that the subject has not attracted a commensurate amount of scholarly attention over the past two decades. There has been some interest, but no comprehensive re-examination of its causes or

[21]   Smith, 'The English peasantry', pp. 366–9; R.W. Hoyle, 'Tenure and the land market in early modern England: or a late contribution to the Brenner debate', *Economic History Review*, 43 (1990), pp. 4–12.

[22]   See, for example, Whittle, *Agrarian capitalism*, pp. 305–15; Hoyle and French, *English rural society*, pp. 12–42.

[23]   Whittle, *Agrarian capitalism*, p. 7.

[24]   French and Hoyle, *The character of English rural society*, pp. 30–1.

[25]   Whittle, *Agrarian Capitalism*, p. 64.

processes of decline.[26] This point can be crudely illustrated by contrasting the sustained interest in the Black Death of 1348–9, which has attracted a cluster of general surveys over the last decade, with the complete absence of any dedicated monograph on the disappearance of villeinage.[27] The last general survey of the latter is still Hilton's classic *The Decline of Serfdom in late Medieval England*, published in 1983, but that was no more than a super- ficial update to the first edition of 1968.[28] Inexplicably, the subject hardly receives any treatment in many recent undergraduate textbooks of late medi- eval England. Pollard acknowledges the 'profound importance' of the decline of serfdom in his wide-ranging survey of fifteenth-century England, yet devotes just two pages to the subject, and it warrants scarcely two sentences in Goldberg's social history of the period.[29] The declining interest in the decay of serfdom may have reached its nadir with S.A. Epstein's broad survey of the economic and social history of later medieval Europe, which devoted just 31 sentences to the subject, compared with the 57 devoted to the Paston family of Norfolk.[30] So, even though the fifteenth century has long since shed its tag as the 'Cinderella century' of English historical studies, the decline of serfdom continues to be its Cinderella subject.[31] On these grounds alone, a new survey is long overdue.

The earliest historians of villeinage wrestled with both the chronology and the causes of its decline, but failed to agree about either: Cheyney and

---

[26] There are some honourable exceptions to this sin of omission: see, for example, E.B. Fryde, *Peasants and landlords in later medieval England c.1380 to c.1525* (Stroud, 1996); Whittle, *Agrarian capitalism*, esp. pp. 37–82; and the various works of Chris Dyer, but most recently 'New serfdom in England', pp. 419–36; and 'The ineffectiveness of lordship in England 1200–1400', in C. Dyer, P. Coss and C. Wickham, eds., *Rodney Hilton's Middle Ages: an exploration of historical themes* (Past and Present Supplement, 2007), pp. 69–86.

[27] For example, N.F. Cantor, *In the wake of plague: the Black Death and the world it made* (New York, 2001); S.K. Cohn, *The Black Death Transformed. Disease and culture in early renaissance Europe* (London, 2002); O. Benedictow, *The Black Death 1346–1353. The complete history* (Woodbridge, 2004); W. Orent, *The Plague, the mysterious past and terrifying future* (New York, 2004); J.P. Byrne, *The Black Death* (Santa Barbara, 2004); J. Aberth, *The Black Death. The Great Mortality of 1348–50* (New York, 2005); J. Kelly, *The great mortality. An intimate history of the Black Death* (London, 2005); J. Hatcher, *The Black Death. An Intimate History* (London, 2007); and B. Gummer, *The Scourging Angel. The Black Death in the British Isles* (London, 2009).

[28] R.H. Hilton, *The decline of serfdom in late-medieval England* (second edition, London, 1983).

[29] Pollard, *Late Medieval England*, pp. 183–5; P.J.P. Goldberg, *Medieval England. A social history 1250–1550* (London, 2004), pp. 193–4.

[30] S.A. Epstein, *An economic and social history of later medieval Europe, 1000–1500* (Cambridge, 2009), pp. 246–8, 264–6.

[31] J. Watts, *Henry VI and the Politics of Kingship* (Cambridge, 1996), pp. 1–2.

Gray concurred that villeinage was showing signs of decay by c.1300; Page contended that it was in rapid decline in the late-fourteenth, and had disappeared by the mid-fifteenth, century; while Cunningham preferred the late-fifteenth century.[32] Part of the problem was that each historian was either looking for different symptoms of the decline, or concentrating upon different periods and areas of the country: Cheyney, Gray and Page concentrated upon the disappearance of labour services, but considered different estates, while Cunningham focused upon key changes in the 'rural relations of production'.[33] Consequently, they tended to pursue the subject along parallel lines.

A succession of influential studies in the 1960s and 1970s sought to address many of the evidentiary and methodological shortcomings of these early exchanges. Hilton re-orientated the subject by emphasizing that there was much more to villeinage than just labour services, extending his analysis to include villein tenures and the array of other personal restrictions. Raftis adopted a similar approach, documenting the nature and chronology of changes in villein tenure, labour services and servile dues on the estates of Ramsey abbey in the fourteenth and fifteenth centuries.[34] The complex and uneven process of the evolution of villein tenures into new forms of contractual tenancies was analyzed in Barbara Harvey's study of the estates of Westminster abbey.[35] Finally, in the 1980s and 1990s many regional and estate studies touched upon aspects of the decline of villeinage, and, in particular, the various chapters of the late medieval volume of the *Agrarian History of England and Wales* provided much useful commentary upon the pace of the decay of its various elements.[36]

From studies such as these, it is apparent that the chronology of decline was very uneven across the country. In some places, villeinage was in full retreat in the fourteenth century, while, in others, it lingered until the mid-sixteenth century: but, in most places, the 1390s to the 1450s emerges as

32   E.P. Cheyney, 'The disappearance of English serfdom', *English Historical Review*, XV (1900), pp. 32–3; T.W. Page, 'The end of villeinage in England', *American Economic Association*, 99 (1900), pp. 60–83; W. Cunningham, *The growth of English industry and commerce* (Cambridge, 1890), pp. 336–9; H.L. Gray, 'The commutation of villein services in England before the Black Death', *English Historical Review*, XXIX (1914), pp. 627–36.

33   The debate is surveyed in Hybel, *Crisis or change?*, pp. 49–50, 107–10.

34   Hilton, *Decline of Serfdom*, pp. 31–2; J.A. Raftis, *The estates of Ramsey abbey* (Toronto, 1957); J.A. Raftis, *Tenure and mobility. Studies in the social history of the medieval English village* (Toronto, 1964).

35   B. Harvey, *The estates of Westminster abbey in the later Middle Ages* (Oxford, 1977).

36   E. Miller, ed., *The Agrarian History of England and Wales, volume III: 1348 – 1500* (Cambridge, 1991), chapter 7, pp. 587–743: hereafter *AgHEW, III*.

the main period of change.[37] It is also apparent that significant gaps in our knowledge still remain. The first is the lack of real precision about the exact chronology of decline between 1300 and 1500. This is mainly due to the genuinely wide variety of regional experience, but it also owes something to the ways in which historians have approached the issue. There is a marked tendency to treat the process of decline anecdotally, rather than to chart the precise chronology of each aspect of villeinage on manor after manor according to a consistent methodology. The general reluctance to adhere to a tight discipline actually exposes some underlying scepticism about its utility. According to King 'to produce a single date at which the last reference to servility is found in any village is not of itself very helpful', while Raftis admits the difficulties of trying 'to find a meaningful sequence' from such material.[38] The second gap is the absence of any coherent or persuasive explanation for the unevenness of the decline from one manor, estate or region to another: historians comment on the local variety of decline without really trying to explain it.[39] Finally, and the most serious omission of all, there have been few attempts to correlate an observed chronology of decline closely with the key socio-economic trends of this period, such as changing land values or patterns of peasant resistance.

The presence of such sizeable holes in our knowledge owes much to the size and the difficulty of the task required to fill them. The construction of a precise and quantified chronology depends upon the survival of a good series of both manorial court and account rolls for individual manors across a wide timeframe, but few such series are extant. For example, P.D.A. Harvey regards the absence of detailed work on the timing of the disappearance of labour services as 'extraordinary', and attributes it to the low survival rate of the detailed documents necessary to discover exactly 'what happened on a particular manor'.[40] Even where sufficient sources do exist, the work required to extract the relevant information from them is time-consuming and technically demanding. As MacCulloch observes, 'chasing villeinage into private archives would require a full-scale research team to face the vast but miscellaneous storehouse of … manorial records scattered

---

37 For a full synthesis of the current state of knowledge, see Chapter Two.
38 E. King, 'Tenant farming and tenant farmers: the East Midlands', in *AgHEW, III*, p. 632; J.A. Raftis, 'Peasants and the collapse of the manorial economy on some Ramsey abbey estates', in R.H. Britnell and J. Hatcher, eds., *Progress and problems in medieval England. Essays in honour of Edward Miller* (Cambridge, 1996), p. 205.
39 Dyer commented upon the unevenness of the decline on the various manors of the Bishopric of Worcester, while acknowledging that the reasons for this are 'uncertain', Dyer, *Lords and peasants*, p. 270.
40 P.D.A. Harvey, 'The peasant land market in medieval England and beyond', in Z. Razi and R.M. Smith, eds., *The medieval manor court* (Oxford, 1996), pp. 402–3.

throughout England.'[41] Yet there is also a lingering sense that some historians are not really convinced that the immense effort is worthwhile: after
all, as there is no doubt that villeinage *did* decline, why dwell for long upon
its exact timing, especially when it is hard to generalize precisely about the
chronology of decline for each of its constituent parts? Far easier, and much
more interesting, has been to explore *why* it declined.

The reasons for the decline of serfdom intrigued the earliest historians
of the subject, although again they failed to reach any agreement. Cheyney
and Page accepted that the commutation of labour services was the defining
moment in the disappearance of villeinage, but they disagreed over its cause.
Cheyney explained it in terms of the widespread leasing of demesnes from
the second half of the fourteenth century, a change in estate policy which
dispensed with the lord's need for labour services, while Page pointed instead
to changes in the supply of money per capita after the Black Death, which
provided the liquidity for the commutation of labour services.[42] In contrast,
Davenport emphasized the general economic and social changes in the wake
of the Black Death that worked to the benefit of villeins, and which then
forced lords to compromise on the main terms of villeinage.[43]

Postan later developed this line of argument into a powerful model of
economic and social change, in which sustained demographic decline in the
century and a half after 1348–9 undermined the value of land yet enhanced
that of labour, thus forcing landlords to bargain away villeinage gradually.[44]
Hilton acknowledged the influence of demography among a wide range of
causes of the decline of serfdom, but, despite his broadly pluralist approach,
he identified the role of class conflict as the key element, and, in particular,
the success of serfs in taking action to resist seigniorial demands.[45] This
position is neatly summarized by Epstein: 'the extent to which landlords
succeeded or failed [to maintain serfdom after 1350] matches the abilities
of the peasants by whatever means to resist those encroachments'.[46] The
primary role of class conflict in determining whether and when serfdom

---

[41] D. MacCulloch, 'Bondmen and the Tudors', in C. Cross, D. Loades and J.J.
Scarisbrick, eds., *Law and government under the Tudors. Essays presented to Geoffrey
Elton* (Cambridge, 1988), p. 93.

[42] Page, 'End of villeinage', pp. 57–8. Cheyney, 'Disappearance of English serfdom',
pp. 34–6.

[43] F.G. Davenport, 'The decay of villeinage in East Anglia', *Transactions of the Royal
Historical Society*, XIV (1900), pp. 128–30.

[44] M.M. Postan, *The medieval economy and society* (London, 1972), pp. 169–73; M.M.
Postan and J. Hatcher, 'Population and class relations in feudal society', in Aston
and Philpin, eds., *The Brenner debate*, pp. 64–78.

[45] Hilton, *Decline of serfdom*, pp. 34–9.

[46] Epstein, *Economic and social history*, p. 246.

declined attains its most graphic expression in the works of Brenner, which provoked what became known as the Brenner Debate.[47]

In the aftermath of the Brenner Debate, which raged in the 1970s and 1980s, many historians have appeared wary of adopting overtly political or ideological stances in their treatment of the subject, although this also reflects a growing distrust of mono-causal explanations for economic change, and a general retreat 'into wider pluralist interpretive models'.[48] Consequently, the decline of serfdom in England has come to be explained as the result of a conjunction of a number of factors. The first, contextual, factor is that villeinage had effectively reached its high point in the thirteenth century, because the development of the common law acted as a subsequent barrier both to the enserfment of new groups of people, and to the relegation of free tenures into villeinage. Thus after 1300 the institution of villeinage could no longer expand. On the contrary, it suffered some attrition from the marriage of female villeins to freemen, whose status and that of their progeny was raised out of servility because 'mixed' offspring were deemed to be free.

After the mid-fourteenth century three other developments accelerated the decline in the number of serfs: the punitively and persistently high mortality rates after the Black Death of 1348–9; the increased mobility of rural serfs, who left their home manors for better tenures, wages and prospects elsewhere; and the granting of manumission, whereby serfs could buy their freedom. Simultaneously, the burdens of villein tenures were gradually released and removed due to the chronic shortage of workers and tenants, depressed land values and inflated wages, all of which forced landlords to make concessions on the incidents and terms of villeinage. Wherever landlords proved slow or reluctant to concede on these terms, villeins resisted their demands actively and passively, collectively and individually.[49] Finally,

---

[47] Brenner, 'Agrarian class structure', pp. 10–63; and 'The agrarian roots of European capitalism', in Aston and Philpin, eds., *The Brenner Debate*, pp. 213–327. In addition to the works cited in n. 20 above, see also the critiques of Brenner's work in Hoyle, 'Tenure and the land market', pp. 4–12; M.E. Mate, 'The east Sussex land market and agrarian class structure in the later Middle Ages', *Past and Present*, 139 (1993), pp. 46–65; Whittle, *Agrarian capitalism*, pp. 21–6, 307–9; French and Hoyle, *The character of English rural society*, pp. 4–12. Brenner's most recent reiteration of his position does not engage with the criticisms of his work and it does not use any of the direct research into villeinage in England published since Hilton (1983): R. Brenner, 'Property and progress: where Adam Smith went wrong', in C. Wickham, ed., *Marxist history-writing for the twenty-first century* (Oxford, 2007), pp. 49–111.

[48] C. Wickham, 'Memories of underdevelopment: what has Marxism done for medieval history, and what can it still do?', in Wickham, ed., *Marxist history-writing*, p. 43.

[49] These arguments are presented in R.H. Britnell, *Britain and Ireland 1050–1530* (Oxford, 2004), pp. 432–5; Rigby, *English society*, pp. 104–44; J. Whittle and S.H.

it has been suggested that an acute shortage of money in the countryside by the middle of the fifteenth century meant that villeins simply lacked the cash to pay their servile dues, which accelerated their disappearance.[50]

There is no doubt that during the fourteenth and fifteenth centuries this powerful combination of demographic, economic and social forces fatally undermined villeinage in England. Yet recent commentators have tended to resist any temptation to weigh or to rank each cause in order of importance. This is probably a function of their desire to seek some shelter from the heat of the Brenner Debate, although it may also reflect the belief that any attempt to create a hierarchy of historical causation is misplaced.[51] Some recent historians who *have* ventured to name their primary cause are not always explicit about the evidentiary or objective grounds upon which their judgement is based. Indeed, their choice often appears to be based upon a particular interpretation of the fundamental nature of human relations. For example, Fryde regarded peasant action – whether fight or flight – against 'oppressive and sometimes hostile lordship' as the main factor in the decline of villeinage, which is consistent with his stated belief that there existed an 'endemic mutual distrust between landlords and peasants beneath a veneer of stability'.[52] In contrast, Campbell has depicted the decline as a complex and varied process of attrition, based in part upon a sense that landlord and villein relations also involved a good deal of compromise and cooperation, both of which are preferable because they 'involve less wear and tear than resistance'.[53]

So, for all these generalisations, there is still much that remains unresolved. Dyer has recently posed two major, but still contentious, questions about the disappearance of villeinage from England: did reactionary landlords attempt to re-impose serfdom after the Black Death of 1348–9? Was serfdom ended by impersonal economic forces or did active social resistance play a significant role?[54] Uncertainty also remains about the process of tenurial change. We know that the villein tenant of the fourteenth century became the copyholder of the sixteenth century, and that the English copyholder possessed more secure proprietary rights than Brenner had supposed. Yet copyholds came in a number of different forms, some of which (copyholds for lives) provided the tenant with less security than others (copyholds

Rigby, 'England: popular politics and social conflict', in Horrox and Ormrod, eds., *Social history*, pp. 77–8.

[50] E.B. Fryde, 'Peasant rebellion and peasant discontents', in *AgHEW*, III, p. 793.

[51] S.H. Rigby, 'Historical causation: is one thing more important than another?', *History*, 259 (1995), pp. 227–42; Rigby, *English Society*, pp. 141–3.

[52] Fryde, *Peasants and landlords*, p. 14.

[53] Campbell, 'The land', pp. 214, 226.

[54] Dyer, 'New serfdom in England', pp. 428, 433.

by inheritance). Why did copyholds for lives emerge in some areas, notably the south and west, and why did copyholds by inheritance come to dominate in others? Why did leaseholds dominate in some places, but not in others? As Smith admits, 'the regional geography of copyhold tenures remains a perplexing and unresolved problem'.[55]

The purpose of this book is to re-assess the decline of serfdom in the century and a half after the Black Death; to address some of the gaps in our knowledge; to confront the unresolved questions about the existence of a 'second serfdom' and about the causes of decline; to consider the implications of this reassessment for our understanding of English serfdom; and, finally, to explore how different types of copyholds and leaseholds emerged out of villein tenure and shaped England's subsequent agrarian development. The first section of the book comprises a survey of the existing literature. Chapter 2 charts the evolution and decline of villein tenure during the fourteenth and fifteenth centuries. Chapter 3 surveys the evidence for the chronology of decline of all the main incidents of serfdom. Chapter 4 considers the arguments for the causes of that decline, focusing particularly upon the influence of economic forces, of attempts to impose a second serfdom, and peasant resistance. This section closes with a brief assessment of the weaknesses of the approaches to the subject so far. Part II opens with a statement of a tighter and more reliable methodology for charting and explaining the decline of serfdom, which is then used as the basis for original research into a sample of 38 manors. The findings are presented and analysed in Chapters 6 to 12. These chapters contain much detailed evidence and close argument, and so each contains a summary statement and conclusion. Part III offers a general Conclusion that re-evaluates the decline in the light of these findings.

---

55 Smith, 'English peasantry', p. 368.

2

The Chronology of Decline: Villein Tenures

Villeinage and serfdom in England in c.1300

Between c.1160 and c.1220 the development of the common law in England established that the title to land held on free tenure could be defended in the royal courts. Land held on tenures which did not have access to the (royal) courts of common law, and whose title was therefore entirely dependent upon the gift or the will of the manorial lord, were defined as unfree (also 'customary' or 'villein').[1] The villein, who held 'unfree' land, did possess a legal right to pursue other actions, such as debt and trespass, in the royal courts, and, in theory, these courts had to the power to protect the villein against assault and maltreatment.[2] However, few villeins were ever allowed to bring such cases before the royal courts, although Hyams suggests that they posed interesting and complex legal questions when they did.[3] Hence villeins could neither defend their title to villein tenure, nor pursue proprietary actions against their lords, under the common law. Instead, all issues relating to the title of villein tenure, or to the status of the villein, could be defended only in the private court of the relevant lord, and therefore, in theory, both villein land and the villein were vulnerable to forfeiture at the arbitrary will of their lord.

It was not just land that was categorized as unfree, but people too. Thirteenth-century lawyers argued that a person was born either free or servile, based upon the principle that genealogy determined legal status: legitimate offspring acquired the status of the father, whereas the status of bastards was uncertain and thus presumed to be free. Those who inherited servile status were called 'serfs [*servi*]' and 'neifs [*nativi*]', the latter a word which overtly reinforced the hereditary nature of their condition. Most tenants of villein land were also personally servile, although contemporary lawyers readily acknowledged that personal status could also be independent of landholding: many landless people were serfs, and a freeman could be a

---

[1]   For general introductions, see Miller and Hatcher, *Rural England*, pp. 101–33; Hatcher, 'Serfdom and Villeinage', pp. 3–14; Rigby, *English society*, pp. 21–34; Faith, *English peasantry*, pp. 259–65; Dyer, 'New serfdom', pp. 423–4.

[2]   Raftis, *Tenure and mobility*, p. 129, n. 3; P. Hyams *King, lords and peasants in medieval England* (Oxford, 1980), p. 143.

[3]   Hyams, *King, lords and peasants*, p. 49.

tenant of villein land – subject to all the restrictions attached to the land – while remaining personally free. Serfs were subject to seigniorial powers of control and discipline irrespective of whether they held villein land. In theory, serfs could be bought and sold; they could be subject to detention or corporal punishment for misdemeanours; their goods and chattels were deemed to belong to their lord; and they could be compulsorily settled on villein land.[4]

The debate about the impact of villeinage on English society and its economy around 1300, sketched in the opening chapter, hinges upon a judgement about the extent to which the full range of its legal restrictions was actually enforced, and the extent to which the theoretical vulnerability of the serf was exploited in practice. According to one school of thought, the emergence of villeinage between c.1160 and c.1220, with the associated tightening of restrictions on the unfree, constituted a legal and practical change of such significance that it was tantamount to the imposition of a new form of serfdom, involving 'the ruthless depression of the economic status' of the unfree peasantry.[5] The nature and burden of rent upon villein land, the range of personal restrictions upon serfs, and the arbitrary and unpredictable powers of the lord all combined to suppress innovation and prevent the accumulation of wealth among unfree peasants in the thirteenth century.[6] Serfdom thus distorted the markets for land and labour in favour of landlords, placing the peasantry 'at a disadvantage in relation to the market, constrain[ing] their social, occupational and geographical mobility, creat[ing] an oppressive atmosphere of insecurity both of their persons and their property, and threaten[ing] any reserves they might accumulate'.[7]

Another school of thought contends that a sizeable gap existed between the strict law of villeinage and the reality of its operation on the ground. They argue that it was not possible to draw or maintain a hard and fast distinction between the free and the unfree. For example, the status of land tenure was blurred along the boundary between free and unfree, and a freeman might hold villein land without becoming personally servile and a villein might hold free tenure without becoming a freeman.[8] Hence, 'the line between servile and free customs was hard to descry outside the theorist's brain', so

---

[4] Miller and Hatcher, *Rural England*, pp. 113–16; Dyer, 'New serfdom', pp. 423–4.

[5] Hatcher, 'Serfdom and villeinage', pp. 3–4; Dyer, 'New serfdom', pp. 419–24.

[6] For a survey of such arguments, see Rigby, *English society*, pp. 104–9, 127–42; Hatcher and Bailey, *Modelling the Middle Ages*, pp. 66–120.

[7] B.M.S. Campbell, 'Land and people in the Middle Ages, 1066–1500' in R.A. Dodgshon and R.A. Butlin, eds., *An historical geography of England and Wales* (second edition, London, 1990), p. 98.

[8] J.M. Kaye, *Medieval English conveyances* (Cambridge, 2009), pp. 359–62.

that, in reality, social relations were governed by 'a jungle of rules'.[9] These rules softened and tempered the full legal force of villeinage. In particular, it is argued that local custom regulated the precise terms on which tenures were held, together with many other aspects of the relationship between lord and serf, both of which reduced the seigniorial scope for arbitrary action. Custom enabled villeins to inherit and dispose of land with a good degree of security, with the result that evictions of villeins were rare, and arbitrary evictions, and seizures of property, seldom known. Sales of serfs, and arbitrary punishments and restrictions upon them, were unusual. In the thirteenth century, custom – the practice of the past – was used as a benchmark for defining, fixing and codifying the precise obligations of villeins, and the meticulous manner in which landlords recorded these liabilities is proof that they felt bound by them.[10] At some times and places custom could work to the advantage of the landlord: at others, to the advantage of the villein. Either way, custom mediated the relationship between lords and villeins, to the extent that 'custom triumphed over caprice' according to Hatcher.[11] While most historians now accept this interpretation, some continue to emphasize that the power of custom did not eradicate all elements of unpredictability, and those that remained invariably operated to the landlord's advantage.[12]

Villein tenure in the early fourteenth century

In c.1300 around one half of all peasant land in England was freehold, and the remainder was held on villein tenure.[13] Many unfree holdings were organized into standardized sizes, an arrangement designed to facilitate the allocation of rents and services, and to preserve the viability of family-based units. Standardized holdings went under a variety of names and fractions thereof, such as virgates (20 to 40 acres), half virgates, quarter virgates; full lands, half lands and quarter lands; bovates, and fractions thereof; and *tenementa* of various sizes, and cotlands, cottages and other smallholdings. The different names and sizes of these holdings reflect the fact that standard sizes varied according to region and estate. The labels given to the tenants

9   Miller and Hatcher, *Rural England*, p. 112; Hyams, *King, lords and peasants*, p. 185.
10   Miller and Hatcher, *Rural England*, pp. 130–1; Hatcher, 'Serfdom and villeinage', p. 10; R.M. Smith, 'Some issues concerning families and their property in rural England 1250–1800', in R.M. Smith, ed., *Land, kinship and life-cycle* (Cambridge, 1984), p. 64; Savine, 'Bondmen under the Tudors', p. 268.
11   Hatcher, 'Serfdom and villeinage', p. 9.
12   Dyer, 'The ineffectiveness of lordship', pp. 73–4.
13   J. Whittle, 'Leasehold tenure in England c.1200–1600: its form and incidence', in B.J.P. van Bavel and P.R. Schofield, eds., *The development of leasehold in north western Europe c.1200–1600* (Turnhout, 2008), p. 140.

of these holdings also reflect their variety of form: *custumari, tenentes in villenagio, villani, bondi, virgatarii, semivirgatarii, consuetudinarii, werkmen, operarii, servi, cotagi, coterelli, croftarii*, and so on.[14] The produce of the land belonged to the tenant, subject to defined payments to the church and, especially, to the lord. The exact composition of 'payments' to the lord varied, but usually comprised a mixture of renders of agricultural produce (such as eggs, capons, malt and grain), labour services, personal incidents and money (see Chapter 3).

In the century before 1350 villein land is identifiable through labels such as 'customary', 'bond', and 'native', and villein tenure is identifiable through phrases such as 'held in villeinage', or 'in bondage', for 'customs and services'. The relationship between lord and tenant was non-contractual, because the villein was *required* to hold the land, and the customs and services were obligatory. The tenant usually held the land 'for himself and his brood [*sequela*]', and the choice of 'brood' emphasizes the hereditary and inferior status of the individual: other transfers deploy the phrase 'to hold for him and his heirs [*sibi et heredibus suis*]' instead. Both versions confirm that the tenant and his family enjoyed rights of inheritance over land held on villein tenure.[15] The exact nature of those rights is seldom stated explicitly, but they were determined by local custom: they were usually either partible (split equally between sons) or impartible (one inheriting son), and, if the latter, either primogeniture (eldest son inherits) or ultimogeniture (youngest son).[16]

Local custom influenced the operation of the land market in other ways, such as the days on which rent was paid and the extent to which a market in customary land had developed. The latter was especially important, and by c.1300 it was already active and extensive particularly in the Home Counties and eastern England.[17] The transfer of land from one party to another – whether kin or non-kin, whether after the death of the tenant [*post mortem*]

---

[14]   See the general introductions in Miller and Hatcher, *Rural England*, pp. 111–33; Rigby, *English society*, pp. 25–34. Regional variations in the names given to standardized holdings are mapped in B.M.S. Campbell and K. Bartley, *England on the eve of the Black Death. An atlas of lay lordship, land and wealth* (Manchester, 2006), p. 37.

[15]   Harvey, *Westminster abbey*, p. 279; Smith, 'Families and their property', p. 63, and R.M. Smith, 'Some thoughts on hereditary and proprietary rights in land under customary law in thirteenth- and early fourteenth-century England', *Law and History Review*, 1 (1983), pp. 95–128; Smith, 'English peasantry', p. 352; Kaye, *Medieval English conveyances*, p. 71. The translation of *sequela* as 'brood' is conventional: to translate it as 'following' is too literal, and 'offspring' does not properly capture the Latin word. See also Kaye, *Medieval English conveyances*, pp. 352–4.

[16]   R.J. Faith, 'Peasant families and inheritance customs in medieval England', *Agricultural History Review*, 14 (1967), pp. 77–88; Smith, 'Families and their property', pp. 38–62.

[17]   Smith, 'Families and their property', pp. 13–21; B.M.S. Campbell, 'Population

or during his lifetime [*inter vivos*] – was formally recorded in the manorial court of the landlord, and it followed a careful and remarkably standardized procedure of 'surrender and admission': the outgoing tenant surrendered the land into the 'hands of the lord [*in manibus domini*]' and 'to the benefit [*ad opus*]' of the incoming tenant, who obtained seisin through swearing an oath of fealty to the lord and paying an entry fine.[18]

Thus custom influenced the management and operation of villein tenures everywhere. Its importance was sometimes recognized in conveyances by the inclusion of a phrase emphasising that customary land was held 'according to the custom of the manor [*secundum consuetudinem manerii*]'. One of its most important, generic, influences was to prevent landlords from behaving arbitrarily and whimsically towards villein landholders, which meant that, in practice, villein land was not seized without good reason.[19] It also enshrined variety in local practice, because the very nature of local custom varied slightly from manor to manor: hence, the precise nature and operation of 'villein tenure' on one manor was subtly different from that on another.[20]

Copyholds and leaseholds in the early sixteenth century

During the course of the fourteenth and fifteenth centuries a momentous change occurred in the nature of land tenancies. In c.1300 villein tenures had constituted around one half of all peasant landholdings in England, but by the early sixteenth century they had disappeared and mutated into various copyhold tenancies and also into leaseholds.[21] According to Barbara Harvey 'the development of copyhold was the most important feature of tenurial history in the fifteenth century'.[22] Allen argues that the creation of copyhold 'amounted to an even greater democratization of property ownership. The redefinition of land ownership laid the basis for yeoman agriculture in

pressure, inheritance and the land market in a fourteenth-century peasant community', in Smith, ed., *Land, kinship and lifecycle*, pp. 107–27.

[18] Smith, 'English peasantry', pp. 343, 352–7; P.R. Schofield, *Peasant and community in medieval England* (Basingstoke, 2002), pp. 52–76. Some historians have argued that the phrase 'to the benefit [*ad opus*]' of the recipient also provided further confirmation of their hereditary right to the land thereafter, see C. Howell, 'Inheritance customs in the Midlands, 1280–1700', in J. Goody, J. Thirsk and E.P. Thompson, eds., *Family and inheritance. Rural society in western Europe 1200 to 1800* (Cambridge, 1986), p. 128.

[19] Hatcher, 'Serfdom and villeinage', p. 15.

[20] P.D.A. Harvey, 'Aspects of the peasant land market in medieval England', in. P.D.A. Harvey, ed., *The peasant land market in England* (Oxford, 1984), pp. 330–2. The nature of rents is discussed in Chapter Three.

[21] Hilton, *Decline of serfdom*, p. 44.

[22] *VCH Oxfordshire*, volume 6 (London, 1959), p. 214.

the later sixteenth and seventeenth centuries'.[23] However, copyhold emerged from the old villein tenure slowly and uncertainly, and is only really recognizable as a distinctive and different form of tenure in the sixteenth century.

Copyhold tenure acquired its name from the practice of providing the tenant with a copy of the manorial court roll entry documenting his or her admission to the landholding and its terms. One copy was presented to the tenant, while the lord kept the other. Thus the tenant acquired a quasi-legal document, which could be (and was) subsequently produced in the manorial court as proof of title to the land.[24] Sixteenth-century copyholds assumed one of three general forms. First, *copyholds of inheritance* could be passed securely onto heirs. Second, *copyholds for a term* provided less security, in the sense that they were held for either a term of years or, more commonly, for the life, or lives, of a stipulated tenant(s), after which they reverted to the landlord.[25] The landlord could then opt to grant the holding to the next of kin at the end of the term, but it was not assured. Third, *tenant right* was a variant on copyhold found mainly in north-west England, in which the tenant enjoyed rights of inheritance, but paid entry fines at variable rates whenever the manor changed hands, as well as when the land was transferred to another tenant.[26]

A fourth form of tenancy, leasehold, had also become more common. Leasehold comprised the temporary grant of land to a tenant on a stipulated term for a fixed annual rent, and, once again, a copy of the court roll grant of the lease was often presented to the lessee. Once the lease commenced, the land was the tenant's chattel property for the duration of the term, as long as the rent was paid and the terms of the contract were observed.[27] Landlords could not arbitrarily seize or alter such tenancies in mid-term, so tenants acquired them with the confidence that they possessed exclusive and secure property rights for the duration of the contract.[28] At the end of the term the land reverted to the lord, who was then free to dispose of it as he deemed fit.

Copyholds as a distinct category of tenure emerged as the courts of common law gradually began to recognize, and to offer more protection, to them. Savine dated such developments to the second half of the fifteenth

---

[23] R.C. Allen, *Enclosure and the yeoman. The agricultural development of the south Midlands 1450–1850* (Oxford, 1992), p. 73.

[24] Hoyle, 'Tenure and the land market', p. 6.

[25] Hoyle, 'Tenure and the land market', pp. 6–7.

[26] R.W. Hoyle, 'An ancient and laudable custom. The definition and development of tenant right in north-west England in the sixteenth century', *Past and Present*, 116 (1987), pp. 25–8, 51–5.

[27] C.M. Gray, *Copyhold, equity and the common law* (Cambridge, Mass., 1963), p. 11.

[28] At least, I have not encountered any seizure or breach of leasehold by the lord before the expiry of a stipulated term. See also van Bavel and Schofield, 'Introduction', in van Bavel and Schofield, eds., *Development of leasehold*, p. 21.

century, when, he argued, the royal courts first made some judgements favourable to the tenants of customary land, and then defended the title to them.[29] However, his argument and chronology have attracted little support. Most historians agree that from the early fifteenth century royal courts did begin to intervene on equitable matters associated with customary tenures, which offered tenants, including leaseholders, some protection against loss if they had been unjustly evicted. Furthermore, by mid-century customary tenants were permitted to take out suits against their lords and to produce evidence from manorial courts for inspection in the royal courts. However, there is no firm evidence that the courts of common law defended the title to such tenancies before the middle of the sixteenth century.[30]

Thus sixteenth-century copyholds and leaseholds were different from villein tenures of the early fourteenth century in a number of ways. They had gradually acquired greater legal protection under the common law. Their 'appearance and dignity' were different in the sense that many of the servile burdens had either lapsed or been replaced with cash renders (see Chapter 3).[31] Finally, they bore more resemblance to contractual tenancies, because the tenant acquired the land through choice rather than compulsion and, in some cases, for a limited period or specified time.[32]

The exact nature and level of the rent package attached to copyholds and leaseholds, including entry fines, varied subtly but importantly. The annual rent might be either fixed in perpetuity or re-negotiable upon the transfer of the tenancy: similarly, entry fines might be fixed at set levels or variable at the will of the lord. This mix of variables, when combined with the variation in the degree of security provided by the different forms of copyhold tenure, combined to determine the local balance of power between sixteenth-century lords and tenants. Hence manors characterized by either relatively insecure copyholds for lives or leases, and by variable rents and entry fines, generally favoured the landlord: in contrast, manors dominated by secure heritable copyholds, and fixed fines and rents, generally favoured the tenant.[33] While such manors could be found everywhere, copyholds for lives were mainly a feature of 'the west country and southern England, running over towards Hampshire and Oxfordshire and through the west midlands', whereas copy-

---

[29] A. Savine, 'Copyhold cases in the early Chancery proceedings', *English Historical Review*, 17 (1902), pp. 296–303.

[30] Gray, *Copyhold*, pp. 13, 33–4, 54, 63–7; Fryde, *Peasants and landlords*, pp. 227–8; A.B. Simpson, *An introduction to the history of land law* (Oxford, 1961), pp. 69–89; S.F.C. Milson, *Historical foundations of the common law* (London, 1969), pp. 127–32; Harvey, 'Aspects of the peasant land market', pp. 328–9; Allen, *Enclosure and the yeoman*, pp. 68–72.

[31] Gray, *Copyhold*, p. 15.

[32] Whittle, 'Leasehold tenure', pp. 139–40.

[33] Hoyle, 'Tenure and the land market', pp. 6–10; Whittle, *Agrarian capitalism*, p. 64.

holds by inheritance dominated in the east Midlands, the Home Counties and East Anglia.[34]

Customary tenures in transition, c.1350 to c.1500

We know a good deal about the nature and operation of villein tenure in the period c.1200 to c.1350, and about copyholds after c.1500. In contrast, our knowledge of the nature and form of tenures during the intermediate period c.1350 to c.1500 is less secure, and consequently our understanding of how the tenurial transformation occurred is patchy. Kettle has commented that the history of tenures in this period has yet to be written, while Smith observes that historians have little idea how different forms of copyhold came to be distributed along those highly distinctive regional lines by the sixteenth century.[35] In short, much has been written about copyhold tenures in the sixteenth century, but much less about where they came from and what immediately preceded them. One of the main objectives of this book is to address that gap in our knowledge. The purpose of this section is to summarize what has been written, and to identify some lines of inquiry for exploration in the case studies which follow.

Our patchy knowledge owes much to the inherent difficulties with the subject matter. The evolution of late-medieval tenures was often gradual, inexact and hard to trace. As P.D.A. Harvey once observed, these tenures exhibit 'great differences between one place and another', thus creating the impression of 'an extraordinary muddle', while Schofield remarked that they 'resist most attempts at generalization'.[36] When considering changes in tenure on one Berkshire manor, Faith observed 'the actual chronology of change is hard to date, and several kinds of tenure existed side by side'.[37] Fryde lamented the variations in these evolving tenurial forms, which he regarded as 'a bewildering variety of practices...a mosaic of variable bargains', even within the same locality or upon the same seigniorial estate.[38] Nor was

---

[34] Quote from Hoyle, 'Tenure and the land market', p. 6. See also Smith, 'English peasantry', p. 368–9; Allen, *Enclosure and the yeoman*, p. 67.

[35] *VCH Shropshire*, volume 4 (Oxford, 1989), p. 110 n. 29; Smith, 'English peasantry', p. 368.

[36] Harvey, 'Aspects of the peasant land market', pp. 329–34; P.R. Schofield, 'Tenurial developments and the availability of customary land in a later medieval community', *Economic History Review*, 49 (1996), p. 257.

[37] R.J. Faith, 'Berkshire: the fourteenth and fifteenth centuries', in Harvey, ed., *Peasant land market*, p. 133.

[38] Fryde, *Peasants and landlords*, pp. 129, 132, 135; Raftis, too, notes the widening variety of tenurial forms in the late fourteenth century, Raftis, 'Peasants and the collapse of the manorial economy', pp. 197–8.

the evolution of these tenures necessarily linear and irreversible, because, for example, unfree land was occasionally converted to leasehold and later reverted back to villein tenure.[39] The problems of variety and fluidity of form are exacerbated by the ways in which tenures were described and recorded in the manorial court rolls of this period. Sometimes the formulae deployed to describe tenures can be bland, imprecise and inconsistent, while some courts did not even bother to record the details of the terms of tenure. It seems as though the amount of detail depended upon the disposition and personality of the person who wrote the court rolls.[40]

Hence tracking the transformation of villein tenures during the course of the late fourteenth and fifteenth centuries is a demanding and thank-less task, so much so that some historians remain cautious, almost pessi-mistic, about our ability to do so with precision.[41] One of the least cautious but best-known interpretations is the work of Brenner, who speculated that three crucial tenurial developments occurred in fifteenth-century England. First, landlords converted large areas of former customary land to leasehold; second, they retained the ability to charge variable entry fines on copyholds; and, third, tenants failed to acquire any real security of tenure. He argued that these characteristics were essential in enabling sixteenth- and seven-teenth-century landlords to evict tenants, to consolidate landholdings and to charge commercial rents, which in turn undermined small peasant holdings and promoted large farms producing for the market using wage labour and innovative techniques.[42] Historians now agree that Brenner seriously under-estimated the complex realities of copyhold and, in particular, the degree of security it offered to the tenant.[43] However, his argument for the expansion of leaseholds, and the role of landlords in promoting them, has not been seriously challenged. He contended that late-medieval landlords appropri-ated vacant customary holdings and added 'them to their demesnes. In this way a great deal of land was simply removed from the "customary sector" and added to the "leasehold sector", thus…substantially reducing the area of land which potentially could be subject to peasant proprietorship'.[44] These

---

[39] M. Bailey, 'The Prior and Convent of Ely and the management of their manor of Lakenheath', in M. Franklin and C. Harper-Bill, eds., *Ecclesiastical studies in honour of Dorothy M. Owen* (Woodbridge, 1995), pp. 7–9. For example, in the early 1350s 20 of the 31 customary virgates at Lakenheath (Suffolk) were either unten-anted or had been converted to leasehold, yet by 1373 23 were once again held on villein tenure and only 2½ were untenanted.

[40] Hoyle, 'An ancient custom', p. 28.

[41] Harvey, 'Aspects of the peasant land market', pp. 329–37.

[42] Brenner, 'Agrarian class structure', pp. 46–50. For a commentary, see Smith, 'English peasantry', pp. 363–6; Hoyle, 'Tenure and the land market', pp. 10–11.

[43] Smith, 'English peasantry', p. 363–6.

[44] Brenner, 'Agrarian class structure', p. 47.

seigniorial appropriations in the fifteenth century enabled their sixteenth-century successors to create large farms and to lease them to capitalist tenants. The lease is thus depicted as a potent weapon deployed to exercise seigniorial control over the ownership of, and the level of rent charged for, customary land.[45]

Customary tenures in the late fourteenth and fifteenth centuries were essentially an intermediate form, no longer villein tenure but not yet recognizable as the stable and distinctive copyholds of the sixteenth century. Yet, despite the 'muddle', and their 'bewildering variety', it is possible to identify with clarity and confidence four important developments. The first is the gradual decay and then final disappearance of many of the characteristic elements of the rent package attached to villein tenures. The chronology of their disappearance is discussed in Chapter 3.

The second development is the spread of the practice of issuing the tenant with a copy of the court roll entry of the transfer of customary land, which is, of course, the origin of the 'copyhold'. The use of copies was already known in the early fourteenth century, although at this date the practice is seldom mentioned and it was probably unusual.[46] By the mid-fifteenth century the practice was so widespread that the phrase 'by the copy [*per copiam*]' began to be included both within the formulae of conveyances and in the description of customary land in rentals and surveys.[47] Fox and Padel reflect the general consensus when stating that holding by copy was 'a later development of the fifteenth, and particularly the sixteenth, centuries'.[48]

Thus, by the second half of the fifteenth century, the written copy of the surrender of, and admission to, customary land had become the basis upon which tenants were able to grant, sell and assign their land to third parties

---

[45] Mate, 'East Sussex land market', p. 52.

[46] Harvey, 'Aspects of the peasant land market', p. 337; P.D.A. Harvey, 'Tenant farming and tenant farmers: the Home Counties', in *AgHEW III*, p. 671.

[47] See for example Dyer, *Lords and peasants*, p. 294; R.H. Britnell, 'Tenant farming and tenant farmers: Eastern England', in *AgHEW III*, p. 621; Harvey, 'Tenant farming and tenant farmers: Home Counties', pp. 671–2; E. Miller, 'Tenant farming and tenant farmers: the Southern Counties', in *AgHEW III*, p. 712; R.A. Tuck, 'Tenant farming and tenant farmers: the Northern Borders', in *AgHEW III*, p. 594; Harvey, *Westminster abbey*, pp. 280n, 284–5; M. Yates, *Town and countryside in western Berkshire c.1327 to c.1600. Social and economic change* (Woodbridge, 2007), pp. 141–2; A. Jones, 'Bedfordshire: the fifteenth century', in Harvey, ed., *Peasant land market*, pp. 192–3, 203; F.G. Davenport, *The economic development of a Norfolk manor* (Cambridge, 1906), p. 69; P.R. Schofield, '*Extranei* and the market for customary land on a Westminster abbey manor', *Agricultural History Review*, 49 (2001), p. 11.

[48] H.S.A. Fox and O.J. Padel, eds., *The Cornish lands of the Arundells of Lanherne, fourteenth to sixteenth centuries*, Devon and Cornwall Record Society, 41 (2000), p. lvii.

securely and safely through the manorial court.[49] Fifteenth-century 'copies' were not a new form of tenure, nor were they yet copyholds: Harvey states that it would 'be wrong to see a tenant's possession of a copy ... as having any technical significance' before c.1500.[50] They were vaguer, untidier and more imprecise than sixteenth-century 'copyholds', and copyhold did not exist as a distinctive tenure until the sustained attention of administrators and lawyers after the late fifteenth century, which gradually introduced greater formality and clarity in tenurial forms.[51] Yet the issue of a copy did represent something different from the original villein tenure: Barbara Harvey suggests that the use of copies emulated 'the freeholder's possession of a charter', and constituted an implied contract.[52]

There remains considerable uncertainty about the pace and extent to which the copy spread between the early fourteenth and mid-fifteenth centuries, and also the extent to which manorial courts became reliant upon the copy as written evidence of a land transfer. Hence we are uncertain about whether the growth of references to copies from the mid-fifteenth century reflects a recent and real change in practice, or simply reflects nomenclature catching up with a practice that had been long established. Faith suspected the latter when speculating that 'the history of [copies] must go back much further than specific references to it by name suggest. When a tenant took land in the manorial court it may often have happened that he was given – or more probably sold – a "copy" of the transaction without the fact being recorded.'[53] This is another area worth of close attention in the case studies which follow.

The third development of significance in customary tenures during the later Middle Ages was the changing language of conveyances. When a tenant was admitted into a villein holding in the early fourteenth century, the language used in the court roll entry explicitly reinforced its inferior status: the common phrases were 'held by him and his brood', and 'held in villeinage ... held in bondage ... for customs and works ... for ancient services'. During the course of the later Middle Ages the use of such servile language within conveyances was dropped and replaced with more digni-

---

[49]   Smith, 'English peasantry', pp. 361, 363–9; Whittle, *Agrarian capitalism*, pp. 76–9.

[50]   Harvey, 'Aspects of the peasant land market', p. 337.

[51]   Hoyle, 'Tenure and the land market', pp. 4–8. Whittle, *Agrarian capitalism*, pp. 74–5.

[52]   Harvey, *Westminster abbey*, p. 284.

[53]   Faith, 'Berkshire', p. 140. Jones, 'Bedfordshire', p. 192 suggests that copies might have been issued to signify the removal of labour services. The use of copies earlier and more widely than previously suspected is suggested by a 1378 rental of the Berkeley estate in Gloucestershire, which describes certain customary lands as held *'per copiam'* or *'per scriptum domini'*, B. Wells-Furby, *The Berkeley estate 1281–1417. Its economy and development* (The Bristol and Gloucestershire Archaeological Society, 2012), p. 106.

fied phrases, such as 'holds according to the custom of the manor', 'by copy of the court roll', 'at the will of the lord', 'leases at farm' and 'by the rod'.[54] By the late fifteenth century words such as 'villein', 'bond' and 'native' were still frequently used to describe land parcels, but they were no longer used to describe the *terms* on which the tenant was being admitted to the land.[55]

The broad consensus among historians is that the decisive change in the vocabulary of conveyances occurred during the early fifteenth century.[56] An excellent example of this process is the withdrawal of the phrase *'in bondagio'* after 1427 from transfers of virgates at Kibworth Harcourt (Leicestershire), as part of a wider agreement between lord and tenants to improve the terms of tenure, and the disappearance of the same from Willington (Bedfordshire) by the early 1380s.[57] However, Mullan and Britnell have recently sounded a cautionary note about this general chronology. They do not read any significance into the 'spasmodic absence of reference to the villein status of customary land in the Winchester pipe rolls' before c.1430, attributing it instead to 'clerical omission' of 'superfluous words' rather than to a real change in the dignity of the tenure: for them, the decisive period of change on the estates of the Bishopric of Winchester occurred much later, between 1430 and 1470.[58] Their caution about how much can be reliably read into the language of conveyances echoes the warning of P.D.A. Harvey, who is uncertain about whether any exact meaning can be inferred from the words used in late-medieval land transfers.[59] The chronology and significance of

---

[54] Page, 'End of villeinage', pp. 83–5. Precisely what *was* the custom of the manor is seldom articulated or recorded, and therefore it has to be inferred from the evidence and the practices revealed by chance in court roll entries, Whittle, *Agrarian capitalism*, pp. 74–5.

[55] For example, 'X holds ten acres of bond land once of Smith's tenement by copy according to the custom of the manor', or 'Y leases a virgate of villein land at farm'. Thus in 1484 in Yoxford (Suffolk) one Thomas Burnham held two and a half acres of 'native' meadowland 'by copy', and another tenant held 30 acres of 'native' arable and pasture 'in lease', A.H. Denney, ed., *The Sibton abbey estates. Select documents 1325–1509*, Suffolk Records Society, volume 2 (1960), pp. 105, 107.

[56] Harvey, *Westminster abbey*, p. 275; Fryde, 'Peasant rebellion and discontent', pp. 814–16; Raftis, 'Peasants and the collapse of the manorial economy', pp. 193–6; Schofield, *Peasants and community*, p. 17.

[57] C. Howell, *Land, family and inheritance in transition. Kibworth Harcourt 1280–1700* (Cambridge, 1983), pp. 51–2; Howell, 'Inheritance customs', pp. 132–4; Jones, 'Bedfordshire', p. 203. See also the formal changes to the form of villein tenure at Battle in the 1450s, E. Searle, *Lordship and community. Battle abbey and its banlieu 1066–1538* (Toronto, 1974), pp. 380–3.

[58] J. Mullan and R.H. Britnell, *Land and family. Trends and local variations in the peasant land market on the Winchester bishopric estates, 1263–1415* (Hatfield, 2010), pp. 63–4.

[59] Harvey, 'Aspects of the peasant land market', pp. 329–30.

changes in the language of conveyances will be explored directly in the case studies which follow.

The fourth and final development of significance is the growth of fixed-term tenures of various kinds. In c.1300 the vast majority of customary land was held on heritable villein tenure: the right of inheritance is identifiable by the ubiquitous phrase 'to hold for him and his heirs [*sibi et heredibus suis*]'.[60] After the Black Death a growing proportion of this villein tenure was formally converted to, and re-granted as, tenures for a finite period of time, after which the land reverted to the lord. The conversion from heredi-tary villein tenure to a customary fixed-term tenancy sometimes involved the removal of all servile incidents and their replacement with a high, but fixed, annual money rent.[61] Fixed-term tenures were essentially economic contracts covering the temporary rather than permanent alienation of land. They are all forms of leases, in a strict technical sense, although three broad sub-categories of fixed-term tenure are identifiable.

The first category comprises the most rudimentary form of fixed-term tenancy, i.e. one held 'at the will of the lord' without any stipulated time-frame for a straight money rent.[62] The phrasing for this type of tenure is usually a variant of 'X holds Y acres of land at the will of the lord rendering Zs. per annum'. Entry fines were not usually charged. In this context, the conspicuous absence of any qualifying statements about the length of term, or about any rights of inheritance, meant that the lord could literally termi-nate at his will. Landlords appear to have used such grants as a temporary expedient, as a means of filling an empty holding quickly for a very short term until it could be re-granted on the old terms. Such were the '*de exitus*' grants popular in the immediate aftermath of the first (1348–9) and second (1361) plague epidemics, whereby a new tenant paid a small sum of money to occupy abandoned customary land until such time as the heir, or another tenant, could be found to hold it on villein tenure.[63] These were the most insecure form of customary tenure, although they were not very common.[64]

The second category of fixed-term tenure was that held for the term of the life of the tenant, or for a stipulated term of lives (usually three). This

---

[60] Dyer, *Lords and peasants*, p. 292; Harvey, *Westminster abbey*, pp. 241–2.

[61] Kaye, *Medieval English conveyances*, pp. 357–8.

[62] Grants 'at the will of the lord' or 'by the rod' had been known since the late thirteenth century, and the use of these particular phrases was designed to signal that these were customary grants and not to be mistaken for free tenure, Smith, 'English peasantry', p. 353.

[63] M. Bailey, *A marginal economy? East Anglian Breckland in the later Middle Ages* (Cambridge, 1989), pp. 224–5; J. Titow, 'Lost rents, vacant holdings and the contraction of peasant cultivation after the Black Death', *Agricultural History Review*, 42 (1994), pp. 100–4.

[64] Hatcher, 'Serfdom and villeinage', p. 15.

had been known as a form of tenancy since Anglo-Saxon times, although before c.1300 it was not a common method of holding customary land.[65] The seigniorial motives for granting life tenancies were varied, although the main one was to generate a good rental income without alienating the land.[66] They are identifiable within manorial court rolls by conveyances containing phrases such as 'to hold to him for the term of his life [*"ad terminum vitam suam"*] at the will of the lord' or 'to hold to him, his wife and his son for the term of their lives [*"ad terminum vite eorum"*] at the will of the lord': the mention of other 'heirs' was conspicuously avoided. Thus, at Coleshill (Berkshire) in the 1420s, the majority of grants of land were to a tenant and his wife 'to hold for their lives according to the custom of the manor at the will of the lord'.[67] Entry fines were usually charged. This form of tenure may have originated in the reversionary right of widows in many places to hold customary land for the rest of their lives after the death of their husband.[68] By c.1500 terms for three lives were the most common form.[69]

Many life tenancies appear to have been created by direct conversions from hereditary villein tenures. For example, in 1361 four villeins paid fines of up to £1 each in the manorial court of South Moreton (Berkshire) to be released from villeinage and to hold their land 'for the term of a life' instead, and in the 1370s seven tenants of Englefield (Berkshire) held their tenements for life.[70] Between c.1350 and c.1420 many hereditary customary virgates on the estate of Ramsey abbey were converted to life tenancies paying just money rent (*arentata*).[71] The scale of such conversions could be significant. At Houghton (Huntingdonshire) between the 1390s and the 1420s around one half of the former customary virgates were granted for money rent for life.[72] The period from the 1390s to the 1450s has been dubbed the 'golden age of the life lease' at Holywell-cum-Needingworth (Huntingdonshire).[73] The loss of perpetual rights of inheritance was evidently of little concern to these tenants. Faith argues that in the land-hungry conditions of the early fourteenth century families had clung to inheritance customs because these

[65] In the early fourteenth century a few customary holdings were held for a term of lives rather than heritably. See, for example, some holdings on the Berkeley estates in Gloucestershire, Wells-Furby, *The Berkeley estate*, pp. 96–7.

[66] Kaye, *Medieval English conveyances*, pp. 236–7.

[67] Faith, 'Berkshire', pp. 156–7.

[68] M.E. Mate, *Women in medieval English society* (Cambridge, 1999), pp. 20–1, 78–80.

[69] Kaye, *Medieval English conveyances*, p. 237.

[70] Faith, 'Berkshire', pp. 137, 151.

[71] Raftis, *Ramsey abbey*, pp. 250 n. 2, and 259–60.

[72] Raftis, *Ramsey abbey*, p. 269, figures for 1394 and 1418.

[73] E.B. Dewindt, *Land and people in Holywell-cum-Needingworth* (Toronto, 1972), pp. 107–9, 134–5. For longer leases, see H.P.R. Finberg, *Tavistock abbey* (Cambridge, 1951), p. 250.

ensured the eventual succession of their heirs to customary land, but they were much less fussed about such rights when the land market slackened after the Black Death: the result was the growing popularity of more flexible forms of tenure and 'the decline of customary inheritance'.[74] However, the exact chronology of this decline is uncertain. The works of Faith, Jones and Raftis reveal unequivocally that tenures for lives were known in the late fourteenth century, although Allen dates their arrival to the early fifteenth century.[75] Hoyle has suggested that they did not become *widespread* until after the late fifteenth century.[76]

The third form of fixed-term tenure was leasehold for a term of years. Leases for years are similar in form and structure to life tenancies, although the latter possessed a social cachet that short-term leases did not.[77] The grant of a lease in the court roll, or its enrolment on the manorial account, invariably deploys one or both of the phrases 'to lease [*dimittere*]' or 'to hold at farm [*teneo ad firmam*]': these phrases are often absent from the conveyances of customary life tenancies. Hence the formula usually appears as 'X leases/holds at farm one virgate of customary land for Y years rendering Zs. per annum'. Leases of customary land were terse and basic, naming the tenant, the property, the length of the term and the annual rent. There were few if any sub clauses. They were created through the direct conversion of a hereditary villein tenure, and the vast majority were held for money rent set at whatever the market would bear in lieu of all servile incidents. However, variants existed. A few were held for a combination of cash and seasonal labour services, and modest entry fines were charged on some leases.[78] The rent days for leases are seldom stated, but one assumes that they were determined by the custom of the manor. Customary leases by copy of the manorial court roll offered the tenant less security than leases of free land, or of demesne land, 'by grant of leasehold', a more formal arrangement in which both parties interchangeably signed and obtained copies of the agreement laying out terms, conditions and covenants. The latter, which arguably gave the lessee parity with the landlord before the law, had been used long before

---

74   Faith, 'Berkshire', pp. 120–1.

75   For Faith and Raftis, see above, fn 70–1; Jones, 'Bedfordshire', p. 203; Allen, *Enclosure and the yeoman*, p. 67.

76   Hoyle, 'Tenure and the land market', pp. 7–8. There is certainly evidence that tenures for lives were relatively recent introductions, and spreading rapidly in the late fifteenth century on the estate of the Bishopric of Worcester, Dyer, *Lords and peasants*, p. 294.

77   Kaye, *Medieval English conveyances*, p. 237.

78   Whittle, 'Leasehold tenure', p. 141; Schofield, 'Tenurial developments', pp. 256–7; M.E. Mate, *Trade and economic developments, 1450–1550. The experience of Kent, Surrey and Sussex* (Woodbridge, 2006), pp. 223–8.

the fourteenth century by freemen and landlords to contract out a wide range of landed resources.[79]

The conversion of villein tenure into leaseholds has not attracted the attention it deserves, even though it is the least complex aspect of late-medieval tenurial change.[80] Historians have tended to regard the spread of leasehold tenure as an important prerequisite to the development of capitalist farming, because it comprised a commercial contract and it established a level of rent that forced the lessee to maximize farm profits. Whittle has distinguished between 'commercial' leases – those held for terms of less than 21 years for a commercial rent per acre – and 'beneficial' leases, held for lower fixed annual rents and granted for long periods in excess of 21 years.[81] Brenner assumed that landlords were the driving force behind the introduction of leases, because they were the main beneficiaries of them. Upon termination of a lease, he argued that landlords enjoyed a number of options: to increase the rent, to change tenant, or to engross the land within their own expanding demesne farm.[82] Commercial, short-term, leases were certainly beneficial to landlords in periods of rising land values and grain prices, such as the sixteenth and early seventeenth centuries. Yet commercial leases could be beneficial to the tenant in different circumstances, such as periods when labour was scarce, and land values falling, because they enabled tenants to reduce their exposure to risk in challenging or uncertain times.[83] Hence, in some circumstances, tenants might have been the driving force behind the introduction of leases. None of this is surprising, because the very flexibility and variety of leases made them highly adaptable to changing needs and circumstance.

Leasehold was already well established in thirteenth-century England, when it was most commonly used to grant individual components of the manorial demesne on a temporary basis to a number of different tenants.

---

[79] See R.W. Hoyle, 'Monastic leasing before the Dissolution: the evidence of Fountains abbey and Bolton priory', *Yorkshire Archaeological Journal*, 61 (1989), pp. 111–38; Kaye, *Medieval English conveyances*, pp. 254–77.

[80] Although there has been some good work on leaseholds: see Mate, 'East Sussex land market', pp. 52–5; Schofield, *Peasants*, pp. 18–19; and van Bavel and Schofield, eds., *The development of leasehold*.

[81] Whittle, 'Leasehold tenure', p. 141.

[82] Brenner, 'Agrarian class structure', pp. 46–50, and also J.E. Martin, *Feudalism to capitalism. Peasant and landlord in English agrarian development* (London, 1986), pp. 102–17. For a critical evaluation of this hypothesis, see van Bavel and Schofield, 'Introduction', pp. 21–2; Whittle, 'Leasehold tenure', p. 139; Hoyle, 'An ancient and laudable custom', pp. 47, 55; J. Broad, *Transforming English rural society. The Verneys and Claydons 1600–1820* (Cambridge, 2004), pp. 50–2.

[83] Schofield, *Peasant and community*, p. 31; Van Bavel and Schofield, 'Introduction', p. 22; M. Muller, 'Peasant land and developments in leasing in late medieval England', in van Bavel and Schofield, eds., *Development of leasehold*, pp. 155–66.

The conversion of parcels of the manorial demesne to leasehold is well documented in the literature.[84] In contrast, hardly any villein tenures were converted to leasehold before c.1350, although thereafter it became increasingly common to convert either odd parcels of former customary tenures, or entire holdings, to leasehold. Following the severity of the Black Death of 1348–9, which killed around 40% of rural land tenants in England, sizeable areas of customary land remained abandoned and untenanted for months or even years on many manors. Faced with the prospect of diminished rent rolls and reduced land occupancy in the early 1350s, more and more landlords began to offer abandoned villein holdings on leases as a way of enticing new tenants with flexible and attractive rent packages, largely free of servile obligations.[85] For example, within a generation of the Black Death bond holdings on the estates of Durham priory had been converted to leasehold, and, as consequence, villein tenure had been transformed.[86]

Hence the area of former customary land converted to leasehold increased after 1348–9 as a means of finding tenants for those parcels of customary land that remained stubbornly vacant.[87] This suited landlords, because it enabled them to find tenants and boost their rent rolls, although the short-term nature of many of the early grants (for terms of a year or two) indicates that the conversions were regarded as a temporary measure to kick start the land market.[88] Yet leases also suited the needs of tenants, because they offered flexible access to land, released from the taint and unpredictability of servile obligations, at a reasonable cash rent and on a fixed-term contract. Furthermore, tenants could thus acquire land without the need to raise the capital sum necessary for any outright purchase, enabling first-timers to obtain a foot on the property ladder.[89] Hence leasehold provided an excellent opportunity for both existing landholders to extend, and for newcomers to acquire, landholdings in a manner that offered relative freedom, flexibility and protection against risk: attractive attributes in uncertain and swiftly

---

[84] See, for example, Mullan and Britnell, *Land and* family, pp. 64–8.

[85] Faith, 'Berkshire', p. 124; Bailey, *A marginal economy?*, pp. 223–31; P.L. Larson, *Conflict and compromise in the late medieval countryside. Lords and peasants in Durham 1349–1400* (London, 2006), pp. 162–3; Whittle, 'Leasehold tenure', pp. 147–8; Muller, 'Peasant land', pp. 163–5.

[86] R.A. Lomas, *Northeast England in the Middle Ages* (Edinburgh, 1992), pp. 191–2; and 'A priory and its tenants', in R.H. Britnell, ed., *Daily life in the Middle Ages* (Stroud, 1998), pp. 112–13.

[87] Bailey, *Medieval Suffolk*, pp. 180–2.

[88] Many short-term leases, 'farms' of a year or two for small fragments of land, are recorded in various places. See, for example, Bailey, *Marginal economy*, p. 223; Mate, 'East Sussex land market', pp. 52–5.

[89] Schofield, 'Tenurial developments', pp. 262, 264.

changing economic conditions.[90] In these circumstances, the tenant held the balance of power in pressing for the lease.[91]

Many of the published estate studies mention the grant of some customary land at lease during the 1350s, and then identify c.1390 to c.1420 as the main period in its growth, without analysing the trend in any detail.[92] A notable exception is Schofield's study of Birdbrook (Essex), where the number of customary holdings converted to leasehold doubled during the course of the 1390s, so that, at the end of the decade, only one standardized holding remained on the old bond tenure.[93] Landlords appear to have been reluctant to relinquish the hereditary villein tenure, judging by the addition of a caveat to some leases that the holding was to be returned to the lord if anyone could be found willing to hold it by 'ancient service'.[94] The sense that landlords, not tenants, were making the greater concession in granting leases is also supported by a tendency everywhere during the fifteenth century for the length of individual leases to increase, as tenants levered greater security of tenure when negotiating re-grants.[95] In some cases leases now stretched to 20, 30 or 40 years, or for the life of the tenant.

The area of former villein land held on leasehold peaked in the first quarter of the fifteenth century. Leasing declined markedly thereafter, both in terms of the levels of income received from, and the area of former customary land held on, leases.[96] What, then, became of the land? Some land was either left uncultivated or absorbed within the demesne when its lease was either abandoned in mid-term or could not be re-let upon expiry. Some leases mutated into tenure for a term of lives: after all, a long lease resembles a life tenancy.[97] Leases for 40 years, common on the estates of Tavistock abbey in

90 Harvey, 'Aspects of the peasant land market', p. 334; Smith, 'English peasantry', p. 361; Larson, *Conflict and compromise*, pp. 165–7. See also Schofield, 'Tenurial developments', p. 262.

91 Larson, *Conflict and compromise*, pp. 191, 201.

92 Raftis, *Ramsey abbey*, pp. 259–60; Finberg, *Tavistock abbey*, pp. 249–52; Dyer, *Lords and peasants*, pp. 292–3; DeWindt, *Land and people*, pp. 101–2, 107–9; Faith, 'Berkshire', p. 127; Bailey, *Marginal economy*, pp. 223–31; Schofield, 'Tenurial developments', p. 257; Harvey, *Westminster abbey*, pp. 254–6, 263–4.

93 Schofield, 'Tenurial developments', pp. 256–60.

94 Harvey, *Westminster abbey*, pp. 263–4; Faith, 'Berkshire', pp. 124–5.

95 In the 1370s the length of leases of former villein land varied between five and ten years at Forncett (Norfolk), with most at seven years, but in the 1430s the range had increased to five to twenty years, with most at ten years, Davenport, *Economic development*, p. 77.

96 Harvey, *Westminster abbey*, pp. 276–7, 281; Dyer, *Lords and peasants*, pp. 292–4; Britnell, 'Tenant farmers and farming: Eastern England', p. 615–16; Fryde, *Peasants and landlords*, p. 229; Whittle, *Agrarian capitalism*, pp. 73–4; Bailey, *Medieval Suffolk*, pp. 199–200, 230–2.

97 Whittle, 'Leasehold tenure', p. 149.

the mid-fifteenth century, had been largely replaced by tenancies for (three) lives at the beginning of the sixteenth century.[98] Similarly, the 'tenant right' copyholds of northwest England during the sixteenth century appear to have originated as long leases.[99] Finally, some customary land was converted back to a heritable tenancy rather than re-granted again at lease. Customary holdings at Birdbrook (Essex), nearly all leased in c.1400, were held on a form of heritable copyhold by 1500.[100] In the second quarter of fifteenth century some leases of customary land for years were re-granted upon expiry 'at fee farm [*ad feodi firmam*]' in some parts of East Anglia.[101] The concept of the fee farm originated in the twelfth and thirteenth centuries, when such grants were widely used in conveyances of free and burghal properties as a means of replacing all attendant incidents and services with a money rent.[102] A *customary* fee farm effectively converted a lease to a hereditary tenure, thus enabling the tenant to hold the land for an annual money rent, free of servile incidents, with customary rights of inheritance. However, these processes remain dimly understood: why did leaseholds decline in importance during the fifteenth century? What determined whether they were converted to a life tenancy or a hereditary tenancy?

Conclusion

Around one half of the land available to English peasants in the early fourteenth century was held on villein tenure. Villeins enjoyed rights of inheritance over this land, but could only defend their title to it in the manorial court of their landlord. By the sixteenth century villein tenure had evolved into fully fledged copyholds and leaseholds. Copyholds of inheritance retained the hereditary principle, whereas those for lives, and leases, did not. The transformation of the villein tenure of c.1300 into the copyholds of c.1550 was a complex and slow process, which remains only partially understood. The precise nature and status of tenures in the fifteenth century are somewhat varied and vague: they had shed many characteristics of villeinage, but their title could still not be defended in the courts of common law, and it was not until the sixteenth century that lawyers defined explicitly what they had become.

98   Finberg, *Tavistock abbey*, p. 250.
99   Hoyle, 'An ancient and laudable custom', p. 27.
100   Schofield, '*Extranei*', pp. 11–12. See also Fryde, *Peasants and landlords*, p. 229, who identifies a shift from leases to hereditary tenures after the 1430s on the estates of the Bishopric of Worcester.
101   Davenport, *Economic development*, pp. 57–8; Britnell, *Britain and Ireland*, p. 437.
102   Kaye, *Medieval English conveyances*, pp. 105–17.

It appears that most copyholds of inheritance emerged through the slow evolution – rather than the conversion – of villein tenure. The general consensus is that after the 1390s hereditary villein tenure gradually shed the various servile incidents that comprised the bulk of the rent package, and dropped the use of phrases such as 'held in villeinage' from conveyances.[103] Likewise, the practice slowly spread of supplying the tenant with a copy of the court roll entry describing the grant of the land, and of using this written record as proof of title in the manorial court, which had become commonplace by the middle of the fifteenth century. The conversion of villein tenure to various types of fixed-term tenure – mainly leases for years and life tenancies – was unusual in the early fourteenth century, but it had become more common by the end of the fifteenth century: these were the forerunners of the copyholds for lives and leases of the sixteenth century.

The pace of tenurial change was notably quicker during two periods: the 1350s, and between the 1390s and 1420s. The massive loss of tenants in 1348–9 meant that some changes were necessary in the 1350s to encourage land occupancy, while after the 1390s falling prices, rising costs and shortages of coin generated difficulties for many agriculturalists. The high turnover in land ownership during both periods created more opportunities for renegotiating the terms and conditions of land tenure, and therefore accelerated a move away from villeinage.[104] After the 1470s, and well into the sixteenth century, the gradual recovery of the economy and the return of agrarian prosperity stimulated new legal interest in the status of customary land under the common law.[105]

The chronology of changes to the rent package attached to customary land is considered in more detail in Chapter 3. Meanwhile, this survey of the current state of knowledge about customary tenures has revealed that the answers to a number of questions about their transformation in the late Middle Ages remain uncertain. Why did some land on villein tenure evolve slowly into hereditary tenures by copy, while other land was converted to fixed-term tenures? Can any real significance be attributed to changes in the language of conveyances of villein land? How far had the practice spread

---

[103] Allen identifies the late fourteenth and early fifteenth centuries as the period of great fluidity in tenurial arrangements, *Enclosure and the yeoman*, p. 65. See also Raftis, 'Peasants and the collapse of the manorial economy', pp. 197, 202–3.

[104] See, for example, Jones, 'Bedfordshire', pp. 203–4; Faith, 'Berkshire', pp. 127, 132–3; Schofeld, 'Tenurial developments', p. 258. At Birdbrook the shift to leasehold between the late 1380s and early 1400s was also associated with a decline in inheritance by kin, and with an increase in people from outside the village holding land, Schofield, '*Extranei*', pp. 4–5.

[105] Harvey, 'Aspects of the peasant land market', pp. 335–6; Schofield, '*Extranei*', pp. 7, 16.

of issuing copies of the court roll entry of land transfers to tenants in the second half of the fourteenth century?

Another set of questions relates to the development of fixed-term tenures. What was the extent and the chronology of their growth in the later Middle Ages? Can tenures for lives be readily distinguished from tenures of inheritance before c.1500 and, if so, were they widespread?[106] To what extent is Brenner correct to assert that landlords appropriated vacant customary holdings and converted them to leaseholds? To what extent did the enthusiasm for leases diminish in the fifteenth century, and what then became of them? Why did the popularity of leases wane? None of these questions have been fully answered, yet they remain crucial to our understanding of tenurial evolution and change. The answers will provide a firm evidentiary basis for attempting to answer the one major question which has so far eluded early modern historians: what explains the clear regional distribution between copyholds for lives and copyholds of inheritance? The case studies which follow attempt to address these issues directly.

---

[106]   Hoyle, 'Tenure and the land market', p. 8 suggests not: 'in the fifteenth and early sixteenth century there was no effective distinction between copyholds for lives or by inheritance: there was only copyhold'.

3

The Chronology of Decline: Servile Incidents

All sections of medieval English society were liable to render various payments and services to a superior lord, which either marked key moments in the life cycle of an individual or were associated with the terms of their landholding. The nobility and gentry paid aid upon the marriage of their lord's eldest daughter, and were liable for military service; freemen paid relief upon entry to a landholding; and all but the poorest paid mortuary (a death duty) to the church. Villeins and villein tenures were also liable for a range of incidents, dues and services, but these differed from those owed by the rest of society in two ways: they were generally more onerous and demeaning, and the lord could – in strict legal theory – impose them arbitrarily. In reality, by c.1300 the arbitrary imposition of servile dues was exceptionally rare, and instead their frequency and duration were determined and largely fixed by local custom. However, there still remained some elements of uncertainty and unpredictability, in the sense that the precise package of dues, and the way in which they were levied, varied from manor to manor; the lord could determine how much was charged for some dues; and the lord might challenge or ignore custom.[1]

This chapter surveys each of the main dues and incidents associated with villeinage in England in c.1300; briefly explains their character, origin and prevalence; and then constructs as tight a chronology of their decline as the current historical literature permits.

Merchet

A person subject to merchet had to obtain the permission of the lord to marry, and, in theory, the lord could either refuse permission or grant it demanding 'whatever he desired'.[2] In practice, and especially from the late thirteenth century, the lord seldom refused permission and invariably received money in lieu of this permission through his manor court. Thus

---

[1] Dyer, 'New serfdom', p. 427; Fryde, *Peasants and landlords*, p. 14; P.R. Schofield, 'Lordship and the peasant economy, 1250–1400: Robert Kyng and the Abbot of Bury St Edmunds', in Dyer, Coss and Wickham, eds., *Rodney Hilton's Middle Ages*, pp. 56–7.

[2] Hyams, *King, Lords and peasants*, p. 187.

merchet was a fine levied upon villein tenants and hereditary serfs as permission for their daughters to marry, and it was one of the most ubiquitous and common incidents of villeinage in England. Merchet was usually regarded in law as a conclusive test of both villein tenure and of servile status. As such, according to Vinogradoff, it was 'the most striking consequence of unfreedom'.[3]

Historians have disagreed on the exact purpose of merchet. It has been variously interpreted as a means of discouraging (or encouraging) marriage outside the manor, in order to exert some control over the size of the local labour force; as a method of regulating marriage and vetting husbands; or as a tax on the dowry of an unfree peasant, and, by extension, upon the alienation of villein chattels from the lord.[4] To some extent, this disagreement can be explained by the existence of different local customs in the approach to merchet, which are further reflected in subtle local differences in liability for merchet. In most places, merchet was liable whenever the daughter of a villein tenant, or a landless serf, married, but, in a few places, sons were also liable whereas, in others, it was required only if a daughter married outside the manor.[5] The size of payments varied widely, from a few pennies to a few pounds, although most fell between 2s. and 10s. Wealthy villeins, widows seeking remarriage, and those wishing to marry freemen were usually charged higher rates, while paupers might be exonerated. The average rate charged on a given manor could rise over time, reflecting some undefined change in underlying administrative, economic or social circumstances. For example, the average fine for merchet increased fourfold between 1308–19 and 1335–45 on the manor of Sutton-in-the-Isle (Cambridgeshire), with a similar increase in the size of fines for marrying without licence, for no

3   Vinogradoff, *Villeinage in England*, pp. 153–6; D.C. Douglas, *The social structure of medieval East Anglia* (Oxford, 1927), pp. 72–5; Hyams, *King, lords and peasants*, pp. 189–90; Faith, *English peasantry*, pp. 263–4; Fryde, *Peasants and landlords*, p. 124; Rigby, *English society*, p. 259.

4   A.E. Levett, *Studies in manorial history* (Oxford, 1938), pp. 245–6; J. Scammell, 'Freedom and marriage in England', *Economic History Review*, 27 (1974), pp. 523–37; E. Searle, 'Freedom and marriage in medieval England: an alternative hypothesis', *Economic History Review*, 29 (1976), pp. 482–6; E. Searle, 'Seigniorial control of women's marriage: the antecedents and function of merchet in England', *Past and Present*, 82 (1979), pp. 3–43; Hyams, *King, lords and peasants*, pp. 187–90; J.M. Bennett, 'Medieval peasant marriage: an examination of marriage licence fines in the *Liber Gersumarum*', in J.A. Raftis, ed., *Pathways to medieval peasants* (Toronto, 1981), pp. 193–246; P. Brand and P.R. Hyams, 'Seigneurial control of women's marriage', *Past and Present*, 99 (1983), pp. 122–33; E. Searle, 'A rejoinder', *Past and Present*, 99 (1983), pp. 148–60.

5   Rigby, *English society*, p. 259; Bailey, 'Villeinage in England', pp. 438–9.

reason that is obviously apparent.[6] Elsewhere, set fines were not unknown, such as the standard tariff of 1s. 3d. for marriages between serfs on the estate of Tavistock abbey.[7]

The requirement to render merchet did not mean that villeins reported their marriages willingly to their lord's manorial court, nor that the seigniorial administration always monitored the liability for merchet tightly. It has been suggested that recorded merchets never comprised more than around one half of the marriages that actually took place among those liable to pay them.[8] As Mate observes, 'a large number of unauthorized marriages could take place before a zealous official caught up with them, if he ever did'.[9] Officials were more attentive to the marriages of heiresses and wealthier villeins, and to the remarriages of widows, than to those of smallholders or the landless. Yet the frequency and ubiquity of 'unlicensed' marriages indicates that officials did monitor and take action against those villeins who failed to report their nuptials. In many cases, the average size of payments for unlicensed marriages was lower than the average size of merchet on the same manor, which suggests that unlicensed marriages were concentrated among the landless and smallholding population.[10] However, unlicensed fines were sometimes significantly higher than merchets, perhaps when the lord wished to create an incentive to report marriages.[11]

Merchet continued to be collected rigorously in the immediate aftermath of the Black Death. Average fines rose in a few places, reflecting either increases in wealth per capita – and by extension the size of dowries – or a seigniorial desire to extract more cash from survivors of the epidemic. The latter seems to have been the case at Halesowen (Warwickshire), where the merchet fine jumped from around 2s. to 6s. 8d. after the Black Death, before its sudden and complete disappearance in 1385 following tension between the lord and his serfs.[12] Elsewhere merchet continued to be charged well beyond

6   E. McGribbon Smith, 'Court rolls as evidence for village society. Sutton-in-the-Isle in the fourteenth century', in M. Bailey and S.H. Rigby, eds., *England in the age of the Black Death. Essays in honour of John Hatcher* (Turnhout, 2012), p. 270.

7   Finberg, *Tavistock abbey*, pp. 77–8.

8   L.R. Poos, R.M. Smith and Z. Razi, 'The population history of medieval English villages: a debate on the use of manor court rolls', in Z. Razi and R.M. Smith, eds., *Medieval society and the manor court* (Oxford, 1996), pp. 318–19.

9   M.E. Mate, *Daughters, wives and widows. Women in Sussex, 1350–1535* (Woodbridge, 1998), pp. 192–3.

10   Scammell, 'Freedom and marriage', pp. 534–5; Bailey, 'Villeinage in England', pp. 439–40.

11   Merchets on the St Albans estates were usually charged between 6d. and 4s., while unlicensed marriages attracted a fee of 6s. 8d., Levett, *Studies in manorial history*, p. 239.

12   Razi, *Life, marriage, death*, p. 132.

the 1380s, although the level of fine began to fall.[13] For example, merchet was usually charged between 3s. 4d. and 13s. 4d. during the third quarter of the fourteenth century on the estate of the Bishopric of Worcester, but then fell to around 2s. in the early fifteenth century, and closer to 1s. in the 1450s.[14]

After c.1400 the declining size of the fine for merchet was accompanied by a decline in its frequency and, finally, by its disappearance. Evidence of its disappearance in the second quarter of the fifteenth century can be found from places as far apart as south Yorkshire, Sussex and the east Midlands.[15] It began to disappear in the 1450s from some manors on the estate of the Bishopric of Worcester, although it survived late into the century on the estate of St Albans abbey.[16] Where it survived so late, its frequency was greatly diminished, and prone to swings in administrative competence and enthusiasm. For example, no merchet was collected between 1435 and 1447 on the Pelham estates in Sussex, yet two sizeable, but isolated, payments were made in 1463.[17] A few estates, such as Battle abbey, were still charging merchet in the early sixteenth century, usually upon serfs rather than upon tenants of customary land, although the frequency was low because the number of serf families had dwindled severely.[18]

Leyrwite and childwite

Leyrwite was known in the eleventh century, although its origins are obscure.[19] By the later thirteenth century it was widely established as a charge upon unmarried female serfs for fornication. Examples of males being presented for leyrwite are exceptionally rare.[20] In some parts of the country, such as East Anglia, it was levied upon the reproductive results of sexual activity, and known as childwite, rather than upon the act of intercourse. Female serfs were not charged for both.[21]

[13] Fryde, *Peasants and landlords*, p. 69; Howell, *Kibworth Harcourt*, pp. 33–4.

[14] Dyer, *Lords and peasants*, pp. 273–4.

[15] Mate, *Daughters, wives and widows*, p. 193; M.E. Mate, 'Tenant farming and tenant farmers: Kent and Sussex', in *AgHEW III*, p. 686; Howell, *Kibworth Harcourt*, pp. 33–4.

[16] Levett, *Studies in manorial history*, p. 244; Fryde, *Peasants and landlords*, p. 176.

[17] Mate, *Daughters, wives and widows*, pp. 192–3.

[18] Mate, 'Tenant farming and tenant farmers: Kent and Sussex', p. 686.

[19] T. North, 'Legerwite in the thirteenth and fourteenth centuries', *Past and Present*, III (1986), pp. 4–5.

[20] Although it happened on the estate of St Albans abbey, see M. Tomkins, 'Park', in (no editor) *The Peasants' Revolt in Hertfordshire 1381* (Hertford, 1981), pp. 66–7.

[21] North, 'Legerwite', pp. 7–8; J. Bennett, 'Writing fornication: medieval leyrwite

Illicit sexual activity was directly punishable in ecclesiastical courts, where the punishments were usually either a fine or penance, and so historians have speculated upon the reasons for the presence of a repeat punishment in manorial courts. Most agree that it represented a form of financial compensation to the lord: perhaps for the alienation of part of the serf's assets to another jurisdiction (i.e. the fine paid to the church court); or for the potential loss of a merchet; or for the loss of a servile asset, since bastards were deemed to be free.[22] Whatever the precise legal principle, leyrwite was both 'a response to moral lapse and a manifestation of seigniorial power'.[23]

Leyrwite was common in the eastern counties, the Midlands and the North, although it was rare in many areas of southern and south western England. On a few estates the lord was entitled to seize any land held by the offender and to dispose of it at will, but most just charged a modest cash sum.[24] Around c.1300 the modal charge was 6d., although the range of fines varied from 4d. to 6s. 8d., and in the eastern counties a regional charge of 2s. 8d. was widely established.[25] The fines were overwhelmingly paid by the women themselves. Bennett has shown that the incidence of leyrwite peaked around 1300, when demographic pressure was most acute in many communities, and that it was imposed mainly upon the poorer elements of society, indicating that communities increasingly used it to discourage sexual activity in a period of demographic crisis.[26] In a few places, such as the estates of Durham priory, it was used to target prostitution.[27] The limited frequency of, and low profits from, leyrwite even at its peak suggest that it did not constitute a significant element of the seigniorial management of villeinage.[28]

After peaking around 1300, leyrwite fell into a steep decline from c.1350. By the late fourteenth century it had disappeared from all but the most conservative estates, and by 1500 it was, in Bennett's phrase, 'a matter of memory, not practice'.[29]

and its historians', *Transactions of the Royal Historical Society*, sixth series, XIII (2003), pp. 134, 141; Bailey, 'Villeinage in England', pp. 440–1.

[22] F. Pollock and F.W. Maitland, *History of English Law*, volume II (Cambridge, 1963), p. 543; Vinogradoff, *Villeinage in England*, p. 154.

[23] Bennett, 'Writing fornication', p. 139.

[24] Page, *Crowland abbey*, p. 109.

[25] North, 'Legerwite', p. 10; E.D. Jones, 'The medieval leyrwite: a historical note upon fornication', *English Historical Review*, 107 (1992), p. 947; Bailey, 'Villeinage in England', pp. 440–1.

[26] Bennett, 'Writing fornication', pp. 142–3, 152.

[27] Larson, *Conflict and compromise*, p. 156.

[28] Jones, 'Medieval leyrwite', p. 947; Bennett, 'Writing fornication', p. 136.

[29] Bennett, 'Writing fornication', p. 134.

Chevage

Chevage [*chevagium*] was ubiquitous on the Continent, but less widespread in England.[30] It literally means 'head money'. Its origins are obscure, and during the thirteenth century the term was applied generically to a number of very different types of exaction, including one paid by freemen to the Crown.[31] The latter explains why chevage was not regarded as a reliable test of villeinage under the common law. In many places during the thirteenth century chevage, also called 'capitage' [*capitagium*], was a payment due from any serf who did not hold land or property on his home manor.[32] On a few manors it was a charge upon immigrants: on others, it was a head charge upon all those landless serfs who lived upon the manor and were not liable to tallage (see below).[33]

The most common form of chevage was a specific payment from a villein to his lord for permission to reside away from the manor. This was usually coupled with the requirement that the migrant returned each year to a session of the manorial court to renew the licence. The denial of the right to move permanently was a fundamental limitation upon freedom.[34] Chevage marked the landlord's rights over those serfs who did move, thus reinforcing the serf's status and enabling the lord 'to retain some hold' over migrants.[35] Not all migrants paid chevage. Some illicit departures were either ignored or unreported, and Fox suggests that before the Black Death most landlords only collected it from those emigrants who wished to retain an interest in their home manor.[36] Some absences were 'presented' each year in the manorial court. The court would then usually order their return, and sometimes bring pressure to bear by either ordering the distraint of goods belonging to the absentee, or fining the nearest relative. In theory the lord could seek out, physically seize and return the absentee to render chevage or to be admitted to a landholding, but such extreme actions were very rare.[37]

---

30   H.S.A. Fox, 'The exploitation of the landless by lords and tenants in early medieval England', in Razi and Smith, eds., *Manor court*, p. 527.

31   R.E. Latham, 'Minor enigmas from medieval records', *English Historical Review*, 76 (1961), pp. 639–45.

32   Fox, 'Exploitation of the landless', pp. 526–33.

33   Latham, 'Minor enigmas', pp. 643–4; Hyams, *King, lords and peasants*, p. 36; E.M. Carus-Wilson, 'Evidence for industrial growth on some fifteenth-century manors', in E.M. Carus-Wilson, ed., *Essays in economic history*, volume two (London, 1962), p. 161; Fox, 'Exploitation of the landless', p. 528.

34   Hatcher, 'Serfdom and villeinage', p. 30; Latham, 'Minor enigmas', pp. 642–3.

35   Vinogradoff, *Villeinage in England*, p. 157; Hyams, *King, lords and peasants*, pp. 34–6.

36   Fox, 'Exploitation of the landless', pp. 527–8.

37   Raftis, *Tenure and mobility*, pp. 139–43; Finberg, *Tavistock abbey*, p. 77.

By c.1300 chevage was known across England without being levied everywhere. Some landlords enforced its collection routinely. By c.1300 regular payments for chevage are recorded each year on the estates of Ramsey and Crowland abbeys, while in some years more than one hundred people are recorded as paying chevage annually on the manors of Glastonbury abbey.[38] In contrast, neither chevage nor presentments for absence feature much at all on the estates of other landlords.[39] This did not mean that no serfs had left the manor, because everything we know about the economy confirms that the geographical mobility of the rural population was high. It is probable that some landlords were indifferent to the departure of their villeins, because it helped to alleviate pressures caused by swollen populations and the full occupancy of villein land. The latter is also suggested by the modest fines for chevage before the Black Death on those estates where it was imposed, usually between 1d. and 6d. per person per annum: the customary render in many places was one capon, whose value was similar. Thus in c.1300 it is probable that only a small proportion of all servile migrants paid chevage in England.

After the Black Death the recorded interest in flown villeins increased sharply on most manors, including those whose officials had shown little or no prior interest. This attentiveness is evident in three ways. First, presentments for absence and chevage payments increased in frequency in many places. As Dyer remarks, 'references to the emigration of serfs increase markedly after 1349'.[40] Second, the level of fine charged for chevage jumped. For example, chevage at Forncett (Norfolk) had been charged at 1d. per head between 1272 and 1306, yet in the second half of the fourteenth century it ranged between 3d. and 3s. 4d.[41] Before 1348–9 on the manors of Ramsey abbey the entire customary population was required to pay a lump sum for chevage annually, but thereafter it became a charge upon individuals at higher rates of between 3s. 4d. and 6s. 8d. each per annum.[42] Higher fines were probably levied on the wealthier serf families, but carried the additional benefit of deterring others from leaving. Finally, greater detail is recorded about the whereabouts of migrants, officials were sometimes ordered to seize them 'by body', and close relatives were threatened with penalties if their kin

[38] Raftis, *Tenure and mobility*, pp. 139–43; Page, *Crowland abbey*, p. 137; Miller and Hatcher, *Rural England*, pp. 43–4.

[39] Bailey, 'Villeinage in England', pp. 448–9.

[40] C. Dyer, 'The social and economic background to the rural revolt of 1381', in R.H. Hilton and T.H. Aston, eds., *The English Rising of 1381* (Cambridge, 1984), p. 24; Larson, *Conflict and compromise*, p. 147.

[41] Davenport, *Economic development*, pp. 72–4.

[42] Raftis, *Tenure and mobility*, pp. 141–4; Raftis, 'Peasants and the collapse of the manorial economy', pp. 202–3.

did not return. Occasionally, the chattels of flown serfs were distrained, and some were physically returned to the manor and forced to swear oaths of servility at its court. Court jurors were occasionally ordered to enquire about the progeny of flown serfs.[43]

The explanation for the rising interest in serf departures after the Black Death is simple enough. In the 1340s landlords might have been indifferent to outmigration from their heavily populated manors, but after 1348–9 they were exposed to shortages of both tenants and labourers, and, in these changed conditions, chevage and presentments for absence offered a ready mechanism for tracking departures. Seigniorial concern about the mobility of villeins found another, highly innovative, form of expression through the government's introduction of extensive and ambitious labour legislation. The Ordinance (1349) and the Statute (1351) of Labourers sought principally to fix wages at pre-Black Death levels, to ensure transparency in the method of hiring, and to compel the able-bodied without land or regular employment to work.[44] Its general effect was therefore to reinforce the hand of land-lords who wished to restrict the flight of their servile population from their manors, but its detailed provisions also gave them a specific new remedy. Before 1351 a flown villein could counter attempts at physical capture and return through the acquisition of a writ of *monstravit*, which permitted him to remain at liberty until a proper trial be held to establish his personal status. However, the Statute of Labourers enabled a landlord to capture and detain a fugitive villein until that trial, thus nullifying the effect of the writ.[45] Consequently, the legislation has been viewed as extending seigniorial powers as 'an endeavour to perpetuate villeinage and to hinder the move-ment towards freedom'.[46]

The increased seigniorial sensitivity to the mobility of serfs after 1349 is indisputable. Historians do not always distinguish carefully between the two methods of reporting this mobility in manorial court rolls, namely present-ments for absence and the payment of chevage. Both provide useful infor-mation about the scale and pattern of migration, but they reflect different degrees of success in managing it. After 1350 the rise in the number of

---

[43] Page, 'Decline of villeinage', p. 56; Levett, *Studies in manorial history*, p. 255; DeWindt, *Land and people*, p. 178; Raftis, *Tenure and mobility*, pp. 141–4; Dyer, 'Economic and social background', p. 24.

[44] B.H. Putnam, *The enforcement of the Statutes of Labourers during the first decade after the Black Death* (New York, 1908); D.L. Farmer, 'Prices and wages 1350–1500', in *AgHEW, III*, pp. 483–90; Fryde, *Peasants and landlords*, pp. 33–6.

[45] Fryde, *Peasants and landlords*, pp. 34–6. For the development of this legislation in subsequent years, see C. Given-Wilson, 'Service, serfdom and English labour legislation 1350–1500', in A. Curry and E. Matthew, eds., *Concepts and patterns of service in the later Middle Ages* (Woodbridge, 2000), pp. 21–37.

[46] Putnam, *Statutes of Labourers*, pp. 3–4.

presentments for absence was probably higher than payments for chevage. Indeed, the names of fugitives are presented with tedious regularity year after year in some court rolls, even though there was little realistic chance of securing either their return or a chevage payment: as Poos states, 'there is almost a whimsical quality to these repeated orders to return escaped serfs'.[47] The sources never explain why some migrants chose the unlicensed route, while others agreed to pay chevage (and why others oscillated from one year to another). Chevage payers probably had some landed interests, such as inheritance rights in prime holdings that they wished to protect, and were therefore keeping one eye on an eventual return to the manor. Some may simply have been disposed to deference, or wished to avoid unwelcome pressure upon their relatives back home.

The number of recorded fugitives – licensed and unlicensed – is supposed to have peaked at the start of the fifteenth century.[48] Certainly, the number of recorded emigrants surged dramatically on a number of manors at this date, although in some cases this looks more like an administrative enforcement wave rather than a genuine flood of migrants.[49] Thereafter, both the number of cases and the level of fines began to fall all across England. For example, the size of chevage payments peaked between 3s. 4d. and 6s. 8d. in the second half of the fourteenth century on the estate of the Bishopric of Worcester, but dropped thereafter to 1s. to 2s. per annum.[50] Chevage dwindled markedly in the second quarter of the fifteenth century, and by mid-century it was rare in the Home Counties and in most of south-east England.[51] In those places where chevage survived, the sums fell to a few pennies by the second quarter of the fifteenth century. Similarly, the number of presentments for absence declined sharply.[52]

Chevage was unusual after c.1450 in England. However, it persisted doggedly until the sixteenth century on just a few estates, notably those of the dukes of Norfolk and Lancaster, of Glastonbury abbey, and on some

[47] L.R. Poos, *A rural society after the Black Death: Essex 1350–1500* (Cambridge, 1991), p. 246.

[48] Z. Razi, 'The myth of the immutable English family', *Past and Present*, 140 (1993), pp. 39–42.

[49] See, for example, Howell, *Kibworth Harcourt*, p. 44; King, 'Tenant farming and tenant farmers: the East Midlands', p. 631.

[50] Dyer, *Lords and peasants*, p. 274.

[51] Harvey, 'Tenant farming and tenant farmers: Home Counties', pp. 675–7; Mate, *Trade and economic developments*, p. 193.

[52] Mate, 'Tenant farming and tenant farmers: Kent and Sussex', p. 686; Mate, *Daughters, wives and widows*, p. 92; King, 'Tenant farming and tenant farmers: the East Midlands', p. 631.

Crown lands.[53] Even here, chevage was confined to low numbers of serfs, and the small fines levied each year were not financially draining. Yet the symbolism was powerful and 'undoubtedly psychologically burdensome, signifying...the yoke of servitude'.[54] Before c.1350 chevage had not been especially common, but, where it survived after c.1450, it had become a tagging and tracking device for the last remaining servile families.

Special licences

A condition of villeinage was a requirement to obtain seigniorial permission to be educated; to take holy orders; and, occasionally, to enter an apprenticeship. This requirement is an extension of the principle that the villein could not leave the manor without permission, providing additional compensation for the loss of a subject.[55] Permission was usually granted in return for a one-off payment.

Little has been written about these licences, which might indicate that they were not especially commonplace. Licences to educate or to apprentice were rare, but usually inexpensive (between 3d. and 12d.). The persistently low fees (3d. to 6d.) charged to educate on the estate of St Albans abbey might indicate that the monks were actually recruiting bright young talent into its own school, with an eye to future employment as clerks within the monastic administration.[56] Fines to enter holy orders were usually higher, for example ranging between 12d. and 6s. 8d. at Kibworth Harcourt (Leicestershire), and a fine of 13s. 4d. was recorded in 1371 at Wolrichston (Warwickshire).[57] Fines to permit serfs to be apprenticed to urban crafts are recorded occasionally in fifteenth-century court rolls, and they were probably linked to contemporary concerns about the effects of urban employment on the supply of labour in rural areas.[58] All of these special licenses are very rare after the late fourteenth century.[59]

[53] Savine, 'Bondmen under the Tudors', p. 248; Davenport, *Economic development*, p. 96; Yates, *Town and countryside*, p. 212.

[54] Mate, 'Tenant farming and tenant farmers: Kent and Sussex', p. 687.

[55] Vinogradoff, *Villeinage in England*, p. 157.

[56] Levett, *Studies in manorial history*, pp. 246–7.

[57] Howell, *Kibworth Harcourt*, pp. 33–4; Cheyney, 'Disappearance of English serfdom', p. 21.

[58] Given-Wilson, 'Service, serfdom', pp. 28–9; Whittle, *Agrarian capitalism*, p. 39.

[59] Howell, *Kibworth Harcourt*, pp. 33–4.

Tallage and recognition

Medieval lords possessed the ability to levy extraordinary contributions or 'aids' from their tenants, in addition to the usual rents and services. By the thirteenth century the occasions upon, and the manner in, which these levies were charged became standardized and subject to limitations, and a distinction was now routinely drawn between the 'reasonable aid' charged upon free tenants, and tallage 'at the will of the lord' levied upon villeins. The latter meant that, theoretically, the lord could determine both the frequency and quantum of tallage.[60] Liability to tallage at will thus reinforced the tenant's submission to the lord, while the uncertainty surrounding its timing and level was demeaning. Consequently, it became one of the most important tests of villeinage, after merchet, under the common law.[61]

In practice, tallage assumed a variety of local forms, as one would expect of a servile incident determined at the will of the individual lord.[62] In general, however, by c.1300 it had ossified almost everywhere into a payment whose terms were predictable. Consequently, irregular and severe tallages are hard to find.[63] In many places both the timing and the quantum had become standardized. For example, in 1233 the lord of a Norfolk manor agreed to make tallage an annual but predictable levy of 12d. at Michaelmas each year on every villein, and in the late thirteenth century the villeins of Oakington (Cambridgeshire) paid £8 tallage annually to Crowland abbey.[64] It appears to have been a charge upon villein *tenants* rather than upon the whole servile population of the manor, because individual assessments – where they have survived – were originally based on either landholding size or livestock. It was payable by socage tenants and leaseholders, as well as villeins, on the estates of Tavistock abbey.[65]

Tallage assumed another form on some estates, widely known as 'recognition', which was a charge upon villeins whenever a new lord acceded to the estate. This was usually a characteristic of ecclesiastical or lesser lay estates.[66] Recognition in this form and annual tallage were usually mutually exclusive, i.e. an estate charged one or the other, although a few estates are known to

---

[60]   Hyams, *King, lords and peasants*, pp. 192–3; Vinogradoff, *Villeinage in England*, pp. 162–3.

[61]   Douglas, *Social structure*, pp. 75–7; Levett, *Studies in manorial history*, p. 193; Hyams, *King, lords and peasants*, pp. 191, 241, 267; Page, *Crowland abbey*, pp. 131–2; Dyer, 'The ineffectiveness of lordship', pp. 23–4.

[62]   Also reflected in the various names used to describe it, usually *tallagium, recognitio, auxillium* and, occasionally, *misa*.

[63]   Vinogradoff, *Villeinage in England*, p. 163.

[64]   Page, *Crowland abbey*, pp. 309–12; Miller and Hatcher, *Rural England*, p. 130.

[65]   Finberg, *Tavistock abbey*, p. 78.

[66]   Levett, *Studies in manorial history*, p. 255.

have charged both.[67] Like tallage, the sums charged were originally variable, but by c.1300 many had become standardized.

The chronology of the decline of tallage is not often charted carefully in existing academic studies. Yet there is a clear trend after the Black Death for the sums demanded to fall in many places. At Oakington (Cambridgeshire) the £8 payable annually in the 1290s had declined to £2 in the 1380s, and at Hurdwick (Devon) it fell from over £10 in 1347 to under £2 in 1387.[68] In the 1350s and 1360s falls in the levels charged for recognition are recorded on the estates of the Bishopric of Worcester.[69] From the late fourteenth century both tallage and recognition had begun to disappear from a few estates, although in the early fifteenth century they remained common enough on many other aristocratic and, especially, ecclesiastical estates, such as Crowland and Westminster abbeys.[70] In 1433 the villeins of the Bishopric of Worcester coordinated an estate-wide boycott of recognition payments and by the 1450s both it and tallage had largely disappeared from many ecclesiastical estates.[71] Tallage is still recorded at the end of the fifteenth century on the estates of the Duchy of Cornwall, and of Battle abbey, but such examples are rare.[72] Exceptionally, the earls of Northumberland were still notionally levying recognition in the early sixteenth century.[73]

Labour services

The seigniorial extraction of labour as rent was an important feature of villeinage. Indeed, labour services were its *defining* feature to the earliest historians of the subject. Labour services had been established as part of the rent package of rural tenants as early as the eleventh century, and by the thirteenth century the type and quantity of services owed by each holding had become fixed in frequency and duration.[74] Thus they provided a secure,

---

[67] Dyer, *Lords and peasants*, p. 224.

[68] Page, *Crowland abbey*, pp. 309–12; Finberg, *Tavistock abbey*, p. 78; E. Miller, 'Tenant farming and tenant farmers: Yorkshire and Lancashire', in *AgHEW, III*, p. 607.

[69] Fryde, *Peasants and landlords*, p. 61.

[70] Davenport, *Economic development*, pp. 46 and 54; Page, *Crowland abbey*, pp. 105–6, 309–12; TNA SC6/872/9 (Stevenage, Westminster abbey manor).

[71] Dyer, *Lords and peasants*, pp. 276, 280; Fryde, *Peasants and landlords*, pp. 142–3, 176.

[72] TNA SC6/819/10 and J. Hatcher, *Rural economy and society in the Duchy of Cornwall 1300–1500* (Cambridge, 1970), p. 61; Mate, 'Tenant farming and tenant farmers: Kent and Sussex', pp. 685–6 (Canterbury and Battle).

[73] Fryde, *Peasants and landlords*, pp. 274–5.

[74] Dyer, 'New serfdom', p. 424; Hatcher, 'Serfdom and villeinage', pp. 9–10.

accessible and cheap, although not necessarily willing or skilled, labour force to work upon the seigniorial demesne.

Labour services fell into one of two basic categories. The first was week, also known as winter or summer, works, which were performed for a specified number of days each week throughout the year, excluding the harvest period, and the tasks required to discharge them could involve any aspect of agricultural labour. Week works were generally the most onerous category of labour service, and the one most strongly associated with villeinage. The second category was variously known as seasonal, harvest or boon works, which comprised specified seasonal tasks, such as ploughing, haymaking or reaping in the harvest. Seasonal works tended to be lighter, they were sometimes more rewarding (because the lord supplied food to the workers as part of the package), and they were not confined to villein tenants (because some freemen, and some serfs who did not hold any land, also owed harvest services).[75]

The contribution of labour services to the overall rent package of the villein holding was modest, and so, in this sense, the earliest historians overestimated their importance.[76] In general, labour services contributed less than 10% of the value of all customary rents on lay manors across large tracts of midland, northern, south-west England and Kent, and they formed the highest proportion – more than 30% – of the rent package in parts of East Anglia, Sussex, Hampshire and Oxfordshire.[77] Within these broad regional variations, the total weight of services, and the balance between week and seasonal works, varied considerably from manor to manor.[78] For example, services tended to feature more prominently on major monastic and episcopal estates. In northern England customary holdings were held almost entirely for labour services on the estates of Durham priory, whereas across lay estates 'labour services hardly existed'.[79]

The uses to which landlords put labour services, the extent to which they used them, and variations in such practices from one estate to another, can be ascertained from the 'works account' contained within the annual manorial account.[80] The account enumerates the number of individual works utilized upon the demesne each year in each category; those 'allowed', i.e. not performed for a permissible reason, such as holy days and remissions to any tenants holding manorial offices; and those which the landlord had chosen not to utilize, which were thus 'sold' to the tenant for a standard

[75] Page, 'End of villeinage', pp. 21–3; Fox, 'Exploitation of the landless', pp. 522–6.
[76] Hatcher, 'Serfdom and villeinage', pp. 10–11.
[77] Campbell, 'Agrarian problem', map 4.
[78] Miller and Hatcher, *Rural England*, pp. 121–8.
[79] Campbell, 'Agrarian problem', p. 38; Lomas, 'A priory and its tenants', pp. 112–13.
[80] M. Bailey, ed., *The English manor c.1200 to c.1500* (Manchester, 2002), pp. 157–61.

cash sum in lieu of the service, a process known as commutation. Thus these works' accounts enable historians to recreate general trends in either the utilization or the commutation of labour services, although the accounts do not explain why a particular policy was adopted.

In a pioneering study, Page argued that most labour services were directly exploited in the period before the Black Death in England, but were then increasingly commuted in the third quarter of the fourteenth century, until hardly any remained in use after c.1430.[81] However, his sample of manors was largely confined to south-east England, and he failed to recognize the extent to which the process of commutation had already advanced by c.1300 in some parts of the country.[82] Cheyney was the first to identify a swing to commutation in the late thirteenth century, and he also noticed that week works were often the first services to be commuted, and that seasonal and occasional works continued to be used. He also linked the chronology of decline to the wider trend in demesne management: labour services were widely used in the thirteenth century when many landlords exploited their demesnes directly, but they were increasingly commuted during the fourteenth and early fifteenth centuries as landlords abandoned direct exploitation for the security of leasing their demesnes.[83]

Subsequent research has broadly confirmed these early generalizations.[84] The utilization of labour services peaked during the second half of the thirteenth century, after which the tide turned. It turned quickly in some places, such as on the Percy estates in northern England where in the early fourteenth century works were extensively and permanently commuted following the decision to abandon direct demesne exploitation.[85] Contradictory trends are evident in the generation after the Black Death, with temporary commutations, or the replacement of services with a money rent, in some places, but the reversal of earlier commutations in others. For example, in 1351 the villeins of Castleford and Methley (Yorkshire) failed to carry out their labour services during the disruption of the Black Death, causing the loss of the lord's corn and the escape of wild animals from local parks, and so officials agreed 'to change the services for the better', allowing the tenants to pay a fixed commuted sum instead: in the event, this *ad hoc* arrange-

---

[81]   Page, 'End of villeinage', pp. 39–47, 60–4, 77–83.

[82]   Gray, 'The commutation of villein services', pp. 627–30.

[83]   Cheyney, 'Disappearance of English serfdom', pp. 32–6. For the reinforcement of this point in later studies, see, for example, Poos, *A rural society*, pp. 242–3; Dyer, *Lords and peasants*, pp. 140–1, 269; Harvey, *Westminster abbey*, pp. 269–70; Mullan and Britnell, *Land and family*, pp. 58–9.

[84]   Hatcher, 'Serfdom and villeinage', pp. 11–12.

[85]   Tuck, 'Tenant farming and tenant farmers: the Northern Borders', p. 593.

ment appears to have become permanent.[86] Similar provision for temporary commutations in the 1350s can be found on numerous other estates, in some instances becoming permanent but, in others, the commutations were reversed soon afterwards.[87]

From the 1370s the pace and permanency of commutations quickened appreciably. By the 1380s labour services had disappeared from many areas of north-east England in general, and the estates of the Bishopric of Durham and Durham priory in particular; they were widely commuted in the 1380s and 1390s on the estates of Worcester cathedral priory, and of the Bishopric of Worcester; from the 1390s Westminster abbey entered a series of formal agreements with tenants on each of its manors to commute services; in the same decade Ramsey abbey promoted a major shift to money rents, which permanently replaced labour services; and around 1400 Battle abbey formally commuted week works for set sums on its estates in southern England.[88] Soon after c.1400 week works had largely disappeared from England.[89] Seasonal works – especially harvest works – proved more resilient in many places, lasting until at least the mid-fifteenth century and sometimes much longer.[90]

The disappearance of labour services actually followed one of three distinct routes, although the differences between the three are not often teased out explicitly enough. The first route is where the lord did not deploy some or all of the available labour services during the agrarian year, but instead chose to 'sell' the unwanted works to the tenant for a set sum in lieu of each unused work. This is 'commutation at the will of the lord', which is commutation as conventionally described and understood: the works were available each year, and recorded as such, but the lord sold some or all of them 'at will' on an annual basis. The second route is a subtle variation on the first, in which the landlord agreed in advance to accept a cash sum in lieu of all labour services as part of a formal agreement with some or all of their tenants,

---

[86] H.S. Darbyshire and G.D. Lumb, eds., *The history of Methley*, Publications of the Thoresby Society, 35 (1934), pp. 135–6, 140.

[87] Page, 'End of villeinage', pp. 52–5; Fryde, *Peasants and landlords*, p. 62; Harvey, *Westminster abbey*, pp. 257, 259. Dyer, *Lords and peasants*, pp. 120–1; Mullan and Britnell, *Land and family*, p. 59.

[88] Page, 'End of villeinage', pp. 55–64; Lomas, *Northeast England*, pp. 177, 191–2; P. Hargreaves, 'Seigniorial reaction and peasant responses', *Midland History*, 24 (1999), p. 59–60; Dyer, *Lords and peasants*, pp. 257–9, 269; Harvey, *Westminster abbey*, pp. 268–70; Raftis, *Peasant economic development*, p. 73; Searle, *Battle abbey*, p. 376; also Mullan and Britnell, *Land and family*, pp. 61–3.

[89] Page, 'End of villeinage', pp. 77–83; Harvey, 'Tenant farming and tenant farmers: the Home Counties', p. 667; Yates, *Town and countryside*, pp. 215–16.

[90] Harvey, 'Tenant farming and tenant farmers: the Home counties', p. 667; Poos, *A rural society*, pp. 242–3; Yates, *Town and countryside*, pp. 215–16; Mullan and Britnell, *Land and family*, pp. 59–60.

usually for a fixed term. These are best regarded as 'negotiated commuta-tions'. The third, and final, route is the permanent or semi-permanent aban-donment of some labour services caused by the rise in uncollectable works attached to villein holdings that had been either abandoned or converted to a contractual tenancy for a money rent, such as leasehold. The works' account might continue to record the theoretical liability of the holding for services, because of an optimistic (or conservative) assumption that it might be restored to villeinage in the near future.[91] These were, in essence, 'decayed commutations'.

Thus the deployment of labour services on demesnes peaked in the thir-teenth century, and declined thereafter. The decline accelerated after the Black Death, especially for the onerous and unpopular week works which had largely disappeared by 1400, although seasonal works proved more durable. Services declined in one of four ways: commuted through an *ad hoc* sale; commuted through a negotiated, and usually enduring, agreement; the abandonment of the holding; and, finally, the conversion of a holding to a contractual tenancy for money, such as leasehold. Landlords generally preferred to retain the option of using services for as long as their demesnes were exploited directly.

Heriot

A heriot was a payment to the lord from the estate of a deceased villein tenant. This acknowledged the lord's legal ownership of the chattels of the villein, while enabling the heirs to inherit them according to either the custom of the manor or their own will and testament. Only villein tenants rendered heriot, so it was a duty based on landed rather than moveable wealth. Heriot was not used in the royal courts as a test of villeinage, because death duties on landholders were not confined to the unfree.[92]

The most common form of payment for heriot was to render the 'best beast' (i.e. most valuable) of the deceased tenant. If the deceased had no livestock, then the lord enjoyed the right to take chattels instead, although most landlords, such as the abbot of St Albans, would accept a cash render in lieu.[93] In parts of East Anglia the cash render payable under these circum-

---

[91] See, for example, the abbot of St Albans' manor of Park, where many labour services disappeared as a consequence of conversions to leasehold, although some grants stipulated that labour services could be restored with a reversion to villeinage at end of the lease, Tomkins, 'Park', p. 73.

[92] Vinogradoff, *Villeinage in England*, pp. 159–60; Hyams, *King, lords and peasants*, pp. 77–9.

[93] Levett, *Studies in manorial history*, p. 198; Tomkins, 'Park', p. 75.

stances was fixed at 2s. 8d.[94] Yet there were important local variations in practice. Tenants of Tavistock abbey did not render a beast as heriot, but were charged a cash sum equivalent to one third the value of their chattels.[95] Elsewhere, a heriot was paid whenever land was transferred to another tenant, not just upon *post mortem* transfers.[96] Sometimes, the payment of a heriot was linked to the assessment of the entry fine if the new tenant was an heir rather than non-kin.[97] In a few places, tenants who did not reside on the manor paid part of their grain crop as a heriot.[98]

Heriot remained one of the most durable incidents of customary tenure, surviving well into the sixteenth century in many places to become a common feature of copyholds.[99] However, two general changes to its implementation are discernible in the fifteenth century. First, its frequency declined, partly as tenants sought ways to evade its payment, such as making deathbed transfers of land, or agreeing to just one heriot when they held multiple holdings.[100] Second, the custom of rendering the best beast was gradually replaced by cash renders, which was more convenient for both lord and tenant. Often the size of the cash render was agreed at the beginning of the tenancy.[101] In general, the size of those renders declined during the course of the fifteenth century.[102]

Entry fines

An entry fine was payable upon succession to, or acquisition of, customary land, and it is invariably recorded in the manorial court roll when the new tenant entered the holding. It may originally have been a render in kind, but from the thirteenth century cash payments were the norm.[103] A variety of

---

94 Bailey, 'Villeinage in England', p. 446.
95 Finberg, *Tavistock abbey*, p. 77.
96 Such as on the estates of Worcester Cathedral Priory, Hargreaves, 'Seigniorial reaction', pp. 58–9; Vinogradoff, *Villeinage in England*, p. 160.
97 Bailey, 'Villeinage in England', p. 446.
98 M. Tompkins, 'Peasant society in a Midlands manor, Great Horwood 1400 to 1600' (PhD thesis, University of Leicester, 2006), pp. 158–9.
99 Fryde, *Peasants and landlords*, p. 269.
100 L. Bonfield and L. Poos, 'The development of deathbed transfers in medieval English manor courts', in Z. Razi and R.M. Smith, eds., *Medieval society and the manor court* (Oxford, 1996), p. 137; Bailey, 'Villeinage in England', p. 446; Dyer, *Lords and peasants*, pp. 285–7.
101 Harvey, *Westminster abbey*, p. 272; Howell, *Kibworth Harcourt*, p. 33; Dyer, *Lords and peasants*, p. 272.
102 Fryde, *Peasants and landlords*, p. 176.
103 Vinogradoff, *Villeinage in England*, p. 162; Levett, *Studies in manorial history*, p. 197.

factors influenced the size of the entry fine, which might be fixed at a set rate per acre or per standard holding, or it might be variable. Fixed rates were usually set by custom or, in the fifteenth century, by negotiated agreement. For example, the equivalent of two years' rent was routinely charged as an entry fine in parts of south-east England, while a year's rent was common elsewhere.[104] Where rates were variable, they were determined by a number of factors: the underlying demand for land, the soil fertility or condition of the holding, and the circumstances of the tenant.[105] For example, the entry fine might be waived, or its level reduced, if the incoming tenant was an heir and had already paid heriot or merchet.[106] A lord might waive his right to an entry fine on consideration of the personal circumstances of the incoming tenant, such as their poverty. Both of these variants confirm the principle that the entry fine was the responsibility of the incoming tenant.

Entry fines were a universal and enduring element of villeinage, which, like heriot, survived the transformation into copyhold tenures. They tended to be high and rising in the land-scarce conditions of the thirteenth century, and low and falling in the land-abundant conditions of the late fourteenth and fifteenth centuries. Entry fines even disappeared in some places after 1349, such as Kibworth Harcourt (Leicestershire).[107] Within this general picture, local trajectories of decline varied. The average payment fell precipitously between the 1340s and 1370s on the estates of Worcester Cathedral Priory, becoming 'a shadow of its former self...almost eliminated as a customary payment'.[108] In contrast, entry fines did not fall markedly until the mid-fifteenth century on the bishopric's estate.[109] Elsewhere in the west Midlands the level of fines halved between the late fourteenth century and the 1430s.[110] The total income from entry fines rose between the 1370s and 1390s on the estate of the Bishopric of Winchester, although the rate of fine per acre and per virgate fell over the same period.[111] In most places the levels

---

104   There is evidence for the custom of charging the equivalent of two years' rent as entry fines in south-east England in the fifteenth century: Mate, *Trade and economic developments*, p. 224; Vinogradoff, *Villeinage in England*, p. 162; Tompkins, 'Great Horwood', p. 161.

105   Miller and Hatcher, *Rural England*, pp. 46–8.

106   Sometimes entry fines might be waived if a merchet or heriot was also due, Page, *Crowland abbey*, p. 31.

107   Howell, *Kibworth Harcourt*, p. 33.

108   Hargreaves, 'Seigniorial reaction', p. 58.

109   For the decline in the incidence and level of entry fines during the fifteenth century on the Bishopric of Worcester's estate, see Dyer, *Lords and peasants*, pp. 271–2.

110   C. Dyer, 'Peasant holdings in west Midland villages 1400–1540', in Smith, ed., *Land, kinship and lifecycle*, p. 281.

111   Mullan and Britnell, *Land and family*, pp. 77–8.

of entry fine began to fall consistently from the 1380s, and reached their lowest point between the 1430s and 1470s.[112]

Entry fines usually survived into the sixteenth century to become an important feature of copyhold tenures. However, their characteristics varied, in ways that mattered much more to sixteenth century tenants than to those of the fifteenth. Where the level of entry fine was variable, landlords could deploy it as a form of 'tax' to reflect the real value of land as prices rose during the sixteenth century. In contrast, landlords were unable to recoup rises in land values in places where the level was fixed by local custom. In some places, landlords had felt compelled to change the arrangements when economic conditions were unfavourable to them in the fifteenth century. For example, in 1471 the lord of Blunham (Bedfordshire) entered a collective agreement to replace variable entry fines with fines fixed at 6d. per acre for arable, and 20d. for meadow, land to the detriment of his successors.[113]

Millsuit

Villein tenants were required to grind their corn at the mill of their lord, rather than at the mill of another lord or at home on hand mills. The lord was therefore able to charge a toll for the enforced privilege, usually by retaining a percentage of the ground corn ('multure'). The rate of multure charged upon villeins usually lay between 3% and 8%, and they also paid a higher rate than other users.[114] Bloch famously argued that this monopoly guaranteed the profitability of seigniorial mills, which thus encouraged lords to invest in expensive watermills and windmills: albeit at the expense of some resentment and resistance from their villeins, who would have preferred to mill elsewhere.[115]

The origins of millsuit are obscure, but there is clear evidence that it was extended and tightened in the late twelfth and early thirteenth centuries as the number of mills in England increased.[116] In some places even the free peasantry were compelled to use the lord's mill, so this incident was not

---

[112] Fryde, *Peasants and landlords*, p. 69.

[113] Jones, 'Bedfordshire', pp. 198–201.

[114] Langdon, *Mills in the medieval economy. England 1300–1540* (Oxford, 2004), p. 277 and appendix 7.

[115] M. Bloch, *Land and work in medieval Europe* (London, 1967), pp. 136–68; R. Holt, *The mills of medieval England* (Oxford, 1988), pp. 36–53; Rigby, *English society*, pp. 133–4; J. Langdon, *Mills in the medieval economy*, pp. 257–75.

[116] R. Holt, 'Whose were the profits of corn milling? The abbots of Glastonbury and their tenants 1086–1350', *Past and Present*, 116 (1987), pp. 8–9, 22; Holt, *Mills of medieval England*, pp. 107–16.

exclusively a feature of villeinage.[117] Millsuit was found widely throughout England, albeit with exemptions and complications, but it was enforced with greatest rigour in northern England. The existence of private and independent mills created competition for seigniorial mills everywhere, and especially in south-east England, so lords used their manorial courts to enforce their monopoly by amercing villeins who milled elsewhere: 6d. was the most common level of fine before 1350.[118] However, the volume and frequency of recorded violations were relatively small, and the average value of seigniorial mills was modest, both of which indicate that lords did not routinely coerce use of their mills. Landlords probably used suit of mill to lift the profits of their mills, but it was not essential to their underlying profitability.[119] In general 'customers came to mills because they wanted to, not because they were forced there'.[120]

After 1350 the incidence of recorded millsuit violations fell sharply everywhere. Langdon found 'only twenty four suit of mill violations ... among the 1,096 courts sampled for fourteen communities' across England.[121] The size of amercements fell on those manors where millsuit was still levied, and, elsewhere, occasional orders are recorded to grind at the lord's mill, supported with threats of financial penalties.[122] The profits of seigniorial mills declined and many fell into disuse: perhaps one half of all demesne mills disappeared in the century or so after 1350.[123] This must have reflected a fall in the level of multure rates, as well as a fall in demand for milling, and the reduced imposition and prevalence of mill suit. Langdon concluded that 'enforcement of suit of mill after 1350 seems to have been limited mostly to the late fourteenth century'. Examples of enforcement from the fifteenth century are very rare.[124]

Villein tenure and personal servility

Before c.1350 manorial documents did not usually distinguish between those who held villein land and those who were personally unfree, because the two

---

[117]   Langdon, *Mills in the medieval economy*, pp. 275–83.

[118]   Holt, *Mills in medieval England*, p. 45.

[119]   J. Langdon, 'Lordship and peasant consumerism in the milling industry of early fourteenth-century England', *Past and Present*, 145 (1994), pp. 3–46; Langdon, *Mills in the medieval economy*, pp. 280–7.

[120]   Langdon, *Mills in the medieval economy*, p. 287.

[121]   Langdon, *Mills in the medieval economy*, p. 286.

[122]   For example, Tomkins, 'Park', pp. 70–1.

[123]   Holt, *Mills in medieval England*, pp. 159–70; Bailey, *Medieval Suffolk*, pp. 233–4.

[124]   Langdon, *Mills in the medieval economy*, pp. 286–7; Miller, 'Tenant farming and tenant farmers: Yorkshire and Lancashire', p. 607; Harvey, 'Tenant farming and tenant farmers: the Home Counties', p. 670.

groups were assumed to be more or less synonymous.[125] This assumption was reasonable enough for practical purposes, although it was not strictly correct. For example, small numbers of freemen held villein tenures, rendering the obligations and rents attached to the land while remaining personally free. The main practical reason for not maintaining a rigid distinction is that the overlap between tenurial and servile villeinage was blurred in places. Heriots and entry fines were attached to the villein holding, but they were not charged upon serfs. Merchet was liable from both serfs and villein tenants. Liability for tallage, recognition, labour services and millsuit was usually attached only to land tenure, although local custom determined whether landless serfs also contributed. Serfs were liable for merchet, chevage and leyrwite, whether they held land or not, and chevage and leyrwite were seldom paid by villein tenants.

After c.1350 manorial court rolls routinely identify those individuals who were personally unfree, labelling them as *nativi*, or *nativi de sanguine*. These were members of families that had long been established locally, whose lineage was proof of their servility. The move to distinguish them explicitly reflects the determination of manorial administrators to keep track of their activities and whereabouts during a period of upheaval and discontinuity. Yet it also reflects the fact that after 1350 the overlap between villein tenure and status was rapidly breaking down. First, villein tenures were increasingly occupied by freemen and, especially, newcomers of indeterminate personal status. Even if the latter had once been hereditary serfs on another manor, they were not classified as such on their new manor. These processes explain how in 1380 only four of the 14 tenants of customary virgates at Combe Bisset (Wiltshire) were also serfs by blood.[126] Second, the conversion of some villein tenures to leaseholds and life tenancies further widened the gap between tenure and status. These were still customary lands, but they were not the old villein tenures, and so 'customary land [had become] separated from serfdom'.[127] Hence, after 1400, officials on the manor of Forncett (Norfolk) made a clear distinction between the 'tenants of customary lands, *terre native tenentes*', and those people who were personally servile or 'serfs by blood, *nativi domini de sanguine*'.[128]

In the fifteenth century the sharper focus upon personal servility is evident in the development of three distinct practices on a small number of estates: the production of servile genealogies; compilations of lists of serfs;

---

[125] Schofield, *Peasants*, pp. 13–15.
[126] J.N. Hare, 'The lords and their tenants: conflict and stability in fifteenth-century Wiltshire', in B. Stapleton, ed., *Conflict and community in southern England* (Stroud, 1992), p. 19.
[127] Raftis, 'Peasants and the collapse of the manorial economy', p. 197.
[128] Davenport, *Economic development*, p. 83.

and challenging serfs who claimed to be free. The first two were designed to maintain track of serf families, on or off the manor, and to establish written proof of their servility. Separate lists of serf families on each manor were occasionally compiled, identifying their lineage, progeny and whereabouts. These might take the form of one-off lists or registers, compiled centrally by estate officials, such as the unique Mintlyng Register of Spalding priory.[129] Jurors on the manors of Durham priory were required to produce a list of serfs annually, an exercise which was eventually dropped in 1470.[130] Using evidence compiled in these ways, lords sometimes explicitly challenged the status of individuals who had long since flown the manor and claimed to be free. The competing claims were settled through special inquests held on the home manor, in which an elected local jury was required to consider the evidence and pronounce, under oath, upon the true status of the individual.[131]

The compilation of written information about serfs by these means was time-consuming, especially when a significant amount of administrative effort was being expended upon a dwindling number of people.[132] It may simply reflect a certain bureaucratic mind set. It certainly represents a conscious attempt to maintain an increasingly outmoded social structure, perhaps by landlords who themselves were socially conservative: their own pride and contempt for serfs might have been part of their motivation.[133] It also reflects a hard-edged determination to profit from serfs financially. Some landlords were clearly using their background information to target wealthy serfs for sizeable one-off payments, such as merchet, entry fines or manumission. The prioress of Amesbury pursued John Halle, the wealthy clothier, MP and mayor of Salisbury (Wiltshire), whom she accused of being one of her serfs, while at Castle Combe (Wiltshire) Sir John Fastolf seized upon the servile origins of a wealthy clothier, William Haynes, to demand a £40 entry fine for a property that had previously attracted a 30s. fine.[134] Such

---

[129]   E.D. Jones, 'Going round in circles: some new evidence for population in the later Middle Ages', *Journal of Medieval History*, 15 (1989), pp. 330–3; M. Bailey, 'Blowing up bubbles: some new demographic evidence for the fifteenth century', *Journal of Medieval History*, 15 (1989), pp. 352–3; Dyer, *Lords and peasants*, p. 270; Raftis, 'Peasants and the collapse of the manorial economy', p. 198.

[130]   Larson, *Conflict and compromise*, pp. 147, 157–8.

[131]   Dyer, *Lords and peasants*, pp. 272–5; Bailey, 'Blowing up bubbles', pp. 351–2; Larson, *Conflict and compromise*, pp. 147–8, 158.

[132]   Hare, 'Lords and their tenants', pp. 19, 21, 23.

[133]   Dyer, *Lords and peasants*, p. 275; Fryde, *Peasants and landlords*, pp. 242–3.

[134]   These examples are from Hare, 'Lords and their tenants', pp. 21–2. See also Carus-Wilson, 'Economic development', pp. 162–3; Hilton, *Decline of serfdom*, pp. 51–4; R.K. Field, 'Migration in the later Middle Ages: the case of some Hampton Lovell villeins', *Midland History*, 8 (1983), pp. 33–5; Fryde, *Peasants and landlords*, pp. 134, 217–18.

examples are striking, although they were confined to very small numbers of serfs. The shortage of ready cash in the mid-fifteenth-century economy would also have inhibited this practice.[135]

The economic revival of the sixteenth century, and the burgeoning wealth of some landholding serfs, encouraged landlords to maintain track of them through chevage or merchet for the prospect of a financial windfall, until the remaining serfs either died out or were manumitted. For example, a spate of manumissions occurred in the mid-1550s on the Duke of Norfolk's estate, and in 1575 Sir Henry Lee received a grant from Elizabeth I to obtain the profits from the manumission of 300 bondmen of the Crown.[136] The sums involved could be large, in excess of £100 a time.[137] It is ironic that serfdom was being abandoned in the second quarter of the fifteenth century in most parts of England, yet a century later it was applied with renewed energy and vigour on the very few estates where it survived. The maintenance of personal servility deep into the sixteenth century on a handful of aristocratic estates was motivated mainly by the prospect of profit. The unwillingness of the House of Lords to pass a bill in 1536 proposing to manumit the few hundred bondmen left in England was due to the simple fact that 'the lords knew that any such sweeping step would be a blow to many highly placed people's exploitable assets'.[138]

The squeezing of wealthy, and sometimes prominent, serfs for cash in the fifteenth and sixteenth centuries has caught the attention and captured the imagination of historians. Similarly, references to *nativi de sanguine* in court rolls of this period are striking. However, it is important to keep all of these examples in a proper perspective: they were exceptional occurrences, and serfs were actually few in number. As Whittle states, 'the significance of the sixteenth-century survival of serfdom pales in relation to the enormous implications of its almost total disappearance in a short period of time at the end of the fourteenth and the beginning of the fifteenth centuries…what we observe in the period 1440 to 1580 is the gradual disappearance of the last vestiges of serfdom'.[139]

[135] Fryde, 'Peasant rebellions and discontents', p. 793; J. Hatcher, 'The great slump of the mid-fifteenth century', in Britnell and Hatcher, eds., *Progress and problems*, p. 244; P. Nightingale, 'Monetary contraction and mercantile credit in late medieval England', *Economic History Review*, 43 (1990), pp. 560–75.

[136] Savine, 'Bondmen under the Tudors', pp. 266–8; Davenport, *Economic development of a Norfolk manor*, pp. 88–97; Hilton, *Decline of serfdom*, pp. 55–6.

[137] Savine, 'Bondmen under the Tudors', pp. 269–77.

[138] MacCulloch, 'Bondmen', p. 100. See also Savine, 'Bondmen under the Tudors', pp. 236–48; Davenport, *Development of a Norfolk manor*, pp. 88–97.

[139] Whittle, *Agrarian capitalism*, p. 46.

Conclusion

When writing of the management of servile incidents in the Home Counties, P.D.A. Harvey concluded that they 'seem to have been generally enforced to the end of the fourteenth century, and to have then fallen mostly into disuse'.[140] Whittle comments that serfdom was common before 1380 and rare after 1420.[141] Surveying the country at large, Fryde observed that 'between about 1380 and 1450 ... [landlords] abandoned most of the demands on the labour of their servile tenants. Personal serfdom gradually dwindled.'[142] Harriss preferred a slightly shorter timeframe: 'in the course of one generation, c.1380–1430, the legal and economic position of the manorial peasantry was transformed'.[143] How do these assessments compare with the evidence presented in this survey?

Of the incidents that were primarily tenurial, week works mainly disappeared between c.1370 and c.1400, and seasonal works thereafter; tallage and recognition largely disappeared in the first half of the fifteenth century; millsuit was rare after c.1390; while heriots and entry fines were reduced in scale during the fifteenth century, but endured to become features of copyhold tenures in the sixteenth century. The terminology of villein tenures gradually shed their servile vocabulary between the 1390s and the mid-fifteenth century, by which time tenures by copy were widely established. The conversion of villein tenures to leaseholds jumped in the 1350s, and peaked in the first quarter of the fifteenth century. From this, it would appear that tenurial villeinage largely disappeared in the half century after 1380.

The difficulties finding tenants in the wake of the pestilence in 1348–9, coupled with heightened seigniorial concerns about migration, meant that the explicit identification of those people who were personally unfree became commonplace in manorial documents: serfs, or neifs, by blood [*nativi de sanguine*]. Of the incidents that were primarily personal, and therefore were charged upon individual serfs if not upon tenants in villeinage, leyrwite and childwite largely disappeared between the 1370s and 1390s; merchet declined significantly in the first half of the fifteenth century; and chevage, including presentments for absence, followed a similar chronology. On a small number of prominent and conservative estates, the tracking of a handful of serf families through chevage continued well into the sixteenth century.

It is possible to hedge these conclusions with numerous caveats, the most important of which are the sheer variety of local experience uncovered by research in the archives, and the difficulty of pinning down a precise chro-

---

[140] Harvey, 'Tenant farming and tenant farmers: the Home Counties', pp. 669–70.
[141] Whittle, *Agrarian capitalism*, p. 37.
[142] Fryde, 'Peasant rebellion', p. 745.
[143] Harriss, *Shaping the Nation*, p. 234.

nology from the limited information provided in many of the published studies. Whatever caveats are applied, the sum of all the evidence indicates that villein tenures effectively disappeared in England between c.1380 and c.1420, and personal serfdom disappeared over a slightly longer time frame, between c.1380 and c.1450. In the next chapter we explore how well this chronology fits with the various causes of its decline identified by historians.

4

The Causes of Decline

In c.1300 around half of all peasant land in England, and half its rural population, were servile. This proportion could not subsequently rise, because the common law presented legal obstacles to any further enserfment of freemen and free tenures. The size of the English population was slashed by around 40% during the first outbreak of the Black Death in 1348–9, and remained stagnant for the next 150 years. Its size is estimated at 2.8 million people in 1377, and slightly lower in the 1520s.[1] Thus the number of serfs fell after 1348–9, and thereafter their proportion within the general population gradually fell until there were hardly any left in the early sixteenth century. Villein tenure, meanwhile, evolved into leasehold and various forms of copyhold. Four main reasons have been advanced to explain the decline of serfdom during the later Middle Ages: manumission; economic pressures; peasant resistance; and migration. Two other associated issues warrant exploration. The first is whether English landlords attempted to impose a 'second serfdom' in the second half of the fourteenth century, which in turn shaped the scale and nature of peasant resistance and migration. The second is whether the distribution of the few remaining bondmen in the Tudor period provides any clues to the causes of decline. The purpose of this chapter is to review critically the current state of knowledge on these subjects.

Manumission

An individual who was personally unfree, as opposed to one who merely held land on villein tenure, was regarded as his or her lord's chattel, obligated and tied to their manor of origin. The legal freedom to leave the lord's fee at will could only be obtained formally through the grant of a charter of manumission from one's lord.[2] Thirteenth-century lawyers disputed whether manumission conferred complete freedom or left some theoretical liabilities for

---

[1] The population of England is estimated to have fallen from around 5 or 6 million people in c.1300 to 2.8 million in 1377, then to 2.3 million in the 1520s, Rigby, *English society*, p. 81.

[2] Hyams, *King, lords and peasants*, pp. 31–2; Kaye, *Medieval English conveyances*, pp. 534–6.

heirs.[3] It is generally assumed that permission was not given lightly or often, because the legal enfranchisement of serfs represented the formal loss of an exploitable asset and thus a diminution in the resource base of a manor. The Warden of New College, Oxford, resisted pressure in the 1520s to manumit one prominent serf family from Colern (Wiltshire) on the grounds that the College statutes prohibited him from alienating either land or bondmen.[4]

The lord usually sought financial compensation for the permanent alienation of servile chattels, thus a charter of manumission was normally purchased. A sum equivalent to one third of the value of the serf's lands and goods was sometimes regarded as an appropriate basis for manumission. Inventories of servile assets survive from the sixteenth century, which presumably must have served as the basis for such valuations.[5] A fifteenth-century manumission cost anything between ten marks and £20 each on the Ramsey abbey estate, although elsewhere a £10 charge appeared frequently.[6]

The patchy survival of records of manumission indicates that such grants were not especially common. For example, only eight are recorded between 1435 and 1454 on the estate of the earls of Stafford, it was hardly known on the estate of the Bishopric of Durham, and Harvey concluded that it was rare generally in the Home Counties.[7] The Bishopric of Worcester granted 74 manumissions between 1380 and 1540, Ramsey abbey (Huntingdonshire) granted 79 manumissions during the fifteenth century, and St Swithun's priory, Winchester (Hampshire), granted 46 across its whole estate between 1350 and the late fifteenth century, the majority within the period 1390 to 1450.[8] Manumissions generally occurred later on ecclesiastical estates, from mid-century on the estates of Ramsey abbey, between the 1470s and 1510s on the estates of the Bishopric of Ely, and between 1505 and 1510 on those of Gloucester abbey.[9] Evidence for manumission is best preserved on the estates of ecclesiastical landlords, although it is unclear whether this indicates a greater willingness to manumit or simply greater efficiency in the keeping of records.[10] Indeed, manumissions were not routinely recorded in manorial court rolls, but were often documented in centralized estate records

---

3   Hyams, *King, lords and peasants*, pp. 129–30.
4   Savine, 'Bondmen under the Tudors', p. 277; MacCulloch, 'Bondmen', p. 106; Hare, 'Lords and their tenants', p. 20.
5   Savine, 'Bondmen under the Tudors', pp. 264–5, 270.
6   Raftis, *Tenure and mobility*, pp. 183–8; Hilton, *Decline of serfdom*, p. 50.
7   Fryde, *Peasants and landlords*, pp. 276–7; Larson, *Conflict and compromise*, pp. 209–10; Harvey, 'Tenant farming and tenant farmers: the Home Counties', p. 670.
8   Dyer, *Lords and peasants*, p. 272; Raftis, *Peasant economic development*, p. 115; Hare, 'Lords and their tenants', pp. 20–1.
9   Raftis, *Tenure and mobility*, pp. 184–5; MacCulloch, 'Bondmen', p. 93.
10 Harvey, 'Tenant farming and tenant farmers: the Home Counties', p. 670.

such as cartularies: original copies of letters of manumission are exceptionally rare.[11] Any study focused exclusively upon manorial records will thus tend to underestimate the scale of manumissions.

The reasons for seeking or granting manumission are seldom given in contemporary documents. The seigniorial motive was generally financial, because a spate of manumissions provided a way of raising ready cash, either to ease financial difficulties or to meet exceptional expenditure. In a financial emergency, serfs 'held the potential of considerable capital gains for the lord'.[12] For example, in 1415 the Duke of Norfolk granted a spate of manumissions across his estate to raise additional cash for his participation in the Agincourt campaign.[13] After c.1450 a small number of landlords, such as the earls of Stafford, pursued the aggressive policy of tracking known serfs with a view to obtaining future financial windfalls through manumission.[14] While most manumissions were financially driven, other motives are sometimes apparent. Some early manumissions were pious acts, while some later ones were granted by lords who recognized the administrative futility of preserving serfdom.[15] Occasionally, the lessee of a manor freed serfs, probably without the lord's consent.[16] Exceptionally, a lord might grant manumission to a serf as a reward for devoted personal service.[17]

The exact motive of serfs in seeking manumission cannot be known, because it is never explicitly stated. All serfs must have desired freedom from the taint of servility and its associated vulnerability to financial squeeze, and so manumission was an attractive prospect because its legal grant of freedom was irreversible. However, the substantial cost of formal manumission must have acted as a major deterrent. Initially, it was probably only attractive to the nouveau riche, those who had left their home manor without permission and accumulated wealth elsewhere as traders, artisans or demesne lessees.[18] But, for the most part, we can only guess why some serfs left their home manor while others stayed, and why some sought formal manumission while others did not.

[11] MacCulloch, 'Bondmen', p. 92.

[12] Raftis, *Peasant economic development*, p. 115.

[13] Savine, 'Bondmen under the Tudors', pp. 269–70; MacCulloch, 'Bondmen', pp. 92, 106; Fryde, *Peasants and landlords*, pp. 134, 276–7.

[14] Fryde, *Peasants and landlords*, pp. 276–7.

[15] D.A.E. Pelteret, *Slavery in early medieval England* (Woodbridge, 1995), pp. 140–1, 259; Hare, 'Lords and their tenants', p. 23.

[16] *CIM, 1387–1393*, pp. 148–9.

[17] M. Bailey, 'Rural society', in R. Horrox, ed., *Fifteenth-century attitudes* (Cambridge, 1995), p. 158; Dyer, *Lords and peasants*, p. 271.

[18] Raftis, *Peasant economic development*, p. 116.

Cheyney stated long ago that the process of manumission contributed little to the demise of serfdom in late medieval England, and few would disagree.[19] Manumissions were expensive, and therefore likely to have been confined to wealthy serfs who could afford them, and who had most to gain socially from the formal acquisition of freedom. Notwithstanding the inherent deficiencies of the high reliance upon manorial records, the number of recorded manumissions is insignificant, and so it is likely that they were the exception rather than the rule in the overall process of decline.

Economic and demographic forces

The argument that economic and demographic forces best explain the decline of villeinage has long attracted support. The Black Death is depicted as the greatest supply side shock to the labour market in recorded history, exposing landlords to the loss of up to one half of their prospective tenants and workers, and causing the value of labour to rise relative to land. This exerted pressure upon landlords to reduce the rent burden attached to land-holdings in order to retain and to attract tenants, and it also exerted pressure on employees to increase wages and to improve conditions of employment. Hence the position of landlords was suddenly disadvantaged, and that of villeins potentially advantaged, in the markets for both land and labour. As Postan argued, 'in the end economic forces asserted themselves, and the lords and employers found that the most effective way of retaining labour was to pay higher wages, just as the most effective way of retaining tenants was to lower rents and release servile obligations'.[20] According to Thomson 'serfdom had virtually disappeared in the years of labour shortage and declining population'.[21] The decline of villein holdings at Birdbrook (Essex) 'follows a pattern consistent with one initiated and, perhaps, dictated by plague'.[22] Freedman concludes that 'the general decline of English villeinage was greatly encouraged, if not caused, by the untenable position of the lords

---

[19] Cheyney, 'Disappearance of English serfdom', pp. 25–7. See T. Lomas, 'South-east Durham: the late fourteenth and fifteenth centuries', in Harvey, ed., *The peasant land market in England*, p. 283; Z. Razi, 'Serfdom and freedom in medieval England: a reply to the revisionists', in Dyer, Coss and Wickham, eds., *Rodney Hilton's Middle Ages*, pp. 184–5.

[20] M. Postan, 'Agrarian society in its prime: part 7, England', in M. Postan, ed., *Cambridge economic history of Europe, volume I: the agrarian life of the Middle Ages* (Cambridge, 1966), p. 609.

[21] J.A.F. Thomson, *The transformation of medieval England 1370–1529* (London, 1983), p. 373.

[22] Schofield, 'Tenurial developments', pp. 255–6.

with regard to enforcing the bondage of their tenants in the demographic aftermath of repeated plagues'.[23]

Do broad changes in the value of customary land support this interpretation? Unfortunately, medieval historians have yet to construct a national series of agricultural land values, which in turn reflects the scarcity of reliable information about rents per unit area, and their changes over time, in contemporary sources. The best potential data are from the rents per acre charged on leaseholds, as these most reliably reflect fluctuations in the real market value for land, but they are problematic: pre-1350 values are rare; some leases relate to demesne not customary land; manorial accounts do not always record individual leases, and, where they do, the rental values often include houses, buildings and closes of undisclosed areas and not just arable land. Hence rental values are hard to win, fragmentary and highly localized. However, leasehold rents from East Anglia cited by Britnell show a slight rise in value between the 1350s and 1370s; a c.20% fall between the 1370s and 1390s; and a relatively stable pattern thereafter, with the exception of a c.15% fall between the 1400s and 1420s.[24] The problems with obtaining good series of rental values per acre have forced historians to concentrate instead upon overall levels of rental income from tenanted land, which were generally buoyant between the mid-1350s and mid-1370s, before falling in the last quarter of the fourteenth century, and slumping again in the mid-fifteenth century.[25] Kitsikopoulos estimates that these 'rents declined by as much as 20%, beginning in the fifteenth century'.[26]

The willingness of tenants to occupy arable land, and by extension the level of rent, was partly determined by the profitability of agriculture, which in turn was heavily influenced by the price of foodstuffs and the cost of labour. Fortunately, we have an excellent series of agricultural wage and price data for late medieval England, which permit the construction of a reliable chronology of changes in the relative value of agricultural wages and prices (i.e. 'real wages'). These provide a useful inverse measure of the profitability of agricultural activity, mainly grain production, and by extension a surrogate measure of agrarian land values. Table 4.1 measures changes in the amount of paid agricultural work needed to buy a fixed quantity of barley. The higher the score, the more profitable was grain production: the lower the score, the lower the profits in producing grain. If we use the data as a surrogate measure for the demand for arable land, then it remained buoyant in the immediate aftermath of the Black Death until the early 1370s. However,

---

[23] Freedman, 'Rural society', p. 94.

[24] Britnell, *Britain and Ireland*, pp. 441–2.

[25] Hatcher, 'The great slump of the mid fifteenth century', pp. 237–72.

[26] H. Kitsikopoulos, 'England', in H. Kitsikopoulos, ed., *Agrarian change and crisis in Europe, 1200–1500* (Abingdon, 2012), p. 39.

it than fell dramatically and consistently between the 1370s and 1390s, by as much as one half, due to the combined effect of falling grain prices and the underlying shortages of labour. Land values then remained stable until another significant fall, of around 20%, between the 1430s and the 1440s.

4.1 Index of the purchasing power of wages, 1340–1470[*]

Decade	Index
1340–47	100
1350–60	128
1360–70	128
1370–80	96
1380–90	72
1390–1400	83
1400–10	80
1410–20	76
1420–30	67
1430–40	70
1440–50	50
1450–60	52
1460–70	59

Source: D.L. Farmer, 'Prices and Wages', *AgHEW, III*, table 5.13.
[*] Units of work need to buy fixed amount barley for five different types of worker.

Thus both the direct and indirect evidence indicate that decisive falls in land values occurred between the 1370s and 1390s, between the 1410s and 1420s, and again between the 1430s and 1440s, with little evidence of recovery before the end of the fifteenth century. Of course, the extent to which these general trends converted into changes in tenancies and rent levels varied according to local conditions, and would have been subject to some time-lags of adjustment. Yet, overall, in the absence of any demographic recovery landlords faced a constant challenge to retain existing tenants and workers on their manors. The most obvious way of meeting this challenge was to improve the terms on which land was held, and to make employment contracts more remunerative: this meant initially reducing the restrictions and constraints of villeinage, and, ultimately, removing them. For example, the productivity of customary labour was significantly lower than hired labour, and the number of works performed fell dramatically in plague years, so it made sense to dispense with them after the mid-fourteenth century.[27]

[27] D. Stone, 'The productivity of customary and hired labour: evidence from Wisbech Barton in the fourteenth century', *Economic History Review*, 50 (1997), pp. 640–56; D. Stone, *Decision-making in medieval agriculture* (Oxford, 2005), pp. 102–3, 251–2.

Thus, overall, economic pressures seem to provide a powerful explanation for the decline of serfdom. Landlords could not swim indefinitely against such a strong, sustained and adverse economic tide, and so they had little option but to concede on elements of villeinage slowly and inexorably.[28] 'The forces of supply and demand proved stronger' than all others.[29] 'Declining prices, declining land values, and rising wage costs, all reduced the power of land-lords to resist concessions to tenant interests.'[30]

These economic conditions were unquestionably adverse to seigniorial attempts to maintain personal servility and unfree tenures on their estates. The point at issue is whether these forces provide a full and sufficient expla-nation for the decline of serfdom. The belief that they do can be tested crudely by comparing the chronology of decline with the basic trends in wages, prices and land values. Villeinage mainly disappeared between c.1380 and c.1450, according to the traditional chronology. The key changes in land values and wages occurred between the 1370s and 1390s, after which market forces were persistently hostile to the preservation of serfdom: hence its inexorable decay after the 1390s.

Yet there are difficulties with accepting this line of argument unreserv-edly. The first difficulty is explaining how villeinage took so long to disappear, given that economic trends after the mid-1370s were so unremittingly unfa-vourable to its existence. The second is explaining why the local chronology of the decline of villeinage varied so much when those basic economic forces were so powerful, and so uniform, across England. Why did it disappear on one manor soon after 1350, yet continue for many more years on another close by? The third is that it assumes that social relations were broadly consensual and thus downplays the potential for social conflict in driving change. Finally, why did similar economic conditions in the seventeenth century result in the *strengthening* of serfdom in parts of eastern Europe?[31] Taken together, these reservations are sufficiently cogent to raise doubts that economic pressures alone were sufficient to guarantee the decline of villeinage. Market forces do not operate in an unrestrained and unfettered manner in complex societies, and the same economic forces do not always result in the same outcome.[32]

---

[28]   Postan, *Medieval economy*, pp. 40–4; Postan, 'Agrarian society', pp. 569–70; Postan and Hatcher, 'Agrarian relations', pp. 68–70.

[29]   Postan, 'Agrarian society', p. 609.

[30]   Britnell, *Britain and Ireland*, p. 433.

[31]   Brenner, 'Agrarian class structure', pp. 46–7.

[32]   Hatcher and Bailey, *Modelling the Middle Ages*, pp. 55–65.

Peasant resistance

Scepticism about assigning the decisive role in the decline of serfdom to economic and demographic forces also draws broadly upon the belief that 'class' conflict is inherent within social relations and acts as the prime mover of economic and social change. Marxist perspectives emphasize that relations between lords and peasants, and the balance of power within those relationships, were based more upon legal coercion than market forces.[33] Thus an inequitable legal construct such as serfdom will inevitably generate conflict between lords and peasants, wherein lie the seeds of its ultimate decline. Conflict and social tension were manifest in myriad ways, but they emanated from either the seigniorial desire to uphold serfdom or the serf's desire to eliminate it. Shortages of tenants and labourers after the Black Death were likely to have increased the incentive for landlords to uphold serfdom firmly, yet the same conditions created justifiable grounds for serfs and villein tenants to anticipate its speedy demise. Therefore social relations deteriorated after 1350 as lords and peasants tussled over the future of serfdom, and its eventual decline in England is proof of the triumph of peasant action.

Hilton drew together these broadly Marxist ideas into a cogent explanation for the decline of serfdom in England. He emphasized the significance of an 'increased self-assertiveness' among peasants, reflecting their determination to throw off the incidents of personal servility and to acquire the trappings of freedom: serfs were socially conservative, in the sense that their objective was to become like freemen rather than to overthrow serfdom *per se*.[34] This assertiveness undermined the desire and capability of lords to enforce serfdom, which consequently dissolved due to the actions of countless individuals, not just because of the impersonal action of the forces of supply and demand in the land and labour markets.

Hilton's influential work inspired other historians to develop and to illustrate his arguments further. Peasant action and protest against lordship is identifiable throughout the Middle Ages, but after 1350 villeins 'seem to have been constantly testing the regime' through 'open and self-conscious opposition to seigniorial control'.[35] This 'rising crescendo of resistance'[36] could take many forms. It could be confined to the manor, or directed towards wider targets and issues: it could involve rebellion or recalcitrance, foment or foot-dragging.[37] In a rising crescendo of research, historians have identi-

---

33 Wickham, 'Memories of underdevelopment', pp. 39–41.
34 Hilton, *Decline of serfdom*, pp. 24–6, 30–1, 35, 50–1.
35 Dyer, 'Social and economic background', p. 30.
36 Poos, *A rural society*, p. 240.
37 Larson, *Conflict and compromise*, pp. 14–17.

fied three broad categories of social action after the Black Death. The first, and best known, emanated from seigniorial attempts to re-impose villeinage in aggressive and novel ways, thus provoking serfs into defiant responses. The second type of social action involved serf protests against the collection or implementation of the established incidents of villeinage, such as labour services or tallage. The third, and final, type of resistance is the most difficult to recover and to document, but it occurred whenever individual serfs took steps to better their personal lot, such as holding out for an improved rent package or leaving the manor for employment elsewhere. In those places where the cumulative impact of these forms of social action and resistance was effective, serfdom did not survive: where it was absent or ineffective, serfdom was consolidated or even reinforced. Hence serfdom disappeared in some places, but was strengthened in others: the decisive factor in determining whether or not it declined was not economic forces, but the precise nature and trajectory of conflict between landlord and tenant.[38]

The first category of social action – resistance to the re-imposition of serfdom – has attracted most attention in published studies. As a legal construct beneficial to landlords, serfdom would be especially vulnerable to manipulation whenever their economic interests were threatened, and those interests were most threatened whenever labour was scarce and land abundant. In theory landlords could manipulate the institution of villeinage to counter the effects of adverse market forces and to maintain their economic position after the Black Death, leaving peasants with the option either to submit or to resist. It can be argued that after 1348–9 landlords all over Europe deployed a variety of coercive tactics to uphold their legal rights over serfs, actions which strained social relations severely and provoked peasant resistance.

There is a long-established historical tradition that this pattern of seigniorial reaction then effective peasant resistance is precisely what happened in England in the generation after the Black Death.[39] Nineteenth-century historians, such as Rogers and Pearson, argued that the immediate response of English landlords was to shackle their villeins and to re-impose serfdom: according to Pearson 'a part of the population was practically brought back into serfdom and constrained to labour by irons and imprisonment'.[40] Hilton, too, stated that 'the first reaction of the lords was repression rather than accommodation' and they were 'pressing hard' on their villeins until at least

---

[38]   Martin, *Feudalism to capitalism*, pp. 57, 72, 78.

[39]   The case is well summarized in Rigby, *English society*, pp. 113–16.

[40]   C.H. Pearson, *English history in the fourteenth century* (London, 1876), pp. 229–30; J.E.T. Rogers, *A history of agriculture and prices in England*, volume I (London, 1866), pp. 26, 81.

the 1370s.[41] Freedman and Bourin suggest that the seigniorial response was so severe that it constituted an attempt to impose a second, or a new kind of, serfdom in late fourteenth-century England. They define 'neo-serfdom' as 'an innovative and adaptable means of seigniorial exploitation related to political, demographic and economic factors', and identify its imposition on a number of occasions in various parts of Europe during the last millennium.[42] Bolton asserts that 'the decades after the Black Death saw exploitation of the peasants in excess of even the bad old days of the thirteenth century', as, in Hargreaves' words, 'peasants were made to pay for the demographic, political and economic crisis'.[43]

What form did this seigniorial reaction take? Bolton contends that English landlords reacted strongly to the new conditions by mobilizing a 'whole battery of weapons at their disposal'.[44] These included control over rents and labour services, some of which were 'increased' and 'intensified' in the third quarter of the fourteenth century.[45] Another weapon was seigniorial control over the manor court, which villeins were compelled to attend.[46] It is assumed that this combination exposed villeins to 'the arbitrary will of determined and unscrupulous landlords', and such landlords became increasingly arbitrary in their behaviour, and in their manipulation of villeins, after the Black Death.[47] Certainly, after c.1350 most manorial courts across the country display a greater interest and precision in recording matters relating to villeinage, and some landlords used them to impose novel and aggressive tactics against serfs, including compelling them to hold land on special conditions of service, or to hold untenanted customary land; reclaiming fugitives though raiding parties or by levying huge fines on their close relatives; and the trial then imprisonment of serfs who claimed to be free.[48] The final weapon was the ambitious new labour legislation introduced immedi-

---

[41] Hilton, *Decline of serfdom*, pp. 36–7, 41.

[42] Freedman and Bourin, 'Introduction', pp. 1–16.

[43] Bolton, *Medieval economy*, p. 213; Hargreaves, 'Seigniorial reaction', p. 52.

[44] Bolton, *Medieval economy*, p. 213.

[45] Hilton, *Decline of serfdom*, pp. 37, 41; R.H. Hilton, *Bondmen made free* (London, 1977), pp. 156–7; R.H. Hilton, *The English peasantry in the later Middle Ages* (Oxford, 1976), pp. 58–60; J.L. Bolton, *The medieval English economy 1150–1500* (London, 1980), p. 213; Brenner, 'Property and progress', p. 96; Fryde, 'Peasant rebellion', pp. 761–2; Razi, 'Serfdom and freedom', p. 186.

[46] Dyer, 'Social and economic background', pp. 28–9; Poos, *A rural society*, p. 244.

[47] Fryde, *Peasants and landlords*, p. 14.

[48] Dyer, 'New serfdom', pp, 428–32; Page, 'End of villeinage', p. 56; Hilton, *Decline of serfdom*, pp. 37–9; Bolton, *Medieval economy*, p. 213; Fryde, *Peasants and landlords*, p. 26; Hargreaves, 'Seigniorial reaction', pp. 52–5; Fryde, 'Peasant rebellions', pp. 760–6; Schofield, 'Lordship and the peasant economy', pp. 60–8; Dyer, 'Social and economic background', pp. 24–32; Larson, *Conflict and compromise*, pp. 86–9, 94–7.

ately after the Black Death, which sought to restrict wage rises and to fix contracts of employment in ways advantageous to employers. The intervention of central government to regulate the labour market was novel in many ways, not least in the creation of a new form of judicial commission (of Justices of Labourers, later Justices of the Peace) to enforce the legislation.[49] It can be argued that this intervention created a new and powerful alliance, in which the growing authority of central government was mobilized to support and reinforce the repressive actions of landlords in the localities.[50]

It is contended that the scale and the nature of this seigniorial reaction provoked serfs to respond with defiance and anger. Razi links the 'seigniorial reaction' directly with a rise in peasant resistance and claims to be free.[51] Martin, too, contends that lordly behaviour caused 'discontent and conflict to become more frequent and widespread, [and] tenants began to move on the offensive against their landlords'.[52] The most high profile peasant rebellion during this period was, of course, the Peasants' Revolt of 1381. To varying degrees Galbraith, Hilton, Fryde, Rigby and Hargreaves all suggest that the Revolt was a collective act of resistance against provocative seigniorial policies during the 1360s and 1370s. In turn, the ferocity of events in 1381 fired a warning shot back to landlords about the possible consequences of persevering with such policies.[53] The Revolt can be depicted as drawing upon 'a

---

[49] Putnam, *Statute of Labourers*, pp. 1–5, 219–24; Hilton, *Bondmen made free*, pp. 154–5, 160–4; R.H. Britnell, 'Feudal reaction after the Black Death in the Palatinate of Durham', *Past and Present*, 128 (1990), pp. 29–30; S.A.C. Penn and C. Dyer, 'Wages and earnings in late medieval England: evidence from the enforcement of the labour laws', *Economic History Review*, 43 (1990), pp. 356–76; R.C. Palmer, *English law in the age of the Black Death, 1341–1381: a transformation of governance and law* (Chapel Hill, 1993); W.M. Ormrod, 'The politics of pestilence', in W.M. Ormrod and P. Lindley, eds., *The Black Death in England* (Stamford, 1996), pp. 155–9; C. Given-Wilson, 'Service, serfdom and English labour legislation 1350–1500', in Curry and Matthews, eds., *Concepts and patterns of service*, pp. 21–37; A. Musson, 'New labour laws, new remedies? Legal reaction to the Black Death crisis', in N. Saul, ed., *Fourteenth Century England I* (Woodbridge, 2000), pp. 73–88; C. Given-Wilson, 'The problem of labour in the context of English government, c.1350–1450', in J. Bothwell, P.J.P. Goldberg and W.M. Ormrod, eds., *The problem of labour in fourteenth-century England* (York, 2000), pp. 85–100.

[50] Dyer, 'New serfdom', p. 434; Wickham, 'Memories of underdevelopment', p. 39; Fryde, *Peasants and landlords*, pp. 33–5, 209–11, 248.

[51] Razi, 'Serfdom and freedom', pp. 186–7. See also Bolton, *English economy*, p. 215, and Fryde, 'Peasant rebellion', pp. 814, 818.

[52] Martin, *Feudalism to capitalism*, pp. 63–6, 72.

[53] V.H. Galbraith, 'Thoughts about the Peasants' Revolt', in F.R.H. DuBoulay and C.M. Barron, eds., *The reign of Richard II: essays in honour of May McKisack* (London, 1971), p. 56. Hilton argued that 'the feudal reaction was not only partially responsible for precipitating the rising (of 1381), but that it faded away as a result of it', Hilton, *Bondmen made free*, p. 231–2; Fryde, *Peasants and landlords*, pp. 39–41;

groundswell of discontent, resentment and opposition to seigniorialism in its various forms of expression'.[54]

The second broad category of peasant resistance after the Black Death was targeted against the continued collection of the established incidents of servility. These were frequently rendered with little or no recorded protest before the Black Death, and indeed continued to be so many times afterwards, but they became increasingly the targets of petty acts of non-compliance, such as refusals to perform labour services, to pay tallage, or to serve in manorial offices.[55] Fryde notes 'a sharp rise in the number of minor delinquencies in the performance of such labour services as still remained'.[56] Some of these were collective refusals, such as in 1353 when 33 tenants of Walsham-le-Willows (Suffolk) failed to turn up for winter works, and another 11 refused to reap as required for the lord during the harvest, preferring to work elsewhere for wages.[57] Similarly, the frequency of collective refusals against labour services increased after 1350 at Holywell-cum-Needingworth, characterized by two notable labour strikes in 1353 and 1386.[58] Other acts of resistance were piecemeal and personal. Again at Holywell-cum-Needingworth, between 1288 and 1339 21 separate refusals to perform labour services are recorded in 19 sessions of the manorial court, compared with 191 cases involving numerous tenants between 1353 and 1403.[59] Resistance is also evident from the appearance of emotive language in the court rolls of many other manors, describing the specific behaviour of named villeins as 'malicious', 'willful', 'contemptuous' or 'rebellious'.[60] Very occasionally, direct protest against particular incidents was followed immediately by collective agreements to remove servile incidents from rent packages.[61]

The third type of resistance emanated from the personal desire of individual serfs to better their situation. Most resistance tends to be low key and sporadic, rather than open conflict.[62] Serfs who after the Black Death would not hold customary land on villein tenure, but who were willing to hold it on a lease or a life tenancy for money rent, were making choices which ran contrary to the interests of their lords, and therefore their action involved

Rigby, *English society*, pp. 116–18; Hargreaves, 'Seigniorial reaction', p. 52. See also Razi, 'Serfdom and freedom', p. 186.

[54] Hilton, *Bondmen made free*, pp. 231–2; Fryde, 'Peasant rebellion', pp. 744, 760–1.

[55] Larson, *Conflict and compromise*, pp. 127–31; Poos, *A rural society*, pp. 247–9.

[56] Fryde, *Peasants and landlords*, p. 32.

[57] Hatcher, *Intimate history*, pp. 253–6, and below, pp. 000.

[58] DeWindt, *Land and people*, pp. 91–2.

[59] DeWindt, *Land and people*, pp. 91–2.

[60] Larson, *Conflict and compromise*, p. 131.

[61] Searle, *Lordship and community*, pp. 380–3.

[62] Larson, *Conflict and compromise*, p. 125.

an element of resistance. Likewise, those serfs who left their home manors seeking land or employment elsewhere, whether they left with formal permission or not, were also acting in a contrary manner. Even though each one of these individual actions was minor and isolated, their cumulative impact was significant. They exacerbated the contraction in the number of serfs after the Black Death, and therefore added to the lords' difficulties in finding tenants and upholding personal servility. However, it is difficult, if not impossible, to be certain whether such acts were motivated by conscious and deliberate opposition to the lord. Was a hard-bargaining tenant, or a flown serf, engaging in either 'conscious political gestures, [or] calculated risks for extra income, or attempts at making life easier' for themselves?[63] Whatever the motive, all such expressions of 'resistance', even those that emanated purely from an individual's determination to improve his or her lot, undermined the edifice of serfdom.

It is undeniable that after the Black Death landlords reacted, and villeins responded, in various ways to the dramatically altered economic and social conditions. It follows therefore that 'rural unrest in the late fourteenth century can be readily explained in terms of the tension between entrenched lordly power and the changes, or potential changes, in peasant society'.[64] There were also widespread concerns about the exclusion of the lower orders from royal justice in the generation or so after 1350, which contributed to a mood of unease and discontent.[65] Thus there are grounds for arguing that the key element in the decline of serfdom was the scale, persistence and strength of peasant rebellion and resistance, which eroded the 'whole structure of servile exactions', and forced landlords to make piecemeal concessions on villein tenures and personal servility.[66] Economic and demographic decline alone could not guarantee such changes, and therefore resistance – whether individual or collective, piecemeal or sustained, active or passive – explains 'the virtual disappearance of villeinage' from England.[67]

Despite the cogency and popularity of these arguments, there are three principal grounds for disputing that they provide a full and sufficient explanation for the decline of serfdom. The first objection is that models based on class conflict underplay the presence of consensus and coopera-tion in society, and they also struggle to explain evidence for conflict within the *same* social class.[68] Thus they over-simplify social relations and fail to

---

[63] Larson, *Conflict and compromise*, p. 17.

[64] Dyer, 'Social and economic background', p. 41.

[65] Harriss, *Shaping the Nation*, pp. 228–9.

[66] Fryde, 'Peasant rebellion', p. 768.

[67] Fryde, 'Peasant rebellion', p. 818; Martin, *Feudalism to capitalism*, p. 78.

[68] Rigby, *Rural society*, pp. 6–14; Hatcher and Bailey, *Modelling the Middle Ages*, pp. 114–20; Larson, *Conflict and compromise*, pp. 14–25.

capture the complexities and contradictions within society. The second is that many elements of the case for a seigniorial reaction are not supported by a strong evidentiary base. Nineteenth-century historians made little attempt to substantiate their strident claims for a second serfdom after the Black Death, and some modern historians have made powerful assertions based on a small corpus of evidence.[69] Anecdotes of aggressive or novel behaviour by landlords are cited as evidence of a reaction, without any proper sense of the frequency and duration of such behaviour. On the few occasions where historians have investigated such policies closely, the case for a reaction looks less strong. For example, Britnell has shown how one of the most powerful landlords in England, the bishop of Durham, launched a feudal reaction against serfs on his estate in the 1350s, but was unable to sustain the policy for long.[70]

The third objection is that the evidence for a seigniorial reaction is not contextualized properly. Few studies establish a sustained and direct link between the adoption of a specific seigniorial policy on a given manor, and the rise in peasant resistance there: instead, generic examples of resistance tend to be collected and aligned broadly alongside generic examples of reactionary policies. Similarly, manors and estates that yield *no* evidence of such tactics, or of resistance, are usually ignored. However, when such examples are considered as part of a balanced assessment of the evidence, the case looks weaker. For example, after reviewing all the evidence from a number of estates in western England, Fryde concluded that a 'unified seigniorial response' is hard to identify, even on manors held by the same landlord, and instead one is left with a sense of a 'variety of different reactions according to local conditions'.[71] It follows that if the existence of a 'seigniorial reaction' is undermined, then so, too, is the case for retaliatory peasant resistance.

Migration

Historians now recognize that medieval rural society was a good deal more mobile geographically than they had once supposed. Poos' observation that 'extensive geographical mobility had already become an integral experience of country life in Essex well before the Black Death', with regular movements of people within ten to fifteen miles of their home manor, applies

---

[69] Hybel, *Crisis or change?*, p. 23; Martin asserts that during the 1370s 'much of the South and Midland [England] was in a state of unrest' as 'all facets of villeinage became the subject of struggles between tenants and landlords', but supports this claim with just a thin footnote, Martin, *Feudalism to capitalism*, pp. 72–3.

[70] Britnell, 'Feudal reaction', pp. 28–47; Britnell, *Britain and Ireland*, p. 432.

[71] Fryde, *Peasants and landlords*, pp. 32, 61–8, 129.

just as readily to other areas of the country in the period after the great epidemic.[72] Migration offered a serf the best prospect of obtaining *de facto* freedom quickly. The migrant serf who resided in a borough for a year and a day acquired right of access to the borough court, and thus acquired a form of freedom, while the serf who moved to a new rural location was not treated there as personally servile.[73] As a newcomer he was regarded as a tenant of customary land, not as a hereditary serf or the chattel of the new lord.

It is widely assumed that the scale of geographical mobility increased after the Black Death. The decline in population created opportunities for betterment elsewhere, whether in landholding or in other forms of employment on more advantageous terms. The incentive for serfs to leave their home manor to seek better terms and conditions elsewhere was heightened by their demeaning status and the refusal of their lords to make sufficient concessions on servile burdens. There is no doubt that an increase in the migration of serfs after the Black Death would have contributed decisively to the decline of serfdom, or that the opportunities and incentives to move rose. Unfortunately, we cannot prove definitively whether the relative level of serf migration did increase after 1348–9, because sufficiently accurate and detailed evidence does not exist. Nor can we be sure about the motives of migrants.

Manorial court rolls are the best source for assessing peasant migration, although incidental references in cases under the Statute of Labourers, and in ecclesiastical courts, can also provide further glimpses into local population movements.[74] All of these sources create a strong impression that mobility did increase after the Black Death in many places. Some immigration can be detected from the careful analysis of manorial court rolls, usually when newcomers became tenants or lessees of customary land, but the most compelling and accessible evidence is their lists of emigrant serfs, either through presentments for absence or for the payment of chevage. Cheyney was the first to remark upon and document the increased, then persistent, listings of serfs who had escaped the manor in post-Black Death manor court rolls.[75] Razi used such evidence to remark that 'the mobility of the peasants was intensified considerably in the post-plague period', and Dyer observes that the record of servile migration increased 'markedly after 1349,

72 Poos, *A rural society*, p. 160.
73 MacCulloch, 'Bondmen', pp. 91–2. A knighthood also brought automatic manumission.
74 Although Poos warns that 'each of these indices of movement is sporadic and uncovers only the tip of a doubtless much bigger iceberg of migration activity', Poos, *A rural society*, p. 163.
75 Cheyney, 'Disappearance of English serfdom', pp. 27–9.

reflecting both the general *wanderlust* of the period, and also the renewed concern of the lords to deal with the problem'.[76]

Earlier historians of villeinage recognized the scale of the movement of serfs, but, for the most part, they did not attribute to it any real significance in precipitating the decline of serfdom.[77] A notable exception was Davenport, who suggested that the scale and permanence of serf departures reflected their 'restless and refractory spirit', which ultimately eroded villeinage.[78] Muller follows Davenport's lead when attributing the disappearance of villein tenure at Brandon (Suffolk) to intense pressure from local peasants, who were 'very mobile and ready to shake off all vestiges of serfdom and villeinage': similarly, Britnell comments that geographical mobility was 'the chief cause' of the decline of personal serfdom in fifteenth-century East Anglia.[79]

Manorial court rolls contain clear evidence for a sudden increase in recorded migrations in the 1350s. Hilton also detected another surge of emigration from the manor in the last quarter of the fourteenth century, and Fryde, Raftis and Razi have all argued that the migration of serfs peaked at the beginning of the fifteenth century.[80] Fryde states that there occurred from this date 'a spectacular increase in the mobility of the peasantry', and Raftis observed that 'suddenly, around 1400 on nearly all Ramsey [abbey] manors, the trickle of emigration burst into a veritable tide. The exodus was largely illegal' and the whereabouts of emigrants was largely unknown.[81] Between 1400 and 1457 a grand total of between c.30 and c.60 serfs left each of the manors on the estate of Ramsey abbey.[82] A similar chronology of departures – although not on the same scale – has been observed on the estate of Crowland abbey.[83] Razi found a similar pattern in Halesowen (Warwickshire), but also noted that the increase in migration after c.1400 was accompanied by a fall in the number of fugitives who subsequently returned to their home manor.[84] By the middle of the fifteenth century the scale of mobility had fallen, and, with it, interest in imposing chevage on many manors.

---

[76] Z. Razi, *Life, marriage and death in a medieval parish. Economy, society, and demography in Halesowen 1270–1400* (Cambridge, 1980), pp. 117–18; Dyer, 'Economic and social background', p. 24.

[77] For example, Cheyney, 'Disappearance of English serfdom', pp. 27–9.

[78] Davenport, 'Decline of villeinage', pp. 140–1, and *Economic development*, p. 129.

[79] Muller, 'Peasants, lords', p. 164; Britnell, 'Tenant farming and tenant farmers: Eastern England', p. 621.

[80] Hilton, *Decline of serfdom*, pp. 33–5.

[81] Fryde, *Peasants and landlords*, p. 116; Raftis, *Tenure and mobility*, pp. 153–4.

[82] DeWindt, *Land and people*, pp. 178–9; Raftis, *Tenure and mobility*, pp. 160–6.

[83] Page, *Crowland abbey*, p. 149; Britnell, 'Tenant farming and tenant farmers: Eastern England', p. 621.

[84] Razi, 'The myth of the immutable English family', pp. 39–43.

This accepted chronology for servile migrations after 1350 is susceptible to challenge. The argument that migrations peaked around c.1400 is based mainly upon chevage evidence from a limited sample (some manors on the estates of Crowland and Ramsey abbeys, and the manor of Halesowen), and it has not been properly balanced against those places where no surge of departures is recorded around 1400: for example, the record of servile migration from Kibworth Harcourt *ceased* around this time.[85] In any event, can we be certain that a surge in *recorded* departures of serfs reflects a *real* increase, and not merely an administrative crackdown? The rise in the number of reported departures in manorial courts of the 1350s undoubtedly reflects sudden and real seigniorial concerns about the difficulties of retaining tenants and labourers on their manors, and it probably reflects a real rise in absolute rates of emigration too.[86] However, chevage is a servile incident, not an infallible measure of migration, and, as such, landlords could choose whether or not to implement it, and serfs could choose whether or not to pay it. In other words, the management of chevage was liable to waves of enforcement or even subtle changes in its usage, caused by changing managerial priorities or zeal, which might explain a sudden surge in recorded departures. Raftis assumes that the sudden burst of departures after c.1400 on the Ramsey manors is a genuine phenomenon, but does not discuss the possibility that its amplitude might be heightened by an estate-wide crackdown on migration. The scale and timing of the exodus across a number of very different Ramsey manors is remarkably consistent, which is highly suggestive of an administrative change, especially when it occurred at a time when the abbey was experiencing a deepening crisis in local land markets, with untenanted lands, tenurial change and refusals to hold customary holdings: developments which would make the abbey especially sensitive to the migration of any residents, and thus more likely to concentrate its attention upon a servile due that created an obstacle to departing serfs.[87]

Whatever the chronology of servile migration between 1350 and 1500, there are two main approaches to explaining why it occurred. The first is to regard it as an unequivocal expression of resistance against villeinage. Hargreaves attributes migration from the estate of Worcester Cathedral Priory to the harshness of seigniorial policies there, which made life intolerable for serfs, and Fryde asserts that the motivation behind most migrations was a burning desire to be free of the shackles of serfdom.[88] Brenner and Razi develop these observations to argue that the scale and timing of migra-

---

[85]   The record of emigration at Kibworth ceases in 1409, Howell, *Kibworth Harcourt*, p. 45.

[86]   Razi, *Life, marriage and death*, p. 119.

[87]   Raftis, *Tenure and mobility*, p. 191.

[88]   Hargreaves, 'Seigniorial reaction', p. 71; Fryde, *Peasants and landlords*, pp. 116–18.

tion at the end of the fourteenth century represented a new phase in peasant resistance to seigniorial impositions: when faced with inflexible or aggressive management, villeins simply voted with their feet, leaving the manor and starting again elsewhere on better terms and conditions.[89] More specifically, emigration from the manor replaced direct action against lordship as the main expression of resistance. Razi contends that direct peasant action had characterized resistance to seigniorial policies before the 1380s, but thereafter it was replaced with 'massive migration'.[90] Similarly, Brenner states that after the Revolt of 1381 'peasants now streamed away from their manors, and their lords could do nothing to stop them'.[91] Indeed, he identifies the success or failure of seigneurs in countering this peasant mobility and resistance as the key determinant of divergent patterns of social development across late medieval Europe.[92]

The argument that serf migrations in the second half of the fourteenth century were primarily a function of 'flight from aggression' would be greatly strengthened if a direct and persistent link could be established between specific evidence for the tough management of serfs on a given manor and a subsequent spate of departures. No such link has been established on the Ramsey abbey estates, which are the main source of evidence for mass migration after c.1400. In fact, many of the fugitives from individual Ramsey manors initially settled on other manors within the same estate, which hardly squares with the notion that their migration was driven by seigniorial oppression.[93] Thus there has been a tendency to assert or to assume a link between aggressive policies and servile departures, rather than to prove one empirically.

The second way of explaining serf migration is to regard it as the pursuit of opportunity rather than as a response to oppression. We cannot know definitively *why* serfs migrated, because the sources provide few explanations for the departures. Some might have been political gestures against oppression, but many could have been motivated by a desire for a better life at a time when the choices available to peasants were widening. Serfs left their home manors for a variety of reasons, many of which had nothing to do with serfdom: a lack of economic opportunity, geographical remoteness, family reasons, disagreeable neighbours, and so on. In reality, the decision to migrate was motivated by a complex interplay of forces, a mix of 'indi-

[89] Cheyney, 'Disappearance of English serfdom', pp. 27–9; Davenport, 'Decline of villeinage', pp. 128, 140–1; Fryde, 'Peasant rebellion', pp. 766–8; Razi, 'Myth', pp. 36–42; Dyer, 'New serfdom', p. 433; Razi, 'Serfdom and freedom', p. 189.
[90] Razi, 'Serfdom and freedom', p. 187.
[91] Brenner, 'Property and progress', p. 97.
[92] Brenner, 'Property and progress', pp. 64, 91.
[93] Raftis, *Tenure and mobility*, p. 156–7, 170–1.

vidual responses to a variety of external stimuli which offered prospects for economic development': as Field states, 'it is unconvincing and misleading to explain all, or even most, rural mobility simply in terms of resistance to lordship or a desire to be free'.[94] Razi recognizes that migration was partly motivated by 'impersonal demographic and economic forces'.[95]

Bondmen under the Tudors

A different perspective upon the decline of serfdom in late medieval England is obtained by considering why it lasted until the Tudor age in some places and not in others. In 1485 at least 400 English manors contained serfs, and at least 104 in 1560.[96] Yet these headline figures disguise a particular and unambiguous pattern in the geographical distribution of those manors across England, a pattern which is consistent in both 1485 and 1560. By 1485 serfdom was virtually dead north of the Trent, and, to the south, it was weakest in the Midlands. Although no longer a common condition, personal serfdom was strongest in the coastal counties of the south east (with the notable exception of Kent), especially Norfolk and Suffolk, and in the wetlands of Lincolnshire and Somerset.

MacCulloch attempted to explain this pattern in a number of ways. He attributed the early disappearance of serfdom from the North and the Midlands to the failure of the classic manorial system to take root in the former, and by what he saw as its weakness in the latter. He argued that serfs were most likely to be retained on manors with a settled, and continuous, history, especially those in river estuaries and valley systems.[97] Yet there are flaws in MacCulloch's general thesis. The extent of classic manorialism in the medieval North was greater than he supposed, and we now know that the extent of villein rents and the proportion of customary land were greater in the Midlands than in south-east England.[98] Furthermore, this level of

---

[94]   Field, 'Migration in the later Middle Ages', p. 41; Britnell, *Commercialization*, pp. 219–21.

[95]   Razi, 'Myth', p. 42.

[96]   These figures, and the following analysis, are taken from MacCulloch, 'Bondmen', pp. 94–5.

[97]   MacCulloch, 'Bondmen', pp. 95–7.

[98]   The dominance of villein tenures in the Midlands is shown in Campbell, 'Agrarian problem', p. 35. The existence of villeinage and classic manorial structures in parts of northern England is evident in, for example, G.A. Wood, 'Field arrangements in the west Riding of Yorkshire in the high Middle Ages' (PhD thesis, University of Leeds, 2003), pp. 91–8; G.A. Wood, M. Purvis, and B. Harrison, 'Irregular field systems and patterns of settlement in western Yorkshire', in T. Unwin and T. Spek, eds., *European landscapes: from mountain to sea* (London, 2003), pp. 169–70.

generalization does not explain the survival of serfdom in c.1500 on some manors in midland England, or its absence from hundreds of other manors in the south-east.

For all the difficulties of generalizing about why serfdom survived in some places and not others, MacCulloch identified one striking and irrefutable pattern. He showed that the survival of serfdom was as much a feature of lay as of ecclesiastical estates, especially in East Anglia, a discovery which ran contrary to the received wisdom that the latter were the most administratively bureaucratic and controlling, and therefore most likely to maintain serfdom.[99] He cites the case of a petition from bondmen on four manors on the estate of the duke of Norfolk, who used the opportunity created in 1546 by the political fall of the third Howard Duke to press for their freedom. They claimed that this particular duke had squeezed his bondmen hard, reviving old and obscure restrictions on schooling and learning, in a manner that was 'much more extreme than his ancestors'.[100] Thus MacCulloch raises two important points, neither of which he was able to develop in a short article. The first is that continuity of ownership or administration of a manor was a significant element in preserving serfdom, and this was as much a feature of Crown lands or the great lay estates as of perpetual institutions such as monasteries. Second, individual lords might have strong personal views about serfs and serfdom, which could be translated into particular and discernible policies on their estates.

Conclusion

Historians have identified four main contributors to the decline of serfdom in late medieval England: manumission, economic and demographic pressures, peasant resistance, and the migration of serfs. In the 1970s and 1980s the causes of the decline of serfdom became something of an ideological battleground among the participants in the Brenner Debate, with the combatants divided between those supporting the primacy of economic pressures, and those promoting the primacy of social conflict, especially increased peasant resistance.[101] Yet the quest for the prime mover in history is beset with difficulties, the most serious of which is the philosophical objection that it is not possible to rank causes according to a hierarchy of importance. Causes

---

[99]   MacCulloch, 'Bondmen', pp. 93–5.

[100]   MacCulloch, 'Bondmen', p. 99. See also M. Fisher, '"A thing without rights, a mere chattel of their lord". The escape from villeinage of a Suffolk family', *Proceedings of the Suffolk Institute of Archaeology and History*, 42 (2009), p. 36.

[101]   T.S. Aston and C.H.E. Philpin, eds., *The Brenner Debate. Agrarian class structure and economic development in pre-industrial Europe* (Cambridge, 1985).

might be usefully ranked according to immediacy, or selected to address the needs of a particular audience, but they cannot be weighted objectively.[102] Another objection is the excessive simplicity of prime mover explanations, which tend to portray causes as operating independently and separately, thus downplaying the complex inter-dependencies and interactions of the real world.[103]

One feature of the work on villeinage in England has been a tendency to generalize broadly about the causes of its decline on the basis of a single case study or a handful of striking examples. This is most obviously true of the earliest research, published at a time when historians were charting the contours of this new field of scholarship without the benefits of a large volume of case studies. Yet it is still observable in the case for 'reaction and resistance' after the Black Death. The second half of the fourteenth century was unquestionably 'a period of agitation, excitement, anger, antagonism and creativity', and many landlords reacted to the shortages of labourers and tenants after 1348–9 by restraining their villeins in various ways and to varying degrees.[104] Some landlords did adopt reactionary policies on their estates in response to the shock of 1348–9, although we do not yet know how sustained and how typical they were. There is imprecision about what scale and type of behaviour is necessary to justify the use of a label such as a 'seigniorial reaction', let alone 'a second serfdom'.

It is already clear that any attempt to impose a 'second serfdom' in England after 1350 was different from the forms of 'second', or 'neo-', serfdom identified in parts of eastern Europe under similar economic conditions in the early modern period. Some eastern-European landlords successfully enslaved their peasantry on a far greater scale than that achieved in late medieval England, because they had a wider range of political, legal and fiscal instruments at their disposal.[105] There can be no question that the seigniorial response in late fourteenth-century England was mild and restricted compared with these 'achievements'.

---

[102]   S.H. Rigby, 'Historical causation. Is one thing more important than another?', *History*, 80 (1995), pp. 227–42.

[103]   Hatcher and Bailey, *Modelling the Middle Ages*, pp. 208–19; Kitsikopoulos, 'England', pp. 40–7.

[104]   Dyer, 'New serfdom', p. 429.

[105]   W. Kula, *An economic theory of the feudal system* (London, 1976), pp. 25–7, 33–5, 127; A. Klima, 'Agrarian class structure and economic development in pre-industrial Bohemia', in Aston and Philpin, eds., *The Brenner Debate*, pp. 193–4; W.W. Hagen, 'Village life in east-Elbian Germany and Poland 1400–1800: subjection, self-defence, survival', in Scott, ed., *Peasantries of Europe*, pp. 145–89; J. Langton, 'The historical geography of European peasantries', in Scott, ed., *Peasantries of Europe*, p. 392; Freedman and Bourin, 'Introduction', pp. 8–12; H. Kitsikopoulos, 'Epilogue', in Kitsikopoulos, ed., *Agrarian change and crisis*, pp. 330–52.

Our understanding of the reasons for the decline of English serfdom can be greatly enhanced by accumulating more evidence to elucidate key developments, and to deploy it in a manner that will test the assumptions about causation. Simply generating more local evidence about the extent and timing of manumission would be useful. Even more instructive would be to explore the presence of any correlation between economic change and the chronology of decline of serfdom; the existence, or not, of a seigniorial reaction; any correlation between recorded resistance to performing established servile dues, and the chronology of migration of serfs from the manor, to the decline of serfdom there; and further exploration of Hilton's belief that the incidents of personal servility, more than tenurial incidents, became the target for resistance. It can also be enhanced by closer exploration of the influence of seigniorial attitudes to villeinage upon the management of serfdom on the ground, and, also, the impact of continuity and discontinuity in the ownership of estates upon the survival of serfdom. The case studies which follow will address these issues.

PART II

Case Studies

5

Reassessing the Decline of Serfdom: Methods and Sources

Part I explored how the decline of serfdom impacted upon the economic and social history of England, and then surveyed current opinion on the chronology and causes of its decline. Part II presents the fruit of new research into this subject. Thus, at one level, this section adds more local examples to the existing stock of knowledge. Yet, at another level, it attempts to go beyond previous research to provide more precision in the chronology and causes of decline by using a different methodology to those deployed in previous studies.

This new approach proceeds from three simple assumptions. The first is that the key characteristics of villeinage on the eve of the Black Death must be explicitly defined if its subsequent decline is to be charted effectively: if they are ambiguous or unstated, then there is no reliable baseline from which to trace the decline. The second assumption is that, having established those key characteristics, the chronology of decline of each of them must be plotted as precisely as the sources allow for each individual manor. Finally, the manors used in the study should be representative of the different types of manor found in England, and they should be located in more than one area of the country, in order to increase the typicality of the research findings.

Once precise chronologies have been constructed for each of the key elements of villeinage on each manor, they can be correlated with major trends in those forces which contributed to the decline of villeinage: manumission, the demand for land, and patterns of peasant resistance and flight. Correlating the precise chronologies on individual manors with each of these underlying social and economic trends provides the most secure basis for evaluating what caused the decline.

A definition of villeinage

Establishing a watertight definition of villeinage ought to be a simple task, yet it eluded both medieval lawyers and early twentieth-century historians. The failure of the latter to agree upon a definition created a major obstacle to the resolution of their debate on the decay of villeinage. The various participants sought to chart its decline by reference to different elements of villeinage, which meant that they were effectively arguing along parallel lines: thus Cunningham looked for specific changes in the rural relations of production, while Cheney focused upon the decline of labour services.[1]

Although no definition of villeinage can be exact, for the compelling reason that there was no exact definition in medieval law, some credible definition of villeinage in the thirteenth century is essential if its subsequent disappearance is to be tracked and then explained. Here we argue it comprised three central elements: a tenant or person who held land on villein tenure; a tenant or person required to render certain pecuniary customs and services to their lord, associated with either their personal status or that of the land they held; and, finally, a condition regarded as inferior and subordinate.

A tenant or person who held land on villein tenure

As we have seen, the title to villein tenure could not be defended under the common law, which meant that a villein tenant could only seek redress in his/her lord's manorial court, with no recourse to any other court or lord. Thus the common law provided villein tenants with no protection against landlords who acted arbitrarily, unfairly or capriciously towards villein property, and therefore villein tenure was in theory insecure and vulnerable to seizure.

Although many practical features of villein tenure and its rent package were decisively altered during the course of the fourteenth and fifteenth centuries, the fundamental legal relationship between lord and customary tenant had not changed.[2] Thus a strict legal interpretation would be to assert that villein tenure did not disappear until either the sixteenth century, when the courts of common law finally and consistently provided remedy to copy- and leaseholders, or even until the early seventeenth century, when the law itself was finally changed to recognize that remedy.[3] Yet medieval historians have not favoured such a narrow and legalistic interpretation, preferring instead to follow Hilton's lead in regarding the transformation of villein tenure into copyhold, or its conversion into a fixed-term tenancy for money rent, as the step changes of significance.[4] They have consistently treated leasehold as a form of tenure distinct from villeinage.[5] Indeed, leaseholds were secure economic contracts, respected as long as the tenant honoured the terms.[6] This approach is reflected in Schofield's observation that in the

---

[1]   Hybel, *Crisis or change?*, pp. 49–50.

[2]   Gray, *Copyhold*, pp. 8, 10, 12.

[3]   See the discussion in Chapter 2, pp. 20–3.

[4]   Hilton, *Decline of serfdom*, pp. 44–51; see also Harvey, *Westminster abbey*, pp. 244–93.

[5]   Rigby, 'Serfdom', p. 463.

[6]   Smith, 'Families and their property', p. 64; Smith, 'English peasantry', pp. 363–9; Schofield, '*Extranei*', p. 12.

1390s tenants in Birdbrook (Essex) 'were unable or unwilling to hold their tenements in villeinage' and so held it on leasehold tenure instead.[7] Medieval landlords themselves were well aware of a significant practical difference. Customary lands converted to life tenancies for money on the Berkeley estate were described as 'held freely by copy'.[8] As the prior of Otterton (Devon) noted as early as 1260, the leaseholder 'is apt to regard himself as a freeman thenceforth'.[9]

This study follows Hilton's lead, and the established practice among medievalists, in regarding the moment when the critical mass of customary land on a manor either shed the main incidents of villeinage, and/or shifted to a fixed-term tenure, as a decisive moment in the decline of serfdom. These forms of customary tenancy were different from villein tenure in three important, practical, ways: they possessed the trappings of simple contracts between lord and tenant, with a formal and explicit statement of the rudiments of that contract recorded in the manorial court roll; the language of the tenancies was more dignified; and their rent package was largely free of the old servile exactions. Consequently, they did not carry the same stigma as villein tenure, which thus made them more attractive to people who were not personally servile, such as freemen, townspeople and even gentry lords.[10] For example, in the 1360s a knight refused to hold some inherited villein land, surrendering it instead to Southwick priory without compensation, on the grounds that he did not wish to be tainted by the requirement to perform rustic services. Contrast this disdainful rejection of villein tenure with Sir Robert Tyrell's ready acquisition in the late fifteenth century of a block of six customary holdings, and the onward sale of this portfolio in 1506 to Thomas Spring, a wealthy merchant of Lavenham (Suffolk).[11] Thus it is justifiable to regard this tenurial transformation as a decisive moment in the decline of villeinage. It amounted to a shift from the non-contractual villein tenure to rudimentary contractual tenancies, a transformation *de facto* with which the common law would eventually catch up.

Hence tracking the extent and the pace of the conversion of villein tenures to fixed-term tenures, or their evolution into a customary tenure without servile incidents, is essential to charting the decline of villeinage on an individual manor. Identifying the moment when this occurred on a given manor

---

7   Schofield, 'Tenurial developments', p. 257.
8   Wells-Furby, *Berkeley estate*, p. 106.
9   Quoted in Finberg, *Tavistock abbey*, p. 251.
10 Dyer, 'New serfdom', p. 433; Mate, *Trade and economic developments*, pp. 193–4; Harvey, 'Aspects of the peasant land market', p. 328. In the north of England such tenures 'differed little, if at all, from those of the freemen who surrounded them', Tuck, 'Tenant farming and tenant farmers: the Northern Borders', p. 594.
11 Kaye, *Medieval English conveyances*, p. 358; Schofield, '*Extranei*', p. 16.

is often difficult and inexact, given the evolutionary nature of the process. However, the task is not impossible, especially if it is broken down into three component parts. The first is to establish as precisely as possible the rate at which customary holdings shed the core incidents of villein tenure. Few published studies track this process with any precision or rigour for each manor, and instead most have tended to provide an approximate timeframe for the decay of a particular incident across a number of manors on the same estate. The dates of the disappearance of each of the main incidents must be pinpointed for every manor, and the context of their decay – sudden or gradual – should be established as far as the extant sources permit.

The second component of the transformation of villein tenure is the scale and timing of its conversion to fixed-term tenancies for money rent. Tracing this development from manorial sources is relatively straightforward. The initial grant of customary land on a fixed-term tenure is usually recorded in the manorial court roll, and thereafter the cash rent due annually usually appears as an individual entry in the rents section of the manorial account. Insecure tenures at will and temporary grants *de exitus* are usually recorded in the account only. Consequently, a good run of court rolls, augmented by some account rolls, enables the broad chronology and approximate extent of conversions of former villein land to fixed-term tenures of various kinds to be reliably reconstructed. However, the reconstruction can seldom be definitive, because there are a number of ways in which the relevant information could leak: for example, not every court session may have survived; some leases were recorded straight onto the account, but not all accounts have survived; and some accounts do not detail each lease individually.

A complementary method of tracking the chronology and extent of conversions of former customary land to fixed-term tenures is to analyse the ways in which labour services were discharged in the 'works' section of the manorial account. This detailed sub-section contains details of all labour services due during the year, and how those works were deployed or discharged. For example, a total of 200 week works might be owed, of which X were used to weed the demesne, Y to mend the lord's hedges, and Z were commuted at will because they were not required. In addition, some works may not have been available to the demesne in a given year, but were instead recorded as 'decayed' or 'allowed' for various reasons. 'Decayed' services related to holdings that either lay abandoned 'in the hands of the lord' or had been formally converted to a money rent. In the latter case, the theoretical liability of the holding for services was still being recorded as a rather pedantic accounting device, reflecting the official stance that conversions to fixed-term tenancies were not formally regarded as a permanent change in tenurial status. From this type of information it is possible to estimate the scale of conversions from villein tenure to fixed-term tenancies in a given year by calculating the proportion of 'decayed' labour services against those nominally liable.

Of course, this technique is entirely reliant upon the existence of a 'works' account' within the manorial account, but these are not always recorded, especially if the demesne was leased and not exploited directly. Even if a works' account is extant, the technique is still reliant upon the scribe maintaining a clear and consistent distinction between 'decays' and 'allowances', the former relating to unavailable labour services, the latter to one-off remissions for existing tenants for permissible reasons. Unfortunately, within the record of decays, accounts seldom differentiate between land that was simply abandoned and that which had been converted to money rent.

The third component is the changing nature of the language used to describe the terms of tenure. As discussed in Chapter Two, in c.1300 conveyances of customary land recorded in manor court rolls routinely used phrases such as 'held in villeinage …' or 'held in bondage …', but such overt servile language was rarely, if ever, a feature of the terms of customary tenures in the late fifteenth century, when phrases such as 'held according to the custom of the manor', 'by copy of the court roll' or 'at the will of the lord' dominated. The latter two phrases still underlined that the title to customary tenure was defensible only in the manorial court, but the deliberate and widespread shedding of 'in villeinage/in bondage' signifies a decisive alteration in the nature of that tenure: namely, the withering of servile incidents, especially labour services, from its rent package. However, historians are uncertain about whether to attribute much significance to subtle changes in such language over much shorter periods of time. For example, does the disappearance of 'in villeinage' from conveyances on a given manor between, say, the 1370s and 1390s, reflect clerical whim or is it reliable evidence of a real change in the dignity of villein tenure? Historians have tended to be cautious and to assume the former, but the assumption is worth testing more systematically.[12] One approach to addressing this uncertainty is to pay careful attention to the timing, nature and permanency of changes to the language employed in the conveyances of villein land recorded within manorial court rolls, and then to correlate them with the chronology of the decline of servile incidents and the spread of fixed-term tenures. Did changes to the language of conveyances and the shedding of servile incidents occur along similar timeframes, or were they markedly dissimilar? A good correlation would indicate strongly that contemporaries recognized a symbolic and substantial change in the 'appearance and dignity' of villein tenure had taken place.

One further, and final, issue is worth addressing within this context: when did the practice of issuing a copy of the court roll entry of the transfer of customary land develop? As we have seen, it was rare in the early fourteenth century but had become well established by the mid-fifteenth century,

---

[12] Mullan and Britnell, *Land and family*, pp. 63–4.

although a few historians suspect that it had spread earlier. Unfortunately, the practice of issuing copies is very hard to recover, because the copies themselves seldom survive and references to them in surviving sources are often a matter of chance. Yet there are incidental references and survivals, sufficient to encourage the belief that an attentive and systematic sifting of the sources for any evidence of the existence of copies before c.1450 might prove instructive. This is *not* to argue that the issue of a copy created a new and distinctive form of tenure, even though it represented the genesis of the copyhold tenure of the sixteenth century. However, by establishing a more reliable sense of *when* the issue of copies became common place, and placing it within the context of other changes to customary tenure, we might develop a better understanding of *why* they emerged.

A tenant or person required to render certain pecuniary customs and services to their lord, associated with either their personal status or that of the land they held

Chapter 3 illustrated how villeinage was associated with a number of pecuniary customs and services attached to unfree land and/or people. None of these customs was a universal characteristic of villeinage, and no one of them provided conclusive proof of villeinage under the common law.[13] However, it is possible to identify the main core of servile incidents, whose subsequent disappearance is therefore indicative of the decline of villeinage. What were they?

Early historians deemed the seigniorial extraction of labour as rent to be the defining characteristic of medieval peasant society, and therefore they regarded the performance of labour services upon the lord's demesne as the central component of villeinage. As we have seen, these services came in a variety of types and forms, and they were not exclusive to villein holdings. Yet week works lay at the core of servility, because they were the most demeaning and unpopular type of service.[14] Week works were the most frequent and most onerous of all labour services: two or more works per week are regarded as especially heavy.[15] Furthermore, they were an uncertain and unspecified service in the sense that the villein did not know in advance what agrarian task would be required in order to discharge it, and such tasks could be unskilled, arduous and unpleasant. In contrast, the tasks associated with other labour services (e.g. weeding, carting, ploughing, harvest works) were specified in advance, seasonally restricted, and less frequently

---

[13]   Hyams, *King, lords and peasants*, p. 187.
[14]   Douglas, *The social structure of medieval East Anglia*, pp. 80–2.
[15]   Miller and Hatcher, *Rural England*, p. 127.

demanded.[16] Finally, and unlike these other, lighter, seasonal services, week works were associated exclusively with villein tenure.

Of the other servile incidents, liability to merchet and, to a lesser extent, tallage came closest to defining villeinage under the common law.[17] Leyrwite and chevage were ubiquitous, personal, servile incidents that recognized overlordship and reinforced the villein's subjugation to the will of the lord.[18] Heriot and millsuit were not exclusively associated with villein tenure, because death duties of various kinds were charged on tenants whatever their status, and millsuit could be a requirement of all manorial tenants; yet both were predominantly servile incidents, and both were widespread throughout England.

Hence the core pecuniary customs and services of villeinage are defined as week works, merchet, tallage, leyrwite, chevage, heriot and millsuit.[19] This definition is not far removed from the opinion of one fifteenth-century lawyer, who regarded the key profits from villeinage as labour services, merchet, heriot and tallage.[20] The presence of each of these incidents on an individual manor, the changes to their management over time, and the chronology of their disappearance, will be the focus of research in the following case studies.

A condition regarded as inferior and subordinate.

Hilton rightly stressed that villeinage was more than just a legal and economic construct, because its cogent and pervasive ideology influenced social attitudes to a significant degree. The relationship between lord and villein was an expression of the subordination of one person to another, and it conveyed powerful messages about social subservience and inferiority.[21] Servitude represented 'a capricious domination … it depended upon certain dramatic images and proofs of subordination for its effectiveness'.[22] The very word *nativus* 'carried the plain implication that the birth and hereditary

---

[16]   Page, 'End of villeinage', pp. 21–3; Mate, 'Tenant farming and tenant farmers: Kent and Sussex', p. 683; Faith, *English peasantry*, pp. 259–65.

[17]   See above, pp. 38, 47.

[18]   Schofield, 'Robert Kyng', p. 63, shows how in the 1390s the abbot of Bury accumulated references to chevage, childwite and merchet from court rolls to prove the villein status of one of his tenants.

[19]   This list of core pecuniary customs is very similar to that complied by Rigby, who regards tallage, merchet, chevage, heriot, millsuit and labour services as the defining characteristics of English serfdom: Rigby, 'Serfdom', p. 464.

[20]   Savine, 'Bondmen under the Tudors', p. 263.

[21]   P.R. Coss, 'Age of deference', in Horrox and Ormrod, eds., *Social history*, pp. 32–3.

[22]   P. Freedman, *Images of medieval peasants* (Stanford, 1999), p. 243.

condition ... mattered', and a *nativus* was both expected and required to recognize his status as personally subjugated.[23]

Status mattered in late medieval England. Freedman develops this point by emphasizing that status is an important element in well being, a fundamental issue of human dignity, not least because it was regarded as such by peasants themselves.[24] When villeins mounted claims to be free, they did so because they regarded their servile status as restricting and degrading.[25] In courtly literature 'villein' was associated with all that was base, vile and unpleasant, and is the source of the word villain, just as 'churl' is the origin of churlish.[26] To be derided as a serf was widely regarded as offensive and insulting.[27] For example, in 1365 the Durham halmote court banned tenants from calling anyone *rusticum*, and other courts handled defamation cases based on similar slurs.[28] In the 1420s the prioress of Redlingfield (Suffolk) readily admitted an amorous affair, but she strenuously denied that her lover was a serf.[29] Even as late as the sixteenth century, some prospective brides were disdainful of servile suitors.[30]

Hence social attitudes towards villeinage, and in particular the notion that the condition was inferior and subordinate, are another defining characteristic of the condition. Identifying and measuring the persistence of such attitudes – and by extension their eventual disappearance – is extremely difficult, because the entries in manorial records that document the day-to-day relationship between lord and villein are formal and dry. They simply do not tell us what people thought, nor do they reveal the attitudes that motivated recorded actions. However, they do document the particular characteristics of villeinage on an individual manor, and they do record the way in which lords managed their relationship with their villeins, both of which offer a window through which to glimpse social attitudes to serfdom. A lord who insisted upon the imposition of harsh or demeaning incidents of villeinage, particularly ones that were not common elsewhere, can be reasonably regarded as adopting a conservative attitude to serfdom. Likewise, the lord who attempted to impose new incidents of serfdom, or who adopted an

---

[23] Hyams, *King, lords and peasants*, pp. 228–9; Vinogradoff, *Villeinage in England*, p. 142.

[24] Freedman, *Origins of peasant servitude*, p. 12.

[25] Dyer, 'New serfdom', p. 427.

[26] Coss, 'Age of deference', pp. 34–5.

[27] Bailey, 'Blowing up bubbles', pp. 350, 357n.; Coss, 'Age of deference', p. 34.

[28] Tuck, 'Tenant farming and tenant farmers: the Northern Borders', p. 593; Larson, *Conflict and compromise*, pp. 64, 158, 187.

[29] She even erased any references to her lover's servile status from court rolls in the priory's possession, Fisher, 'A thing without rights', p. 33.

[30] MacCulloch, 'Bondmen', p. 98.

aggressive or confrontational approach to the management of villeinage (as a standing policy or as a new one), can be deemed to have had strong ideas about the inferior condition of villeinage.

Thus the nature and range of the incidents of villeinage on a given manor, and, especially, the manner in which lords chose to manage them, convey something of significance about underlying social attitudes. For example, the requirement that a villein obtain seigniorial permission, or pay a fine in lieu of that formal permission, to enter holy orders, to be educated, or to enter into an apprenticeship was relatively rare, but it was a particularly demeaning incident, because it overtly targeted the serf's opportunities for self-improvement and upward social mobility, and because it pointedly avoided the use of the generic incident of chevage which could just as readily have been employed to cover the associated absence from the manor. The combination of its relative scarcity and demeaning nature means that its continued imposition after 1350 would be indicative of a conservative and disdainful attitude to serfs.

By deploying this rationale, we can identify a number of other practices that are indicative of such attitudes in the second half of the fourteenth century: an insistence that serfs claiming to be free, or seeking to leave the manor, swear an oath recognizing their status in front of other tenants in the manorial court; physical seizure and/or incarceration of migrant serfs; the imposition of hefty or increased fines for the core incidents of villeinage; and unusually demeaning or restrictive conditions of service or tenure.[31] In the fifteenth century some lords constructed elaborate genealogies of serf families to facilitate the administrative task of keeping track of them and proving their servile lineage, while others pursued and extorted the descendants of long-departed villeins.[32] Even some contemporaries viewed such practices as outmoded. In *The Parson's Tale* Chaucer criticized the legal doctrine that serfs have no goods except those derived from their lord and the application of this principle to pursue flown villeins for financial purposes, regarding such behaviour as indicative of 'harde lordshipes'.[33]

Chronology, correlation and causation

The three-pronged definition of villeinage in the early fourteenth century provides a baseline from which to establish a precise chronology of its decline

---

[31] Dyer, 'New serfdom', pp. 429–32; Schofield, 'Lordship and the peasant economy', pp. 60–7.

[32] Hare, 'Lords and their tenants', pp. 21–5; Fryde, *Peasants and landlords*, pp. 217–19, 243–8.

[33] Fryde, *Peasants and landlords*, p. 217.

on a given manor. The first objective is to trace and date, as best we can, the evolution of villein tenures into contractual tenancies: what is the scale and timing of the shift to fixed-term tenancies? Do changes in the language of conveyances of customary land correlate closely with either these conversions or the disappearance of servile incidents from the rent package of the original hereditary tenures?

The second objective is to establish a precise chronology for the disappearance of the core incidents of villeinage (week works, merchet, tallage, heriot, chevage, millsuit and leyrwite) on each manor, and to chart, as far as the sources allow, the date when each was levied for the last time. Establishing definitively the last date of an individual incident can be difficult, given the inevitable gaps that occur in the extant sources of even the best-documented manors, and so reconstructing the declining frequency of exactions, and changes in their management, is also important. Manorial court rolls are essential for the record and management of merchet, leyrwite, recognition and millsuit, and they are usually reliable sources of information about tallage and chevage. Account rolls are essential for reconstructing the utilization of labour services, and are sometimes important sources of information about chevage and tallage.

The third objective is to assess social attitudes towards villeinage, based upon the ways in which lords managed the relationship with their serfs. To what extent was the management of villeinage aggressive or novel, to what extent was it pragmatic and accommodating? Is there evidence for attempts to impose new forms of service, or to manage existing customs in new ways, in the second half of the fourteenth century as part of a seigniorial reaction? The emphasis will be upon considering such examples firmly within the context of the long-term management of villeinage upon that particular manor. Once again, manorial court rolls are essential for this purpose, although other estate records are usually more revealing about the construction of serf genealogies and the extent of manumission.

Having reconstructed the chronology of decline of the core incidents of villeinage on an individual manor, the fourth objective is to compare evidence for the main social and economic changes which are assumed to have caused the decline of serfdom. The main economic changes are indicated by the land, price and wage data discussed in Chapter 4. These national series are augmented wherever possible by local rent data from individual manors, so that the local experience of villeinage is correlated with local indices of change. Unfortunately, the latter are hard to win, which explains why historians have yet to construct a national rent series to compare with their comprehensive and reliable data for prices and wages. The main social trends are indicated by the scale, timing and nature of recorded peasant resistance to servile incidents, especially labour services, and by the scale and timing of emigration from the manor: both are fully documented in manorial court rolls. Correlating a precise chronology of decline with shifts in the key social and economic forces provides a more secure basis for assessing the reasons for the decline of villeinage.

The sample for the case studies

How should we select a sample of manors to be used this study? Manors came in many shapes and sizes, and they were held by different types of land-lord.[34] In c.1300 the majority of English manors were 'small', i.e. comprising fewer than 500 acres of land. These constituted 65% of the 1,031 manors documented in the Hundred Rolls of 1279; 'medium' manors (500 to 1,000 acres) constituted 21%; and 'large' manors (more than 1,000 acres) 14% of the manorial sample. The aggregate area of land occupied by large (41%) and medium (30%) manors was greater than that of small (29%) manors. The Hundred Rolls also reveal a strong correlation between the size of a manor and the social status of its landlord. Large manors were mainly found on the estates of the upper nobility, including bishoprics and the wealthy monasteries. Small manors were strongly associated with gentry lords, including the lesser monastic houses.[35]

There is also a clear correlation between the size of a manor and the extent of villein tenure. The Hundred Rolls reveal that the proportion of villein land was highest on large manors (51% of the total land area of the manor, including free tenancies and the lord's demesne), and lowest on small manors (32%).[36] The tendency for the proportion of villein land to dwindle with the size of the manor is also evident when the figures are reworked with the demesne omitted. On large manors 69% of all tenant land was held in villeinage (thus 31% free), compared with 60% on medium manors, and 54% on small manors.[37] Campbell identifies a similar pattern using an even larger sample of lay manors, drawn from the period 1300–49 and using the evidence of Inquisitions Post Mortem: free land comprised 60%, and villein land 40%, of tenant land on all manors, but, on the smallest manors, the proportion of free land rose to 70%.[38]

---

[34] See the general surveys of variations in manorial type in Miller and Hatcher, *Rural England*, pp. 19–22; Rigby, *English society*, pp. 40–5; Bailey, *English manor*, pp. 5–10.

[35] Kosminsky, *Studies in the agrarian history*, pp. 97, 108.

[36] Kosminsky, *Studies in the agrarian history*, p. 101.

[37] The total acreages are 113,514 acres (villein) and 51,947 acres (free) on large manors; 60,544 acres (villein) and 40,952 acres (free) on medium manors; and 46,902 (villein) and 40,169 (free) on small manors, Kosminsky, *Studies in the agrarian history*, p. 101.

[38] Campbell, 'Agrarian problem', pp. 26–7.

Thus in c.1300 small manors were the most common manorial type in England; they were concentrated in the hands of lords of lesser wealth and status; and they contained the lowest proportion of villein land. Yet this type of manor has received little attention in published studies of villeinage, which have concentrated instead upon the large manors and estates of the greater lords. The history of villeinage has been largely written from the perspective of the largest, but least typical form of, manor. There is a pragmatic and compelling explanation for this bias: fewer records survive from the small manors, and the best survivals are usually from the large manors of the great estates. Whatever the reason, the ubiquity and numerical importance of small manors dictates that they must be well represented within our sample.

The sample must also contain manors held by a good cross-section of landlords. Noble landlords wielded significant political power, and may well have approached villeinage in a different manner from less powerful gentry lords. Likewise, perpetual institutions such as monasteries enjoyed continuity of manorial ownership, which might have enabled more consistent management policies than on lay estates experiencing frequent changes of ownership: MacCulloch suggested that continuity of ownership was an important element in explaining where serfdom persisted into the sixteenth century.[39] Thus extending the sample across a number of seigniorial estates will increase its typicality, as well as helping to determine whether broad similarities in the management of serfdom are apparent within particular categories of lordship. This will also be a novel approach, because most detailed studies of villeinage are based on a single estate.

Two other factors should be considered when constructing an appropriate sample of manors: geography and sources. Manorial forms varied by region, not just by landlord. Large manors with large demesnes and a high proportion of customary land were more characteristic of the south and east Midlands, and less of East Anglia, while villeinage was virtually absent from Kent.[40] Hence the sample cannot be narrowly confined to a single region. Finally, there must be a sufficiently good corpus of manorial documents – especially court rolls – from each manor to sustain a meaningful investigation into the decline of villeinage, irrespective of the location and type of manor, or the status of its landlord.

The sample used in the following study reflects these considerations and criteria. It contains examples across the range of manorial types, but especially from small manors where villeinage was not especially prominent. It includes manors located in regions with different social structures, to enable direct comparisons between areas where villeinage was lightly established in

[39]   MacCulloch, 'Bondmen', p. 96.

[40]   Rigby, *English society*, pp. 40–5; Campbell, 'Agrarian problem', p. 35.

c.1300 with those where it was prominent. The sample also includes manors from different types of estates, especially those held by landlords of lower status: the latter were numerically the most important in medieval England, but they are the least understood because of the fragmentary nature of their archives. Finally, it includes manors from the same estate, in order to assess the consistency of a landlord's management of villeinage across the manors in his possession.

More precisely, the sample comprises 38 manors concentrated in two discrete geographical areas: East Anglia, where villeinage was not especially prominent in c.1300, and eastern Oxfordshire/western Buckinghamshire, where it was. This enables a contrast to be drawn between one region with a classical manorial structure, and a high proportion of villeins, with another region with a loose manorial structure and a high proportion of freemen. The sample is further subdivided into two categories, based upon the quantity and temporal distribution of extant court rolls from each manor. Category A comprises the best-documented manors, those for which a very good series of court rolls is extant across the late fourteenth and fifteenth centuries, and for which some accounts also survive. Such a rich archival base enables each manor in this category to be subjected to a rigorous individual case study based on the methodology described above. There are 15 manors in Category A, located in either the south Midlands or East Anglia:

East Anglia

Walsham and Walsham High Hall, two manors held by gentry landlords, and Walsham Church House, held by a minor ecclesiastical lord. These three manors comprised all the manorial holdings in Walsham-le-Willows (Suffolk).

Cratfield (Suffolk), Dunningworth (Suffolk), Forncett (Norfolk) and Staverton (Suffolk), all part of the estate of the earls, (from 1397 dukes), of Norfolk.

Chevington (Suffolk) and Fornham All Saints (Suffolk), held by the abbot of Bury St Edmunds.

Aldham (Suffolk), held by the de Vere earls of Oxford.

South Midlands

Tingewick (Buckinghamshire), held by a minor ecclesiastical landlord until 1391, then by New College, Oxford.

Upper Heyford (Oxfordshire), held by a high-status gentry family until 1382, when it was granted to New College, Oxford.

Cuxham (Oxfordshire), Holywell (Oxfordshire) and Kibworth Harcourt (Leicestershire), held by Merton College, Oxford.

Category B comprises 23 manors, many of them held by lower-status landlords and/or characterized by a lower proportion of customary land. Inevitably, the survival of source material is not as rich as from manors in Category A. Short runs of court rolls and/or the odd account or rental are usually all to have survived from the smaller lay manors, which cannot sustain the type of full and detailed reconstruction undertaken for the Category A manors. However, all the manors in Category B have left a run of court rolls good enough to provide a reliable snapshot of the profile of villeinage on a manor over a representative period of time. The manors are:

East Anglia (Suffolk unless stated)
Badwell Ash, Barton Magna, Beeston (Norfolk), Debach, Drinkstone, Fornham St Martin, Harkstead, Harleston, Higham, Holbrook, Iken, Lackford, Lidgate, Norton, Thorpe Morieux, Runton and Beeston Felbriggs (Norfolk), Runton Hayes (Norfolk), Winston and Withersfield.

South Midlands
Akeley (Buckinghamshire), Hardwick Russells (Buckinghamshire), Radclive (Oxfordshire), Weedon Vale (Buckinghamshire).

Details about the structure and lordship of each manor, and the range and quantity of extant sources, are all contained in the Appendix. The inclusion of such details avoids the pitfalls that can emerge in court-roll studies whenever historians are not explicit about the degree of completeness of their series. McGribbon Smith has argued that the most reliable court-roll studies are those which are explicit about the number of court sessions used in the research, and those which draw upon a variety of manors in different regions under more than one type of lordship.[41] The case studies which follow meet both of McGribbon Smith's tests. They draw upon the evidence contained within nearly 3,500 sessions of manorial courts and more than 400 manorial accounts.

The analysis of the 15 manors in Category A is split into six separate case studies, which form Chapters 6 to 11. These chapters are highly detailed and closely argued, and they will mainly interest the specialist and the dedicated enthusiast. The analysis of the 23 manors in Category B is perforce less detailed and more broad-brush in its approach, and is contained within Chapter 12. Each chapter contains accessible summary sections, and also a conclusion, which will enable the less zealous reader to grasp the main findings of each case study. The Conclusion to the book, which comprises Part III, brings together all the main strands and themes of the case studies, and re-assesses the passage from bondage to freedom in their light.

---

[41]   McGribbon Smith, 'Court rolls as evidence for village society', pp. 267–9.

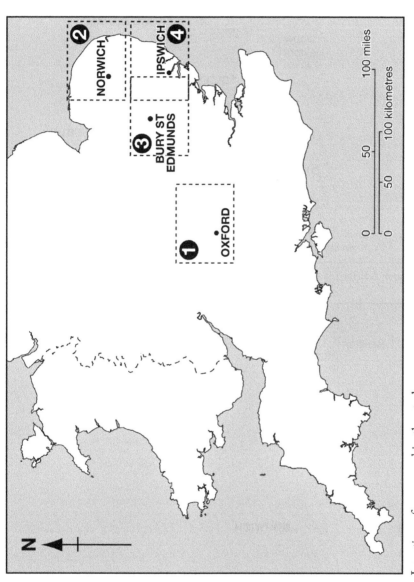

Location of areas used in the study

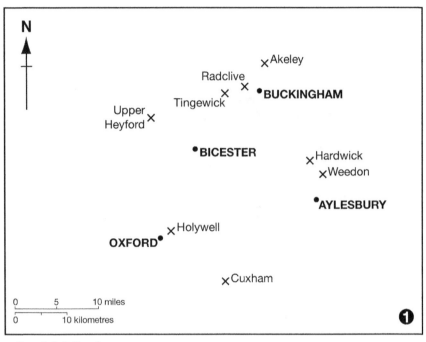

1 South Midlands manors

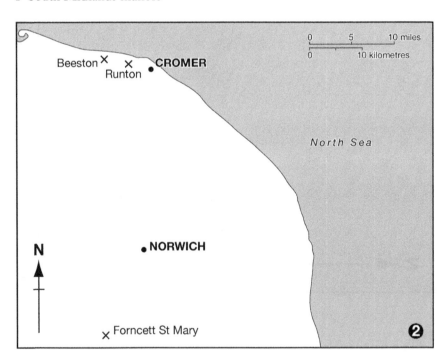

2 East Anglian manors: Norwich region

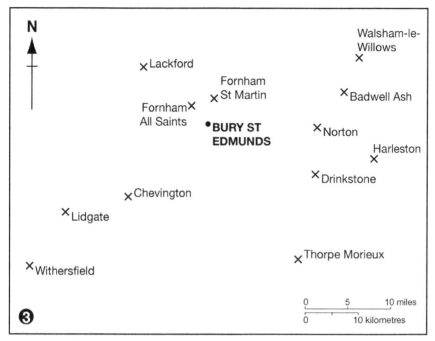

3 East Anglian manors: Bury St Edmunds Region

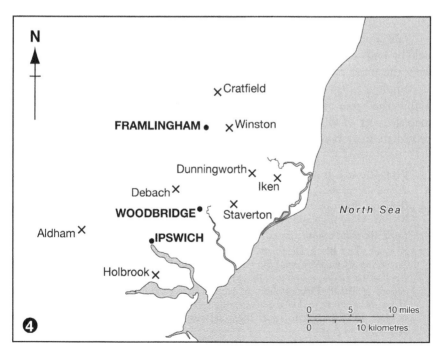

4 East Anglian manors: Ipswich region

6

Walsham-le-Willows

Walsham-le-Willows (Suffolk) is situated 13 miles north east of Bury St Edmunds, and in the fourteenth century it was split into three separate manors. The main manor was medium-sized, with an arable demesne of 350 acres, just over 200 acres of free land, and a sizeable but indeterminate area of customary land.[1] It was held by a succession of lay lords from the upper ranks of the gentry, although its exact descent is obscure and for periods it was held in trust.[2] The other two manors were small. High Hall was held by lesser gentry until its absorption into the main manor in 1379, and Church House was held by Ixworth priory.[3] The court roll series for Walsham and Walsham High Hall are full, exceptionally so for gentry-held manors, and they have already formed the basis of two excellent studies of the community during the passage of the Black Death.[4] The fourteenth-century records have also been translated, edited and published.[5] The unpublished run of court rolls from the fifteenth century is just as good, and it is supplemented by a run of manorial accounts. Furthermore, a set of fifteenth-century court rolls has survived from Church House manor.

Walsham offers an excellent case study for two reasons. First, manors held by lords of gentry status, where villeinage tended to be less prominent, were the most common type of manor, but they seldom leave an archive as complete as this. Second, the survival of sources from all three manors within the same vill provides an exceptional opportunity to compare the management of villeinage, and the chronology of its decline, upon three proximate manors in different ownership.

[1]   F. Hervey, ed., *Pinchbeck Register of the abbey of Bury St Edmunds and related documents, volume 2*, (Brighton, 1925), pp. 202–4.

[2]   R. Lock, *The court rolls of Walsham-le-Willows, volume 2, 1350 to 1396*, Suffolk Records Society, 45 (2002), pp. 10–11.

[3]   Lock, *Walsham volume 2*, p. 12.

[4]   R. Lock, 'The Black Death in Walsham-le-Willows', *Proceedings of the Suffolk Institute of Archaeology and History*, 37 (1992); Hatcher, *Intimate history*. There are c.235 courts 1351–4, 1359–1400, 1404, 1407–14, 1423–64, 1467–1500, Lock, *Walsham volume 2*; SROB HA504/1/10.1 to 10.12; HA504/1/11.1; HA504/1/12.1 to 12.25; HA504/1/13.1 to 13.30; HA504/1/14.1 to 14.13; HA504/1/15.1 to 15.20; HA504/1/16.1 to 16.13; HA504/1/17.1 to 17.22. There are also 25 accounts 1373 to 1455, SROB HA504/3/1 to 15.12.

[5]   R. Lock, *The court rolls of Walsham-le-Willows, volume 1, 1303 to 1350*, Suffolk Records Society, 41 (1998); and Lock, *Walsham volume 2*.

Walsham manor

Customary land tenures

The extant sources do not permit an exact calculation of the area of customary land at Walsham, although the high volume transacted in the court rolls indicates that it was large. In the 1340s the market in customary land was characterized by a high turnover of small parcels: the combined effects of this active land market and partible inheritance had long since broken down any standardization that may once have existed among the villein hold-ings.[6] Villein tenure was held 'in bondage …' or 'in villeinage for services and customs', and owed a small cash rent, labour services, entry fine, heriot, merchet, millsuit, childwite and recognition.[7]

The Black Death claimed nearly half the population of Walsham in 1349, yet most of the customary land was quickly reoccupied.[8] The vast majority of this land continued to be held as a heritable villein tenure. The use of 'in villeinage/bondage' continued in conveyances until the 1370s, and, on a single occasion in 1366, the grant was to the villein tenant 'and his brood (*sequela*)' rather than to 'him and his heirs'.[9] During the course of the 1370s 'in villeinage' was replaced with the phrase 'by the rod', and then during the 1380s the phrase 'at the will of the lord' was also added routinely.[10] In 1386 the court noted that the customary land granted to John and Catherine Peel had been 'formerly held in bondage'.[11] By the early fifteenth century the use of 'customs and services' was also, gradually, dropped, so that most grants were now simply 'by the rod at the will of the lord'.[12] The first explicit reference in the court rolls to the title to customary land being based upon the written record of the transaction occurs in 1464, although as early as the 1390s accounts referred to grants 'as appears in the court rolls'.[13] In the early

---

[6] Lock, *Walsham volume 2*, pp. 13–15.

[7] The phrase '*in villeinagio*' is most frequent, although '*in bondagio*' is common enough. Occasionally the phrase 'at the will of the lord' was also included in the formula, see, for example, Lock, *Walsham volume 1*, pp. 110–12, 123.

[8] Lock, *Walsham volume 2*, p. 17.

[9] For the continued use of 'for him and his heirs in villeinage for services and customs' during the 1350s and 1360s, see Lock, *Walsham volume 2*, pp. 50, 55, 57, 69, 73, 86. The reference to the overtly servile 'brood' is on p. 82.

[10] During the 1370s 'for him and his heirs by the rod for services and customs' became the common format, see Lock, *Walsham volume 2*, pp. 103, 105, 108, 116, 125, 127; the addition of 'at the will of the lord' in the 1380s is evident on, for example, pp. 143–4.

[11] Lock, *Walsham volume 2*, p. 153.

[12] For some early examples of this formula, see SROB HA504/1/12.23.

[13] For the first reference to a tenant copy of the court entry of their land transaction, see court held January 1467 when William Smith showed a copy of a transaction

fourteenth century court officials had requested to see charters of customary land.[14]

Conversions of customary land to fixed-term tenures were very unusual. There were none in the 1350s, but between 1360 and 1375 nine grants of land were made 'for a term', seven for short terms of years and two for terms of lives. In every case, the grant was for odd parcels of land directly from the lord's hands, indicating that this form of tenure was being used to dispose of land that had been untenanted for some time. For example, in 1365 John Terwald acquired all the land formerly held by William Coppelowe 'at lease for the term of his life', because 'the land has been in the lord's hands for seven years as no-one was willing to hold it'.[15] After 1375 very few leases are recorded in the court rolls, although some *ad hoc* leases appear in the account rolls. The manorial account of 1390–1 records the decay of c.15% of all rents of assize, and of c.20% of labour services, thus confirming that most of the original customary land – perhaps 80% – was still occupied on a form of villein tenure.[16] The remaining c.20% was either abandoned or leased. The same account notes that 39s. 4d. rent was received from 'land in the lord's hands leased to various men'.[17] For much of the fifteenth century the proportion of customary land thus held changed little: hereditary tenancies continued to dominate land transfers in the court rolls, other forms of tenure hardly feature, and the structure and level of rental income remained broadly the same.[18]

Hence the majority of the original customary land continued to be granted on a hereditary tenure, and less than 20% was converted to fixed-term tenures. However, the nature of that hereditary tenure changed significantly in the last quarter of the fourteenth century. The use of 'in villeinage' disappeared from land grants during the 1370s, and the servile incidents attached to these holdings first declined and then disappeared by the 1390s (see below). The

from the May court of 1464, SROB 504/1/14.6 and 14.8; SROB HA504/3/3 (1390–1 account).

[14] Lock, *Walsham volume 1*, pp. 199, 258.

[15] Lock, *Walsham volume 2*, p. 69 (November 1362); p. 73 (October 1363); p. 80 (July 1365); pp. 86–7 (August 1366); p. 98 (September 1368); p. 101 (January 1369); and pp. 113–14 (September 1371).

[16] In 1390–1 rents of assize amounted to 204s., of which 29s. were decayed in the lord's hands, SROB HA504/3/3.

[17] SROB HA 504/3/3.

[18] For example, the proportion of labour services allowed as uncollectable (either because the holding was untenanted or converted to leasehold) remained fairly constant in subsequent accounts (see table 6.3), as did the sales of labour services: compare the £11 16s. 3d. raised in 1426–7 (SROB HA504/3/15.1) with the £10 18s. 3d. in 1451–2 (HA504/3/15.12). Finally, income from leases held steady, see SROB HA504/3/3 (1390–1); HA504/3/5B (1406–7); HA504/3/15.1 (1426–7).

manor court had dispensed much earlier with formal distinctions in the status of tenants when performing fealty to a new lord. In 1361, and again in 1391, tenants swearing fealty to a new lord were distinguished according to their tenurial status, but on all other such occasions they were listed without distinction.[19]

6.1 Last recorded dates of key incidents of villeinage at Walsham (all three manors), 1350 to 1499

Manor	Capit.	Chev.	Pres. for absence	Child.	Heriot	Merchet	Millsuit	Recogn.	Tallage
Walsham 1350–1499	None	1439	1392	1396	1477	1398	1398	1375	None
High Hall 1350–1381*	None	None	1365	None	1374	None	None	None	None
Churchhouse 1409–1499	None	None	None	None	None	None	None	None	None

Presentments for dues, for which no fine or pardon was collected, are not captured in this table with the exception of absences.

* In 1379 High Hall was absorbed into Walsham manor.

Incidents of villeinage

Recognition was imposed for most of the fourteenth century as a collective charge on all customary tenants at the accession of a new lord of the manor, although the sum varied on each occasion. They rendered 6s. 8d. in 1316, 13s. 4d. in 1325, and then £5 in 1331, when the new lady, Roesia de Pakenham, immediately waived this 'customary fee'. In 1361 they paid 40s., when the homage pointedly stated that recognition payment was neither a fixed amount nor at the lord's will, 'but only as much as at the courtesy of the homage'.[20] Their courtesy extended to 40s. in 1369, and to a nominal 1d. in 1375 on the accession of the next lord.[21] No seigniorial complaint or concern is recorded, and recognition was not levied again (see table 6.1). Millsuit was imposed episodically before the Black Death, but then disappeared for decades until just three cases immediately preceded its disappearance in the 1390s (see table 6.2).

---

[19]   Lock, *Walsham volume 2*, pp. 59, 105, 122, 170–1.
[20]   SROB HA504/1/3 m. 15 and Lock, *Walsham volume 2*, p. 59.
[21]   Lock, *Walsham volume 2*, pp. 59, 106, 122, 136, 170.

6.2 Frequency of merchet, heriot, childwite and millsuit
on Walsham manor, 1325 to 1499

Period	Merchet	Heriot	Childwite	Millsuit
1325–48*	53	48	29	8
1350–74	23	22	7	o
1375–99	20	17	2	3
1400–24	o	4	o	o
1425–49	o	9	o	o
1450–74	o	o	o	o
1475–99	o	1	o	o

Merchet, heriot and childwite are fines only (including if waived); millsuit includes
fines and presentments.

* 1325–48 to avoid distortions to frequency caused by the pestilence in 1349.

6.3 Utilisation of key labour services on Walsham manor, 1390 to 1434

Year	Weeding	Winter	Harvest	Harvest boon works	Ploughing	Demesne sown acreage
	Total 191 D/S/U%	Total 973 D/S/U%	Total 754 D/S/U%	Total 127 D/S/U%	Total 46 D/S/U%	
1390–1	16/82/2	22/13/65	27/12/61	19/15/66	o/o/100	237 acres
1396–7	16/68/16	20/37/43	28/19/53	23/13/64	o/o/100	223 acres
1402–3		25/20/65	28/21/51	21/20/59	o/o/100	223 acres
1406–7	20/34/46	27/1/72	30/1/69	23/1/76	o/o/100	237.5 acres
1426–7	14/86/0	22/78/0	26/74/0	19/81/0	o/100/0	Leased
1433–4	20/80/0	25/75/0	30/70/0	20/80/0	o/100/0	Leased

Total = total of works owed
D = works decayed or allowed as a percentage of total
S = works sold as a percentage of total
U = works used by the manor as a percentage of total

Source: SROB, HA 504/3/3, 4, 5a, 5b, 9, 15.1.

Heriot proved a durable incident (see table 6.2), widely collected in the
fourteenth century, although its frequency halved after the Black Death.
During the first half of the fifteenth century its frequency waned further,
and its final appearance in 1477 was an isolated occurrence. Tenants increasingly avoided its payment through death-bed surrenders of land, but by the

6.1 Values of customary arable land at Walsham 1340s to 1480s (d. per acre)

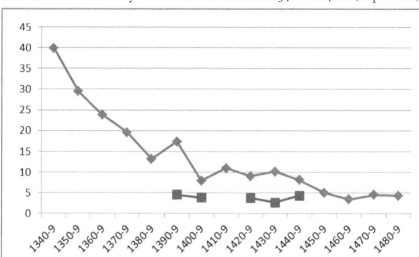

Starred line = mean entry fine in d. per acre; squared line = mean value in d. per acre of demesne land at lease.

1480s heriot was not even levied when a tenant died holding unfree land.[22] Entry fines survived, and their variable rather than fixed nature benefited the tenant in the economic conditions of the fifteenth century. The mean entry fine per acre fell two-thirds between the 1340s and 1380s, and by the 1460s had fallen to a mere 10% of that in the 1340s (graph 6.1).

Many of the key labour services continued to be enforced until the early fifteenth century, although the weight of week works was not heavy. Between 1390 and 1407 the proportion of winter and harvest works utilized each year fluctuated between 41% and 69%, and those not used were commuted at will (see table 6.3). The manor retained labour services for as long as the demesne was exploited directly, and only ceased utilizing them completely after 1426 when the demesne was leased: all remaining services were then commuted for cash. In the 1480s ploughing services were still being commuted at will each year.[23]

Peasant resistance to labour services was limited (see table 6.4). Instances of withholding of services are recorded in 12 years in the period 1325–48, and in a grand total of 16 years after 1350, over half of which cases involved just a

---

[22] See the death of Ellen Ermite in November 1488, SROB HA504/1/17.6: for several examples of death-bed transfers, see the courts held in 1491 and 1493, HA504/1/17.11 to 17.14.

[23] See, for example, the 'sales' of ploughing works in the August court of 1481, SROB HA504/1/15.17.

6.4 Incidence of recorded non-performance of labour services
on Walsham manor, 1353 to 1407

Year	Non-Performance of Labour Services
1353	11 refuse to reap, 33 refuse to winter work
1354	1 withholds
1359	1 withholds
1360	1 withholds
1362	1 withholds, 13 glean lord's corn badly
1363	1 withholds
1365	3 withhold
1373	11 refuse to reap, 5 refuse to cart
1384	1 withholds
1385	2 withhold
1386	4 reap lord's corn badly
1389	1 withholds
1390	1 withholds
1391	1 refuses and withholds
1392	3 withhold
1407	17 refuse to make hay

6.5 Frequency of chevage and presentments for absence
on Walsham manor, 1325 to 1499

Period	Total number of annual presentments for absence	Total number of annual chevage cases	Mean fine per case
1325–48	16	8	6.25d.
1350–74	18	0	0
1375–99	3	0	0
1400–24	0	1	4d.
1425–49	0	15	2d.
1450–74	0	0	0
1475–99	0	0	0

single individual.[24] Collective and organized refusals occurred on three occasions before 1348 and on four occasions afterwards.[25] The court of October
1353 reported that 33 tenants had failed to turn up for winter works, despite
reminders from the reeve, and another 11 had refused to reap as required for

[24] Lock, *Walsham volume 2*, pp. 42, 43, 54, 56, 62, 73, 78, 143, 151, 163, 170, 172, 179.
[25] There were collective refusals in 1334 (17 individuals), 1335 (nine) and 1348 (six).

the lord during the harvest, preferring to work elsewhere for wages. The scale of, and the defiance behind, these refusals constituted a serious challenge to the authority of the lord, Sir Thomas Pakenham, yet his response was canny rather than punitive: 14 of the 33 villeins were pardoned, because they had performed some services, while the amercements imposed upon the reapers were all waived on condition that there was no repetition during the following harvest. In 1362 13 tenants were each amerced between 6d. and 18d. for gleaning badly during the harvest; in September 1373 16 tenants would not fulfil either their reaping or carting services; and in 1407 17 refused to perform their haymaking services.[26] There were no other strikes or go-slows.

Merchet was imposed frequently before the Black Death, when it was payable by customary landholders as well as serfs.[27] The average fine was high by East Anglian standards (mean = 7s. 6d. in the period 1325–48), and rose marginally after the Black Death (mean = 8s. 2d. in 1350–74) before falling off in the last quarter of the century (mean = 6s. 5d. in 1375–99). Fines tended to be higher for landed widows who chose to remarry, or for female serfs who were marrying off the manor. The frequency of merchet halved between 1325–48 and 1350–74 (see table 6.2), due to the fall in population and a shift to charging just serfs, not villein tenants: there is no record of a villein tenant being charged after 1349. It still remained a regular and remunerative incident at the end of the fourteenth century, which makes its sudden and complete disappearance after 1398 difficult to explain (see table 6.1). In 1385 the court had called for all serfs who had married without licence to be presented, but this is the only hint of difficulties enforcing merchet.

Childwite was a regular imposition before the Black Death, when occasionally it was imposed upon villein tenants who were personally free as well as serfs.[28] The fine charged was the standard East Anglian sum of 2s. 8d., which did not alter after the Black Death. The frequency of childwite halved after the Black Death (see table 6.2), although it was still imposed regularly enough between 1350 and 1374: its frequency then fell markedly before its disappearance in 1396 (see tables 6.1 and 6.2).

The Walsham court paid little attention to flown serfs, judging by the modest total of just 16 separate presentments for absence in the period 1325–48, and 18 between 1350 and 1374 (see table 6.5). Chevage was charged occasionally before 1350, but not once in the second half of the fourteenth century. Between 1350 and 1500 a total of twelve different people were presented for absence from the manor, one of whom was in the lord's service elsewhere, and five of whom subsequently returned to the manor. In the 1350s only

---

[26] Lock, *Walsham volume 2*, pp. 68, 117–18; SROB HA504/1/10.4.

[27] In 1334 four women were amerced for merchet 'because they hold customary land', Lock, *Walsham volume 1*, p. 169.

[28] See, for example, Lock, *Walsham volume 1*, pp. 190, 270.

two men were presented for absence albeit repeatedly (see table 6.5).[29] There is evidence of an administrative crackdown in 1361, when seven men were presented, mainly members of the Clevehog and Osbern families, and some of the presentments were repeated in each of the next three years until one of them, William Osbern, appeared in court.[30] No further presentments were made until another short crackdown in the early 1390s, then nothing about fugitives is mentioned until 1423.[31] In that year the court levied its first chevage payment (4d.) upon Isabel Torold, *nativa de sanguine* living in nearby Hepworth. Between 1424 and 1439 she dutifully paid 2d. chevage each year, whereupon the payments abruptly stopped.[32] Thereafter, all interest in flown serfs ceased. The initial surge of interest in the early 1360s, the minor revival in the early 1390s, and the eventual withdrawal of interest in Torold in 1439, had all coincided with the accession of new lords to the manor.[33]

Attitudes to serfdom

There are no presentments for educating villeins nor for entering into holy orders, nor any evidence for serf genealogies and manumissions. Successive lords of Walsham neither capitulated on villeinage nor enforced it aggressively. The handling of the labour strikes in 1353 was deft, because the lord asserted his authority while acknowledging villein concerns. The attitude towards flown serfs was pragmatic to the point of relaxed, because it is hard to believe that after 1350 only twelve of them left Walsham. Managerial action is only apparent in the 1360s, when, after a short wave of presentments against absentees, William Osbern 'was taken by the bailiff' and then required to find pledges to guarantee that he would stay on the manor in future. He did so.[34] A new lord of the manor in 1391 pointedly segregated *nativi* from other tenants when receiving fealty, and, while absent tenants were distrained to perform at the next court in the usual manner, absent serfs were distrained and a note added against each of their names: 'in mercy or writ being sued'. This provided a basis for pursuing the Osbern siblings for

---

[29]   John Peyntour (who never returned) and John Patel (who did), Lock, *Walsham volume 2*, pp. 33, 41.

[30]   Water Robhood, William and Henry Osbourn, William Clevehog (all eventual returnees), John Rampoyle (serving with the lord of the manor in Parham, east Suffolk), and John and Nicholas Clevehog (non-returnable), Lock, *Walsham volume 2*, pp. 61, 67, 72, 76, 79.

[31]   Lock, *Walsham volume 2*, pp. 170, 179.

[32]   SROB HA504/1/12.1 to 12.22.

[33]   Robert de Ufford (July 1361); Sir Henry Green and others (March 1391); and William de la Pole (February 1441), Lock, *Walsham volume 2*, pp. 59, 170, and SROB HA504/1/12.23.

[34]   Lock, *Walsham volume 2*, pp. 79, 83, 90, 93, 94, 104.

their absence from the manor for a short period, but then the matter was dropped.[35] These are isolated and exceptional instances.

In only one documented case did the lord challenge the status of a tenant. In the early 1380s Elias Typetot failed repeatedly to attend the manorial court of Walsham, while pursuing a number of legal actions in the courts of other manors. Such behaviour was the prerogative of the freeman, and so in March 1385 the Walsham court amerced him 6s. 8d. for his failure to attend (the normal levy was 3d.), and an additional 40s. for the 'unlawful' litigation. Elias countered with an explicit claim to be a freeman, which prompted the court to order the seizure of all his land and goods until he could prove it. Neither party repeated these confrontational tactics, there is no evidence that the order to seize was actually carried out, and Elias maintained a low profile until his death three years later.[36] In fact, there is ample evidence to suggest that he was indeed a hereditary freeman, who also happened to be the tenant of some villein land.[37]

Challenging the status of Elias Typetot was an aggressive stance to adopt against a freeman, although it drew upon the ambiguities that arose when a freeman held villein land and also, perhaps, upon the administrative uncertainties that arose when manors changed hands frequently. It is probable that the lord had decided to take a tactical stance against a habitual offender whose wider conduct he deemed contemptuous of his court, a stance which should be placed within the context of an on-going vigilance about villeins initiating actions in the courts of other lords.[38] The court also remained watchful until the early fifteenth century of the purchase of free land, and of customary land pertaining to another manor, by its villeins. Such purchases had to be recorded in the court rolls, after which the land was re-issued to the tenant to hold at will with the payment of a nominal annual rent of increment. By the later fifteenth century such land was described as soiled.[39]

Summary of chronology and key indicators
Customary land was quickly and extensively reoccupied after 1349 on hereditary villein tenure, thanks to the presence of a deep pool of prospective tenants.[40] Odd parcels of land that remained untenanted until the 1360s were

---

[35]　Lock, *Walsham volume 2*, pp. 170–1.

[36]　Lock, *Walsham volume 2*, pp. 117, 120, 146–8, 162.

[37]　Lock, *Walsham volume 2*, pp. 4–5.

[38]　See July 1404, SROB HA504/1/10.4.

[39]　Examples of the purchase of free or extra manorial villein land are recorded in Lock, *Walsham volume 2*, pp. 64–5, 92. The resultant increased rent payments are exemplified in the 1390–1 account, SROB HA504/3/3. References to soiled land are in SROB HA504/1/16.2 and 17.1.

[40]　Lock has estimated that around 500 adults survived the Black Death in Walsham. There were around 100 tenants of the manor in 1350, a figure which remained

converted to leaseholds and tenures for a term. Between the 1370s and the 1390s the nature of villein tenure changed decisively. The use of 'in villeinage' disappeared from conveyances, and listings of tenants no longer distinguished between the free and the unfree. Recognition disappeared, millsuit hardly featured, and merchet and childwite fell in frequency and became fixed upon the personally unfree rather than customary landholders. All that remained were labour services, although by 1400 around half of them were sold rather than used in any given year, and in the 1420s all were formally and finally commuted. Personal servility also disappeared in the 1390s with the disappearance of childwite, merchet and presentments for absence.

How does this chronology correlate with the key indicators of the causes of decline? There are no recorded manumissions. Recorded migration of serfs from the manor was insignificant: between 1350 and 1500 just one person was amerced for chevage, and a dozen were presented for absence, half of whom either returned to the manor subsequently or remained in the service of the lord. Presentments for absence peaked in the early 1360s. The lax approach to recording departures probably owed something to the steady supply of tenants on the manor, which after 1350 remained constant at around 100.[41] Neither the scale nor the chronology of recorded departures from Walsham correlates with the chronology of villeinage's decline.

There is little evidence for either a seigniorial reaction or social unrest at Walsham.[42] Resistance to the continued performance of labour services was serious during the early 1350s, but minor and piecemeal thereafter, with just 14 individual cases of withdrawal of labour services, and four cases of collective refusals, between 1350 and 1500. Week works were extensively sold by 1400 and they formally disappeared in the 1420s when the demesne was leased. Hence there is little to indicate that active social resistance caused villeinage to decline.

The evidence for local land values is highly reliable and complete (see graph 6.1), based on the changing levels of entry fines and leasehold rents per acre. These reveal that between the 1340s and 1460s land values fell by 90%, with a precipitous fall of 40% between the 1340s and 1360s. The fall by the 1360s must have created pressure to reduce the burdens of villeinage between the 1370s and 1390s. However, the correlation is not exact and, indeed, the final disappearance in the 1390s of three key servile incidents corresponds with a discernible recovery in land values in that decade, and, of course, week works continued long after the main fall in land values. Hence,

more or less constant over the next two centuries, Lock, *Walsham volume 2*, pp. 13, 17–18, 20.

41   Lock, *Walsham volume 2*, p. 13.
42   Lock, *Walsham volume 2*, p. 20.

while changing land values exhibit the best correlation with the decline of villeinage, the pattern is not especially close.

Walsham High Hall[43]

Villeinage was relatively prominent at Walsham High Hall, which is unusual for a small manor of this type. In 1325 villeins comprised 46% of all tenants.[44] Before 1348–9 customary landholdings were small and non-standardized, and they rendered week works and other labour services, merchet, childwite, heriot and recognition (see table 6.6). The formulae of conveyances were similar to the main manor, usually appearing as 'in villeinage for customs and services'. In the 1350s and 1360s most grants of land continued to be described in this way, but by 1381 the phrase 'in villeinage' had been dropped. At this date High Hall had been absorbed into the main manor, and thereafter the formulae for conveyances on the two were the same. Only two conversions to fixed-term tenures are recorded after 1349, both to leasehold in a single court in 1372.[45] Some remaining labour services were added to those of Walsham upon the merger of the manors in 1379, after which their management follows that of the main manor.[46]

6.6 Frequency of merchet, heriot, childwite and millsuit
on Walsham High Hall manor, 1325 to 1381

Period	Merchet	Heriot	Childwite	Millsuit
1325–48*	7	6	4	0
1350–81+	0	2	0	0

Merchet, heriot and childwite fines only (including if waived); millsuit includes fines and presentments.

* 1325–48 to avoid distortions to frequency caused by the pestilence in 1349.
+ 1350–81 High Hall was absorbed in the main manor in 1379 and its last separate court was held in 1381.

During the early fourteenth century recognition had been collected from customary landholders upon the accession of a new lord, but the practice

[43] There are 42 courts extant between 1325 and 1348, Lock, *Walsham volume 1*, pp. 96–316; there are also c.13 courts 1351–5, 1359, 1365–6, 1371–4, 1379, 1381, Lock, *Walsham volume 2*.

[44] Lock, *Walsham volume 1*, p. 96.

[45] Lock, *Walsham volume 2*, pp. 44, 48, 56, 115, 140.

[46] SROB HA 504/3/5a.

ceased completely after 1349.[47] One presentment for childwite was made after 1350, but nothing was paid, and chevage also disappeared (see table 6.6).[48] Six separate presentments for absence had been made in the period 1325–48, and then eight in three different years (1354, 1356 and 1365) between 1350 and 1381: the eight post-1350 presentments related to five males, none of whom ever returned to the manor (see table 6.7).[49] Merchet was levied consistently on both male and female villein landholders before 1349, attracting an average charge of 40d., i.e. around half the level of that charged on the main manor. A couple of attachments to answer for merchet were recorded in the wake of the epidemic in 1350, and another in 1371, but no merchet was actually imposed or paid after the Black Death (see tables 6.1 and 6.6).[50] Only two heriots are recorded after 1349.[51]

6.7 Frequency of chevage and presentments for absence
on Walsham High Hall manor, 1325 to 1381

Period	Total number of annual presentments for absence	Total number of annual chevage cases	Mean fine per case
1325–48	6	10	1d.
1350–81	8	0	0

The number of villein tenants diminished rapidly after the Black Death. The 19 villein tenants recorded in 1325 had dropped to five in 1351, and only two in 1379.[52] There are no recorded manumissions. There was no seigniorial reaction, and no evidence for any resistance to, or tension over, serfdom. Just a single instance of withdrawing labour services is recorded (in 1354), but no other expressions of resistance.[53]

---

[47] See Lock, *Walsham volume 1*, pp. 44, 96, for the collection of recognition before 1349.

[48] Lock, *Walsham volume 1*, pp. 332–3 for presentment of childwite in 1350.

[49] Lock, *Walsham volume 2*, pp. 42, 48–9, 80–1.

[50] The three presentments for merchet were made in 1350 and 1371, Lock, *Walsham volume 1*, pp. 332–3; Lock, *Walsham volume 2*, p. 114.

[51] Lock, *Walsham volume 2*, pp. 86–7, 118.

[52] Lock, *Walsham volume 2*, pp. 38, 136.

[53] Resistance to labour services had been more commonplace in the period 1325–48, occurring in 14 of those 24 years: collective strikes are recorded in 1327, 1330, 1343 and 1346.

Walsham Church House[54]

The manor remained in the hands of Ixworth priory – a middling-sized monastery – throughout the fourteenth and fifteenth centuries. No sources are extant before 1409, so we cannot know how villeinage evolved before that date. However, in, or after, 1409 there are no references to any of the main incidents of villein tenure, with the exception of two cases of withholding an unspecified labour service in 1409 and 1414. The extant court rolls contain not a single reference to any aspect of personal serfdom. There are no recorded migrations, no disputes or tensions over villeinage, and no manumissions.

Tenants are described as either 'free' or 'tenants of villein land', and there are no serfs by blood. The formulae for tenancies are the same as on the main manor. Some leases of customary land appear in the late 1410s, but such grants diminish from the 1430s and thereafter expiring leases were converted to fee farms. Similarly, some hereditary tenures were also converted to fee farms, so that during the 1440s and 1450s around one half of all grants of customary were on the standard hereditary tenure, while the remainder were fee farms. This was clearly a device to convert some hereditary tenancies to permanent negotiated commutations, presumably in response to tenant demand. The number of such grants diminished thereafter, leaving conventional hereditary tenures as the main form of grant.[55]

Conclusion

A very good corpus of documentary sources has survived from all three manors of Walsham-le-Willows, each held by middling- to lower-status landlords. This enables the chronology of the decline of villeinage to be tracked across the whole of this rural community, rather than just on a single manor. Villein tenure and personal servility declined rapidly on Walsham manor between the 1370s and 1390s, and both had already disappeared from Church House when its extant court records commence in 1409. On the small lay manor of High Hall, which had a relatively high proportion of villein tenants in the early fourteenth century, chevage, childwite, merchet and recognition all disappeared after 1349, and heriot was dramatically reduced in frequency. Manumission, peasant resistance and migration were negligible during this period on all three manors. Land values fell 40% between the 1340s and 1360s

---

54 There are c.32 courts 1409, 1413–14, 1417, 1421, 1424–5, 1429, 1446–7, 1452, 1456–7, 1463, 1468–72, 1476, 1480–6, 1488–93, 1497–9, SROB HA504/1/13.23, and HA504/1/21 to 22.8.

55 See, for example, SROB HA504/1/21A.4, and 21A.5; HA504/1/13.23.

at Walsham main manor. By 1400 villeinage had all but disappeared from the vill of Walsham-le-Willows.

The most striking feature of this case study is the consistency of the experience of villeinage across all three manors. Villein tenure shed servile incidents during the course of the second half of the fourteenth century at Walsham and High Hall, and Church House must have followed the same course. Conversions to fixed-term tenures were rare, and the formulae of conveyances for customary land were very similar. The range of dues owed by villeins had been similar at Walsham and High Hall, although the rate of decline after 1349 was quicker on the smaller manor, with chevage, childwite and recognition disappearing with the Black Death, and merchet greatly weakened. If anything, the smaller manor, with its low-status lord, struggled more than the larger manor to hold onto servile incidents. There was no seigniorial reaction, little recorded migration, and few recorded social tensions over villeinage.

How do we explain the general consistency in the management and experience of villeinage across all three manors? The joint ownership of High Hall and Walsham after 1379 was an obvious factor, although before that date, when they were held by two different lords, there were no grounds for any active cooperation or collusion. Nor are there any obvious reasons for Ixworth priory – an autonomous and different type of landlord – to manage villeinage in a similar fashion at Church House. Hence the only credible explanation is a local 'domino effect', whereby the chronology and nature of decline of villeinage on the main manor triggered the same reaction on the two smaller manors. Walsham was the overwhelmingly dominant manor within the vill, and the early and rapid disappearance of villeinage there caused the same to happen on the other two manors: landlords of lowly status were incapable of maintaining villeinage on their small manors if it was in decline on larger, proximate, manors. In this respect and within this context, seigniorial attitudes to serfdom could not overcome contrary market trends: if the main manor in the locality allowed villeinage to wither, other manors had to follow suit if they were to retain their tenants.

7

Merton College, Oxford

Merton College, Oxford, was established in 1262 and its estates were mainly scattered across the southern Midlands.[1] Two of the three manors in this case study were conventional demesne manors, but they were situated a considerable distance from one another. Cuxham (Oxfordshire) lies six miles north east of Wallingford, and twelve miles from Merton College itself, and the manor was small but dominated by its demesne and unfree holdings: there were few free tenures. Kibworth Harcourt (Leicestershire) was a large manor, but it was detached from the main estate and situated 12 miles south east of Leicester. Merton acquired both manors soon after its foundation.[2] The third manor, Holywell, had been acquired in 1266, and was a much smaller manor, located just outside Oxford.[3] Cuxham and Holywell were chosen for study because of their excellent surviving archives, their relative geographical proximity, and their contrasting manorial structure. Kibworth is added to the case study because much is already known about it from Cecily Howell's detailed research, and because its detachment from the main estate enhances the scope for comparison with two manors close to Merton itself.

Cuxham[4]

Customary land tenures
Before 1348–9 villein tenure dominated peasant landholding in Cuxham. A custumal of 1298 listed 21 villein tenants (13 half virgates, each of 12 acres,

[1] R.H. Hilton, 'Kibworth Harcourt. A Merton College manor in the thirteenth and fourteenth centuries', in W.G. Hoskins, ed., *Studies in Leicestershire agrarian history*, Transactions of the Leicestershire Archaeological Society, 24 (1949), pp. 22–5; J.R.L. Highfield, ed., *The early rolls of Merton College, Oxford*, Oxford Historical Society, 18 (1964), pp. 41–3.

[2] Cuxham was acquired in 1268, Kibworth in 1270, see Highfield, *Merton College*, pp. 41–2.

[3] Highfield, *Merton College*, p. 41.

[4] There are records for c.59 courts 1351–63, 1377–1411, 1436–48, 1458, 1466, 1474–89. Merton College, Oxford, 5916 to 5941. 9 *compoti* 1350–9, c.60 farmers' accounts 1395–1495. Merton College, Oxford, 5875, 5879 to 5887, 5888 to 5891.

and eight cottars) and five free tenants.[5] The rent package on the core half-virgate holdings was dominated by week works (around two days per week), payments in kind (various grains and poultry), entry fine and heriot, and they rendered merchet and millsuit, but little in the way of money rent: the cash equivalent of the services on each half virgate was estimated at 20s. per annum.[6] They were held on an hereditary tenure 'in bondage' or 'in villeinage'.[7] Occasionally, half virgates were held for the term of a life.[8] Villein cottages, and small parcels of customary land, were not held heritably, but instead for either the term of the life of the tenant or three lives.[9]

In the 1340s all of the customary landholdings had been occupied and 'rents' from peasant-held land generated just under 45s. annually. The impact of the Black Death was severe, because many holdings were relinquished in the epidemic but then lay unoccupied for a number of years. In 1351 rental income was barely one third of its pre-Black Death level 'and no more for want of tenants due to the pestilence', and in 1352 nine of the thirteen half virgates still lay abandoned.[10] By December 1354 tenants had been found for seven of these nine vacant holdings, but only after a significant adjustment to the rent package. Each of the seven, newly-occupied, half virgates now rendered a money rent (between 9s. and 13s. 4d. per annum) in lieu of most of the old villein incidents, along with just one reaping work (to be performed by two men) in the harvest, one weeding and one haymaking service: the entry fine was either waived or significantly reduced.[11] The remaining two half virgates remained vacant until 1358, when a tenant was admitted to one

---

5   P.D.A. Harvey, ed., *Manorial records of Cuxham, Oxfordshire, c.1200–1359*, Oxfordshire Record Society, 50 (1976), pp. 109–10.

6   P.D.A. Harvey, *A medieval Oxfordshire village. Cuxham 1240 to 1400* (Oxford, 1965), pp. 119–21, 130, 139. For millsuit and merchet, see Harvey, *Manorial records of Cuxham*, pp. 657 and 685.

7   The formula varied until the 1320s, when the use of 'in bondage' became commonplace, Harvey, *Manorial records of Cuxham*, pp. 635, 649, 652–3, 655, 657, 666, 678–9. Heirs were routinely admitted to half virgates before 1348–9, although the conveyance seldom stated explicitly that the grant was 'for him and his'. One transfer does confirm explicitly 'to him and his heirs according to the custom of the manor', Harvey, *Manorial records of Cuxham*, p. 666.

8   For example, Hugo le Carter was admitted to a half virgate 'in bondage for the term of the life of the said Hugo according to the custom of the manor', Harvey, *Manorial records of Cuxham*, p. 679.

9   Harvey, *Manorial records of Cuxham*, pp. 635, 641–2, 658, 663–4, 675, 678, 685. Property on this tenure did not usually render heriot.

10   In 1344–5 rents of assize were 44s. 10½d., and 15s. 10d. in 1350–1, Merton College, Oxford, 5870 and 5879. Cuxham may have lost 60% of its population between 1348 and 1377, Harvey, *Cuxham*, pp. 135–6. Merton College, Oxford, 5916, court held March 1352.

11   Merton College, Oxford, 5916 and 5917. For example, in the court held January 1353 William Amy was admitted to one half virgate rendering 10s. rent and suit

of them on a similar package, although he held explicitly for the term of three lives, namely his own and those of his wife and son.[12] In 1363 eleven, and in 1389 twelve, out of the thirteen half virgates were held for money rent.[13]

Thus in the immediate aftermath of the Black Death the customary land market at Cuxham could only be revived through the conversion of half virgates to money rents. The revival caused rental income to boom from the standard 45s. per annum in the 1340s to £7 10s. 1½d in 1359, because the shift to a cash rent in the 1350s included a compensatory payment for the loss of labour services, merchet and tallage.[14] Some of the first grants for money rent in the early 1350s were hereditary tenures, described explicitly as 'for him and his according to the custom of the manor'.[15] Yet increasingly half virgates were converted to fixed-term tenancies for money: for example, in 1353 three grants were explicitly for terms of lives, John Benet obtaining a half virgate for three lives, and William Amy and John Alynot each for their own life only.[16] A couple of leases for years were also granted.[17] Very rarely, a half virgate was granted to new tenants on the old terms, i.e. heritable for labour services, heriot, merchet, entry fine and no money rent. Thus Robert and Isabel Burdon received one '*native*' half virgate 'to hold according to the custom of the manor rendering services and works as anciently owed [*inde debita ut antiqua*]'.[18] This arrangement did not last long, and the holding was converted to a money rent when it next changed hands. The phrase 'in bondage' disappeared completely from all conveyances of customary land immediately after the Black Death.

The variety and fluidity of tenurial forms in the 1350s and 1360s had greatly diminished by the end of the fourteenth century, when half virgates were now overwhelmingly held for a term of lives, rendering a money rent instead of services. For example, in 1393 John Teverell was granted a half virgate for 9s. per annum and a heriot, held 'for the term of his and his wife's lives according to the custom of the manor', and a year later John Goding received

---

of court each year, together with two days in the harvest, and also weeding and haymaking for one day each. The entry fine was waived.

[12] Merton College, Oxford, 5920, court held April 1358.

[13] Merton College, Oxford, 5921 (1363) and 5923, court held February 1389.

[14] Merton College, Oxford, 5870 (1344–5) and 5887 (1358–9).

[15] Merton College, Oxford, 5916, court held May 1353 (half virgate to John Dyker), and 5917, court held December 1354 (five grants of half virgates).

[16] Merton College, Oxford, 5916, court held January 1353.

[17] For example, one term of 20 years, and another of 40 years, Merton College, Oxford, 5922, court held October 1377; and 5923, court held September 1393.

[18] Merton College, Oxford, 5924, court held April 1410; see also John and Elizabeth Thresher in court held June 1411.

a cottage and a smallholding for the term of three lives.[19] In the 1430s and 1440s some new grants merely stated that the land was held 'according to the custom of the manor', with no details of the term, but this looks more like scribal omission than any change in the nature of the tenure: in other cases grants are unequivocally grants for lives.[20] In 1448 all the standardized holdings were recorded explicitly as held for terms of lives, and in 1474 Robert Hall was granted a virgate for three lives 'at the will of the lord according to the custom of the manor'.[21] Exceptionally, in 1466 two grants of customary land were for a term of years.[22]

The relatively full levels of occupancy achieved in the 1360s were maintained until a dip in the 1420s, when four of the 13 virgates lay abandoned in the lord's hands: the land market recovered again, because in 1448 12 were tenanted, yielding total rent of c.£7 per annum.[23] In 1398 tenants held 'by copy [*per copiam*] according to the custom of the manor', and the court later charged two tenants 'without copy' a small conveyance fee to rectify the omission.[24] The college's own copy of the terms of the grant of one half virgate to Thomas May in 1438 has survived by chance.[25] In 1442 100 acres of demesne land were leased to the tenants *'per copiam'*.[26]

Thus during the 1350s tenants were successfully found for some vacant customary half virgates at Cuxham by converting them to fixed-term tenancies for a money rent, a heriot, token seasonal labour services, and an entry fine.[27] Other half virgates continued to be granted on a hereditary tenure,

[19]   Merton College, Oxford, 5123, courts held September 1393 and September 1394: Goding held for his, his wife's and son's lives. Grants for the term of three lives were becoming established elsewhere in fifteenth-century Oxfordshire, *VCH Oxfordshire*, volume 6, p. 214.

[20]   Merton College, Oxford, 5925 to 5931 (1430s and 1440s). See 5926, where Thomas May held a messuage and one and a half virgates 'to himself and his wife, and his two sons according to the custom of the manor', court held February 1438.

[21]   Merton College, Oxford, 5925 to 5931 (1430s to 1448); 5934, court held October 1474.

[22]   Such grants were extremely rare. Geoffrey Roger 'took from the lord' a tenement 'for 40 years', and William Boteler 'took from the lord in court' two acres of customary land for the term of six years, court held February 1466, Merton College, Oxford, 5933. There is no explicit use of the words 'lease' or 'farm'.

[23]   Merton College, Oxford, 5888, undated rental bound next to 1426–7 collector's account, and 5931 (1448).

[24]   Merton College, Oxford, 5123, court held November 1398. In 1466 John Wrothe and Thomas Benet each held a cottage *'sine copiis'* and were amerced 2d. to provide them, Merton College, Oxford, 5933.

[25]   Thomas May acquired a half virgate in February 1438, and a copy of the transaction on a small piece of parchment has been preserved in the College archives, Merton College, Oxford, 5926 (court) and 5927 (copyhold).

[26]   Merton College, Oxford, 5889.

[27]   Prior to the Black Death cottages held for a term of lives were not subject to

but these too had been converted to money rent in lieu of services. Yet by the 1390s the vast majority of the old customary holdings were now held for a term of lives, and hereditary tenures had largely disappeared. Furthermore, a copy of the court roll entry was already firmly established as the means of confirming the title to the land. Most tenants were immigrants after the Black Death, and therefore were not classified as serfs by blood. In the 1390s tenants failing to perform suit of court were described as either 'free' or 'native', until 1401 when the word 'native' was replaced by the phrase 'tenants according to the custom of the manor'.[28] In 1458 tenants were categorized as either free or tenants at will.[29] The contractual tenancies attracted a new type of tenant to customary land, including the rector of Cuxham church.[30]

Incidents of villeinage

Presentments for failure to use the demesne mill were common before the Black Death, but rare thereafter (see tables 7.1 and 7.2).[31] In 1385 the court warned its tenants (the 'homage') about the requirement to observe millsuit, and the next year it amerced three men for their failure to do so.[32] This was the last record of millsuit here. Tallage was occasionally levied before the Black Death, and merchet was frequently recorded, but neither appears at all thereafter.[33] A formal act of fealty was required on the election of a new Warden of Merton College, but no recognition payment was made (see tables 7.1 and 7.2).[34]

In the wake of the Black Death a spike of illicit departures was presented in the manorial court, including six individuals in the March court of 1352 (see table 7.3). In January 1353 the bailiff was presented to attach the flown serfs at the next court, but he claimed to be unable to respond because none of the fugitives had any close relatives remaining on the manor.[35] No chevage was paid, and by 1357 only one person, John Alynote, was presented for absence each year. There are no references to flown villeins in any of the

---

heriot, see Harvey, *Manorial records of Cuxham*, pp. 658, 664. Hence heriot was added to this form of tenure after the epidemic.

[28] Merton College, Oxford, 5923, court held January 1391; 5124, court held November 1401.

[29] Merton College, Oxford, 5932, court held May 1458.

[30] In 1474, Master Richard Colyns, late Rector, who died seized of two half virgates, Merton College, Oxford, 5934.

[31] For examples of millsuit before 1348–9, see, for example, Harvey, *Manorial records of Cuxham*, pp. 609, 613, 629, 654–5, 664–5, 673.

[32] Merton College, Oxford, 5123, courts held April 1385 and March 1386.

[33] For tallage, see Harvey, *Cuxham*, p. 132–4. For merchet before 1348–9, see Harvey, *Manorial records of Cuxham*, pp. 608, 634, 655–6, 667, 672–3, 685.

[34] Harvey, *Manorial records of Cuxham*, p. 688.

[35] Merton College, Oxford, 5916.

7.1 Last recorded date of incidents of villeinage at Cuxham
and Holywell, 1349 to 1496

Manor	Capit.	Chev.	Pres. for absence	Child.	Heriot	Merchet	Millsuit	Recogn.	Tallage
Cuxham 1351–1496	None	1440	1440	None	1474	None	1386	None	None
Holywell 1349–1456	None	None	None	None	1449	None	None	None	None

7.2 Frequency of chevage, merchet, leyrwite, heriot, tallage
and millsuit at Cuxham, 1350 to 1474

Period	Chevage	Merchet	Leyrwite	Heriot	Tallage	Millsuit
Pre-1349	/	/	X	/	/	/
1350–74	o	o	o	2	o	o
1375–99	o	o	o	7	o	3
1400–24	o	o	o	4	o	o
1425–49	6	o	o	2	o	o
1450–74	o	o	o	I	o	o

/ = recorded pre-1348–9, X = not recorded

7.3 Recorded flight of serfs from Cuxham, 1351 to 1440

Year	Presentments for absence	Chevage
1351	6	o
1352	5	o
1354	I	o
1356	I	o
1357	I	o
1436	4	o
1439	o	3
1440	I	3

late fourteenth-century courts.[36] Even when John Eustace abandoned his half virgate in 1404 'and removed himself from the lord with his moveable goods and chattels', there was no presentment to retrieve or attach him. Then in 1436, after decades in which migrants were not recorded, four serfs were suddenly presented for their absence from the manor, and charges for

---

[36] Merton College, Oxford, 5916 to 5923.

chevage (between 2d. and 6d.) were levied on three of them in 1439 and again in 1440.[37] All interest then ceased.

Labour services collapsed in the 1350s with the rapid swing to contractual tenancies. Immediately prior to the Black Death each half virgate in villeinage had owed around 100 labour services per annum, most of which were directly utilized.[38] The introduction of money rents in the 1350s swept away most of the onerous labour services, which explains why manorial accounts after 1349 contain no sub-section detailing the utilization of works. However, most money rents usually included a requirement to find two men for one day in the harvest, and to work for one day weeding and then making hay. These token services persisted, because it is possible to deduce from an undated rental (probably from the early 1420s) that each half virgate still rendered two days' labour service per year. The rental also states that the demesne lessee was eligible to a total of 30 days of labour service from all the tenanted lands, and a separate account of the 'collector of rents' in 1426–7 valued those 30 days at 10s., which implies that these few, surviving, services were commuted.[39] Some collective refusals to perform works had occurred in the late 1320s, but after 1349 the court rolls contain no such entries.[40]

Heriot was applied to both the original villein tenure and the new tenancy for terms of lives, and its incidence only started to decline in the late fifteenth century (see table 7.2). By that time, cash heriots – many of them stipulated in advance as part of the tenancy agreement – had largely displaced the render of the best beast. Many of the earliest grants of the new contractual tenancy had not included liability for heriot, but thereafter it became commonplace. For example, in 1377 the rector of Cuxham acquired three half virgates, but he was to owe 'no heriot, because he holds for a term of years and not according to the custom of the manor'. However, in 1400 Thomas Christmas was liable for a heriot of 5s. on his half virgate, even though he held 'for the term of his life according to the custom of the manor'.[41] Yet,

---

[37] Merton College, Oxford, 5925 to 5932.

[38] Harvey, *Cuxham*, pp. 82–5.

[39] Merton College, Oxford, 5889, contains around 30 loosely-bound farmers' accounts from fifteenth-century Cuxham. The rental is bound next to Wiliam Bayly's collector's account for 1426–7, which itself refers to the existence of such a rental. The half virgates are identifiable by their standard rent of c.9s. per annum, although one fetched 5s. and John Hutte held two for 22s. Four were noted as lying in the lord's hands.

[40] Harvey, *Cuxham*, pp. 128–9.

[41] Merton College, Oxford, 5922, court held October 1377; 5923, court held November 1400.

by the 1470s and 1480s, heriots were once again being omitted from some new grants.[42]

Entry fines had been levied at between 20s. and 40s. per half virgate before the Black Death, but they were extensively waived, or reduced to a nominal level, in the 1350s and 1360s. Thereafter, the fixed-term tenancies were liable to the payment of a variable entry fine, but the sums were routinely lower than those charged before the Black Death. The highest recorded entry fine is 26s. 8d. plus 6 capons, but many were substantially lower: by the late fifteenth century fines did not usually exceed 3s. 4d. per half virgate.[43]

Attitudes to serfdom

There is no evidence for a conservative or aggressive approach to the management of serfs. The manor seldom held more than two courts a year in the late fourteenth century, and just one in the fifteenth.[44] The manor was leased in 1359, and thereafter probably remained at lease without interruption until the early sixteenth century.[45] After 1359 it is not entirely clear whether Merton still ran the manorial courts or whether this task was delegated to the farmer of the demesne, although the former seems likely.

Summary of chronology and key indicators

In the summer of 1353 70% of the main customary holdings at Cuxham still lay abandoned, due to a combination of the high mortality of the Black Death in 1348, an absence of ready replacements, and the subsequent departure of six servile adults. Faced with this acute crisis, the college offered the empty holdings on more attractive terms. The phrase 'in bondage' disappeared immediately from all conveyances, and the main liabilities associated with villein tenure – week works, tallage and merchet – were all replaced with a money rent on the majority of holdings. As a result of these conces-

---

[42] Merton College, Oxford, 5925 and 5932 (1430s), and 5934 to 5938 (1470s and 1480s).

[43] Harvey, *Cuxham*, appendix VI. The waiving of fines in the 1350s is evident in Merton College, Oxford, 5916 to 5918; the highest fine was recorded in the January court of 1380, 5922; 3s. 4d. was paid in the November 1477 court, and 2s. in the court held October 1488, 5937 and 5940.

[44] Manorial accounts list the number of courts held each year, see, for example, Merton College, Oxford, 5884 (1353–4, one court), 5886 (1357–8, two courts), and 5887 (1358–9, two courts). Single courts per annum in the fifteenth century are the norm, see, for example, 5933 to 5941.

[45] Harvey, *Manorial records of Cuxham*, p. 2. The lease of 1361–8 is mentioned in Harvey, *Cuxham*, p. 94, there is firm evidence for the lease of the demesne from 1391, but no documents survive from the period 1368 to 1391. Although there are some gaps in the fifteenth-century series, all the extant material confirms that the manor was continuously leased thereafter, Merton College, Oxford, 5888 and 5889.

7.4 Mean annual rent charged upon new grants of half virgates held
on contractual tenancies at Cuxham, 1340–9 to 1480–9

Decade	Number of grants	Mean rent (d.)
1340–9	–	240*
1350–9	8	132
1360–9	no data	–
1370–9	3	102
1380–9	2	134
1390–9	3	81
1400–9	5	115
1410–9	no data	–
1420–9	no data	–
1430–9	7	105
1440–9	no data	–
1450–9	no data	–
1460–9	1	96
1470–9	4	110
1480–9	1	108

* Monetary value of services attached to holding from graph 7.1.

sions, the manor was successful in attracting new tenants, many of whom
came from outside the village.[46]

Thus by c.1360 the standardized holdings were held for a money rent,
either for a term of lives or heritably. Occasional attempts were made subsequently to restore some of the holdings to the old tenure, but these were
short-lived. The leasing of the demesne after 1359 probably removed any
residual interest in restoring labour services. By the 1390s all the original
half virgates had been converted to life tenancies for a money rent. Millsuit
disappeared in the 1380s. Heriot was the only main incident of villeinage to
survive the transformation of villein tenure into money rent.

The value of customary land fell dramatically in the immediate aftermath
of the Black Death. In the 1340s the various servile incidents attached to
each half virgate were rated at a cash equivalent of 20s. per annum, yet in
the 1350s the mean money rent charged on new grants was 11s., a fall of 45%.
The level had fallen further to around 9s. in the early fifteenth century, then
held steady (see table 7.4). After the early 1350s hardly any out-migration
was recorded from the manor. There was no seigniorial reaction. Merton
did not pursue a managerial policy which was aggressive or confrontational

[46] Harvey, *Cuxham*, p. 137.

7.1 Value of customary arable land at Cuxham, 1340s to 1480s (d. per acre)

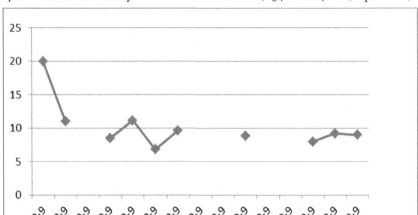

to its serfs. There was no overt or recorded peasant resistance. Merton had effectively conceded on villeinage within a decade of the Black Death.

Holywell[47]

Customary land tenures
Holywell was essentially a rectorial manor, constructed from the glebe and other endowments attached to the parish church, which was appropriated by the college for its own use. It possessed a small demesne and an unknown number of tenants, most of whom were cottagers and none of whom held any agricultural holdings larger than six acres.[48] Freemen were routinely requested to attend the manor court.

Land transfers are recorded in the court rolls, but hardly any include formulae describing the terms on which the land was held: they simply describe the nature of the holding and the principal parties in the transaction. Some land was granted 'for services' in the 1350s, when the jurors occasionally questioned whether such land was also liable for heriot.[49] In

---

[47] For Holywell there are c.15 courts from 1338 to 1347, Merton College, Oxford, 4544 to 4548, then c.50 courts from 1349–66, 1377–89, 1438–62, 1474, 1485–8, 1496, Merton College, Oxford, 4549–4559; and c.60 accounts from 1372–1473, Merton College, Oxford, 4523–4536.

[48] *VCH Oxfordshire*, volume 4 (London, 1979), pp. 272–3.

[49] Merton College, Oxford, 4549, court held December 1349; 4551, court held December, 1355; 4551b, court held May 1357.

· 7.5 Frequency of chevage, merchet, leyrwite, heriot, tallage
and millsuit at Holywell, 1333 to 1474

Period	Chevage	Merchet	Leyrwite	Heriot	Tallage	Millsuit
1333–41	0	0	0	0	0	0
1350–74	0	0	0	0	0	0
1375–99	0	0	0	0	0	0
1400–24	–	–	–	–	–	–
1425–49	0	0	0	1	0	0
1450–74	0	0	0	0	0	0

1357 a messuage and half an acre of land was granted for the term of a life.[50]
Some mid-fifteenth-century courts are slightly more informative about the
terms of tenure, describing some parcels of land as held 'for him and his
according to the custom of the manor', and recording the existence of life
tenancies.[51] Manorial accounts of the early 1380s refer to 'rents of assize,
as contained in the new rental', then in 1383–4 a note was added to this
section which stated that 'there are in the lord's hands certain tenements
and they are leased according to the custom of the manor'.[52] It is impossible
to reconstruct the precise nature and evolution of land tenancies from such
fragments of information. However, the language is strongly indicative of
the presence of some customary land, and of the conversion of some of these
holdings to life tenancies.

Incidents of villeinage
Irrespective of the original extent of villeinage at Holywell, its burdens were
light. This may have owed something to its close proximity to Oxford: the
court occasionally reminded its tenants that they were governed by the
custom of the manor, not the customs of the borough of Oxford.[53] There are
no recorded servile incidents in the court rolls of the 1330s and 1340s, and
thereafter the only incidents are heriot, entry fines and a few seasonal labour
services. Liability for a cash heriot upon the death of the tenant is recorded
occasionally, but there is no record of its actual collection.[54] Entry fines
continued to be paid in the fifteenth century, at a level usually equivalent
to one year's rent. Peasant land was held 'for services', and sundry expenses

---

[50] Merton College, Oxford, 4551b, court held May 1357.
[51] Merton College, Oxford, 4555b, court held April 1449.
[52] Merton College, Oxford, 4530.
[53] Merton College, Oxford, 4549, court held May 1349; *VCH Oxfordshire*, volume 4,
pp. 271–2.
[54] Merton College, Oxford, 4556, court held December 1449.

incurred through the deployment of a few harvest works on the demesne are mentioned in the 1377 account, but otherwise there are no other references to labour services or to commutation.[55] Indeed, after 1378 the demesne harvest was reaped entirely (and expensively) through hired labour.[56] By 1409 the manor was leased, an arrangement which continued for the rest of the century.[57]

Between the 1350s and 1380s the court rolls usually recorded an annual payment entitled 'amercements of the messor not appearing in the issues of the court'.[58] The sums varied between 3s. and 12s. each year, and they most likely related to agricultural offences rather than incidents of villeinage.[59] In the 1350s successive millers charged 'unjust' tolls upon people grinding their corn at the lord's mill, but there are no cases of millsuit.[60] There are no other references to any kind of villein incidents (see table 7.1).

Attitudes to serfdom
No evidence exists for a conservative attitude towards serfdom or of aggressive management of serfs.

Summary of chronology and key indicators
Villeinage was present at Holywell, but it was not the dominant form of tenure and, in any event, it was not burdensome. The extant sources are plentiful but lacking in detail, especially on matters of tenure. Therefore it is difficult to reconstruct the chronology of change with precision. Yet it is clear that some of the original villein tenures mutated into tenure for a term, and that the only incidents of villeinage recorded after the Black Death were heriot and a few seasonal labour services. No meaningful series of land values can be constructed. There is no evidence for manumissions, flight or social tension.

Kibworth Harcourt[61]

Prior to the Black Death 24 half virgaters paid around 6s. rent each year, owed labour services valued at 3s. 4d., and were liable for heriot, merchet,

---

[55] Merton College, Oxford, 4517, 4526; *VCH Oxfordshire*, volume 4, p. 273.

[56] Merton College, Oxford, 4525 to 4533.

[57] Merton College, Oxford, 4535 to 4536.

[58] See, for example, court held October 1352, Merton College, Oxford, 4550.

[59] The practice was also known at Cuxham, where it covered agricultural offences rather than issues of lordship, Harvey, *Manorial records of Cuxham*, pp. 654–60.

[60] Merton College, Oxford, 4549, court held December 1349; 4550, court held June 1349; 4551b, court held May 1357.

[61] This analysis draws upon Hilton and Howell's published work on Kibworth. As

tallage, entry fines, a common fine and head penny payments: serfs were also charged for permission to enter holy orders.[62] Labour services were entirely commuted from at least the 1280s, when the demesne land was permanently leased to local people.[63] Entry fines were no longer charged after 1349, levies for entering holy orders ceased in 1371, merchet was regularly charged until its disappearance in the early fifteenth century, and likewise payments of the common fine until 1448. The isolated imposition of a sizeable tallage in 1423 provoked a refusal to pay among the tenants. Migrants were presented in most years until 1407, when the chief pledges refused to do so. The practice was resumed for one year only in 1440, when the villein status of three families was under question. Heriot prevailed throughout the fifteenth century, although increasingly it became a cash render.[64]

In the aftermath of the Black Death villein land was quickly reoccupied on hereditary tenure. In the 1350s and 1360s there is little evidence of conversions to fixed-term tenures, even though such developments were widespread nearby. At this time Merton was well served by an able and experienced steward of its Leicestershire lands, Simon Pakeman, and Howell suggests that this experience helped him to resist any initial pressure to concede on villein tenure.[65] The relative buoyancy of the land market in Kibworth aided his stance, because new tenants were found quickly for the vast majority of half virgates.[66] Half virgates were heritable and held 'in bondage' for much of the fourteenth century, until the 1390s when this phrase was increasingly replaced by 'held at the will of the lord according to the custom of the manor'. The use of the phrase 'at the will of the lord' did not mean that Kibworth tenants were suddenly vulnerable to forfeiture according to seigniorial whim, because it was qualified by the local manorial custom of impartible inheritance: hence an embryonic copyhold by inheritance became the main form of tenure at Kibworth.[67]

The changes to the vocabulary of tenures after the 1390s were closely associated with a marked slackening in the demand for land, a difficulty which by the 1420s had become acute.[68] Displays of dissent and refusals to hold land increased in this period, which in turn hastened the pace of tenurial change. The imposition of aspects of villeinage, or perhaps the manner of

a result, there are no precise dates for the disappearance of individual incidents, nor any enumeration of their frequency after 1350.

[62] Hilton, 'Merton College manor', p. 32; Howell, *Kibworth Harcourt*, pp. 17, 31, 33–5.

[63] Hilton, 'Merton College manor', p. 32; Howell, *Kibworth Harcourt*, p. 19.

[64] Howell, *Kibworth Harcourt*, pp. 31, 33–5, 44, 50.

[65] Howell, *Kibworth Harcourt*, pp. 38–9; Howell, 'Inheritance customs', p. 130.

[66] Howell, *Kibworth Harcourt*, pp. 42–4.

[67] Howell, 'Inheritance customs', pp. 132–3.

[68] Howell, *Kibworth Harcourt*, pp. 50–2.

its imposition, was occasionally a source of tension between Merton and its tenants.[69] In 1427 the college agreed to reduce the level of cash rent by 3s. 4d. per virgate, and to replace the demeaning phrase 'holds in bondage' with 'at the will of the lord' on all customary tenures, not just new grants, an agreement which was formally reiterated in 1439.[70] The lower rent levels, fixed as part of this agreement, were frozen for the next three centuries.[71] No references to 'in bondage' are found at all after 1440.

Conclusion

Although Cuxham, Holywell and Kibworth Harcourt were part of the same estate, the history of villeinage on each of them is very different. Villeinage was never prominent at Holywell, and hardly features after 1350. It was extensive at Cuxham before the Black Death, but then largely disappeared in the 1350s. In contrast, villein tenure and personal servility survived intact at Kibworth until the early fifteenth century. Thus the management of villeinage across the three manors had little in common. The only similarities are that labour services disappeared at a relatively early date on all three, and that heriot also persisted and mutated into a cash payment during the fifteenth century. A sudden interest in migrants in the late 1430s at both Cuxham and Kibworth is the sole example of an estate-wide initiative associated with serfdom.

The absence of a consistent, estate-based, approach to villeinage confirms Howell's sense that Merton ran its estate in a 'non-directive' manner and without a clearly defined, central, policy. This approach meant that villeinage was bound to evolve differently on individual manors. The administration of Kibworth was largely devolved to the college's steward of estates in Leicestershire, who enjoyed considerable autonomy to determine policy there. The incumbent at the time of the Black Death was highly experienced, which Howell suggests was influential in ensuring the quick and full reoccupation of the customary holdings in its wake, which in turn meant that villeinage was retained with few changes until the early fifteenth century.[72] The estate steward responsible for Cuxham in the 1350s (John le Bruyn) was also highly experienced, but, in direct contrast, he swept away the original villein tenure and replaced it with money-based tenures by the end of the decade.[73] Little

---

69   Howell, *Kibworth Harcourt*, pp. 45, 50.

70   Howell, *Kibworth Harcourt*, pp. 50–3.

71   Howell, 'Inheritance customs', p. 134.

72   Howell, *Kibworth Harcourt*, pp. 38–9, and 'Inheritance customs', p. 130.

73   Le Bruyn ran every extant court at Cuxham between April 1343 and the late 1350s, Merton College, Oxford, 5914 to 5920.

attempt was made to uphold personal serfdom after 1350, probably because few of the original villein families remained in Cuxham. Even a highly experienced steward could not maintain villeinage in the 1350s if there were simply not enough prospective tenants in the locality.

Villein tenure evolved differently across the three manors. The full reoc-cupation of customary holdings in the wake of the Black Death at Kibworth meant that villein tenure initially changed little there. However, in the 1420s a combination of a slack land market and peasant resistance forced Merton to make lasting concessions: villein tenure remained heritable, but its rent level was reduced and the demeaning phrase 'in bondage' was removed from conveyances. In stark contrast, the majority of the former customary holdings at Cuxham still lay vacant five years after the Black Death, and were only re-tenanted when converted to money rents and life tenancies. The choice of life tenancy, rather than another form of fixed-term tenure, was informed by local precedent, because in the early fourteenth century cottages and, very occasionally, half virgates in Cuxham had been granted for life. Its popularity spread after the mid-1350s, until by the 1390s it had completely displaced hereditary tenures. The evolution of villein tenure at Holywell is more difficult to reconstruct, but changes in the 1350s and 1360s were not as dramatic as at Cuxham. Fixed-term tenures were used whenever customary land proved difficult to tenant, and by the mid-fifteenth century life tenancies were the most common form.

These different trajectories of villeinage on three manors within the same estate have three explanations, which themselves provide an insight into why the decline of villeinage was so varied across England. First, the character of villeinage on each before the Black Death was markedly different: it was prominent at Cuxham and Kibworth, but weak at Holywell. Thus differing starting points help to explain differing trajectories of decline after 1350. Second, after the Black Death Merton College did not adopt a consistent and coordinated policy towards the management of villeinage across its whole estate. The absence of such a policy is somewhat surprising, given that a perpetual institution such as Merton, with its continuity of landholding and bureaucratic administration, had greater capacity to implement it than most medieval landlords. Indeed, before the Black Death the college's policy *had* been 'rigorously to exploit the obligations of its unfree tenants, so as to preserve the structure of unfree holdings and its own rights, and to draw a financial profit from them'.[74]

Finally, after the Black Death it was local conditions, not a fixed central policy, which primarily determined the way in which villeinage was managed across the estate. The presence of a pool of prospective tenants at Kibworth

[74] R. Evans, 'Merton College's control of the tenants at Thorncroft 1270–1349', in Razi and Smith, *Medieval society*, p. 254.

meant that there was little pressure for radical changes to villein tenure during the second half of the fourteenth century. When these conditions changed in the early fifteenth century, the college was forced to concede on the terms of customary tenure and the management of personal servility. Conversely, the stark absence of replacement tenants in the early 1350s at Cuxham forced dramatic tenurial change, and the sweeping away of villeinage. There were forces at work beyond the power of even a bureaucratic landlord to control.

8

Aldham

Aldham (Suffolk) was held continuously through the later Middle Ages by the de Vere earls of Oxford.[1] It formed part of a cluster of demesne manors in north Essex and south Suffolk, close to one of the earls' principal residences at Castle Hedingham (Essex). As a medium-sized manor, with a high proportion of villein land and held continuously by a single aristocratic family, Aldham provides a good example of the type of manor where villeinage should have been strongly and conspicuously upheld.[2]

Customary land tenures

In the early fourteenth century there were more than 200 acres of customary land at Aldham, organized into 28 standardized holdings: four 15-*acreware*, sixteen 8-*acreware*, three 4-*acreware* and five 1-*acreware* holdings. The area of free land is not known, although it was probably greater than the customary area, and some land was held on mollond tenure (an intermediary tenure between free and unfree).[3] Each 15-*acreware* villein holding owed a nominal cash rent, ploughing service on six acres of demesne, and a total of 17 week and 42 harvest works each year; each 8-*acreware* holding owed a nominal cash rent, ploughing service on three acres of demesne, and 11½ week and 42 harvest works; while the smaller holdings owed no ploughing services, but carried a heavier relative burden of other labour services.[4] All customary holdings were liable for heriot, merchet, millsuit, entry fine and chevage: there is no evidence for childwite or tallage. Before 1349 the formula for describing the terms of villein tenure was inconsistent, but it was usually

---

[1] Its archive comprises 5 accounts, 1328–9, 1413–14, 1415–16, 1431–2, 1527–8; two rentals, 1442, 1447, CUL Vanneck Mss, box 2. c. 165 courts, 1350–71, 1377–1408, 1415–59, 1468–76, 1486–8, 1504, CUL Vanneck Mss, box 1, SROI HA68/484/135, HA68/484/315.

[2] For the manorial descent see W.A. Copinger, *The manors of Suffolk. Seven volumes* (London and Manchester, 1905–11), volume 3, pp. 132–3.

[3] Bailey, *Medieval Suffolk*, pp. 36, 46, 48–9 for mollond tenure.

[4] The customary landholdings, and their attendant labour services, are laid out in the works' account of the *compotus* of 1328–9, CUL Vanneck Mss, box 2.

held heritably 'in villeinage …' or 'in bondage for services and customs'.[5] All customary land was fully occupied in the 1340s, and granted overwhelmingly on hereditary villein tenure.[6]

The land market remained active in the wake of the Black Death. Many heirs were admitted into their customary holdings, or, if none were forthcoming, then the land was soon granted to other willing tenants. Yet there was also some initial reluctance to hold land on hereditary villein tenure: in October 1350 three villeins abandoned their holdings and left the manor, and then in the summer of 1351 widespread complaints about the weight of labour services forced the estate steward to respite temporarily some services from all villein holdings on the manor.[7] After 1353 any customary land that still lay untenanted was converted to leasehold, either for a short term of years or for the life of the tenant. The latter was especially popular, although the court-roll entries are explicit that these were 'at farm': for example, in 1355 Nicholas Skilman acquired one messuage and an 8-*acreware tenementum* 'at farm' for life, rendering 6s. 8d. per annum and no services.[8] The move to leases proved popular and successful, because a steady stream of such grants continued during the second half of the fourteenth century, whose flow only began to diminish at the beginning of the fifteenth. After the 1360s the vast majority of leases were for terms of years, usually less than ten, although leases for life were still granted occasionally.[9] Most leases were described

---

5   This phrase dominates the conveyances recorded in the many pre-Black Death court rolls. However, on a single occasion an 8-*acreware tenementum* was granted to John Dore 'to him and his by the rod at the will of the lord for customs and services', CUL Vanneck Mss, box 1, court held December 1342.

6   In the first half of the fourteenth century two grants of customary holdings at leasehold are recorded. In 1319 Nicholas le Charect abandoned an 8-*acreware* holding because of his poverty, which was then leased for two years for 9s. per annum 'because no one will hold it for services and customs', and in 1321 the lease was renewed for 12s. rent; in 1329 a single 4-*acreware tenementum* was leased for 40d: CUL Vanneck Mss, box 1, courts held July 1319 and March 1321; 1328–9 account, CUL Vanneck Mss, box 2.

7   SROI HA68/484/135, court held October 1350, Robert Berte abandoned a 15-*acreware* holding, and John Berte and John Dore each abandoned 8-*acreware* holdings. In June 1351 the estate steward Thomas de Chabham handled 'a plea from various unfree tenants on various manors of lord John de Vere, Earl of Oxford, concerning the waiving of part of the labour services which they used to perform before the pestilence and which now, as is well known, they lack the ability to perform in their entirety'. The extract is quoted in R.E. Horrox, ed., *The Black Death* (Manchester, 1994), pp. 286–7.

8   SROI HA68/484/135, court held July 1355. In the same court, Roger Brook was granted William Berte's tenement at farm for 3 years, paying 9s. 6d., and Robert Norys acquired the lease of an 8-*acreware* tenement for nine years, paying 8s. rent and a 40d. entry fine.

9   Only two examples exist after 1377, CUL Vanneck Mss, box 1. Henry Smith

as held 'at farm', although that granted to William Chesewright was additionally 'at the will of the lord'.[10] Leases were granted for fixed money rent only, but, very occasionally, for a mixture of harvest works and a lower cash rent.[11] The evolution of tenures was not always smooth or continuous: for example, Kynges *tenementum* was leased in 1383, but by 1407 it had reverted to an hereditary tenure.[12] However, the general trend was towards leasehold, so that by the last quarter of the fourteenth century the majority of grants were at lease.[13] A sizeable minority, perhaps one third, remained on hereditary villein tenure. During the 1350s this form of tenure shed the use of 'in villeinage … in bondage', and conveyances settled into a consistent format: 'to hold for him and his by the rod at the will of the lord for services and customs'.

After c.1400 a significant change occurred. Re-grants of customary land on both leasehold and the original hereditary tenure declined markedly, and instead most land was now granted as a hereditary tenancy held for a straight money rent. The rent level was set at whatever the market would bear, a modest entry fine was also due, again set around the level of those previously charged for leaseholds rather than at the higher levels associated with the old villein tenure; and, finally, the tenant owed suit of court. There were no other incidents, and the grant was simply 'at the will of the lord for him and his heirs', which confirmed both the hereditary principle and the lord's right to determine the title within his own manorial court: these were effectively negotiated commutations.[14] The court rolls label grants in this form as 'new rents'. They first became popular in the first decade of

---

was granted an 8-*acreware tenementum* for the term of his life in July 1378, and Nicholas Crembell received a package of land on the same term in October 1391.

[10] CUL Vanneck Mss, box 1, court held December 1383, where William was granted a cottage and 4 *acreware* for 2s. per annum, and a 20d. entry fine. In December 1400 Henry Glovere's 'new' lease of a six-acre parcel of demesne was a farm held 'by the rod at the will of the lord'.

[11] An 8-*acreware* holding was granted to a new tenant in 1361 for 5s. (about half the going rate) and harvest services, SROI HA68/484/135, court held March 1361. Only two examples are recorded after 1377: the court held in November 1381 granted an 8-*acreware* holding at farm for three years for 5s. and 'harvest works' per annum, and in February 1385 another was granted for 10s. per annum and 4½ harvest boon works. In July 1390 3 acres of molland tenure were leased solely for harvest services, CUL Vanneck Mss, box 1.

[12] In December 1383 Kynges was held 'at the will of the lord' at farm for 18s. per annum, but in September 1407 it was granted to 'heirs and assignees by the rod at the will of the lord according to the custom of the manor for services and customs', CUL Vanneck Mss, box 1.

[13] The absence of accounts means that it is not possible to calculate a more exact proportion.

[14] The first recorded grants on this tenure occurred in 1399, when two *tenementa* lying in the lord's hands were granted for 10s. and 13s. 4d. per annum, CUL

the fifteenth century, and from the late 1410s they had become the most common form of new grant.[15]

The changing nature of customary tenures at Aldham is captured in the manorial account for 1415–16, which records rental income under four headings: 'rents of assize, and various farms of the demesne and native land, £20 17s. 1d.' (which were mainly leases of demesne parcels); 'new rents, £10 18s. 4d.'; 'new rents at the term of a life, 10s.'; and 'farms of lands of diverse men, 23s.'[16] Based on these valuations, the hereditary tenure for a money rent ('new rents') was now the single most important category. The account contains no separate section for the sale of works, which reinforces the point that labour services had been commuted by negotiation through the growth of leases and the new tenure. A rental of 1442 did not bother with any fine tenurial distinctions, simply listing land as either free tenancies or customary tenancies 'by the rod', and the next surviving rental, from 1477, did the same. These 'customary tenures by the rod' are the forerunners of the heritable copyholds of the sixteenth century.

8.1 Last recorded date of the main incidents of villeinage
at Aldham, 1350 to 1504

Manor	Capit.	Chev.	Pres for Abs.	Child.	Heriot	Merchet	Millsuit	Recogn.	Tallage
Aldham 1350–1504	None	1469	1459	None	1408	1392	1353	None	None

Incidents of villeinage

Millsuit was enforced until 1353 then disappeared (see table 8.1). Just six merchet payments were imposed in the second half of the fourteenth century, and the charges were unusually low, ranging from 6d. to 12d. (see table 8.2). The single exception was the last recorded merchet, levied in 1392 upon the daughter of Thomas Mervyn who paid 12s. to marry a freeman of Edwardistone (Suffolk).[17] Heriot was levied on just nine occasions after

Vanneck Mss, box 1, court held July 1399. They are identical to what other manors called 'fee farms', see pp. 33–4, 173.

[15] Three grants were made on this tenure in the court held September 1406; two more in September 1407; two in October 1418; four in February 1419; and one in November 1419, CUL Vanneck Mss, box 1.

[16] CUL Vanneck Mss, box 2.

[17] CUL Vanneck Mss, box 1, court held December 1392.

1350, and finally disappeared after 1408, reflecting the decline of the original villein tenure, the use of death-bed transfers, and the custom of waiving heriot if the incoming tenant was an heir who paid an entry fine. Heriot was not liable from the new hereditary tenures. There is no evidence for tallage or childwite after 1350. Entry fines continued to be paid on admission to all customary tenures, although leaseholds and tenures 'by the rod' paid lower fines than villein tenure.

8.2 Frequency of merchet, heriot, childwite and millsuit
at Aldham, 1350 to 1499

Period	Merchet	Heriot	Childwite	Millsuit
Pre-1349	/	/	X	/
1350–74	4	4	o	6
1375–99	2	2	o	o
1400–24	o	3	o	o
1425–49	o	o	o	o
1450–74	o	o	o	o
1475–99	o	o	o	o

/ = recorded pre-1349, X = not recorded

Labour services were actively used before 1349: for example, in 1328–9 the majority of week and harvest works were utilized on the demesne.[18] As we have seen, in 1351 one third of specified works due from each of the main customary holdings was postponed for a fixed period of three years, following a plea for relief from villeins across the estate of the earl of Oxford.[19] This agreement also followed directly upon an incident in which 12 villeins had 'reaped badly' on the demesne during the harvest of 1350. 13 serfs again reaped badly during the harvest of 1358, for which they were amerced a total of 6s.[20] Unfortunately, we do not know what a villein had, or had not, to do to 'reap badly', but it implies a 'go slow' or wilfully shoddy work of some kind. No other instances of individual or collective resistance to labour services are recorded subsequently. After c.1360 the rise of leaseholds reduced the availability of labour services to the demesne, although, in the absence of any manorial accounts, we do not know whether the demesne continued to utilize the dwindling number of works owed by those holdings still held in villeinage. It seems very unlikely. When, in 1400, the demesne was parcelled

[18] CUL Vanneck Mss, box 2.
[19] SROI HA68/484/135, court held June 1351, reprinted in Horrox, ed., *Black Death*, pp. 286–7.
[20] SROI HA68/484/135, courts held April 1351 and November 1358.

8.3 Incidence of chevage, and mean size of levy, at Aldham, 1350 to 1499

Period	Number of chevage cases	Mean fine per case
1350–1374	2	7.5d.*
1375–1399	1	8.0d.
1400–1424	13	6.7d.
1425–1449	25	21.9d.
1450–1474	5	10.2d.
1475–1500	0	–

* Capons, where rendered, are nominally rated at 6d. each.

8.4 Recorded flight from Aldham, 1350 to 1469

Year	Number of people presented for absence	Number of people charged for chevage
1350	3	1
1351	3	0
1353	4	0
1354	1	0
1360	5	0
1367	5	0
1368	7	1
1369	3	0
1370	2	0
1371	2	0
1385	1	0
1386	1	0
1387	1	0
1388	1	0
1389	1	0
1395	0	1
1400	2	2
1404	0	2
1405	0	2
1406	0	2
1407	0	2
1416	0	2
1418	2	0
1422	2	0
1424	0	1
1426	2	0
1427	3	0

1428	3	0
1429	3	0
1430	3	0
1432	3	0
1433	0	2
1434	0	2
1436	0	2
1439	1	2
1440	0	1
1441	0	2
1442	0	2
1443	0	3
1444	0	6
1445	0	3
1446	3	0
1447	3	0
1448	3	0
1449	3	0
1450	3	0
1451	3	0
1452	1	0
1453	1	0
1455	1	0
1458	0	1
1459	1	0
1468	0	2
1469	0	2

into a number of separate leases, none mentioned the availability of any labour services.[21] Neither labour services nor their sale are mentioned in the account of 1413–14, which indicates that all works had now disappeared.[22]

In the 1350s and 1360s the Aldham court presented the whereabouts of flown serfs with some care, although only two chevage payments were actually rendered. After 1368 interest waned, as the number of presentments for absence fell and chevage was not charged again until 1395 (see table 8.4). Then, from the late 1390s, the manorial authorities maintained a close interest in around three migrant serfs each year, and chevage was charged more consistently (averaging c.7d., see table 8.3). After 1433 the administration targeted members of the Crembell family, two of whom had moved some distance

21 CUL Vanneck Mss, box 1, court held December 1400.
22 CUL Vanneck Mss, box 2.

to the area around Woodbridge (Suffolk). The Crembells were successfully pursued for escalating charges for chevage (see below), with the result that in the period 1425 to 1449 the mean fine levied for chevage was three times higher that it had been between 1400 and 1424 (see table 8.3). This squeeze was not sustained beyond the late 1440s, when the number of chevage cases, and the amount paid, dwindled. After 1469 all interest in migrants ceased: no presentments for absence or chevage are recorded thereafter (see table 8.4).

Attitudes to serfdom

No servile genealogies and manumissions are extant, and there were no fines for permission to educate sons or to enter religious orders. The management of all servile incidents in the second half of the fourteenth century was low key and pragmatic, and neither assertive nor confrontational. Indeed, the manorial regime was widely accommodating to its villeins. The widespread conversions of villein tenure to leasehold, and the willingness to relieve some labour services in 1351 reflects flexible and understanding lordship. When in 1365 Matilda Rogge pleaded that she could no longer perform 'the ancient services' due from her 8-*acreware* holding, due to 'incapacity, poverty and her family situation', the terms of her tenure were immediately switched to a lease for the term of her life, paying 5s. 8d. annually with harvest services only.[23] Chevage was seldom levied, despite the leakage of people from the manor in the 1350s and 1360s (see table 8.4), and even the modest 3d. imposed upon John Bert in 1368 was a discount rate 'on condition that he return to the manor of the lord each year during the harvest'.[24]

The only exception to this accommodating approach to villeinage was the stance taken in the late 1360s against two departed serfs. Nicholas Mervyn was recorded as absent from the manor from 1365, but he willingly returned to a court session in 1369 'and made his oath that he would obey the lord and his bailiff, and that he will come to bind himself to the lord whenever and wherever he wishes': the lord required two pledges in support of the oath, but placed no further conditions on the agreement. Roger Miller swore the same oath two years later.[25] If considered in isolation, these extraordinary oaths can be credibly interpreted as a move to impose new forms of service as part of a wider seigniorial reaction.[26] Yet, when they are considered within the specific context of the management of villeinage in general, and chevage in particular, at Aldham during this period another interpretation suggests

[23] CUL Vanneck Mss., box 1, court held October 1365.
[24] CUL Vanneck Mss, box 1, court held November 1368.
[25] CUL Vanneck Mss., box 1, courts held December 1369 and September 1371.
[26] Dyer, 'Social and economic background', p. 24.

itself. The oaths were unquestionably demeaning in both their public nature and in the conditions they imposed, but they are the only two of their kind, and they were made within two years of each other. As neither man is ever recorded as paying any chevage for his absence from the manor, it would appear that an accommodation had been reached with the estate steward of the day: Mervyn and Miller would not have to pay chevage as long as they returned when called upon to work, most likely during the harvest.

After c.1400 chevage was the only servile incident to survive. The responsibility for managing flown serfs was initially vested in the lessee of the demesne, a policy which, judging from the modest number of presentments and chevage payments in the first two decades of the fifteenth century (see table 8.4), was not especially successful. The rise in the number of presentments in the 1420s corresponds with a tighter administration of the manor, exemplified in 1422 by a direct order to the demesne lessee to seize the absent Crembell brothers, their chattels and their 'brood', under the threat of a penalty.[27] This aggressive posturing was elevated to a sustained policy after 1433, when Richard de Vere, brother of the incumbent earl of Oxford, assumed responsibility for the management of the manor.[28] The first court he attended recorded extracts from fourteenth-century court rolls relating to serf families, whose purpose was to establish both a ready checklist of serfs and written evidence of their servility.[29] Even the great nobles understood the need to scrutinize the records of their manorial courts in order to establish written proof of servility.[30]

The intense scrutiny of serf families had two discernible outcomes. First, it led to the successful and lucrative pursuit of the two Crembells, who rendered escalating sums of chevage: 12d. each in 1436, 24d. in 1439, 40d. 1441, peaking at 10s. in 1442.[31] They paid the sums, despite living some distance from Aldham. Second, the lord attempted to establish the servile origins of other long-departed families, presumably in order to extract sizeable chevage payments from them as well. In particular, administrative scrutiny fell upon three families. Nicholas Skylman, whom the lord accused of being

---

[27] CUL Vanneck Mss., box 1, courts held August 1418 and September 1422.

[28] John de Vere became earl of Oxford in 1417, at the age of nine, in succession to his father, Richard. The Richard who attended the court of 1433, and who was active in in directing its business, was John (the 12th earl's) youngest brother, J. Ross, *John de Vere, thirteenth earl of Oxford, 1442–1513. 'The foremost man of the kingdom'* (Woodbridge, 2011), p. 18.

[29] CUL Vanneck Mss., box 1, court held March 1433.

[30] Some advice to this effect is documented in F.R.H. DuBoulay, *The England of Piers Plowman. William Langland and his vision of the fourteenth century* (Woodbridge, 1991), p. 48.

[31] CUL Vanneck Mss., box 1, courts held October 1436, June 1439, September 1441, and September 1442.

a descendant of one of his serfs, was physically captured in October 1436 and forced to appear before an inquest jury at the Aldham court. Nicholas denied servile status and claimed to be of free descent: the jury, comprising tenants of the manor, promptly dismissed the charge and proclaimed his free status. A similar case against William Dedwell went the same way.[32]

In the late 1450s John de Vere, 12th earl of Oxford, decided once again to target fugitive serfs. John wrote personally to the steward of his lands in Suffolk with specific instructions to conduct an inquiry into the personal status of the Mervyn family, who had long lived in nearby Copdock (Suffolk), and his extraordinary letter is attached to the court roll for February 1459:

> We sesyd serteyn men be side owr manor of Aldham for bondmen called Mervyns and by ther evydens we cannot fynde that they sholde be so. Wherefore we pray yow to keepe a couwrt at our manor aforesaid in all godly haste at ther costs and that ye make an inquerry among owr tenants there whedyr they can fynde in ther conceyns that they be bondmen or nowght.[33]

The manorial jury, again comprised of local tenants, looked to its conscience and found in favour of the three Mervyn brothers. At the next court, in June 1459, John Bedwall faced a similar inquiry, and, once again, the lord's allegations were dismissed. Yet the evidence from earlier courts provides grounds for doubting the reliability of these verdicts. The Skylmans, Mervyns and Bedwalls had all been well-known serf families in fourteenth-century Aldham, whose members had been presented for leaving the manor without permission.

These events at Aldham between the 1430s and 1450s are unusual but suggestive. The targeting of three servile families, through the imposition of high levels of chevage on some, and the seizure and trial of others, was aggressive and demeaning. The seigniorial motive must have been financial: this was a period of sustained financial difficulties for many landlords, some of whom would have eyed wealthy serfs as an attractive and legitimate way of easing their plight. We do not know why the manor targeted the Crembell family, but the willingness of the long-departed Crembells to pay escalating fines for chevage from the mid-1430s has two possible explanations. The first is that they were subjected to physical intimidation by the earl's officials. Certainly, the bodily seizure of the three Mervyn brothers in 1459 must have involved overt intimidation by members of the earl's retinue, who may have felt less restrained in their actions during the political meltdown of the late 1450s. The second possible explanation is that the Crembells regarded

---

[32]   CUL Vanneck Mss, box 1, court held October 1436.

[33]   SROI HA85/484/315, court held February 1459.

the payments as worthwhile to secure the active protection and patronage of their powerful lord during a period of deteriorating law and order, and growing factionalism, in East Anglia.[34] In effect, they paid a voluntary tax whose escalating size they deemed worthwhile in the circumstances. Whatever the reasons, it is striking that John de Vere observed the law strictly when attempting to establish the personal status of the fugitives, in the sense that the alleged serfs were tried by a properly constituted jury in the manorial court baron, and the verdict of that jury was upheld and respected. The lack of success might well have contributed to the disappearance of personal servility from Aldham: all vestiges disappeared soon after.

Summary of chronology and key indicators

The growth in leases after c.1360 was significant at Aldham, even though the exact scale is not possible to quantify precisely: certainly, by c.1400 the majority of former villein tenures had been converted to leasehold. During the course of the fifteenth century both leaseholds and the surviving villein tenures were gradually converted into, or replaced by, a heritable tenure for money rent with no servile incidents. By mid-century these were already known locally as tenures 'by the rod', and are readily identifiable as an embryonic form of copyhold by inheritance. The early demise of villein tenure reduced the frequency of the incidents of villeinage: only heriot and chevage survived into the fifteenth century. Personal serfdom was not enforced with any vigour or consistency in the second half of the fourteenth century, although the revival of chevage in the second quarter of the fifteenth century reflected a managerial decision to identify and to track four servile families closely.

No usable or reliable data for land values are available from Aldham. Yet it is clear that the timing of the key tenurial changes correlates well with the huge loss of tenants induced by the first outbreak of the Black Death. Conversions to leasehold were deemed to be the best way of increasing and then maintaining land occupancy in its aftermath. The initial peak in the recorded departure of serfs during the 1350s and 1360s indicates that the effects of this demographic shock were exacerbated to a degree by out-

---

[34] For examples of the growth of disorder and factionalism in East Anglia between the 1430s and 1450s, see R.A. Virgoe, 'The murder of James Andrew: Suffolk faction in the 1430s', *Proceedings of the Suffolk Institute of Archaeology and History*, 34 (1980); P.C. Maddern, *Violence and social order. East Anglia 1422–1442* (Oxford, 1992), pp. 154–66; H. Castor, *Blood and Roses. The Paston family and the War of the Roses* (London, 2004), pp. 38–81, 238–81.

migration.[35] Similarly, the nature and timing of resistance to week works indicates that it too reinforced the pace and nature of tenurial change. The pleas from villeins in 1351 for some relief from labour services, and the collective resistance to reaping in both 1350 and 1358, reinforced graphically the problems of utilizing the main labour services, thus increasing the willingness of estate officials to accept the swing away from villein tenure.

Conclusion

In the early 1350s the earl of Oxford experienced severe difficulties in finding tenants for some of the standardized, customary, holdings at Aldham: he also faced some out-migration of serfs and collective resistance to week works. This combination of forces immediately after the Black Death reinforced the difficulties of finding enough tenants to hold all customary land on villein tenure, and collectively triggered the conversion of a growing proportion of the main customary holdings to leases from the 1360s: thereafter, villein tenure was unlikely to be restored. Not even a powerful noble lord, such as the de Veres, could maintain villeinage against such powerful adverse currents. Thus the experience of Aldham underlines the difficulties of separating out individual strands of causation in explaining the decline of villeinage.

The example of Aldham is also illustrative of the varied and complex role played by estate administration in the decline of villeinage, which defies facile generalizations. There was no seigniorial reaction here in the generation after the Black Death. On the contrary, from the moment in 1351 when the steward of estates conceded to a petition for a relaxation of week works from villein tenants, the de Veres surrendered villein tenure with hardly a fight. Leases increasingly replaced the old villein tenures during the 1360s and 1370s, when the management of personal servility was extraordinarily lax. For example, no cases of merchet, nor any presentments for absence/chevage, are recorded between 1377 and 1384, despite the high survival rate of court rolls, and the reality that marriages must have taken place, and that serfs must have been absent, during this eight-year period.

At one level, Aldham illustrates how the huge loss of tenants in 1348–9 – reinforced by subsequent out-migration and some focused, collective, resistance to week works – forced landlords to concede quickly and submissively on villeinage. But the dramatic decline of villeinage in the second half of the fourteenth century was not quite its end. At the beginning of the fifteenth century the estate administration enforced personal servility upon a handful

---

[35]   The number of recorded departures in the 1350s to 1360s was around three or four each year, peaking at seven in 1368, which is equivalent to tenanting one quarter of the 28 available customary landholdings.

of servile families through chevage, a policy which had not been much pursued thitherto. Its policy became more aggressive between the 1430s and the 1450s, manifest in a tougher approach towards flown serfs, the collection of written evidence of servility from earlier manorial courts, and the new tactic of seizing, and challenging the status of, targeted individuals. The seigniorial administration had decided to identify and label as large a body of surviving serfs as possible at Aldham, in the same way that the dukes of Norfolk had done on their manors at the beginning of the century (see Chapter 11).[36] It then sought to target a handful of individual serfs, most of whom had long since left the manor and who now apparently enjoyed financial comfort, with a view to obtaining money through the mechanism of chevage. There is also a sense in which some of those departed serfs *chose* to pay chevage, because they deemed it beneficial to them.

The reason for a more aggressive approach to migrant serfs in the second quarter of the fifteenth century is not made explicit in the source material. It certainly coincided with John de Vere's coming of age in 1428, and therefore the moment when he became personally involved in the management of his estate. The subsequent deployment of his brother Richard to take an active role in estate administration, searching for written evidence of serfs, and John's personal intervention in the case of the Mervyn brothers, strengthens the argument that the policy was directed by the earl himself. It may simply be the case that John's personal attitude towards serfdom was much more conservative than that of his predecessors. Yet the crumbling of royal authority in the provinces between the 1430s and the 1450s may have been another factor in shaping his policy, because it enabled nobles to push the bounds of acceptable behaviour. Likewise, the deterioration of the wider economy at the same time may have forced him to pursue any policy that generated more cash from his estate. John de Vere was reasonably wealthy in the 1430s, but he had not yet acquired all of the estates that were due to him, and so it could have been the weight of financial pressure on the earl's household that forced a policy of squeezing servile assets across the estate.[37]

[36] See pp. 236–8.
[37] Ross, *John de Vere*, pp. 23–5.

9

Tingewick and Upper Heyford

Tingewick (Buckinghamshire) is situated six miles west of Buckingham, and it was held by a middling Norman monastery – the priory of St Faith, Longueville – until 1391 when it was acquired by New College, Oxford.[1] Upper Heyford (Oxfordshire) lies eight miles west of Bicester. In the first half of the fourteenth century it was part of the estate of Robert de Lisle, first Lord Rougemont, but from mid-century it was held jointly by his sister (Alice Seymour) and her husband. The reversion of the title to the manor was sold to New College in 1380, who duly acquired it upon Alice's death in 1382.[2] The two manors thus had three main attributes in common: they were both large and classic manors containing a significant proportion of customary land; they were situated relatively close to each other; and they were both acquired around the same time by New College.

The particular interest in this case study is twofold. The first is to contrast the management of villeinage on two classic manors held by two very different landlords: one an absentee monastic landlord and the other an upper-ranking gentry lord. The second is to observe how, or if, New College then altered the approach to villeinage, and whether it tried to impose a uniform estate policy on its newly acquired manors. New College was itself a recent creation, founded in 1379 by William Wyckham, bishop of Winchester. He created a handsome landed endowment for his college through the purchase of a number of manors from a variety of different landlords, mainly located in Buckinghamshire, Oxfordshire and Wiltshire. Not all were acquired simultaneously. Hence New College offers a case study of an institutional landlord that was acquiring most of its estate at a critical moment in the decline of villeinage.

Tingewick[3]

Customary land tenures

Customary land dominated peasant landholding at Tingewick. In 1311–12 'the rents of the customars' totalled £5 5s. 11d., compared with just 9s. 8½d.

---

[1]   *VCH Buckinghamshire*, volume 4 (London, 1969), pp. 249–50.
[2]   *VCH Oxfordshire*, volume 6, pp. 137, 198–99.
[3]   There are c.100 courts from 1382–1457, 1477, 1489–1500, New College Oxford, 4133

rent from free tenants.[4] 23 customary virgaters each paid 2s. 6d. rent per annum, 16 half virgaters paid 15d., and 11 cotlands 1s., and they also owed capons and hens. In addition, there were six bordars and 11 coterell holdings. The scale and type of labour services attached to these categories of holding are indeterminable from the surviving sources, but they were valued as equivalent to the money rent on each category of holding.[5]

The earliest court rolls are extant from the 1380s, at which time these holdings were held on a mixture of hereditary and life tenancies. There was no reference to holding 'in villeinage/bondage' in the standard formulae of conveyance.[6] There is no evidence for the conversion of any villein tenures to leasehold.[7] By the early fifteenth century hereditary tenure had become the dominant form.[8] In the 1430s the court noted that one such tenancy was held *'per copiam'*.[9] The descriptive formula used in land transactions changed little during the fifteenth century. In mid-century tenants held 'for him and his according to the custom of the manor for ancient rents, works and customs', although by the very end of the century it was simply 'for him and his according to the custom of the manor'.[10]

There are no indications of any acute shortages of tenants or low occupancy of these customary lands. Decays and arrears of rent remained small and manageable throughout the fifteenth century, and land did not obviously stick in the lord's hands for long. In the early 1400s a handful of tenants refused to hold their land, but replacements were immediately and readily

---

to 4139; and c.100 reeve's and farmer's accounts from 1378–1495, New College Oxford, 7087 to 7188.

4   New College, Oxford, 7086.

5   So that the labour services on each virgate were valued at 2s. 6d. per annum, 15d. on the half virgates, and 1s. on the cotlands, New College, Oxford, 7097.

6   For example, in October 1382 tenants were granted customary land 'for him and his according to the custom of the manor and he undertakes ancient services', while in the next court John Pecher obtained two messuages and half virgates 'for the term of his life according to the custom of the manor' New College, Oxford, 4133. Tingewick lies just beyond the boundary of western and southern England where in the sixteenth century copyholds for lives were commonplace, Hoyle, 'Tenure and the land market', p. 6.

7   Customary tenants were also prohibited from sub-letting their holdings according to the custom of the manor, New College, Oxford, 4137, court held April 1451. Leasehold was also uncommon on the priory's manor at Great Horwood, Tompkins, 'Great Horwood', p. 174.

8   The pattern of granting some tenancies for lives initially, but then settling upon tenancies by inheritance, was also a feature of Great Horwood, Tompkins, 'Great Horwood', pp. 167–9.

9   New College, Oxford, 4137, court held April 1438.

10   See, for example, courts held November 1447, New College, Oxford, 4137, and June 1477, New College, Oxford, 4139.

found.[11] All these indicators show that the demand for land, and the supply of tenants, remained steady on this manor.

Incidents of villeinage

There is no evidence for the imposition of tallage or recognition, nor any reference to the enforcement of millsuit (see table 9.1). However, the court did continue to uphold some manorial customs relating to milling. For example, hand mills were suppressed in order to reduce competition for the demesne mill, and the miller was instructed to grind the grain belonging to the tenants before that of outsiders.[12]

9.1 Last recorded date of the key incidents of villeinage at Tingewick and Upper Heyford, 1350 to 1500

Manor	Capit.	Chev.	Pres. for absence	Child.	Heriot	Merchet	Millsuit	Recogn.	Tallage
Tingewick 1382–1500	None	1416	1446	1417	1499	1426	None	None	None
Upper Heyford 1350–1496	None	None	1379	None	1496	1377	1485	None	None

Surviving manorial accounts reveal that labour services continued to be deployed during the third quarter of the fourteenth century, until they were entirely and permanently commuted in 1380. Just one *compotus* survives from before the Black Death, which neither records any commutation of works nor provides any indication of how they were utilized. There was still no recorded commutation in the 1370s, although there is evidence for the deployment of some works during the harvest.[13] The decision to commute all labour services in 1380–1 was the consequence of the decision to lease 128 acres of the demesne arable for six years.[14] When this lease expired in 1386 the whole demesne was packaged into a single leasehold tenancy, initially held by 'the tenants of the vill'; upon acquisition of Tingewick in 1391 New College simply continued with this recent policy of leasing the demesne.[15]

---

[11] New College, Oxford, 4135, see the examples of William Braunston and Richard Bingham, court held July 1401; John Clerk, court held January 1403; and John Cook, court held December 1403.

[12] New College, Oxford, 4137, courts held July 1446 and April 1447 (handmills); and court held September 1440 (outsiders). The suppression of handmills is distinct from imposing fines for evading millsuit.

[13] New College, Oxford, 7086 to 7088.

[14] New College, Oxford, 7089.

[15] New College, Oxford, 7097.

In 1386 the fixed sum covering the commutation of all labour services (£5 6s. 5d.) was formally added to the rents of assize in the account for 1386–7, where it subsequently appeared each year as a standing item.[16] In 1433 this commuted sum was noted as being 'at the will of the lord'.[17] No resistance to labour services, or to the payment of the set sum, is recorded. In 1402–3 the requirement to render capons and hens, part of the rent package on the original villein tenure, was converted to a money rent, based on a flat rate of 2½d. per capon and 1½d. per hen.[18]

9.2 Frequency of chevage, merchet, heriot, childwite and millsuit
at Tingewick, 1375 to 1499

Period	Chevage	Merchet	Heriot	Childwite	Millsuit
1375–99	1	1 (24d.)	31	0	0
1400–24	6	11 (44d.)	53	1	0
1425–49	0	2 (66d.)	55	0	0
1450–74	0	0	9	0	0
1475–99	0	0	13	0	0

Heriot was routinely enforced on landholdings throughout the whole period, declining in frequency only after the middle of the fifteenth century (see table 9.2). It was due whenever a tenant relinquished one of the major customary tenancies (virgate, half virgate, cotland), not just upon the tenant's death – the exception was when a widow was admitted to a holding for the term of her life following her husband's death. The custom was to render the best beast, although tenants without animals paid cash or rendered chattels such as brass pots; those surrendering more than one holding simultaneously paid a heriot for each one. When land was transferred *inter vivos* between non-kin, it was not uncommon for the incoming tenant to pay the heriot on behalf of the vendor.[19] By the fifteenth century heriot payments were

---

[16] New College, Oxford, 7097 to 7110.

[17] Arrears presented periodic difficulties for the manorial administration at Tingewick, but they usually related to the lease of the demesne. Arrears of other rents were small and infrequent. The reeve was elected annually from among the virgaters, and the post attracted full remission of the cash rent and the commuted sum for labour services attached to the holding. In addition, the lord occasionally waived payment of the commuted sum owed by the coterell tenants, see New College, Oxford, 7097. The 1433–4 account is New College, Oxford, 7139.

[18] 12s. 9½d. was thus raised in 1402–3, based on 35 capons and 44 hens, New College, Oxford, 7110.

[19] For an example of such a payment, see the half virgate acquired by John Seman, court held December 1403, New College, Oxford, 4135.

sometimes combined with the entry fine for admission to a holding, a practice which contributed to the declining frequency of heriot and which also
represented a concession beneficial to the tenant.[20]

Entry fines were routinely charged, although the level was variable and
therefore determined by the lord. For example, those charged for virgates
varied from six capons to 100s., and half virgates from 20d. to 10s.[21] In
general, entry fines for virgates were usually between 6s. 8d. and 13s. 4d., and
those for half virgates between 5s. and 6s. 8d.[22] The largest entry fines were
usually charged on those holdings which had been relinquished into the
lord's hands then immediately re-granted to new tenants.[23] Unfortunately,
they cannot be utilized to provide a reliable indication of land values over
time, because of the growing practice of combining the entry fine with the
heriot.[24]

Just one case of leyrwite is recorded, in which Alicia Taylor's punishment
was to relinquish her tenancy of a cottage and two acres. The holding was
transferred to her lover, John Basyngam, who immediately conveyed it to a
third party. John was charged an entry fine of 10s., when the usual fine varied
between 3s. 4d. and 6s. 8d., so the enforced transaction served as a *de facto*
financial penalty.[25]

Merchet was actively levied until its final appearance in 1426 (see table 9.1).
There are no payments for marrying without licence. The fine for merchet
ranged from 12d. to 10s., with a mode of 3s. 4d (see table 9.2). It was usually
paid by the bride's father. The wording employed in five successive grants of
merchet between 1407 and 1411 differed from the standard formula in a highly
unusual manner. For example, William Carter paid 40d. in 1407, in return
for which his daughter, Agnes, became free ('*imposterum sic libera*') from all
elements of servitude and bondage, a grant which extended to all her brood
and belongings ('*sequela sua et omnibus bonis et catallis suis*'); similar grants
were also made to John Wyot and Nicholas Hankyn for their daughters. In

---

[20]   See, for example, New College, Oxford, 4137, court held April 1430.

[21]   These lower and upper figures for virgate entry fines are taken from courts held
in January 1397 (capons) and March 1419 (100s.); and half virgate fines from July
1400 (20d.) and October 1382 (10s.), New College, Oxford, 4133 to 4136.

[22]   The annual rent for virgates was 2s. 6d. before the commutation of labour
services, and 5s. after, and 15d. for half virgates (2s. 6d. after commutation). At
Great Horwood, on the same estate, entry fines were very high at the end of
the fourteenth century, but then were dramatically reduced in the first decade
of the fifteenth, Tompkins, 'Great Horwood', p. 163. There is no such pattern at
Tingewick.

[23]   See courts held March 1419 and July 1424, New College, Oxford, 4136 and 4137.

[24]   This practice was especially prominent in the first quarter of the fifteenth century,
New College, Oxford, 4135 and 4136.

[25]   New College, Oxford, 4136, court held February 1417.

9.3 Recorded flight of serfs from Tingewick, 1382 to 1446

Year	Number of people presented for absence	Number of people charged for chevage
1382	4	0
1383	4	0
1385	4	0
1387	6	0
1392	5	0
1393	5	0
1394	5	0
1395	6	0
1396	6	0
1397	6	0
1398	6	0
1399	0	1
1400	6	0
1401	6	0
1404	6	0
1406	6	0
1413	5	0
1416	0	6
1423	3	0
1434	1	0
1435	1	0
1439	9	0
1440	9	0
1441	9	0
1446	9	0

1411 Carter again paid 40d., although this time the grant for Margaret, his other daughter, confirmed that she could marry and was henceforth free of legal interference (*'sine calumnia'*) from the lord and his successors.[26] This is the language of manumission, although the fees charged here are much lower than those usually charged for manumission. The marriage of a female villein effectively marked the end of the lord's direct interest in her (unless she married one of his serfs), a 'loss' which the merchet payment was partly meant to recognize, but this is subtly different from an explicit grant and confirmation of personal freedom. These unusual merchets then abruptly

[26] New College, Oxford, 4135, courts held September 1407; June 1409; and July 1411.

ceased, and the phraseology returned to a conventional format.[27] Perhaps the estate steward during this short period was liberally minded, legally astute … and a little too zealous.

Presentments for absence were a regular feature of the court series from 1382. A maximum of six serfs were presented in any given year, a modest number in comparison with the fifty customary holdings on the manor. Chevage was much rarer, collected on just seven occasions, once in 1399 and the remainder in 1416. Most serfs paid between 1d. and 4d., although John Geffes and William Michell paid 6s. 8d. to permit an undisclosed number of their sons to be absent from the manor for one year. Its sudden imposition in 1416, and its equally sudden disappearance, has no obvious explanation, beyond dramatic swings in estate policy. Presentments for absence from the manor were made consistently between the 1380s and 1400s, albeit featuring the repetitious listing of the same half a dozen names each year (see table 9.3). There was no recorded surge of emigrations after 1400. The number of presentments waned between the mid-1410s and the mid-1430s. There followed a final enforcement wave between 1439 and 1446, at which point presentments abruptly stopped. No aggressive or coercive tactics were deployed to recover flown serfs: no pressure was brought to bear on individuals, and financial penalties for failure to respond were threatened on three occasions but never followed through.[28]

Attitudes to serfdom

There are no fines for permission to educate sons, to enter apprenticeships or holy orders; no servile genealogies; and no aggressive pursuit of wealthy flown villeins. Villeins were not permitted to hold free land without seigniorial licence – such permission was not usually withheld, as long as the tenancy was recorded, and a small rent of increment (equivalent to 1d. per acre per annum) charged.[29]

A single instance of behaviour cited as contemptuous or rebellious is documented, when in 1398 William and John Geffes fled the manor along with all their goods and chattels to settle in Bloxham (Buckinghamshire). They were amerced a hefty 13s. 4d. and 6s. 8d. respectively, although the money was not collected. Instead, the sums were formally recorded on the manorial *compotus* as owed to the lord, but their collection was postponed

---

[27] New College, Oxford, 4136, court held November 1418, which records straightforward payments 'to marry whoever she wishes'.

[28] In February 1383 the homage was threatened with a 3s. 4d. fine if it failed to attach flown serfs by the next court; a 10s. fine was threatened in September and again in December 1398, New College, Oxford, 4134.

[29] John Robyns, *nativus domini*, was permitted to hold 3 acres of free land 'for the term of his life', upon payment of 3d. per annum, New College, Oxford, 7115.

each year 'at the will of the lord' as an incentive for their continued good behaviour ('*se bene gerant*').[30] This device, together with the omission of their names from lists of flown serfs in the early 1400s, indicates that they had returned to Tingewick.[31]

The general interest in flown serfs diminished markedly between the 1410s and 1430s, until a sudden revival in 1439. In the January court of that year the homage named nine absentees, presumably in response to an instruction from the steward to present upon the matter. However, six of the nine were actually the names of people who had featured regularly among the lists of absentees during the 1390s: in other words, the homage had mischievously trotted out the same old names from nearly 50 years before in a marvellously subtle act of defiance.[32] It then pronounced – presumably with a collective straight face – that these flown serfs were dead. The steward, inscrutable to the end, simply ordered the homage to enquire further upon the matter and to report to the next court. The charade continued until 1446, when all interest in flown villeins ceased. The surge of interest in the 1440s was clearly an administrative push rather than a surge of emigration.

The highest single charge for merchet (10s.) was imposed upon the widowed Agnes Robyn in 1407, who was then permitted to marry whoever she chose as long as she continued to remain a tenant. This is the only example of a restrictive caveat attached to a merchet, and it followed a short period when a number of tenants had refused to hold their land; at that particular moment, New College would have been especially sensitive to the possible departure of a wealthy landholding widow like Agnes.[33]

The only evidence for tension in the relationship between lord and serfs occurs during a short period in the late 1390s. The amercement and pursuit of the Geffes for contempt in 1398 was one symptom; the levying of chevage in 1399, one of only two years on record, and the threat of a penalty of 10s. upon the whole homage for not producing flown serfs, are two other symptoms.

---

[30] New College, Oxford, 7115.

[31] This example emphasizes the importance of assessing the management of villeinage within as wide an administrative context as possible. If the evidence of the court entry is taken in isolation, it could be reasonably utilized to exemplify the aggressive handling of migrant serfs. Yet studying a good series of court rolls over a longer period of time reveals that this was a unique event, and the chance survival of the relevant account reveals that the amercements were actually waived.

[32] John Veysy, Henry Tristram, Richard Geffes, Joanna Wyot, John Franks and William Martin were all regularly presented in the 1390s, and their names all featured again in 1439 – compare, for example, court held January 1394, New College, Oxford, 4134, and court held April 1439, New College, Oxford, 4137.

[33] New College, Oxford, 4135, court held September 1407. Her husband, William Robyn, had died in April 1406.

Finally, the only recorded example of a tenant paying a fee to evade serving as reeve (6s. 8d.) occurs at this time.[34]

Summary of chronology and key indicators

A gap in the court-roll series prevents the detailed study of Tingewick in the quarter century after the Black Death. When the court roll series begins in 1382, phrases such as 'in villeinage' did not feature in the conveyances of customary land, the main labour services had been permanently commuted, and tallage and millsuit were not recorded. The disappearance of labour services was linked directly to the decision to lease the demesne. From this date, only heriot was regularly enforced. By the early fifteenth century the customary holdings were held heritably, and by the 1430s the use of the copy of the court-roll entry as evidence of title was established. The court rolls indicate that New College attempted to tighten personal servility soon after acquiring the manor in the 1390s, although it is not known whether this reflected an institutional commitment to upholding serfdom or simply a response to a shortage of tenants at that time. Presentments for absence were much more common than chevage, which ceased after 1416, while merchet dwindled in the first quarter of the fifteenth century until it, too, ceased in 1426. An attempt to revive an interest in flown serfs in the 1430s met with passive non-cooperation. Thus villein tenure had effectively disappeared by the 1380s, and personal servility, already limited to half a dozen families, limped on until the 1420s.

Upper Heyford[35]

Customary land tenures

Upper Heyford was a large manor held by a succession of high-status gentry lords until the late fourteenth century. It comprised a sizeable demesne, around 170 acres of freehold tenure, and over 700 acres of customary land.[36] Unlike Tingewick, we do know what happened at Upper Heyford in the immediate aftermath of the Black Death and before New College acquired it in 1382.

In the 1340s 35 standard customary virgates were held 'in bondage' or 'in villeinage', each rendering 12s. rent annually, owing 10 summer and 35 harvest works, and carrying liability for tallage, merchet, heriot, chevage, entry fine

---

34   New College, Oxford, 4134 and 4135.

35   There are c.55 courts extant from Upper Heyford dating from 1350–80, 1436, 1443, 1463–75 and 1485–96, New College, Oxford, 3821–3825. These are complemented by c.23 accounts between 1342 to 1396, New College, Oxford, 6272–6295.

36   *VCH Oxfordshire*, volume 6, pp. 199–200.

and millsuit.[37] In 1351, nearly three years after the Black Death had struck, 23 of those 35 virgates still lay abandoned.[38] Odd parcels of these vacant holdings were temporarily leased to any willing takers, usually for three years, until permanent tenants could be found for the entire holding.[39] Over the next five years a handful of tenants did come forward to occupy virgates on the old terms.[40] Some had been attracted by inducements, such as reduced rents and remission of entry fines.[41] Despite these enticements, around one half of the original virgates still remained unoccupied in the late 1350s.

In 1359 the accession to the manor of Alice de St Mauro, as widow of the previous lord, Sir Thomas Seymour, coincided with a decisive new approach to the acute problem of vacant holdings. By 1362 14 of the 35 virgates were still held on the original villein tenure, but 18 were now tenanted for a straight money rent (around 11s. per annum) on leasehold, leaving just three virgates untenanted.[42] During the late 1360s and 1370s the number of virgates held on villein tenure diminished further, from 14 in 1362 to nine in 1371.[43] Thus the introduction after 1359 of fixed-term tenancies for money proved successful at attracting tenants for those customary virgates that had remained untenanted since the Black Death, thus increasing the occupancy levels of land and restoring rental income. In 1344–5 a full rent-roll had generated £19 4s. 7d. from 'assize rents of bond lands and cottars'. After collapsing in the early 1350s, rental income from peasant holdings recovered to £19 10s. 6d by 1380–1, although it was now entitled 'rents and farms, and the relaxation of works'.[44] This provides a clear example of the way in which an increase in rental income after the Black Death is more likely to be explained by the

---

[37] New College, Oxford, 3821, court rolls 1316 to 1347, and New College, Oxford, 6273, works' account (1342–3). Accounts from the 1280s indicate 31 virgates, *VCH Oxfordshire*, volume 6, p. 198.

[38] New College, Oxford, 6279 (1351).

[39] New College, Oxford, 3821, courts held 1350 and 1351.

[40] New College, Oxford, 3821, see, for example, the court held May 1354, and the grant of land to Edmund, parson of the church, '*per antiquam tenuram*' in June 1356; court held July 1367.

[41] New College, Oxford, 3821, court held November 1354, when John de Rodeston was granted remission of his entry fine, and of rent and services for the next year, on admission to a messuage and virgate. On other occasions cash rents were reduced from the set 12s. per virgate to 5s. and 3s. 4d. per virgate, court held May 1357.

[42] New College, Oxford, 3821, courts held April and August 1362.

[43] When only nine virgaters paid to commute their labour services for the year, New College, Oxford, court held June 1371.

[44] New College, Oxford, 6271 (1342–3 account), 6275 (1344–5) and 6281 (1380–1); *VCH Oxfordshire*, volume 6, p. 198.

changing structure of customary rents than any aggressive seigniorial reaction.[45]

The formulae used to describe the mix of customary tenancies which emerged here between the 1350s and 1370s were fluid and sometimes imprecise. One virgate was granted simply 'at the will of the lady', and therefore looks like an insecure tenancy at will.[46] The terms of another grant stated simply that the tenant obtained seisin, and was required to perform suit of court and to render a capon as an entry fine.[47] However, two trends are clear. The first is that the language used to describe the dwindling number of virgates held on hereditary villein tenure had changed decisively by the 1360s: the phrase 'holding in bondage' disappeared permanently, to be replaced with 'to him and his according to the custom of manor'.[48] After the 1350s there are no references to 'bond' or 'native' land.

The second trend is the decisive swing from leaseholds to tenancies for lives. Many of the earliest fixed-term tenancies, granted in the 1350s and early 1360s, were 'leased at farm' for terms of years.[49] From the late 1360s most virgates were re-granted as a life tenancy with a standardized rent package, as and when an existing lease for years expired, or as a hereditary villein tenure was relinquished.[50] These were held 'for the term of the life of the lady of the manor', for a cash rent of around 12s. per annum; one day mowing and one reaping service; liability for heriot; suit of court; and a requirement to keep the holding in good repair.[51] The linking of the length of the grant to the life of the manorial lady, rather than to the life of the tenant, is unusual, but it aligned the tenancies to Alice de St Mauro's claim to the manor as a widow for her lifetime.[52] As a result, by the early 1370s just nine of

---

[45]   See the discussion below, pp. 306–7.

[46]   New College, Oxford, 3822, court held February 1379.

[47]   New College, Oxford, 3821, see courts held June 1369; June 1371; and November 1375.

[48]   New College, Oxford, courts held 1368 and 1371.

[49]   New College, Oxford, 3821, courts held April and August 1362.

[50]   One messuage and one virgate was leased for seven years in May 1367; in December 1368 another was granted 'at farm'; and in May 1372 another virgate was leased for three years. In the June court of 1369 five virgates previously at lease were 'returned to the lady's hands' upon their expired term and then converted to the new tenancy, New College, Oxford, 3821.

[51]   These terms are best exemplified in the simultaneous expiry and re-grant of eleven virgates on exactly the same terms in the June court of 1369, New College, Oxford, 3821. For another example, Peter Smith was granted one virgate for 14s. per annum, a capon as an entry fine, owing heriot and suit of court, to hold for the term of the life of the lady of the manor, New College, Oxford, court held November 1375.

[52]   Alice held the manor from 1359 for her lifetime only, although the reversion was

the 35 customary virgates remained on hereditary villein tenure, while most of the rest were held on the cash-based life tenancy.

The evolution of this life tenancy after the death of Alice in 1382 is difficult to trace, because of a gap in the court-roll series after 1380. When the series begins again in the mid-fifteenth century, the description of the terms on which the former customary virgates were held is frustratingly terse: usually the formula is 'for himself according to the custom of the manor', without elaborating upon the exact nature of that custom. The absence of any reference to heirs is strongly suggestive of a tenure for the term a life. Occasionally conveyances stated that such tenancies were held at the will of the lord.[53] A list drawn up in 1485 of the rents owed by all tenanted virgates is silent on the nature of the tenancy.[54] However, seventeenth-century sources from Upper Heyford are clear that local copyholds were 'lifehold'; similarly, sixteenth-century copyholds at neighbouring Lower Heyford were held for two lives.[55] From all this evidence, it appears that, after a period of tenurial flux in the 1350s and 1360s, the majority of customary holdings at Upper Heyford had been converted to tenure for the term of a life by the early 1370s. It is highly likely that they remained as such thereafter.

Manorial accounts indicate a major decline in the land market during the 1380s, because in 1391 15 of the 35 virgates were abandoned, and, as a consequence, rental income had fallen to £12 17s. 2d., or 45% of its level in 1380–1.[56] However, in 1485 all 35 virgates were tenanted and held for cash rents, raising the rental income to £17 6s. 3d., and this level of rent remained constant until the seventeenth century.[57] Over the course of the fourteenth and fifteenth centuries the number of tenants fell markedly. In the 1340s 35 tenants held 35 virgates, yet there were 21 tenants in 1400 and just 11 in 1485.[58] The extent to which holdings were engrossed during the fifteenth century was considerable.

Incidents of villeinage

Heriot was the most frequent and enduring servile incident, surviving the conversion from hereditary villein tenure to life tenancies for money in the 1370s and then enduring into the sixteenth century (see table 9.4).

granted to New College in 1380 and acquired by them in 1382, *VCH Oxfordshire*, volume 6, p. 198.

[53] For example, New College, Oxford, 3824, courts held June 1466, May 1467, February 1469 and August 1488.

[54] New College, Oxford, 3825.

[55] *VCH Oxfordshire*, volume 6, pp. 188, 201.

[56] New College, Oxford, 6291 (1390–1).

[57] New College, Oxford, 3825; *VCH Oxfordshire*, volume 6, p. 200.

[58] New College, Oxford, 6273 (1342–3), 6299 (1399–1400), 3825 (1485).

9.4 Frequency of chevage, merchet, heriot, childwite and millsuit
at Upper Heyford, 1350 to 1499

Period	Chevage	Merchet	Heriot	Childwite	Millsuit
Pre-1348–9	/	/	/	X	/
1350–74	o	5	9	o	1
1375–99	o	2	7	o	o
1400–24	–	–	–	–	–
1425–49	–	–	–	–	–
1450–74	o	o	8	o	o
1475–99	o	o	12	o	1

/ = recorded X = not recorded pre-1348–9

A heriot of the best beast was rendered whenever a customary virgate was relinquished, whether *post mortem* or *inter vivos*. Discretion on whether to collect the heriot was exercised in individual cases. In December 1368 one horse was collected as a heriot after the death of John Heyward, but, upon the admission of his son to the holding, it was returned to him as a gesture to encourage him to stay there.[59] From the middle of the fifteenth century cash payments begin to appear, replacing the best beast, and a tenant who held more than one virgate was permitted to render just one heriot to cover them all, rather than one for each holding.[60] The latter reflects the growth of the engrossment of holdings and the continued challenges of finding and retaining tenants.

Millsuit also survived the wholesale conversion to contractual tenancies, although it was imposed very infrequently (see table 9.4). In December 1372 Richard Fisher and other tenants were presented for not milling at the lady's mill for the previous six months, but Richard countered that he was a freeman and therefore was not required to perform millsuit. The lady's counsel was sought, and in July 1373 it was decreed that all tenants holding land 'according to the custom of the manor' were required to mill at the lady's mill under a penalty of 40d. No other presentments are recorded until 1485, when two men were each amerced 2d. for 'milling their grain away from the mill of the lord without licence and without reason'.[61]

---

59 New College, Oxford, 3821, court held December 1368.

60 See, for example, court held April 1473, New College, Oxford, 3824.

61 New College, Oxford, 3825, court held July 1484: '*a molindeno domini sine licencia et sine ratione*'.

Merchet was regularly charged before the Black Death.[62] Seven present-ments and fines for merchet are recorded between 1350 and 1377 (see table 9.4), and the sums are generally high, between 6s. 8d. and 10s. each, which represents a sharp rise on the pre-plague average. In June 1371 two women were charged 13s. 4d. each, but the lady 'by her special grace' reduced the fine to 10s. Merchet is not recorded after 1377. The manor also allowed servile wills to be proven, without charge, again through 'the special grace' of the lady.[63]

The court paid little attention to servile migrants before the Black Death: there are no presentments for absence and just one payment for chevage.[64] After 1350 there were regular presentments for unauthorized absences from the manor, usually between three and five people each year, although chevage was never paid again (see table 9.5). The use of aliases complicates attempts to establish the total number of people thus presented, but it was no more than a dozen between 1350 and 1380. On each occasion the homage was ordered to attach flown serfs, but only three ever returned. Close relatives were occasionally directed to attach their kin, and the homage was some-times threatened (but never charged) with a penalty for failure to return them. The futility of most of the presentments is exemplified by the case of John Page, who was doggedly presented as absent for 30 years, but who never once paid chevage and never returned.[65] The last recorded presentment for absence was in 1380, although the court series is then disrupted, so we cannot know whether New College focused on absences when they first acquired the manor in 1382. However, just as with merchet, there was no interest in migrants at all when the series resumes again in the mid-fifteenth century.

Each standardized virgate on villein tenure owed 45 summer labour services per year, a mixture of summer week and harvest works, and they were valued at c.6s. per annum. Each virgate also rendered 12s. as money rent. In 1351 74% of these labour services were uncollectable, because the holdings which owed them were untenanted.[66] The introduction in the early 1360s of new cash tenancies, free from labour services, meant that these losses became permanent. In addition, tenants who still held their virgates on the old terms usually commuted their services for a cash payment each year through application to the manorial court. For example, in 1365 14 virgaters

---

[62] Ten are recorded in the 23 extant courts pre-1348–9, averaging 2s. 10d., New College, Oxford, 3821.

[63] New College, Oxford, 3821, courts held June and October 1371.

[64] 12d. chevage is recorded in the August court, 1347, New College, Oxford, 3821.

[65] New College, Oxford, 3823 and 3824.

[66] The 6s. value is from July 1367 court, New College, Oxford, 3821; New College, Oxford, 6279.

9.5 Recorded flight from Upper Heyford, 1350 to 1380

Year	Number of people presented for absence	Number of people charged for chevage
1350	1	0
1351	3	0
1353	3	0
1354	4	0
1355	3	0
1356	3	0
1362	3	0
1367	4	0
1368	4	0
1369	2	0
1371	5	0
1372	5	0
1373	5	0
1374	5	0
1375	5	0
1377	4	0
1378	4	0
1379	4	0
1380	5	0

each paid 5s. for release from their labour services for the year, and in 1367 nine virgaters each paid 6s. to do so.[67]

By the 1370s this combination of conversions to fixed-term tenancies and annual commutations at will had resulted in the virtual disappearance of labour services. The permanence of these arrangements is evident in the manorial *compoti* from the 1380s, which contain no works' accounts and no separate section for the sale of labour services. Instead, the rents and farms section of the account included money paid for 'the relaxation of works'.[68] A few harvest works were still owed. Even the grants of virgates on contractual tenancies from the 1360s included the requirement to perform a single mowing and a reaping service, which continued to be used. Manorial accounts from the 1380s and 1390s include payments for harvest expenses to 'men and women' reaping around 25 acres of the demesne corn as part of a 'great boonwork', and in the 1380s around one quarter of the demesne

[67] New College, Oxford, 3821, courts held June 1365 and July 1367.
[68] New College, Oxford, 6281 to 6287.

grain was reaped each harvest by such boon works (see table 9.6).[69] Failure
to perform labour services is recorded on just four occasions, three of them
in 1353.[70] The demesne was exploited directly until it was leased in the late
1390s.[71]

9.6 Demesne area harvested by labour services at Upper Heyford,
1380 to 1388

Year	Demesne sown area (acres)	Acres reaped by customary labour	Percentage reaped by customary labour	Percentage reaped by hired labour
1380–1	67.25	18	27%	73%
1383–4	73	27.5	38%	62%
1384–5	79.25	28	28%	72%
1386–7	94	20	21%	79%
1387–8	108.25	23	21%	79%

Source: New College, Oxford, 6281, 6283, 6285, 6286, 6287.

Tallage was levied before 1348–9, although not annually: for example, the
'customars' rendered 13s. 4d. in 1315–16 'and no more because of poverty',
most likely a reference to the severe famine that gripped the country that
year.[72] There is no clear evidence for the payment of tallage after the Black
Death in either account or court rolls. However, in August 1372 two 'assessors
(*taxatores*)' were amerced 6s. 8d. for contempt after refusing to undertake
their task. This was an exceptional, not a standing, manorial office, although
its precise purpose is unknown. Elsewhere, 'assessors' were associated with
the collection of tallage or recognition, and so this might have related to the
final, and unsuccessful, attempt to collect tallage at Upper Heyford.[73] If so,
it was foiled through direct peasant resistance, and the unwillingness of the
lady to press the matter.

[69] New College, Oxford, 6281 to 6287.
[70] Three tenants had not reaped in the harvest of 1353, court held November 1353.
The wholesale conversion to leasehold in the 1360s reduced the scope for refusals,
and just one more is recorded, when Thomas Fisher failed to show for two days
in the harvest despite a clear instruction from the bailiff, New College, Oxford,
3821, court held October 1373.
[71] New College, Oxford, 6299.
[72] The reference is from a court held in 9 Edward II. See also courts held February
1340, and January 1343, New College, Oxford, 3821.
[73] New College, Oxford, 3821, court held August 1372. For the appointment of
'assessors' to collect tallage or recognition on other manors, see pp. 183, 192.

Attitudes to serfdom

There are no fines for permission to enter holy orders, or to seek education or apprenticeships, and no evidence for the construction of servile genealogies. The decision in the early 1360s to convert to tenancies for a term coincided with increased activity in the management of personal servility, especially absentees. In early 1362 estate officials brought direct pressure to bear upon the close relatives of two flown serfs by threatening a penalty of 6s. 6d. unless the serfs returned to the manor and occupied customary land – however, the threat was not repeated, and nothing materialized.[74] In August 1362 Alicia, widow of John Maisterjohan, was ordered to be attached by body and chattels 'to make fealty at the will of the lady' after leaving the manor. She duly attended the October court and swore on oath that she would not leave, and that she would occupy a customary holding. At first, Alicia was true to her word, but by June 1368 she had left the manor after marrying one Walter Heynes of 'Duchenhall'. Court officials court sought the advice of the lady of the manor on the next steps, and still awaited instructions in 1372. Any resolution of the matter is not documented.[75]

The only other serfs who attracted attention in a manner similar to Alicia Maisterjohan were the Parkin brothers, William and John (alias Heyward), who were presented as flown in 1367 and who returned to the manor in April 1368. Both had been absent from the manor for some while, but in June 1368 they formally submitted themselves to the lady as her *nativi* and agreed to hold customary holdings: John was duly admitted into a messuage and virgate on the old terms. In October 1368 a list of their children was recorded in the court roll, then John died in December 1368, and his eldest son, John, succeeded him into the holding. The lady waived the entry fine, and immediately returned the heriot (a horse) to John junior. However, the family matriarch, the widowed Agnes, was required to swear in court that her children were of full age, and to guarantee that none would either leave the manor or marry without licence.[76]

At first glance, this sequence of events looks like an attempt to impose serfdom in a novel and demeaning way, and a local example of the wider 'seigniorial reaction'. Upon closer inspection, however, a more nuanced and interesting interpretation suggests itself.[77] The court recorded that the brothers' lengthy absence from the manor before 1368 was due to their employment on the nearby manor of Rousham (Oxfordshire), which belonged to Sir William Shareshull, the legal architect of the Statute of

---

[74]   New College, Oxford, 3821, court held April 1362.

[75]   New College, Oxford, 3821 and 3822.

[76]   New College, Oxford, 3821 and 3822.

[77]   This case is discussed in detail in M. Bailey, 'Was there a seigniorial reaction in England between 1350 and 1381?' (forthcoming).

Labourers – an arrangement which carried the approval of the previous lord of Heyford, Robert de Lisle, who was Alice's de Mauro's brother. In other words, the various parties had struck a deal to cover this absence, which may have included a commitment from the Heywards to return one day. In the early 1370s, their children reneged on the deal, abandoning their holdings and emigrating, and manorial officials were powerless to prevent them. Thus this case study does not provide a convincing example of seigniorial asser-tiveness and oppressed serfs in the wake of the Black Death. If anything, it illustrates that novel seigniorial manipulation of serfs was rare, short-lived and unsuccessful; that serfs made personal choices that could involve collab-oration with their lords; that landlords competed with each other openly and pragmatically for both labourers and tenants; and that any evaluation of the so-called 'seigniorial reaction' should concentrate less on types of behaviour and more on their scale and duration.

Summary of chronology and key indicators
By the mid-1370s personal servility was in serious retreat: childwite and chevage were never paid, and merchet was rare. Around the same time only one quarter of the 35 customary virgates were still held in villeinage. Even then, the use of 'in villeinage' did not appear in conveyances, nearly all labour services were converted to money rent, tallage ceased to be owed, and millsuit was exceptional. The majority of virgates had been converted to a fixed-term tenancy for the life of the lady of the manor, owing a straight monetary rent, two nominal seasonal services, millsuit and heriot.[78] Villeinage had effec-tively disappeared. In the 1370s the two main practical differences between a virgate held in villeinage and one held on the tenancy for a term was the annual rent level and security of tenure: villein tenures had security of inher-itance, but paid around 7s. rent more each year. By the 1480s all virgates were now held for money rent 'according to the custom of the manor', without any detail about the nature of that custom – it was almost certainly a tenancy for life.

The data for land values at Upper Heyford are rudimentary (see table 9.7). In the 1340s each virgate had owed 12s. per annum, together with labour services rated at 6s. This notional cash value of 18s. per virgate in the 1340s can be compared with the mean rent level charged on new grants of virgates on money rents in subsequent decades: 11s. 2d. in the 1360s, 12s. 6d. in the 1370s, and 9s. 5d. in the 1480s.[79] Thus land values fell nearly 40% between the 1340s and 1360s, then stabilized in the 1370s, before declining again by the

---

[78] New College, Oxford, 6281 (account for 1380–1).

[79] The mean values for the 1360s and 1370s are based on the annual money rent charged on all new grants of virgates on contractual tenancies recorded in the court rolls. The mean for the 1480s is based upon a rental of all 35 virgates

late fifteenth century. The correlation between the fall in land values, and the main changes to both tenures and personal servility, is strong.

9.7 Rental values of virgates granted on contractual tenancies
at Upper Heyford, 1340 to 1489

Decade	Value per virgate
1340–9	18s. 0d.
1360–9	11s. 2d.
1370–9	12s. 6d.
1480–9	9s. 5d.

Failures to perform labour services were insignificant. The collapse of labour services in the 1350s pre-dated the leasing of the demesne in the 1390s. Recorded emigration was not heavy: just five different men fled the manor between 1350 and 1355, and a further four men and one woman between 1367 and 1371. The migration of five serfs in the early 1350s, when around 23 of the 35 virgates remained unoccupied, compounded the losses of population in the Black Death, but over half of the customary landholdings of the manor would still have been untenanted even if those serfs had stayed as tenants. The next recorded surge in departures occurred in the late 1360s, when many virgates were now occupied (albeit on fixed-term tenancies). The decision in the early 1360s to convert the twenty or so abandoned virgates from villein tenure to tenure for the term of a life largely free of labour services was resoundingly successful in increasing the occupancy of customary land. Yet over the next ten years the same manorial administration tried to force its flown serfs to return to Upper Heyford to hold customary land on the old terms. The severance of the close link between unfree tenure and unfree status thus resulted in the more aggressive management of personal servility during the 1360s. The management of fugitives at this time, and the surge in recorded migrants in the late 1360s, were linked to the lady of the manor's unsuccessful attempts to increase the occupancy of virgates in villeinage. Ironically, the attractiveness of acquiring a virgate on villein tenure at Upper Heyford was greatly diminished by the presence of many life tenancies for money rent on the manor.

The inability to find tenants for more than one half of the customary virgates for the whole of the 1350s, and the sizeable fall in land values between the 1340s and 1360s, testify to a severe shortage of tenants in the aftermath of the Black Death at Upper Heyford. The scale of recorded migration in

documented in 1485. No details of the rents of individual virgates are contained within the manorial accounts, which just provide grand totals.

the 1350s was sufficient to reinforce, but insufficient to dictate, the course of tenurial change. At least three serfs left the manor in the 1360s in preference to staying and holding virgates on villein tenure. Thus the loss of tenants in 1348–9, and the shortage of replacements during the 1350s, was the single most important factor in the decay of villeinage within a generation of the Black Death at Upper Heyford.

Conclusion

Tingewick and Upper Heyford were classic medium/large manors, each with hundreds of acres of customary land organized into large, standardized holdings. On both manors the use of 'in villeinage' had disappeared from conveyances within a generation of the Black Death. Severe shortages of tenants in the 1350s at Upper Heyford resulted in experimentation with a variety of forms of tenure, including leases and tenures for a term, and in the 1360s there were some attempts to re-convert some of these contractual tenancies back to villeinage. However, by the 1370s, after this period of flux, the majority of customary holdings had been converted to tenure for the term of a life, and remained as such thereafter. In contrast, demand for land in the immediate aftermath of the Black Death had been more robust at Tingewick, where the vast majority of customary land continued to be held as hereditary tenures. However, the old incidents of villeinage were quickly dropped, so that by 1380 heriot was the only servile incident still attached to these tenures.

Both the prior of St Faith, and the Seymours, struggled to maintain villeinage on these manors in the third quarter of the fourteenth century. Concessions on the main incidents of villeinage were made at Tingewick, while villein tenure was converted to fixed-term cash tenancies at Upper Heyford. Hence villein tenure in its original form had virtually disappeared from both manors by the time New College acquired them. The college did not attempt to turn back the tenurial clock by re-imposing week works or imposing any other servile dues on landholdings, instead, it accepted the local tenurial conditions – tenures for a term at Heyford, and tenures by inheritance at Tingewick, mainly for money rent – as it found them. There is some evidence in the late 1390s and 1400s for closer and more active management of personal servility at Tingewick, which must have reflected a deliberate attempt to tighten up this area soon after the college's acquisition of the manor in 1391.[80] It was probably prompted by some local difficul-

---

[80] Similar signs are evident at Great Horwood in the 1390s, Tompkins, 'Great Horwood', pp. 206–7.

ties finding tenants, although it might have reflected a strong institutional conviction about servility.

New College was certainly active in upholding personal servility well into the sixteenth century on its Wiltshire manors and, as a consequence, it has acquired a reputation among historians for conservative lordship.[81] Yet this case study shows that the college did not persist with policies that were aggressive towards serfs across the whole of its estate. Personal servility did not feature prominently during the first half of the fifteenth century at either Tingewick or Upper Heyford, and, despite a final attempt to revive chevage at Tingewick in the 1440s, it had disappeared entirely by mid-century.[82] The contrast between the disappearance of serfdom on these two manors, and its survival and active management into the sixteenth century on the college's Wiltshire manors, underlines the real difficulties in maintaining a unitary and fixed policy towards serfdom across the whole of an estate. The difficulties were partly a consequence of the wide geographical dispersal of the estate: local circumstances and conditions affecting serfdom were very different from one area to another. Yet they were predicated upon the success or otherwise of previous lords in preserving villeinage on the manors before New College acquired them.

William Wyckham acquired manors for New College as, when, and where the opportunities to do so presented themselves. As the college added each new manor to its portfolio, it had to take the state of serfdom as it found it and adopt a pragmatic approach. Serfdom could not be re-imposed on those manors where it had already disappeared, and it could not be sustained for much longer on those manors where it was already severely weakened. Where serfdom remained a strong feature of the manors it acquired in the 1380s and 1390s, New College proved willing and able to sustain it.

[81]   Savine, 'Bondmen under the Tudors', p. 277; Hare, 'Lords and their tenants', p. 22.
[82]   This interest in migrants in the early 1440s was probably an estate-wide policy. The college acquired the manor of Great Horwood around this time, and made a 'half-hearted' attempt to enforce personal servility, Tompkins, 'Great Horwood', pp. 206–7.

10

The Abbot of Bury St Edmunds

The abbey of Bury St Edmunds was one of the wealthiest and most renowned Benedictine monasteries in medieval England. Its extensive estates were scattered across East Anglia, but were mainly concentrated around the abbey in west Suffolk, where it also enjoyed additional judicial powers through the Liberty of St Edmund. Its landed endowment was internally subdivided between each of the abbey's main obedientiaries, who ran their allotted manors independently. The abbey of Bury St Edmunds is often depicted as a highly conservative landlord, whose relationship with its tenants was characterized by recurrent conflict.[1] Certainly, the strong presence of villeinage on its manors contrasted starkly with its relative absence, and the high levels of freedom, throughout most of East Anglia. This case study focuses upon two large manors, Chevington (Suffolk) and Fornham All Saints (Suffolk), with a high proportion of customary land. Both formed part of the internal estate of the abbot himself, which comprised around a dozen demesne manors, and both were situated close to Bury itself. Thus they provide an opportunity to observe the management of serfdom on two classic manors held by a powerful and conservative lord.

Chevington[2]

Customary land tenures
In the 1270s the manor of Chevington comprised around 340 (arable) acres of villein land, nearly 450 acres of free land, and 460 acres of demesne arable.[3] In the 1340s the former were organized into four 30-*acreware tenementa*, fifteen 15-*acreware*, four 8-*acreware* and four 'coterills' (cottagers), all held

---

[1] M.D. Lobel, 'The 1327 rising at Bury St Edmunds and the subsequent trial', *Proceedings of the Suffolk Institute of Archaeology and History*, 21 (1933), pp. 215–31; R.S. Gottfried, *Bury St Edmunds and the urban crisis: 1290–1539* (Princeton, 1982), pp. 231–6; M. Statham, *The book of Bury St Edmunds* (Buckingham, 1988), pp. 55–7; Schofield, 'Robert Kyng', pp. 50–7.

[2] This study of Chevington is based on c.220 courts from the period 1352–1500, SROB E3/15.3/1.1a to 1.40(b); 40 accounts from 1351 to 1461, SROB E3/15.3/2.9 to 2.42; and two rentals dating from 1389, 1478–9, SROB E3/15.3/3.1 and 3.2.

[3] Hervey, ed., *Pinchbeck Register*, volume II, pp. 155–8. This extent gives the demesne as 460 acres of arable.

'in villeinage for services and works'.[4] They were liable for childwite, heriot, merchet, millsuit, entry fine and recognition, and rendered nominal cash rents and a range of labour services, including three categories of ploughing services, and an annually variable number of week and harvest works.[5] Each 30-*acreware* holding owed around 130 week, and 80 harvest, works annually, each 15- and 8-*acreware* holding owed around 60 week works, and the coterills owed 36 works: the level of harvest services was modest for the smaller holdings, around a dozen each.[6] The burden of labour services was heavy: in total, the demesne could expect to have up to 2,000 week, and 1,000 harvest, works at its disposal each year.[7]

The Black Death made a severe and sustained impact on customary landholding. In the 1340s all 23 of the standardized *acreware tenementa* had been occupied, but by the end of 1352 only four were tenanted on the old terms, and hardly any heirs had claimed their landed inheritance.[8] The level of occupancy remained low for the next decade, with just five of the 23 occupied on villein tenure in 1360 and nine in 1366.[9] Put another way, in 1360 – eleven years after the pestilence had struck – nearly two thirds of the main villein holdings were still untenanted.[10] Hence the abbot of Bury St Edmunds faced a mounting crisis of landholding at Chevington. Some

---

4   For examples of this phrasing, SROB E3/15.3/1.1b, court held March 1353; E3/15.3/1.6b, court held January 1359; and E3/15.3/1.7b, court held March 1363.

5   The exact annual rent owed by each category of holding is not known, but in 1336–7 rents of assize totalled a mere £4 16s. 1½d. This figure is low considering that it includes rents for peasant holdings which amounted to comfortably in excess of 400 acres.

6   See, for example, the works' account in SROB E3/15.3/2.2d (1336–7).

7   The exact number of works was variable from year to year, because tenants were required to perform a fixed number of services per week between moveable religious feasts.

8   In the 1330s and 1340s two of the 23 holdings were leased each year for money rent, the other 21 were held on villein tenure, SROB E3/15.3/2.2d to 2.7. The works' account of 1351–2 records 2 ex 4 30-*acreware* holdings abandoned in the lord's hands, 13 ex 15-*acreware* and 4 ex 4 8-*acreware*, SROB E3/15.3/2.9. The court held in December 1352 notes the failure of heirs to take holdings, which thus remained abandoned in the lord's hands, SROB E3/15.3/1.1a.

9   The court rolls document the trickle of heirs admitted into holdings during the 1350s: for example, the admission to one 15-*acreware* holding in 1353, and to another in 1356, in both cases held 'in villeinage for services and works' and rendering a 5s. entry fine, SROB E3/15.3/1.1b, court held July 1353, and 1.3, court held November 1356. In some cases, the holdings were later abandoned again. The works' account in 1359–60 records 3 ex 4 30-*acreware*, 11 ex 15 15-*acreware*, and 4 ex 4 8-*acreware* in the lord's hands, SROB E3/15.2/2.10b. And in 1365–6 3 ex 4 30-*acreware*, 7 ex 15 15-*acreware*, and 4 ex 8-*acreware* were still abandoned, SROB E3/15.3/2.10d.

10 In 1360 eight of the 23 were tenanted, of which five were on villein tenure and three on leaseholds for years.

concessions had been offered, such as a heavily reduced entry fine in 1356 to encourage Robert Wynston to re-occupy the 30-*acreware tenementum* he had earlier abandoned, but otherwise there were few inducements to prospective tenants, such as temporary remission of labour services or conversions of vacant *tenementa* to leasehold.[11] The second visitation of pestilence in the late summer of 1361, which killed at least two free, and three customary, tenants in Chevington, proved to be a watershed.[12] In 1362 one empty 30-*acreware* holding was converted to leasehold for a term of six years, an annual rent of 40s. and no labour services, and in 1366 more grants of complete holdings at lease followed.[13] Between 1351 and 1361 rental income from the lease of peasant holdings had generated 29s. per annum, but thereafter income from this source increased rapidly to £5 8s. in 1366, then to £8 11s. in 1374.[14] This significantly increased the total income received from peasant rents, from just over £5 in the late 1330s to nearly £10 in the mid-1360s.[15] By 1380 16 of the 23 *acreware tenementa* were held on leasehold, generating rent of £11 17s. 10d.[16] Most of these leases were held for cash rents only, usually for terms of seven to ten years and with a clause requiring the proper maintenance of the buildings. One tenant held a 15-*acreware tenementum* for a modest rent of 5s. per annum and a requirement to perform harvest works, rather than the usual 10s. and no works, but few others found the prospect of any labour services attractive.[17]

Thus, by the early 1380s, around 70% of the former customary holdings were leased. The rental charge per acre on leaseholds had fallen 18% between the 1340s and 1370s, but thereafter held steady (see graph 10.1). The standard term of a seven-year lease was gradually supplanted during the first half of the fifteenth century by 10- to 20-year leases, and by mid-century some

---

[11]　The Wynston example is from SROB E3/15.3/1.3, court held November 1356. Only 27 acres of customary land are recorded as held at leasehold in 1360, E3/15.3/2.10b (1359–60).

[12]　SROB E3/15.3/1.7a, court held September 1361.

[13]　SROB E3/15.3/1.7b, court held December 1362, and /1.9b, court held October 1366.

[14]　SROB E3/15.3/2.9 (1351–2) to /2.10c (1360–1); E3/15.3/2.10d (1365–6), and /10e (1373–4).

[15]　In the late 1330s rents of assize generated £4 16s. 1½d., and the lease of one villein holding added 10s., SROB E3/15.3/2.2d. In 1365–6 rents of assize were the same, minus 10s. for decayed (uncollectable) rents, and income from leases of villein land yielded £5 8s. 0d., E3/15.3/2.10d.

[16]　SROB E3/15.3/2.11 (1379–80).

[17]　See SROB E3/15.3/1.12, court held November 1367. Other, rare, examples of leaseholds paying reduced cash rents and owing some (usually harvest) services can be found in courts held October 1394, E3/15.3/1.29b; July 1395, E3/15.3/1.30; and the leet of 1402, E3/15.3/1.34a.

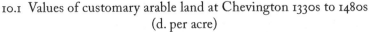

10.1 Values of customary arable land at Chevington 1330s to 1480s
(d. per acre)

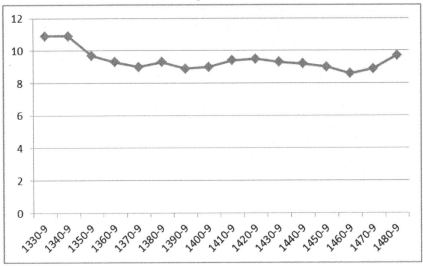

Mean decennial value of customary arable land at lease.

40-year leases were appearing.[18] The format of leasehold changed little, except that from the 1410s some lessees gained the ability to assign the lease to others during its term.[19]

In the early 1380s most of the c.30% of customary holdings which had not been converted to leasehold were still held on an hereditary villein tenure. The formula used in their conveyance had changed during the course of the 1360s, when the phrase 'in villeinage for services and works' was replaced by 'holding to him and his heirs at the will of the lord for services and customs'.[20] This amended wording was retained thereafter with little change. In the early fifteenth century, for example, the format was 'to hold to him and his at the will of the lord by the rod for services and customs', although

[18] For example, new leases for 20 years were granted in courts held October 1417 and June 1418, SROB E3/15.3/1.34b, and 40 year leases were issued in the court held May 1460, SROB E3/15.3/1.35.

[19] Evidenced by the grant to a tenant 'and his assignees', see, for example, courts held May and October 1414, SROB E3/15.3/1.34b. Prior to this, tenants had to seek seigniorial permission, and pay a small fee, to assign a leasehold to another tenant during the term of the lease, see, for example, court held October 1396, E3/15.3/1.30.

[20] SROB E3/15.3/1.12, court held November 1367; and E3/15.3/1.14, court held June 1371.

10.1 Last recorded date of incidents of villeinage at Chevington and
Fornham All Saints, 1349 to 1499

Manor	Capit.	Chev.	Pres. for absence	Child.	Heriot	Merchet	Millsuit	Recog.	Tallage
Chevington 1350–1499	None	1403	1418	1387	1440	1420	1358	1470*	None
Fornham 1350–1423	None	1395	1399	1376	1394	1397	None	1400*	None

* Presentments only

occasionally the phrase 'and to his assignees' was inserted.[21] In the early 1390s
the manorial court referred to the existence of 'copies' of the terms of landholding.[22]

In the last quarter of the fifteenth century a significant change occurred
to the nature of customary tenancies. As leases expired they were increasingly re-granted as a hereditary fee farm, which secured in perpetuity for
tenants the replacement of servile incidents with a money rent and the right
of inheritance. The first such grant had been made in 1439, when an abandoned 15-*acreware tenementum* was granted to John Powle and to 'his heirs
and assignees at fee farm by the rod for 12s. per annum', owing suit of court
and 6d. entry fine; a second grant, on the same terms, was made in 1446.[23]
Although conventional leases continued to be granted during the mid-
fifteenth century, from the 1470s fee farms took over rapidly. For example,
in 1473, when William Spede's lease of a 15-*acreware tenementum* expired,
the land was re-granted on a fee farm to John Hakwrong, 'his heirs and
assignees by the rod at the will of the lord according to the custom of the
manor, rendering to the lord 10s. 6d. per annum and suit of court'. Further
grants soon followed, in most cases representing direct conversions upon the
expiry of a lease.[24]

Incidents of villeinage

Millsuit was enforced fitfully in the 1350s, and then abandoned after 1358
(see table 10.1). Childwite was imposed at the standard rate of 2s. 8d. on
seven occasions after the Black Death, but not at all between 1361 and 1381.
Four of the seven levies were concentrated in the 1380s, including the last

---

[21] For an example of the conventional wording, see SROB E3/15.3/1.34b, court held
1415; for examples of the extension to assignees, see courts held July 1435, and
February 1439, SROB E3/15.3/1.35.

[22] SROB E3/15.3/1.28, court held June 1392.

[23] SROB E3/15.3/1.35, courts held June 1439 and February 1446.

[24] SROB E3/15.3/1.35, courts held May 1473, April 1474, November 1476, May 1479.

one in 1387 (see table 10.2). Merchet was not imposed extensively, scarcely survived the fourteenth century, and eight of the thirteen recorded incidents were actually for marrying without licence. Fines tended to be modest, lying somewhere between 3s. and 6s. 8d., with a mean of 4s. for merchet and 4s. 11d. for marriages without licence. The average charge for unlicensed marriages rose across the late fourteenth century (see table 10.3), indicating a deliberate policy designed to encourage the proactive reporting of marriages. Unusually, the manorial administration managed to extract a payment of 5s. 4d. from Joanna Harfoot in 1384, even though she had departed the manor to live in Culford (Suffolk); their ability to extract payment was probably helped by the fact that the manor of Culford was also part of the abbot of St Edmunds' estate.[25]

10.2 Frequency of merchet, heriot, childwite and millsuit
at Chevington, 1350 to 1499

Period	Merchet	Heriot	Childwite	Millsuit
Pre-1349	/	/	/	/
1350–74	4	11	3	12
1375–99	8	2	4	0
1400–24	1	4	0	0
1425–49	0	1	0	0
1450–74	0	0	0	0
1475–99	0	0	0	0

Merchet, heriot and childwite fines only (including if waived); millsuit includes fines and presentments./ = recorded pre-1349, X = not recorded pre-1349.

10.3 Incidence of merchet, and mean size of levy,
at Chevington, 1350 to 1499

Period	Number of merchets	Mean levy	Number of marriages without licence	Mean levy
1350–1374	2	48d.	2	36d.
1375–1399	2	52d.	6	67d.
1400–1424	1	40d.	0	0
1425–1449	0	0	0	0
1450–1474	0	0	0	0
1475–1499	0	0	0	0

Heriot was levied only upon the death of a customary tenant, but it was not applied to leases or fee farms. Most renders between 1350 and 1401

[25] SROB E3/15.3/1.21, court held July 1384.

comprised a cash payment of 2s. 8d. or 3s., and thereafter only the best beast was claimed. Heriot hardly featured after 1400, withering as leaseholds displaced customary tenures. Entry fines were levied on villein tenure and fee farms, but not on leaseholds. Levels of entry fines varied from one land transaction to another, indicating that the court took account of individual circumstances, especially in the immediate aftermath of the Black Death. No court rolls survive before 1352, but it is likely that the level of entry fines fell after 1349, given the difficulties recruiting tenants, and a continued fall in the 1360s and 1370s is strongly evident (see table 10.4). The small size of the sample after this date reduces the reliability of the data, but the recovery in the level of fines in the fifteenth century, and the emergence of a standard rate of 24d. per acre, indicates the stabilization of the local land market and the popularity of fee farms.[26]

10.4 Entry fines per acre for standardized villein *tenementa* at Chevington, 1350 to 1489

Decade	Number of transactions	Entry fine per acre
1350–9	13	11d.
1360–9	6	8d.
1370–9	1	2d.
1380–9	1	8d.
1390–9	1	8d.
1400–9	1	12d.
1410–9	3	28d.
1420–9	1	5d.
1430–9	7	10d.
1440–9	1	20d.
1460–9	4	21d.
1470–9	3	24d.
1480–9	1	24d.

In the 1340s the burden of labour services was onerous, especially upon the four 30-*acreware tenementa*. The majority of week, and the vast majority of harvest, works were routinely deployed upon tasks on the demesne (see table 10.5). After the Black Death the number of works available collapsed with the abandonment of many of the large customary holdings, although the manor continued to use most of those that were still available. Even so, by the 1380s barely one fifth of week works, and one quarter of harvest works, were utilized. When the demesne was finally leased in 1398, the remaining

---

[26] C. Dyer, 'A Suffolk farmer in the fifteenth century', *Agricultural History Review*, 55 (2007), pp. 10–12.

10.5 Utilization of main labour services at Chevington, 1336 to 1461

Year	Week Works Allowed/Sold/Used			Harvest Works Allowed/Sold/Used			Demesne Sown Area (acres)
1336–7	33%	10%	57%	11%	15%	66%	512¾
1339–40	34%	5%	61%	25%	13%	64%	495
1351–2	51%	4%	45%	28%	20%	59%	423½
1352–3	56%	4%	42%	28%	1%	76%	439½
1359–60	39%	6%	55%	16%	81%	0	444
1365–6	55%	5%	40%	[ms. damaged]			475½
1373–4	68%	1%	31%	[ms. damaged]			368
1379–80	68%	17%	15%	79%	0	21%	368
1381–2	92%	0	8%	80%	0	20%	409
1382–3	82%	0	18%	80%	0	20%	444
1383–4	80%	0	20%	73%	1%	26%	362
1386–7	75%	0	25%	76%	0	24%	365
1391–2	82%	1%	17%	71%	0	29%	262
1392–3	79%	0	21%	71%	1%	28%	289
1394–5	80%	0	20%	77%	0	23%	253
1395–6	73%	0	27%	77%	0	23%	242
1396–7	78%	2%	20%	74%	0	26%	254
1398–9	None			None			Leased
1400–1	None			None			Leased
1406–7	None			None			Leased
1409–10	None			None			Leased
1414–15	None			None			Leased
1416–17	None			None			Leased
1419–20	None			None			173
1421–2	None			None			Leased
1437–8	None			None			Leased
1449–50	None			None			Leased
1456–7	None			None			Leased
1460–1	None			None			Leased

Source: SROB E3/15.3/2.2 (d) to E3/15.3/2.42.

week works were commuted for £4 8s. 4d., and they were never deployed again.[27] Some harvest works were still utilized. As the number of *tenementa* held on villein tenure declined further in the fifteenth century, and by extension the number of liable services fell, so receipts from sales of works dropped to 74s. 2d. in 1416, and then to 49s. 9d. in 1455.[28]

[27] SROB E3/15.3/2.22.
[28] SROB E3/15.3/2.28; E3/15.3/2.39.

10.6 Incidence of recorded non-performance of labour services
at Chevington, 1352 to 1427

Year	Non-Performance of Labour Services
1352	1 withholds, 2 reap badly
1354	3 withhold
1356	6 withhold, 3 plough badly
1357	2 withhold, 2 refuse, 2 plough badly
1358	7 withhold
1359	1 withholds
1360	1 withholds, 1 refuses to plough, 4 collect corn badly, 1 ploughs badly
1361	2 withhold
1362	2 withhold
1365	1 withholds, 3 plough badly
1367	2 withhold, 2 collect lord's corn badly
1370	1 withholds
1371	1 withholds, 1 works badly
1372	3 withhold, 3 collect lord's corn badly
1373	1 withholds
1374	5 withhold
1375	18 refuse to reap
1378	3 withhold
1383	1 withholds
1384	1 withholds
1386	1 withholds, 1 reaps badly
1387	1 withholds
1390	2 withhold
1393	3 withhold
1394	3 withhold
1396	1 withholds
1404	4 withhold
1411	4 refuse to perform boon works
1412	7 refuse to perform boon works
1416	9 refuse to perform boon works
1427	2 withhold

These are recorded amercements (including pardons), not presentments.

Peasant resistance to labour services after 1350 was sustained yet low key, in the sense that cases of non-performance are recorded in many years between 1350 and 1400, but they mainly comprised isolated and minor actions by one or two individuals (see table 10.6). Likewise, the level of amercement charged was not high, usually between 3d. and 12d. per person. A rise in resistance to labour services occurred between 1356 and 1358, at a time when the peasant labour force was still reeling from the disruption caused by the Black Death. Many of the cases between 1352 and 1372 involved tenants who attended the labour service as required, but then worked badly or slowly. Collective resistance against labour services was uncommon, and confined to a substantial protest against harvest works by 18 tenants in 1375, and to lesser, joint, protests between 1412 and 1416 against the same. The cases recorded after the leasing of the demesne in 1398 related overwhelmingly to specific services, such as the 'alebene' and boon works owed by free and molland tenants, and by small numbers of leaseholders, not just villein tenants. Although no targeted opposition to labour services is recorded in the summer of 1381, the proportion of labour services acknowledged as uncollectable by the authorities jumped from 68% in 1379–80 to 92% in 1381–2, indicating that the manorial officials recognized the prudence of not utilizing them in the months after the Revolt.[29]

10.7 Incidence of chevage, and mean size of levy, at Chevington,
1350 to 1500

Period	Number of chevage cases	Mean fine per case
1350–1374	8	8.6d.
1375–1399	66	8.1d.
1400–1424	12	3.7d.
1425–1449	0	0
1450–1474	0	0
1475–1500	0	0

A standard charge of 40s. recognition was due from the homage of Chevington whenever a new abbot of Bury St Edmunds was elected. It was raised in 1362 without any difficulty, but there is no record of its imposition in 1383 upon the controversial election of Abbot John Timworth, which had fanned the flames of local discontent in the build-up to the Peasants' Revolt of 1381.[30] Recognition was restored with the election of William Cratfield in 1389, although only 10s. was actually paid and repeated demands for the shortfall of 30s. went unheeded.[31] Recognition was again requested in 1415, 1429, 1446 and 1470, but the tenants resisted the demand with increasing

---

[29] SROB E3/15.3/1.20, court held September 1381.
[30] SROB E3/15.3/1.7b, court held December 1362; and E3/15.3/1.21 and 1.22. For Timworth and the Revolt, see Gottfried, *Bury St Edmunds and the urban crisis*, pp. 232–3.
[31] SROB E3/15.3/1.28, courts held October 1390 and November 1391.

vehemence, and it is unlikely that it was ever paid on any of these occasions (see below).

The manor routinely presented migrant serfs for absence, although chevage was rare before the 1370s. The combined total of presentments and chevage payments peaked between 1388 and 1396, then chevage ceased abruptly and finally in 1403 (see table 10.8). The mean size of chevage remained constant at around 8d. during the second half of the fourteenth century, then dropped to 3.7d. just before disappearing in the early fifteenth century (see table 10.7). For a period (1365 to 1387) chevage payments were recorded in the annual *compoti* rather than the court rolls, and the shift to the latter coincided with a substantial rise in the volume of both presentments for absence and charges for chevage. This follows the realisation that landlords could manage absence better through their courts.[32]

The tactics deployed in managing departed serfs varied over time. In the early 1350s and the 1370s the court's quest for information was low key, involving little more than an instruction to the homage to attach known absentees.[33] At other times, the court was more persistent in its demands for information, and brought pressure to bear on residents to force the return of migrants. For example, in 1356 the court ordered the seizure of the goods and chattels of John Wynston, who lived close by at Chedburgh, and it also ordered a further six, named, migrants to find pledges from among the resident population to act as guarantors for their return.[34] Wynston took the threat seriously, because he attended a subsequent court to agree to stay in Chevington in future; the abbot's administrators insisted upon the additional insurance of three pledges for his compliance and the threat of a 40s. penalty.[35] Similarly, the spike of presentments in the April court of 1381 reflects a sudden change to a very aggressive approach, including the threat of a communal 10s. fine if the homage failed to produce migrants at the next court; in 1389 a personal pledge was amerced 3d. in successive courts for his failure to secure the return of one absentee; and, in the same year, William Riche paid chevage to formalize his absence, yet he was still required to return to the next leet under the threat of a £5 penalty.[36] The tougher approach proved successful, judging by the rise in the number of presentments and chevage payments in the late 1380s and 1390s (see table 10.8).

---

[32]   SROB E3/15.3/2.10d to 2.17.

[33]   See, for example, SROB E3/15.3/1.1a and 1.1b, and /1.16, 1.19a and 1.19b.

[34]   SROB E3/15.3/1.3 and 1.4, courts held June and November 1356.

[35]   SROB E3/15.3/1.5, court held September 1357.

[36]   SROB E3/15.3/1.19d, court held April 1381; /1.26, court held July 1389.

10.8 Recorded flight from Chevington, 1352 to 1418

Year	Number of people presented for absence	Number of people charged for chevage
1352	5	0
1353	4	1
1356	8	0
1357	8	1
1361	1	0
1362	1	0
1363	1	0
1365	0	1*
1366	0	2*
1369	1	—
1370	1	—
1372	1	—
1373	1	3*
1374	1	—
1375	1	—
1378	1	—
1379	0	3*
1381	12	2*
1382	0	2*
1383	9	2*
1384	6	1*
1385	5	1*
1386	6	2*
1387	3	1*
1388	8	7
1389	6	6
1390	5	9
1391	11	5
1392	9	4
1393	12	6
1394	0	5
1396	4	10
1400	0	3
1401	0	3
1402	2	3
1403	0	3
1418	2	0

* Between 1365 and 1387 chevage payments were recorded in the manorial account.

Attitudes to serfdom

There were no payments for permission to educate, to serve apprentice-ships or to enter holy orders, and no compilation of serf genealogies. Villein tenures and personal servility had all but disappeared by c.1400. These bare facts appear to indicate a pragmatic approach to serfdom at Chevington. Yet the manorial court rolls also yield examples of the aggressive management of fugitives, and a stubborn insistence upon the payment of recognition long after all other pecuniary customs had lapsed, which are indicative of a hard line on serfdom.

This mixed approach to villeinage, in which the lord combined a broadly conciliatory approach with targeted areas of challenge, is exemplified by a case in 1358. John Page had been employed as a worker on the lord's demesne [*famulus*], but then his father, Walter, was presented for removing him from the manor to work elsewhere. John returned to his employment with the lord immediately, swearing an oath that he would remain on the demesne and be available 'at the will of the lord and his bailiffs'.[37] At one level, this is an illustration of aggressive lordship. The abbot's officials were using the general terms of the Statute of Labourers to strengthen their position to retrieve a villein who had departed in mid-contract, and then subjecting him to a demeaning oath confirming his status in front of the whole court. Yet, at another level, the handling of this incident was pragmatic. The same officials had chosen to handle this case through the manorial court, rather than to send it on to the higher court of the Justices of Labourers, and they also chose to pardon both Walter and John, rather than to amerce them, despite the fact that John was in clear breach of his contract. Thus, from their perspective, they were seeking to promote some goodwill by dealing with the matter locally, expeditiously and lightly. This case also exemplifies the terminological and evidentiary problems in determining the existence or not of a seigniorial reaction. Do we interpret this as an example of a landlord exploiting the terms of the Statute of Labourers to help him impose a new form of servitude upon his manor, or should our interpretation be altogether more nuanced?

Forceful handling of migrant serfs is evident in two waves during the second half of the fourteenth century. From the late 1350s manorial officials began to target individuals whom they suspected of itchy feet, at the time when the difficulties in finding tenants for many vacant customary holdings were protracted. Between 1362 and 1364 three people – John Porchet, Joanna Goding, and Richard le Maister – were compelled to find pledges to stand surety that they would neither permanently depart the manor nor remove themselves from the lord's service, and, additionally, they were threatened

---

[37] SROB E3/15.3/1.6a, court held in Easter week, 1358.

with sizeable penalties of £20, £5 and £10 respectively.[38] The official bark was worse than its bite. The only case of any action being taken against a fugitive was the seizure of chattels on a single occasion; the threats of penalties soon disappeared, and none were actually imposed.[39]

The second wave began in April 1381, when the manorial court suddenly paid a renewed interest in the whereabouts of flown serfs, to a degree that is striking and unusual. This burst of interest was due to the personal initiative of John de Lakenheath, a monk who was active in estate administration during the vacancy that followed the death in 1379 of Abbot John de Brinkley.[40] His managerial zeal was ill-timed, because it made him a prime target for the rebels in Bury St Edmunds during the Peasants' Revolt one month later, and it cost him his life.[41] The first court held after the Revolt was judiciously low key, and for the next couple of years the court flagged its interest in flown serfs without pursuing them. Yet, once the tensions generated by the Revolt had eased, officials reverted to a more active and aggressive approach: they pressed hard for details of the progeny of flown serfs, resurrected the practice of personal pledges and the threat of hefty penalties for non-compliance, and enforced chevage payments robustly (see table 10.8).[42] This included explicit directives to establish the names of the progeny of flown serfs, such as those of John Eustace and Thomas Harmer, who had settled in Thaxted (Essex) and Bury St Edmunds respectively.[43]

The aggressive management of migrant serfs in the late 1380s and 1390s proved successful at increasing the revenues generated from chevage (see table 10.7). On one occasion the treatment of a serf was overtly demeaning.

---

[38] SROB E3/15.3/1.7b, court held July 1362 (Prochet); /1.8, court held June 1363 (Goding); and /1.9a, court held October 1364 (le Maister). The officials were justified in having concerns about the Goding family – John Goding abandoned his holdings and fled in October 1370, SROB E3/15.3/1.15.

[39] In 1361 manorial officials seized the goods and chattels of Robert Wynston after he had abandoned his 30-*acreware tenementum* and flown the manor, and promptly gave them to the tenants who replaced him, SROB E3/15.3/1.7a, court held January 1361 – see also /1.9a, court held June 1365, for a follow up to this case. When John Goding abandoned his holding, fleeing the manor in 1370, no action was taken, /1.15, court held October 1370.

[40] SROB E3/15.3/1.19d, court held April 1381, which mentions de Lakenheath's role in directing decision-making.

[41] A mob stormed the abbey at the height of the Revolt, and demanded that de Lakenheath be handed over. He surrendered voluntarily in order to save the abbey from ransack, but was roughly executed in the market square at Bury St Edmunds. He was described as keeper of the barony of St Edmund: E. Powell, *The rising in East Anglia in 1381* (Cambridge, 1896), p. 19; R.B. Dobson, ed., *The Peasants' Revolt of 1381* (second edition, Basingstoke, 1983), pp. 245–6, 250.

[42] SROB E3/15.3/1.24, courts held June 1387; /1.25, court held June 1388; /1.26, court held July 1389; /1.27, court held November 1389.

[43] SROB E3/15.3/1.32, court held December 1395.

In 1388 John Prochet was forced to recognize his servile status in front of the court, and then to swear an oath that he would return to the manor in the near future to hold a tenement in bondage. He was also threatened with a £5 penalty for non-compliance, backed by personal pledges. Yet Prochet never returned, despite occasional reminders from the court, although he did continue to pay chevage each year – perhaps this regular payment, together with the reckoning that John had settled on another abbatial manor, Rickinghall Inferior (Suffolk), persuaded officials not to press harder.[44] Given the tougher approach to migrants in the 1390s, and the policy's evident success in yielding some additional chevage payments, the abrupt abandonment of chevage after 1403 is unexpected.

In the fifteenth century successive abbots of Bury St Edmunds were determined to uphold their right to levy a recognition fine upon all their customary tenants, including leaseholders, a charge which duly recognized their personal overlordship at the time of their election while raising a welcome windfall upon assuming office. During the course of the fifteenth century this determination was the source of sustained and mounting tension with the tenants of Chevington, and its eventual outcome was highly symbolic of the changing balance of power.

Recognition had been paid without documented complaint in 1362, but on the next recorded occasion in 1389 Salman Melk and Henry Smallwood were appointed to assess and then collect the fixed 40s. fine.[45] A year later nothing had been paid, resulting in a 3d. amercement on each collector, with a 3s. 4d. penalty. This action yielded an initial payment of 10s., but late in 1391 Melk and Smallwood were ordered to pay the 30s. arrears by Christmas or face a 13s. 4d. penalty.[46] The following June they were each amerced 6d., and given an amended deadline of Michaelmas 1392 under a 2s. penalty. When they again failed to pay, the manorial administration further extended the deadline to Christmas 1392, without imposing either amercement or penalty.[47] After another reminder in 1393 to raise the outstanding 30s., the next year they were amerced 4d. each, placed under a penalty of 12d., and told to produce the arrears by the next court.[48] A final call for payment in 1395 was countermanded by a marginal note in the court roll, which stated that the sum had been respited by order of William Barwe.[49] Barwe was a

---

[44]   SROB E3/15.3/1.26, court held October 1388. Then see /1.27, courts held November 1389 and June 1390, and /1.28, court held November 1391.

[45]   SROB E3/15.3/1.27, court held November 1389.

[46]   SROB E3/15.3/1.28, courts held October 1390 and November 1391.

[47]   SROB E3/15.3/1.29a, court held October 1392.

[48]   SROB E3/15.3/1.29a, court held November 1393; E3/15.3/1.29b, court held October 1394.

[49]   SROB E3/15.3/30, court held July 1395.

senior estate official, who became Cellarer of the abbey in 1401. The administration had backed down, although its decision to respite, or postpone, the
fine rather than to cancel it meant that it had not conceded on the principle
of recognition.

Recognition was next charged in October 1415, when it was accompanied
by the wildly optimistic directive to collect the payment by the feast of King
Edmund himself, 20 November 1415. Three assessors and collectors were
appointed this time, but it made no difference – four years later they were
each amerced 6d. and threatened with a 40s. penalty for their failure to raise
a penny.[50] Nothing more happened, which implies that the administrators
had simply given up. Then in 1429 the election of Abbot William Curteys
prompted the appointment of another three men to assess and collect the
40s. recognition by Michaelmas.[51] No further mention is made of it during
Curteys' abbacy. Given the tenants' attitude to recognition in the 1390s, and
their success in evading most of its payment, it seems unlikely that it was
paid thereafter. It is much more likely that Curteys, who was to prove one of
the most able administrators in the abbey's history, recognized the futility of
pressing the matter. In 1446 the homage initially refused to elect anyone to
assess and collect the recognition due to Abbot William Babbington; once
they had done so at the next court, the matter did not appear again in the
court rolls.[52]

No attempt was made to impose recognition in 1453 after the election
of John Bohun, which may partly explain the open defiance which greeted
the attempt in 1470 of Abbot Robert Ixworth to resurrect it. The homage
informed the steward bluntly that it refused to appoint collectors; the steward
blustered that their behaviour was gravely contemptuous, and ordered the
bailiff to seize their goods and chattels. When the steward raised the matter
again in the next court, and encountered a second blunt refusal, he again
pointed out the great contempt this behaviour conveyed towards their lord
abbot, and reminded the homage that recognition was owed 'according to
the custom of the manor'. Another order to the bailiff to distrain goods in
lieu of the payment was an empty, but procedurally correct, gesture.[53] The
steward, presumably at Abbot Ixworth's insistence, raised the matter in 1475
and again in 1480 – on the latter occasion, the incensed homage of Chevington refused explicitly either to elect a collector or to work for the lord
('*necque ad laborandum domino*'). Their stinging and overt refusal must have

---

[50]   SROB E3/15.3/1.34b, courts held October 1415, and September 1419.

[51]   SROB E3/15.3/1.35, court held May 1429.

[52]   SROB E3/15.3/1.35, courts held February and July 1446. The tenants of the abbot's
       manor of Hargrave also refused to pay recognition in this year, Dyer, 'A Suffolk
       farmer', p. 16.

[53]   SROB E3/15.3/1.35, courts held 1470 and 1471.

struck a chord, because recognition was never again requested.[54] The world order had unquestionably changed forever when the mighty abbot of Bury St Edmunds had to resort, unsuccessfully, to an appeal to the custom of the manor in order to try and impose his rights within his own manorial court.

Summary of chronology and key indicators
In the 1340s the standardized villein holdings were fully occupied at Chevington, yet in 1360 only 40% were tenanted, all on the old terms. The untenanted holdings were then offered on leases for money rent, with no incidents of villeinage, which resulted in a dramatic rise in the rate of occupancy. By the 1370s nearly all of the old customary holdings were occupied, c.70% of them on leasehold for money rent. Between 20% and 25% were still held nominally on hereditary villein tenure, although the terms of that tenure had become diluted. In the 1360s both millsuit and the use of 'in villeinage' in conveyances disappeared, in the 1380s liability for merchet and heriot declined to the point of irrelevance, and in the 1390s most remaining labour services were formally commuted. Only recognition remained, payable by all holders of customary land whatever its form of tenure. Leases were the dominant tenure until the mid-fifteenth century, when their attractiveness waned and they were displaced by fee farms. Fee farms were hereditary tenures for a money rent, which permanently removed servile incidents from the rent package.

This chronology of tenurial change corresponds closely with the main fluctuations in land values. Leasehold values per acre at Chevington fell by 18% between the 1340s and 1370s, then held steady thereafter (see graph 10.1). The data for entry fines are sparse, given the small number of *tenementa* held on the old terms, although the average level fell sharply in the generation after 1350, picked up in the fifteenth century, and then held constant (see table 10.4). Thus two separate sets of evidence for land values identify the 1340s to the 1370s as the period of greatest decline. The resilience of land values during the fifteenth century, together with the absence of sizeable or sustained rent arrears, indicates that the local land market stabilized after its dramatic collapse during the third quarter of the fourteenth century.[55]

The recorded number of flown serfs first peaked in the late 1350s (see table 10.8), then fell away before peaking again during the late 1380s and 1390s. The first peak of departures comprised eight serfs at a time when 18 of the main customary holdings remained vacant. Therefore migration from the manor must have exacerbated the loss of tenants, and the fall in land values, after the Black Death. The second peak was higher, with 18 absentees recorded in 1393, but it does not correlate with any observable patterns in either land occu-

54   SROB E3/15.3/1.35, courts held 1475 and 1480. Dyer, 'Suffolk farmer', p. 16.
55   Dyer, 'Suffolk farmer', p. 7 shows that manumissions were limited.

pancy, or land values, or tenurial change. Hence it must have been caused by either a surge in unexplained departures or a change in administrative policy associated with the management of serfs. It was almost certainly the latter. In the 1380s and 1390s the abbot's officials were attempting to impose personal servility through a variety of means, including the increased use of chevage, but then in 1403 such efforts and payments ceased abruptly, unexpectedly and permanently. The lord had effectively abandoned personal servility at Chevington and the labelling of serfs as *nativi* thereafter was rare.

Peasant resistance offers only a partial explanation for the disappearance of villeinage from Chevington. It certainly explains the decline of recognition, which was stubbornly and collectively resisted by all of the tenants of customary land, including leaseholders. All other dues withered on the vine in the last quarter of the fourteenth century, when landholdings held in villeinage were already a minority. Resistance made little contribution to the disappearance of week works, which were mainly undone by the huge swing to leases in the 1360s. The few that survived this swing subsequently disappeared in 1398 with the leasing of the demesne.

Thus villein tenure was severely weakened by the 1370s, and had disappeared by the 1390s. As it waned, so the landlord attempted to impose personal servility more actively upon an identified pool of hereditary serfs by blood. After some success, the policy was unexpectedly and inexplicably dropped in 1403. Overall, the abbot of St Edmund managed villeinage at Chevington pragmatically and realistically, although with selected moments of challenge and confrontation.

Fornham All Saints[56]

Customary land tenures

In 1283 the abbot of Bury St Edmunds' manor of Fornham All Saints comprised c.400 acres of free land, 437 acres of demesne arable, 136 acres of molland, and c.175 acres of customary land.[57] There were 16 main customary holdings, comprising five 16-*acreware tenementa*, eleven 8-*acreware*, together with ten 'coterells'(i.e. cottagers).[58] In the early fourteenth century the

---

[56]   There are c.65 courts from 1350–5, 1366–76, 1381–7, 1391–1400, 1415–23, SROB E3/15.6/1.7 to 1.17 and E3/15.7/1.7 to 1.15; and c.50 accounts 1350 to 1470, SROB E3/15.6/2.21 to 2.63 and E3/15.7/2.5 to 2.15.

[57]   BL Add. Ms. 34689, ff. 8–11.

[58]   BL Add. Ms. 34689, ff. 10–11 and the works' account of the 1351–2 account, SROB E3/15.6/2.21. The 16-*acreware* holdings owed anything between 1½d. and 24d. cash rent, and the 8-*acreware* holdings owed anything between 1½d. and 6d. Mollond holdings are also recorded, which explains why the works' account has seven

larger holdings each rendered annually a small (non-standardized) cash payment, 1½d.for *sesilum*, 10d. for *bedrepsilum*, 52 week works, and a variety of ploughing, harrowing, carrying and reaping services.[59] They were liable for heriot, merchet, childwite, recognition, entry fine and millsuit, and they were held for 'him and his brood in villeinage for services and works'.[60]

In the 1340s all 16 customary holdings and ten coterells were occupied on villein tenure.[61] Heirs were very slow to claim these holdings in the aftermath of the Black Death.[62] By 1352 only two (8-*acreware*) out of the 16 main customary holdings were held in villeinage, eight had been converted to leasehold during the previous year, and the rest lay untenanted, a situation which remained unchanged ten years later.[63] A decision in 1351 to convert one vacant 16-*acreware tenementum* to leasehold was explained by the failure of anyone 'to come to hold [it] after the death of Robert Shyerwynd', indicating that such conversions were not the landlord's preferred option.[64] By 1368 ten of the 16 were leased, with just a single 8-*acreware* holding remaining on hereditory villein tenure.[65] When the latter changed hands in 1370, it was described as 'held to her and hers at the will of the lord for services and customs', i.e. without the 'in villeinage' phrase that had been a constant feature of pre-Black Death grants.[66]

By the 1380s villein tenure had virtually disappeared from Fornham All Saints, because the great majority of customary land had been converted to leases for a term, usually of between seven and ten years. In 1396 only one holding – a single coterell – was held in villeinage, which meant that just one week work was available to the demesne that year out of a possible 858

(rather than five) 16-*acreware* holdings rendering ploughing and carrying works, and 17 (rather than 11) 8-*acreware* holdings rendering ploughing works.

[59] BL Add. Ms. 34689, ff. 10–11 and the works' account of 1351–2, SROB E3/15.6/2.21. The free and customary tenants were required collectively to reap 45 acres of corn as their reaping services.

[60] SROB E3/15.6/1.5 and 1.6.

[61] The works' account in 1347–8 and contemporary court rolls confirm the full occupancy of the villein tenures, SROB E3/15.7/2.3; the holding in bondage is evident from court rolls, such as SROB E3/15.7/1.1 to 1.6.

[62] See the courts held in October 1349 and January 1350, SROB E3/15.6/1.7.

[63] These figures are calculated from the decays recorded in the works' accounts for 1351–2 and 1360–1, and the details for the lease of lands, SROB E3/15.6/2.21 and 2.28. For example, the 1360–1 works' account noted that the week works due from all five 16-*acreware*, and from nine of the eleven 8-*acreware tenementa*, were decayed because 'in the hands of the lord due to the pestilence'. The initial surge to leaseholds is recorded in the court held in March 1351, SROB E3/15.6/1.9.

[64] SROB E3/15.6/1.9, court held March 1351.

[65] SROB E3/15.6/2.32. The situation remained much the same in the later 1370s, see E3/15.6/2.34b.

[66] SROB E3/15.6/1.15, court held November 1370.

works. Very few other grants on villein tenure are recorded in the court rolls. In the 1340s rental income from the peasant sector had generated just over £13 per annum, but in the 1390s the expansion of leases had now raised this figure to over £16.[67]

By the mid-1390s subtle changes to the structure of holdings on leases are observable. The practice of leasing customary *tenementa* as complete holdings had begun to give way to the practice of breaking them up into smaller parcels. For example, in 1396 only six of the original 16 *tenementa* were still leased intact, and the remaining ten had been broken up into individual parcels and repackaged into separate leases. For example, one lease comprised '24 *acreware*' made up from various different holdings, and two other leases comprised two large packages (one of 30 and another of 56 acres) compiled from 'the land of diverse *tenementa*'.[68] This characteristic is still evident in the 1400s and 1410s.[69] Its purpose is not clear, although the practice would have enabled lessees to construct more compact and consolidated holdings.

No court rolls survive after 1423 so it is difficult to determine exactly how leases developed subsequently. However, there is no doubt that they still dominated tenures in the mid-fifteenth century, judging from the evidence of manorial accounts. Rental income from leases of customary land rose from c.£9 in the 1390s to c.£15 in the 1450s, dropping to just over £12 in the early 1470s.[70]

Incidents of villeinage

Millsuit does not feature after the Black Death, childwite and merchet were rare, and heriot declined rapidly (see table 10.9). Neither merchet nor illegal marriages were frequent, although the charges for both rose in the last quarter of the fourteenth century (see table 10.10). None of these incidents survived after 1400 (table 10.1). Only ten cases of chevage are recorded after 1350, and none after the mid-1390s (see table 10.11). Presentments for absence

---

[67]   Rents of assize in the 1340s were £11 2s. 6d., with negligible decays, plus 41s. 4d. from leases of peasant land, SROB E3/15.7/2.3. In 1399–1400 rents of assize fetched the same, minus 83s. in various decays, plus leases of peasant lands of £9 4s. 2d., SROB E3/15.6/2.38.

[68]   SROB E3/15.6/2.35.

[69]   SROB E3/15.6/2.45, account of 1409–10. At this time the only remaining labour services were a few ploughing and reaping works, which were all commuted.

[70]   The dominance of leases in mid-century rentals is explicit in SROB HA 528, Hengrave Hall Deposit 114. The manorial accounts detail individual leases until the mid-1440s, when the manor was leased, and thereafter just a consolidated total of leased income is recorded. Leases are entered separately from rents of assize until 1476–7, when all rental income from peasant landholdings was rolled into one figure, see E3/15.7/2.8 to 2.19.

10.9 Frequency of merchet, heriot, childwite and millsuit
at Fornham, 1350 to 1424

Period	Merchet	Heriot	Childwite	Millsuit
Pre-1349	/	/	/	/
1350–74	5	6	2	0
1375–99	7	2	1	0
1400–24	0	0	0	0

Merchet, heriot and childwite fines only (including if waived); millsuit includes fines
and presentments.
/ = recorded pre-1349, X = not recorded pre-1349

10.10 Incidence of merchet, and mean size of levy,
at Fornham, 1350 to 1424

Period	Number of merchets	Mean levy	Number of marriages without licence	Mean levy
1350–1374	2	24d.	3	39d.
1375–1399	2	80d.	5	58d.
1400–1424	0	–	0	–

10.11 Incidence of chevage, and mean size of levy,
at Fornham, 1350 to 1424

Period	Number of chevage cases	Mean fine per case
1350–1374	6	7d.
1375–1399	4	6d.
1400–1424	0	–

were rare before 1370, then increased from the late 1370s as the lord's officials
intensified their interest in fugitive serfs, but ceased abruptly after 1400 (see
table 10.12). Recognition was demanded upon the accession of a new abbot
throughout the late fourteenth century, at a fixed sum of 45s. levied upon all
customary tenants, including leaseholders.

Week works, and the majority of all other labour services, effectively
disappeared in the wake of the Black Death. In 1351–2 87% of week works
were unavailable, because all but two of the main customary holdings were
either abandoned or leased. The number of available works never recovered
(see table 10.13). During the 1350s the manor utilized a few of the week

10.12 Recorded flight from Fornham, 1350 to 1399

Year	Number of people presented for absence	Number of people charged for chevage
1350	2	0
1354	2	0
1370	1	1
1371	0	1
1373	0	2
1374	0	2
1375	0	2
1376	1	2
1383	3	0
1384	3	0
1386	2	0
1387	5	0
1388	1	0
1391	5	0
1394	4	0
1395	5	0
1396	10	0
1398	9	0
1399	9	0

10.13 Utilization of week works at Fornham, 1351 to 1396

Year	Allowed/decayed	Sold	Used	Demesne arable sown
1351–2	87%	8%	5%	297 acres
1360–1	87%	10%	3%	327 acres
1367–8	88%	12%	0	300 acres
1376–7	93%	7%	0	292 acres
1395–6	100%	0	0	296 acres

works owed by those two *tenementa*, but from the mid-1360s all were sold. Refusals to perform labour services were rare and minor.[71]

Attitudes to serfdom

Although few holdings were held on villein tenure after the 1350s, the lord sought to maintain control over hereditary serfs, and there is evidence of a hardening attitude in the last three decades of the fourteenth century. The imposition of chevage for the first time in the early 1370s was accompa-

---

[71] SROB E3/15.6/1.7, court held October 1349, when one tenant was amerced 1d. for not appearing at a labour service.

nied initially by the threat of a heavy financial penalty (20s.) if the migrant did not return each year, although the penalties were never imposed and such threats were soon dropped.[72] Similarly, the increase in presentments of flown serfs in the 1380s and 1390s (see table 10.12) was accompanied by direct instructions to the homage to enquire of their whereabouts.[73]

A handful of flashpoints, mainly dating from the 1380s and 1390s, suggest strongly that the abbot had decided to adopt a firmer approach to the management of villeinage. It applied to both serfs by blood and to the lessees of customary land. For example, in the 1380s the manorial administration targeted the West family, who held one 8-*acreware* holding on villein tenure, by charging higher entry fines, seeking information about their flown relatives, and imposing a large merchet, until the harassed joint tenants abandoned the holding in 1386 and left the manor to start a new life in Norfolk instead.[74] In 1382 Adam Roger and Robert Harry refused to serve as messor and reeve respectively, which resulted in the seizure of Harry's customary holding in 1383. At the same time Robert Wolnard and John Warde abandoned their landholdings but remained on the manor, and were ordered to reoccupy.[75] In fact, Warde lived as a landholder in Fornham until his death in the summer of 1423, although in 1396 he was amerced 12d. for refusing to present certain 'articles' to the court.[76] In another flashpoint, John Crouch refused to swear his standard oath to the court as a customary tenant in 1397, and was promptly amerced 6s. 8d.[77] A further indicator of a more aggressive approach to villeinage is the rise in the average fines charged for merchet and illegal marriage in the last quarter of the fourteenth century (see table 10.10).

The most interesting indication of a tougher stance towards villeinage is the abbot's attempts to impose recognition upon all the customary tenants of the manor, including leaseholders. The standard levy at Fornham was 45s., which before the Black Death had been paid promptly upon the election of a new abbot.[78] In the later fourteenth century 45s. was demanded, despite the smaller tenant base, but payment was sluggish following the election of

---

[72] SROB E3/15.6/1.15, court held November 1379 for the penalty on John West. The change of policy is evident from courts held in 1373, E3/15.7/1.8, and in the mid-1370s, E3/15.6/1.16.

[73] See, for example, SROB E3/15.7/1.10, court held December 1394, and /1.11, court held October 1395.

[74] Bailey, *Medieval Suffolk*, pp. 196–7.

[75] SROB E3/15.7/1.9a, courts held November 1382 and July 1383.

[76] SROB E3/15.7/1.11, court held June 1396; E3/15.7/1.15, court held June 1423.

[77] SROB E3/15.7/1.12, court held February 1397.

[78] SROB E3/15.7/1.1, where full and prompt payment was made in 1335 upon the election of Abbot William Bernham.

abbot John Timworth in 1383.[79] In 1389 Timworth was succeeded by William Cratfield, whose attempts to collect his recognition met with stubborn and sustained resistance. Adam Roger, one of the two appointed assessors and collectors in 1389, died five years later without raising a single penny, and so in 1395 two new assessors were appointed in his place.[80] The three assessors were each amerced around 8d. annually between 1396 and 1398 for their failure to collect, and they were also placed under the threat of a 6s. 8d penalty.[81] In 1399 abbot Cratfield changed his tactics, shifting away from the narrow focus upon the three assessors and targeting all of the customary tenants instead, first distraining them all for non-payment, then imposing a collective amercement of 18d. coupled with the threat of a 6s. 8d. penalty. We do not know how the impasse was resolved, but Cratfield died soon afterwards, and there is no evidence that any payment towards the 45s. recognition was ever made.[82]

In the 1380s and 1390s the estate officials led a concerted administrative drive to track migrants and to impose merchet upon serfs, and recognition upon all customary tenants. The attempt failed. There is a gap in the court series in the first decade of the century, but when it resumes between 1413 and 1423 every vestige of villeinage had disappeared from Fornham All Saints.

Summary of chronology and key indicators
In the 1340s all 16 of the standardized customary holdings in Fornham All Saints had been occupied on villein tenure, but by 1362 only 13% were thus held, half were leased, and the remaining 37% were either untenanted or leased in small parcels. In 1368 land occupancy had edged closer to 70%, when just a single standardized holding remained on villein tenure. The huge swing to leases caused the collapse of week works, which ceased to be used at all after 1361, and the dramatic decline of millsuit and heriot. Most customary arable land continued to be held on leases until the documentary record ceases in the 1470s. By the end of the fourteenth century, only recognition survived as a charge upon customary landholders. Manorial officials made some attempts to impose personal servility in the 1380s and 1390s through an increased interest in flown serfs, and higher charges for merchet, although they were unable to impose any charges for chevage. After c.1400 all interest in personal servility ceased.

After the Black Death the demand for large, integral, holdings on the old villein tenure slumped at Fornham All Saints. The lack of tenants in

79 Failure to pay is noted in courts held in July 1383, SROB E3/15.7/1.9a, and also in January 1384 and November 1386, E3/15.6/1.17 and 1.18.
80 SROB E3/15.7/1.10, courts held December 1394 and October 1395.
81 SROB E3/15.7/1.11 to 1.13.
82 SROB E3/15.7/1.13 and 1.14.

10.2 Values of customary arable land at Forham 1340s to 1460s (d. per acre)

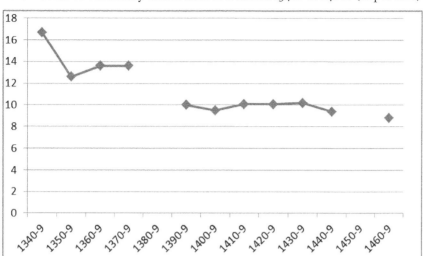

Mean decennial value of customary arable land at lease.

the 1350s is striking, and forced the landlord to convert customary land to leasehold in order to attract new tenants. The profound shock to the land market is reflected in the 25% fall in the value of customary land at leasehold between the 1340s and the 1350s (see graph 10.2).[83] Only two people are recorded annually as having left the manor in the 1350s (see table 10.12), so the shortage of tenants was not exacerbated by flight. There was no resistance to labour services, because few holdings were tenanted. There are no signs of a seigniorial reaction in the third quarter of the fourteenth century. The disappearance of villein tenure correlates directly with the dramatic fall in land values over the period of the Black Death.

The next major fall in land values occurred between the 1370s and 1390s, when they dropped a further 27% (see graph 10.2). This double dip in the customary land market must have again raised fears about a potential loss of tenants, although this time the seigniorial response was more aggressive and proactive. Officials actively sought the names of flown serfs, information which might enable them to pressurize families into holding land on the manor, and they dealt firmly with any recalcitrance or dissent among the customary tenants. The attempt to collect recognition – the last surviving servile tenurial incident – in the 1380s and 1390s was optimistic, and it failed as a consequence of staunch and collective peasant resistance to it. The aban-

---

[83] The figure for the 1340s is based on 18 acres at lease, recorded in the account of 1347–8, SROB E3/15.7/2.3.

donment of personal servility in the first decade of the fifteenth century appears to have been a centralized estate decision, although it followed two decades of lower land values, some out-migration, and piecemeal resistance to the aspects of serfdom.

Conclusion

In the immediate aftermath of the Black Death the abbot of Bury St Edmunds encountered severe difficulties in finding tenants for the large, standardized, customary holdings at both Chevington and Fornham All Saints, most of which remained unoccupied until the late 1350s. The solution was to convert the empty holdings to leasehold tenure, a decision which resulted in a rapid rise in occupancy rates during the 1360s. The scale and duration of the failure to find tenants on both manors, and the lord's initial reluctance to convert to a money-based rent, are both striking. Prospective tenants might have been discouraged by the large size of the standardized holdings, and their liability for a heavy load of week works, especially in a period of acute labour shortages and in a region where small and lightly burdened villein holdings were the norm. There is also the possibility that tenants were staging a coordinated and tactical boycott of these holdings across the abbot's estate, although this suggestion cannot be substantiated. Certainly, the initial reluctance to convert them to leasehold looks like a fixed central policy, as the abbot held out for the restoration of villein tenure. The respective stances of lord and tenant during the 1350s are clear enough: tenants did not wish to hold large holdings on villein tenure, but the landlord would only convert them to leasehold when he had no other alternative.

The huge swing to leases from the late 1350s undermined the close association between tenurial and personal unfreedom, which may explain why the abbot's officials began to target hereditary serfs from the 1360s at Chevington and from the 1370s at Fornham. There are strong similarities in the management of villeinage across both manors, such as the crackdown on fugitive serfs in the 1380s and 1390s, and the dogged pursuit of recognition payments. The aggressive attitude to personal servility in these two decades is consistent with the treatment of serfs on other abbatial manors at this time, most notably Robert Kyng of Hinderclay.[84] This consistency is strongly indicative of coordinated estate policy, as is the abrupt disappearance of personal servility soon after 1400 on both manors.

During the second half of the fourteenth century the seigniorial approach

---

[84] Schofield, 'Robert King', pp. 51–7. It is not clear from Schofield's fascinating study whether interest in serfs disappeared after 1400 at Hinderclay in line with the experience at Chevington and Fornham.

to the management of villeinage on these two manors is mixed and rather contradictory. On the one hand, by 1370 villein tenure had declined to the point of irrelevance, because most customary land was held on leasehold, and because week works, millsuit and heriot were in sharp decline on the few holdings that remained on villein tenure. There is little evidence for a seigniorial reaction in the third quarter of the fourteenth century, which means that the recorded increase in annual revenue from the Chevington court between the 1340s and the 1360s/1370 requires some other explanation.[85] On the other hand, during the 1380s and 1390s, the treatment of some serfs was novel and aggressive, and the pursuit of recognition was confrontational. Such behaviour reinforces the stereotypical image of the abbot of Bury St Edmunds as an uncompromising and reactionary monastic landlord. Indeed, if there was a 'seigniorial reaction' on this estate, then it occurred during the 1380s and 1390s, after which personal servility was suddenly and completely abandoned. The relegation of villeinage to an insignificant form of tenure by the 1370s, and the disappearance of personal servility in the 1400s, were remarkable, especially when other ecclesiastical and lay landlords managed to maintain remnants of both on manors close by.[86]

This case study suggests a number of wider observations about the decline of serfdom. First, it reinforces the advantage of studying individual manors over extended timeframes, and the disadvantage of cherry picking examples from short periods. For example, our understanding of the management of personal servility on both manors would have been very different if the study had just been restricted to the 1380s and 1390s. Second, it underlines the need to explore the existence or absence of estate-based policies in the management of serfdom. Fornham All Saints and Chevington formed part of a core of abbatial manors that were relatively close to each other, and to the abbey at Bury St Edmunds, and they reveal clear evidence for a consistent, estate-wide, policy directed from the centre. It contrasts with Merton College, which did not impose such consistent managerial discipline across its geographically dispersed manors. Third, it shows unequivocally that even the abbot's high status and extended judicial powers were insufficient to uphold serfdom after 1349. The policies of the abbot in the 1380s and 1390s indicate a real desire to maintain the final vestiges of serfdom, and proactive attempts to do so, but they failed. There is no evidence that the abbot attempted to supplement his seigniorial powers with the extended judicial powers available to him through the Liberty of St Edmund.

The last point merits closer consideration. Why did villeinage disappear so quickly from two manors of such a powerful landlord, especially one who was eager to maintain servility? An answer might lay in the size of the gap

[85] C. Dyer, *Everyday life in medieval England* (London, 1994), p. 208.
[86] See, for example, Norton, Walsham and Aldham.

that emerged between tenurial and personal servility, and the speed with which it opened up, soon after the Black Death. The inability to find tenants for the majority of the main customary landholdings immediately after the Black Death may have owed something to the fact that they comprised just a small proportion of the total land available to peasants on both manors, so that locals could afford to be choosy about the terms on which they might occupy them. Whatever the reason, villein tenures were swept away in the 1360s in favour of leaseholds, a process which demonstrated graphically to all the abbot's villeins that villein tenure was not immutable. The collapse of the firm base of servile tenure undermined the abbot's position and restricted his options, because it meant that the attempts thereafter to impose personal serfdom were exposed as just that: personal. The Revolt of 1381 was as severe on the estates of Bury St Edmunds abbey as anywhere in England, and its focus and ferocity was unquestionably linked to more aggressive policies towards serfs in the preceding weeks. However, a narrow focus upon the Revolt misses the wider issue. The inability to restore villein tenures after 1350 increased the difficulties of upholding personal servility thereafter. Even the power and the standing of the abbot of Bury St Edmunds could not overcome the constraints imposed upon him by the dramatic upheavals of the mid-fourteenth century.

Between the 1340s and the 1390s the pool of serfs at Chevington and Fornham shrank considerably. We cannot measure the extent exactly, nor weigh the causes precisely. However, it is evident that during the 1380s and 1390s the abbot's officials spent considerable time and energy, with no little opportunity cost, pursuing a dwindling number of serfs for servile incidents that yielded diminishing sums of money. For example, the total income from all merchet, chevage and childwite fines in the last quarter of the fourteenth century from both manors amounted to little more than £6. A judgement about whether this modest return justified the investment of administrative time and energy must have been finely balanced. The disappearance of personal serfdom soon after 1400 indicates that the balance had suddenly and decisively tipped. Why? It may just have been that the incumbent abbot, William Cratfield, decided that upholding serfdom was no longer worth the effort. If so, his decision may have been influenced by wider changes in the running of the estate. The demesne at Chevington was leased in 1398, as part of a broader shift to demesne leasing on the Bury abbey estates in the 1390s and 1400s.[87] Direct demesne management required a sizeable infrastructure

---

[87] Dyer, 'Suffolk farmer', pp. 7–8 shows that a small area of demesne returned to direct exploitation episodically thereafter. The demesne at Fornham remained in direct cultivation, although the scale of operations fell markedly between the 1390s and 1400s. For example, nearly 300 acres of demesne were cultivated in 1395–6, but only 195 acres in 1401–2, SROB E3/15.6/2.35 and 2.39b.

of administrators and record-keepers to make it work effectively, and the major scaling down of this bureaucratic structure would have exacerbated the difficulties in tracking and managing serfs. There are strong grounds from the evidence presented here for associating the decision to cease imposing personal incidents upon serfs with the decision to run down the scale of direct demesne exploitation.

The disappearance of personal servility after c.1400 on both manors meant that the attention of estate administrators shifted to the management of tenures. Leases continued to dominate at Fornham All Saints until the 1470s, although we cannot know what became of them thereafter. At Chevington their conversion to fee farms during the final quarter of the century at was extensive and striking. It must indicate rising dissatisfaction with some aspects of conventional leases among either tenants or estate administrators. Fee farms were beneficial to tenants, because they preserved the advantages of leaseholds over villein tenures (money rents, and no servile incidents), while adding the security of hereditary rights and the irreversible removal of week works. The conversion of leases to fee farms represented a further concession from the landlord, and a further weakening of the seigniorial position. Yet the scale of the conversions is striking, and it does not suggest any reluctance on the part of the abbot. This raises the possibility that the lord was eager to secure tenants, and to reduce both the uncertainty and the hassle of finding tenants upon the expiry of every lease for a term of years, during the Great Slump of c.1440 to c.1470. The conditions of depressed rental income, reductions in land occupancy and mounting arrears could have created a situation in which tenants saw an opportunity to press for further concessions on tenure, and in which it suited landlords to make those concessions. Fee farms fixed the level of annual rent on customary holdings in perpetuity at a value appropriate to the depressed conditions of the land market. This decision reduced the scope of later lords to reap the benefits of rising land values when the market recovered in the sixteenth century.

11

The Dukes of Norfolk

The Bigod earls of Norfolk acquired extensive lands within East Anglia soon after the Norman Conquest, which by the thirteenth century were administered from their splendid baronial seat at Framlingham (Suffolk).[1] In the fourteenth century the title eventually passed to the Mowbray family, and in 1397 earl Thomas Mowbray was elevated to become the first duke of Norfolk. The last Mowbray duke, John, died in 1476, and in 1483 the title and lands were bestowed upon the Howard family.

This case study is based upon the substantial archive relating to three manors on this estate, and also upon F.G. Davenport's study of a fourth, Forncett St Mary (Norfolk). Forncett lies twelve miles south of Norwich, high on the clay interfluves. Cratfield, Dunningworth and Staverton were small- to medium-sized manors in east Suffolk. Dunningworth and Staverton were located near the coast, the former at the neck of the river Alde near what is now Snape bridge while the latter is further downriver, off Butley creek. Staverton manor extended across the settlements of Eyke, Wantisden and Bromeswell. Cratfield is a short distance north of Framlingham.

The choice of this estate for a case study is partly a function of the quality of its archive, but it is also due to the reputation of the sixteenth-century Howard dukes for their aggressive and exploitative management of their bondmen.[2] Serfdom was preserved as long, and the bondmen were squeezed as hard, on this estate as anywhere in sixteenth-century England. Hence it would be especially instructive to try and uncover any antecedents of this policy: had the estate always adopted a conservative and demanding approach to villeinage? If so, did its villeins resist? If not, when and why did the estate begin to adopt its tough stance against serfs?

[1]   See M. Morris, *The Bigod earls of Norfolk in the thirteenth century* (Woodbridge, 2005), pp. 31–42.
[2]   MacCulloch, 'Bondmen', pp. 99–100.

Dunningworth[3]

Customary land tenures

Dunningworth was a small/medium manor.[4] Customary holdings came in varying sizes, and the principal 8-*acreware* holding carried winter and harvest works, together with some light harrowing, weeding and ploughing services. It was also liable for a cash rent, merchet, millsuit, entry fine, capitage, chevage and tallage, and, on rotation, the manorial offices of reeve, messor and warrener. In the early fourteenth century villein land was variously described as held '*de bondagio*' or '*in villeinagio* … for him and his heirs at the will of the lord for services and customs'. No villein land was converted to fixed-term tenures before 1349, although the lord permitted licensed sub-letting between tenants.[5]

The survival of court rolls during the 1350s is patchy, but, from the extant courts, it is evident that many villein holdings were re-granted on the old terms. However, the use of '*de bondagio*' in the formula for conveyances soon disappeared, so that by the 1370s the phrase 'to hold for him and his heirs making services and customs' was well established, and it was used consistently thereafter.[6] The wording was amended slightly in the 1460s to 'seisin to hold to him and his heirs by the rod at the will of the lord performing services and customs'. The manorial account of 1391–2 reveals that around one half of all customary land was still held on hereditary villein tenure. For example, 49% of all labour services were still theoretically available for use on the demesne (table 11.6), and the annual income derived from assize rents had fallen to around 60% of its pre-Black Death level.[7]

By the 1390s the remainder of the customary land was held as either a tenancy at will, at leasehold or lay untenanted. The 1391–2 account includes rent of 70s. 1d. 'from the issues [*de exitus*] of diverse lands and tenements that exist in the hands of the lady after the deaths of their tenants', i.e. customary land held on a tenancy that could be terminated at will.[8] The phrase 'after the deaths of their tenants' must refer back to the epidemic of 1349, although it is not clear why this temporary arrangement persisted for so long. On

---

3   This case study is based upon c.280 extant courts from the periods 1353–67, 1375–1489, and 1496–1500, SROI HD1538/207/2 to 9. A number of pre-1350 accounts are extant, but only three after that date, namely 1390–1, 1397–8, 1475–6, TNA SC6/995/15 and SROI HD1538/206/6 and 7.

4   The arable demesne was c.100 acres, with undisclosed but large areas of marsh and heath, and c.200 acres in villeinage.

5   TNA SC6/995/15 to 24; SROI HD1538/207/1 and 2.

6   SROI HD 1538/207/3 and 4.

7   The level in the 1390s (just under £9) was appreciably lower than it had been in the 1290s (£14 9s. 7½d.), TNA SC6/995/15 to 24; SROI HD1538/206/6.

8   SROI HD1538/206/6.

most estates, '*de exitus*' tenancy was a temporary measure in the 1350s and it was quickly replaced with more secure fixed-term tenancies, such as leases for years. However, leases remained uncommon at Dunningworth, despite occasional bursts of activity:[9] for example, six leases – involving a total of c.12 acres and for short terms of years – were granted in successive courts in 1363 and 1364, followed by another flurry in 1383.[10] Exceptionally, a lease might be granted for the life of the tenant or the life of the lord of the manor.[11]

In the fifteenth century the overwhelming majority of grants of customary land were on a hereditary tenure, and new grants at lease or at will became increasingly rare.[12] After 1461 no new leases for years were granted. When officials sought tenants for customary land that remained stubbornly abandoned, they invariably resorted to the grant of a hereditary fee farm for cash.[13] From the mid-1420s expired leases and tenures at will began to be re-granted as a hereditary fee farm, held by the tenant 'and his heirs at the will of the lord'.[14] For example, in 1424 Robert Sheringham obtained eight customary acres at lease for the term of the life of the lady of the manor, which he duly surrendered after her death in 1426: he was then immediately re-admitted on a perpetual fee farm.[15] From the 1460s explicit references to fee farms diminish, and thereafter most land grants adopt the language of the conventional hereditary tenure instead. The difference between a fee farm and a conventional hereditary tenure was simply that the former paid a commercial money rent in perpetuity in lieu of all services.[16]

[9] For isolated examples, SROI HD1538/207/1, court held July 1358, and 207/2, court held January 1364. Some land was converted to cash rent and four harvest services, 207/3, court held February 1380.

[10] HD1538/207/2, courts held October 1363 and January 1364; and 207/3, court held March 1383.

[11] William Justice received a cottage and eight acres for the term of the life of the earl of Norfolk, and John Snelling leased a tenement and two acres for the time of his life, HD1538/207/3, courts held May 1380 and December 1381.

[12] A few parcels of villein land were granted at leasehold in short bursts, such as the flurries of small grants in the mid-1420s, and again in the mid-1440s. For example, in 1446 John Blanchflower was granted 4 acres 3 roods of customary land for a fixed cash rent, 'which had existed in the lord's hands for many years for want of tenants', and another grant at farm was made the following year. Otherwise, leases were rare. See SROI HD1538/207/6, courts held February and June 1424; and 207/7, courts held December 1446 and June 1447.

[13] In the second quarter of the fifteenth century, such grants abound: see, for example, grants made in the courts held July and October 1439, SROI HD1538/207/6. For later examples, see SROI HD1538/207/8, courts held October 1482 and April 1485.

[14] SROI HD1538/207/6, courts held September 1425, August 1426 and October 1426.

[15] SROI HD1538/207/6, courts held June 1424 and January 1426.

[16] In other words, the phrase 'to hold to him and his heirs at fee farm [*ad feodi firmam*] at the will of the lord' began to disappear, to be replaced with grants

Hence by the 1390s around one half of the original customary land was held on an evolving form of villein tenure: the remainder was mainly on insecure tenancies at will, although a small proportion was either leased or untenanted. Between the 1420s and the 1460s these less secure tenures were converted to hereditary fee farms, which from the 1460s were seldom distinguished from conventional hereditary tenure. Thus by c.1500 the over-whelming majority of the customary land at Dunningworth was held on hereditary tenure. In May 1382 eight (16%) free, and thirty (61%) customary, tenants performed fealty to the new lord, together with eleven (23%) serfs. In 1426 35 free and customary tenants, and eight (19%) serfs, were recorded, then seven serfs in 1436.[17] Thereafter (in 1448, 1462 and 1476) no distinction of status was made between those performing fealty.

Incidents of villeinage

Millsuit had been regularly enforced before 1349, most notably in 1347 when an enforcement wave resulted in the amercement of eleven men, but it is not recorded subsequently and by the 1390s the demesne mill was no longer functional (see table 11.2).[18] Neither childwite nor heriot was ever imposed on this manor.

Capitage and tallage had been levied frequently before 1349, usually every year (see table 11.8). The patchiness of the series of account rolls makes it impossible to track their disappearance precisely, although there is no evidence whatsoever for any attempt to collect tallage after 1349 (see table 11.8). The very nature of capitage, a fee of 1d. payable from each serf residing on the manor but not holding land directly from the lord, meant that it was likely to vary from year to year, but before 1349 stable sums of either 12d. or 16d. were charged annually, which indicates that they had mutated into a fixed communal levy: whatever, an annual charge of this size upon the community was not onerous, although it might have been irksome. Capitage was still levied in the 1390s at the reduced but fixed sum of 5d. per annum. It was usually collected through the manorial *compotus*, alongside rental payments, although on a single occasion the court roll noted that John and

---

offering 'seisin to hold to him and his heirs by the rod at the will of the lord making services and customs'. The only difference is that the former fee farms paid a more commercial rent, reflecting their origins in leaseholds. The re-grant of a fee farm using the latter formula is recorded in the April court of 1480, SROI HD1538/207/8. The survival of some land held at fee farm is documented in the court of April 1489, HD1538/207/9.

[17] SROI HD1538/207/6, courts held January 1426 and December 1436. John de Mowbray had been restored to the Dukedom in late 1425, but died in 1432. He was succeeded by his son, John, in 1432. Dunningworth must have remained forfeit until 1436.

[18] See SROI HD1538/207/2, court held June 1347; TNA SC6/995/25.

11.1 Last recorded date of key incidents of villeinage at Cratfield,
Dunningworth and Staverton, 1350 to 1499

Manor	Capit.	Chev.	Pres. for Abs	Child.	Heriot	Merchet	Millsuit	Recogn.	Tallage
Cratfield 1401–1497	None	1497	1474	None	None	1485	None	None	None
Dunningworth 1350–1499	1392	1500	1477	None	None	1497	None	None	None
Staverton 1350–1485	1405	1485	1477	None	1351	1485	1357	None	None

11.2 Frequency of merchet, heriot, childwite and millsuit
at Dunningworth, 1318 to 1499

Period	Merchet	Marriage without licence	Heriot	Childwite	Millsuit
1318–48*	3	3	0	0	13
1350–74	2	0	0	0	0
1375–99	12	7	0	0	0
1400–24	18	5	0	0	0
1425–49	7	1	0	0	0
1450–74	2	0	0	0	0
1475–99	4	0	0	0	0

* 23 courts 1318–19, 1332–3, 1343–8

11.3 Incidence of merchet, and mean size of levy,
at Dunningworth, 1318 to 1499

Period	Number of merchets	Mean levy	Number of marriages without licence	Mean levy
1318–1348	3	16d.	3	96d.
1350–1374	2	24d.	0	0
1375–1399	12	42d.	7	56d.
1400–1424	18	52d.	5	(nd)
1425–1449	7	23d.	1	80d.
1450–1474	2	24d.	0	0
1475–1499	4	24d.	0	0

Henry Dawys paid 1d. each for not holding land from the lord.[19] There are no references to capitage after 1400. Tallage disappeared after 1349.

Labour services had been an important component of the rent package on villein tenures, and at the beginning of the fourteenth century the majority were routinely utilized on the demesne (see table 11.6). Allowances were few, and just a small assortment of unused works were sold. None were used in the 1390s when the demesne was leased. In 1391 nearly half the winter and harvest works were recorded as uncollectable, and by 1398 these had been written off permanently.[20] The remaining week works, those attached to the holdings still held on villein tenure, were all commuted at will at a standard rate. All that remained were a few harvest services that continued to be made available to the lessees of the demesne, judging from the occasional entries in the early fifteenth century documenting refusals to perform them.

Merchet had originally been a charge upon the marriage of the sons and daughters of all villein tenants.[21] It was routinely imposed before the Black Death, but its incidence then fell in the third quarter of the fourteenth century before picking up decisively again. The manorial administration was either slack or reluctant to charge merchet on villein tenants while the land market remained fragile after the Black Death, but then implemented a policy of enforcing it upon serfs by blood. After 1375 merchet was closely and effectively managed (see table 11.3), judging by its high frequency (see table 11.2), and the manor even succeeded in extracting a large merchet of 10s. from John Bele, a long-term absentee from Dunningworth who also rendered chevage.[22] The average size of the charge increased with the frequency, doubling from c.24d. in the period 1350–74 to around 50d. between 1375 and 1424. In 1394 the whole homage was amerced 2s. for concealing a known marriage.[23] After c.1430 the management of merchet changed. The last unlicensed marriage occurred in 1430, the last male merchet was levied

[19] SROI HD1538/207/3, court held May 1380.
[20] A change in the accounting system for labour services occurred between the 1391–2 account and that for 1398–9. The former recorded the full range of services owed from the ancient villein holdings, even though in reality half of them had not been available since 1349 because the land had converted to contractual tenancies. The 1398–9 account recognized reality by only accounting for the labour services owed by tenants holding on villein tenures, hence the number of available services in the works' account had dropped by half. SROI HD1538/206/6 (1391–2); TNA SC6/995/25 (1398–9).
[21] The charge upon sons and daughters is unusual, but it was consistently upheld. The clarification that it was originally a charge upon all villein tenants, whatever their personal status, appears in the court of June 1347, SROI HD1538/207/2.
[22] SROI HD1538/207/3, court held May 1389.
[23] SROI HD1538/207/3, court held November 1394.

in 1431, and the frequency of female merchets fell. From the mid-fifteenth century the standard fine on females was lowered to 2s. Exceptionally, in 1497 the estate administrators accepted a cow as a merchet.[24]

11.4   Number of chevage cases, and mean fine, at Dunningworth, 1318 to 1499

Period	Number of chevage cases	Mean fine per case
1318–1348	0	0
1350–1374	2	60.0d.
1375–1399	7	23.3d.
1400–1424	47	10.5d.
1425–1449	51	4.2d.
1450–1474	42	4.6d.
1475–1499	99	3.9d.

Chevage is not recorded in the first half of the fourteenth century, and even in the second half the incidence of chevage, and presentments for absence, were strikingly low (see table 11.4). Just nine cases of chevage, and 18 presentments for absence, are recorded between 1350 and 1399, and in many years neither were recorded (see table 11.5). Chevage attracted large fines on the few occasions when it was collected: for example, Robert Bele paid 40d. to live in Westleton, and Thomas Wolnoth paid 6s. 8d. for one year's absence to live in Orford.[25]

After c.1400 the number of presentments for absence and chevage payments increased sharply. In the first decade of the fifteenth century there were 15 presentments for absence (compared with ten in the 1390s) and 30 chevage payments (compared with four in the 1390s, see table 11.5). The sudden increase appears to offer support for the argument that peasant migration rose sharply after 1400 across England. However, another explanation for the sudden rise at Dunningworth is possible. The increase coincides with the accession of a new lord in 1401, and similar increases in the number of chevage cases and presentments are apparent again in 1427, 1448, 1477 and 1485, all of which followed the accession of new lords to the manor.[26] Hence the spikes in chevage look more like enforcement waves rather than genuine surges of migrants. The requirement for all tenants to appear at the first manorial court of a new lord to swear fealty highlighted

---

[24]   SROI HD1538/207/9, court held October 1497.

[25]   SROI HD1538/207/ 2, court held June 1359 (Bele), and court held October 1363 (Wolnoth). His death is reported in the October 1387 court, SROI HD1538/207/3.

[26]   New lords acceded in SROI HD1538/207/4, court held June 1401; 207/6, court held January 1426; 207/7, court held November 1448; 207/8, court held October 1475.

absentees, and provided a pretext for the estate steward to press the homage for information about them, which often yielded new details about known fugitives and additional names. For example, after the fealty performed in 1426 to John Mowbray as the new Duke of Norfolk, one Sayena Miles was discovered living in Yoxford, and additional information was elicited about two branches of the Dawes family, one of whom had settled in Southwold, and the other who lived 'close to the bridge' in Yarmouth under an assumed name.[27] Similarly, John Myles of Dedham regularly paid chevage in the early 1470s, yet after the accession of, and fealty to, the dowager Duchess Elizabeth in 1476, it was discovered and reported that he had five sons.[28] Chevage continued to be levied into the sixteenth century.

The mean size of levy for chevage in the late fourteenth century was very high, averaging 5s. in the third quarter of the century and nearly 2s. in the fourth quarter (see table 11.4). The combination of high charges and low frequency at this time suggests that officials only bothered with those cases where it knew that a fee could be successfully extracted. This situation changed during the early fifteenth century, when the average charge fell sharply to 10.5d., before settling at around 4d., and when the frequency rose. Thus chevage evolved from an occasional but lucrative levy to a frequent but less lucrative one. Indeed, the manorial administration was increasingly focused upon chevage as the key incident of personal servility, especially after the accession of the first Howard Duke of Norfolk in 1485.

The requirement to perform the office of warrener lapsed straight after the Black Death, and thereafter the role was filled as necessary by salaried officials.[29] In contrast, elections to the offices of reeve and messor continued well into the fifteenth century, based on a rotation of the main customary holdings. Tenants could, and did, pay a fine to excuse themselves from the office of reeve at a standard rate of 30s., which had been established in the early fourteenth century.[30] However, an increasing number of holdings liable for this election were either abandoned or leased, so that in 1400 the homage complained that just two holdings now shared the burden of supplying the reeve; consequently, the fine to avoid the office was formally reduced to 13s. 4d., and, soon afterwards, such fines were dropped.[31] Elections to these two

[27] SROI HD1538/207/6, courts held January 1426 and October 1428.

[28] SROI HD1538/207/8, courts held December 1471, October 1474 and October 1475.

[29] For a pre-Black Death election of the warrener by the homage, see court held July 1313, SROI HD1538/207/2. For subsequent evidence of a salaried official, see TNA SC6/995/25; SROI HD1538/207/6, court held October 1437.

[30] SROI HD1538/207/3, courts held November 1382, November 1383, and October 1384; SROI HD1538/206/6 (1392–3).

[31] SROI HD1538/207/4, court held October 1400 for the reduction to 13s. 4d., and the absence of fines subsequently.

11.5 Recorded flight of serfs from Dunningworth, 1349 to 1500

Year	Number of people presented for absence each year	Number of people charged for chevage each year
1349	1	0
1359	0	1
1363	1	1
1364	1	0
1380	1	0
1384	1	1
1387	2	0
1388	1	1
1389	1	1
1390	1	0
1393	4	0
1395	2	1
1397	1	1
1398	2	1
1399	0	1
1400	0	3
1401	1	6
1402	1	5
1403	3	2
1404	2	4
1405	0	3
1406	4	1
1407	4	2
1408	0	2
1409	0	2
1410	0	2
1411	0	2
1412	0	2
1413	0	2
1415	0	2
1417	0	2
1418	0	2
1419	0	3
1423	2	0
1426	3	0
1427	3	1
1428	3	3
1429	3	3
1430	0	2

1431	2	2
1432	1	2
1434	3	2
1435	3	3
1436	3	3
1437	3	2
1438	3	2
1439	1	2
1440	1	2
1441	1	2
1442	1	2
1443	1	3
1444	1	3
1445	1	3
1446	1	3
1448	1	6
1453	0	5
1454	0	5
1456	0	5
1457	1	4
1458	1	4
1459	0	3
1460	0	3
1461	1	1
1462	0	2
1463	1	1
1470	0	1
1471	0	3
1475	0	2
1477	1	6
1478	0	5
1479	0	5
1481	0	5
1483	0	5
1484	0	5
1485	0	10
1486	0	10
1488	0	10
1496	0	8
1497	0	7
1498	0	7
1499	0	7
1500	0	7

11.6 Utilization of the week works and harvest labour services
at Dunningworth, 1301 to 1392

Year	Winter Works Decayed/Sold/Used			Harvest Works Decayed/Sold/Used			Demesne Area Sown (acres)
1301–2	0	26%	74%	2%	24%	74%	
1302–3	19%	10%	71%	7%	0%	93%	79¾
1305–6	19%	52%	29%	9%	24%	67%	
1391–2	51%	49%	0	40%	60%	0	Leased

Decayed and allowed.

Sources: TNA SC6/995/22 to 25; SROI HD1538/206/6.

offices continued until the 1470s, although the role of the reeve was vastly reduced with the leasing of the manor and the appointment of a salaried bailiff to perform many of the reeve's former functions. In the 1490s the pretence of electing a reeve had been dropped, although the messor and a rent collector were still notionally elected.[32]

11.1 Values of customary arable land at Dunningworth
1340s to 1470s (entry fines d. per acre)

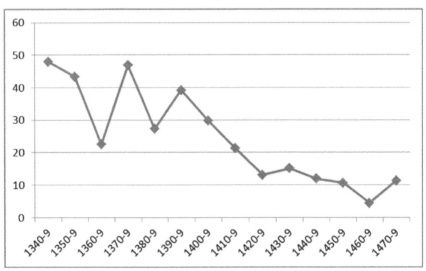

[32] SROI HD1538/207/9.

Entry fines were charged whenever villein land changed hands, and also at the start of a lease. Entry fines on the latter were nominal. The level of entry fine on heritable tenancies was variable. The mean entry fine per acre (of arable land) at Dunningworth peaked in the 1340s at 48d. per acre (see graph 11.1), which was high by East Anglian standards. It dropped 53% between the 1340s and the 1360s, but recovered strongly in the 1370s and remained volatile until the 1390s. Thereafter it fell consistently, dropping dramatically between the 1390s and 1420s (66%), then reaching its nadir in the 1460s.

Attitudes to serfdom

No manumissions are recorded, and no serfs were fined for entering holy orders or to obtain permission to be educated. Two paid to be apprenticed to two different burgesses of Ipswich, although the fines were small.[33] In 1458 the deputy steward of the duke of Norfolk's estate compiled a single list of all known serfs associated with the manor and their progeny, whose preamble indicates that earlier lists had been made.[34]

There is little evidence for any tension over villeinage in the generation after the Black Death, apart from some low-level resistance to harvest services in the early 1350s (see table 11.7). This is unsurprising, given that nearly half the labour services had lapsed and enforcement of most other servile incidents was lax. However, the renewed attention to merchet after the 1370s, and to chevage after c.1400, correlates with a pronounced rise in tension between lords and tenants over aspects of villeinage.

11.7 Non-performance of labour services recorded at Dunningworth, 1353 to 1459

Year	Nature of refusal
1353	3 not come in harvest
1354	6 not come in harvest
1355	4 not come in harvest
1379	2 withhold ploughing services
1383	1 not come to work
1401	1 not come in harvest
1409	2 detain ½ harvest work
	Tenants of Langwade withhold services
1428	Tenants of Langwade detain services
1459	1 not perform services

[33] John Milys was apprenticed at the age of 13 years to John Burre, grocer and merchant of Ipswich, for seven years for a flat fine of 12d., court held May 1451, SROI HD1538/207/7, and Nicholas Miles paid 4d. (probably an annual rate) for continuing to be apprenticed to Thomas Grubbe, 207/8.

[34] SROI HD1538/207/13, the 'names of niefs by blood' were 'updated [*renovat*]' this year.

Some of these disputes emanated from the manorial administration's determination from the late 1370s to impose chevage and merchet upon hereditary serfs by blood. In the 1380s and 1390s this led to two separate claims to freedom from people who had been labelled serfs. Thomas Payn was unsuccessful, and, as a result of his 'false claim', he was fined 13s. 4d. for contempt.[35] In contrast, John Wysman contested a sizeable fine for merchet in 1385 by claiming to be free, and, although one inquisition jury initially found against him, in 1399 a second jury pronounced him a free man.[36] On three occasions serfs engaged in behaviour which was described as 'contemptuous': in 1397 the two Dawes brothers clashed with the messor; in 1402 John Mengy refused to perform suit of court; and in 1406 John Dawes left the manor, probably after a warning not to do so.[37]

11.8 Payment of capitage and tallage at Dunningworth, 1275 to 1399

Year	Capitage (d.)	Tallage (d.)
1275–6	16d.	0
1279–80	16d.	0
1282–3	16d.	30s.
1289–90	16d.	30s.
1291–2	12d.	30s.
1292–3	12d.	30s.
1295–6	12d.	30s.
1296–7	12d.	39s. 4½d.*
1301–2	12d.	39s. 4d.
1302–3	12d.	39s. 4½d.
1305–6	12d.	0
1391–2	5d.	0
1398–9	5d.	0

* 'of which the vill of Langwade 9s. 4½d. this year the first.'

Sources: TNA SC6/995/15 to 25; SROI HD15/206/6.

Tighter administration is also evident in 1396, when the customary tenants failed to respond to requests to draw up a new rental, and regular

---

35 SROI HD1538/207/3, court held May 1394.

36 Bailey, 'Blowing up bubbles', pp. 351–2.

37 SROI HD1538/207/3, court held July 1397; and 207/4, courts held September 1402, and August 1406. John Mengy was amerced 12d. for refusing to performing suit and dues for various holdings in 1402, had still not responded in March 1409, when seizure was ordered of 25 acres of land held by him. However, in February 1410 he served as a presentment juror in the court.

reminders over the next six years were ignored, and so in 1402 they were collectively amerced 2s. and threatened with a 10s. penalty for future non-compliance. An incidental reference in 1409 indicates that the task had only just been completed, 13 years late.[38] After c.1400 overt and sustained examples of conflict receded. Resistance to labour services was rare (see table 11.7), and limited in scope, with just one collective refusal to perform some seasonal works in 1409. Similarly, displays of defiance were now isolated and unrelated to servility, such as when Reginald Tottyng was amerced 20s. for foul-mouthing the bailiff in response to a demand for the arrears of rent on his lease.[39] Fifteenth-century serfs did not resist the payment of chevage or merchet, the two remaining incidents of serfdom.

The court remained sharply watchful of the purchase of free land by *nativi*. The practice was permitted, but only upon the formal enrolment of the acquisition in the court rolls, and the subsequent payment of an incremental rent. Hence when Nicholas Miles bought a parcel of free land in Tunstall he formally reported the purchase to the court, which imposed a small incremental rent.[40] These increments were then recorded in the manorial *compoti* under rents of assize.[41] Most serfs did not report such purchases proactively to the court, and so they were chased and sometimes threatened with a penalty to do so. The regulation of this practice continued well into the 1430s.[42]

The determination to maintain personal servility in the fifteenth century did not extend to any obvious economic discrimination against the serfs of Dunningworth. In the 1390s and 1400s the demesne arable was leased separately for £8 to John Snelling, a serf of the manor, and in 1424 the whole manor was leased for an annual rent of £21 to five men, one of whom, John Wysman, was another serf.[43]

---

[38] SROI HD1538/207/3, courts held May 1396, November 1398, July 1399; 207/4, courts held in September 1402, and September 1409. See also the agreement to reduce the fine to avoid the office of reeve, above p. 205.

[39] SROI HD1538/207/8, court held September 1464.

[40] SROI HD1538/207/3, court held February 1392.

[41] See the shop held in Orford by Thomas Wolnoth, and John Dawys' messuage in Tunstall, in 1399, TNA SC6/995/25.

[42] Nicholas Miles himself had been threatened with a 40s. penalty for failure to report another such purchase in 1377, SROI HD1538/207/3, court held June 1377. See also court held April 1391. For continuing watchfulness thereafter, see SROI HD1538/207/6, courts held October 1432 and December 1436.

[43] SROI HD1538/206/6, TNA SC6/995/25; SROI HD1538/207/4, court held September 1403 for reference to Snelling as farmer of the demesne. The lease of 1424 is recorded in 207/6, court held November 1424.

Summary of chronology and key indicators

By the 1390s around one half of all customary land at Dunningworth was still held on an hereditary villein tenure, although it bore little resemblance to the old tenure: 'in bondage' was no longer used in conveyances, tallage and millsuit had disappeared, all week works were commuted at will, and merchet was no longer charged on customary landholders. The other half was mostly held on tenancies at will and leases, although some had been abandoned. During the fifteenth century these fixed-term tenancies were gradually converted back into hereditary tenures, so that by c.1500 the latter were the dominant form of tenure of customary land at Dunningworth.

Personal servility was not much enforced during the third quarter of the fourteenth century, after which chevage and merchet were suddenly and rigorously imposed. Around 1400 there were around a dozen servile families, and, although the manor kept close tabs on their whereabouts, the number gradually dwindled to eight in the 1450s, and five in c.1500. During the sixteenth century these five families were still tracked for payments of chevage and merchet. Meanwhile, the tenant base of the manor remained steady. In 1382 48 tenants performed fealty, 43 in 1426, and 49 owed fealty in 1448.[44]

There is no evidence for a seigniorial reaction in the third quarter of the fourteenth century, and little evidence for peasant resistance. There are no refusals to render tallage, few examples of resistance to labour services, and hardly any recorded departures before the 1390s. The move to impose personal servility more rigorously in the 1380s and 1390s, and to require all customary tenants to produce a rental, did provoke some direct responses, which led to the abandonment of elections to, and payments in exoneration from, the office of reeve. It had no discernible impact upon the collection of chevage and merchet, which continued throughout the fifteenth century. There are no recorded manumissions.

The number of chevage cases and presentments for absence rose soon after 1400, and peaked in the late 1480s. This pattern is best explained by a combination of a heightened interest in chevage as the means of tracking departed serfs, and the accession of a new lord to the manor. In other words, the frequency with which migration is recorded is as likely to reflect fluctuations in administrative zeal and priorities as genuine fluctuations in departures.

The chronology of the decline of villein tenure correlates well with general trends in the value of land. Land values fell by over one half between the 1340s and 1360s, fluctuated between the 1370s and 1390s, then fell sharply again over the next two decades: they reached their nadir in the 1460s. Their

---

[44] SROI HD1538/207/3, court held May 1382; 207/6, court held January 1426; 207/7, court held November 1448.

dramatic fall across the period of the Black Death corresponds directly with the disappearance of the phrase '*in bondagio*' from villein tenures, the decay of the main incidents of villein tenure, and the conversion of just under half of the former villein tenures to grants 'of issues' and leases. The trough in the land market during the mid-fifteenth century corresponds with the shift towards more secure tenures and fee farms. The management of personal servility was tightened during the 1390s, corresponding with a sharp downturn in the land market, but otherwise its changes do not correlate well with either land values or peasant resistance. The ebbs and flows of enforcing chevage and merchet are best explained by fluctuations in either estate policy or administrative efficiency.

Cratfield[45]

Customary land tenures

A full series of court rolls is extant from 1401, but all that has survived from before that date is a handful of accounts. Unfree land was categorized as either molland, native, *werkelond* or land of increment, and most land transfers were small, although a few standardized villein holdings of 16- and 20-*acreware* still existed. By 1401 the formula for conveyances of customary land did not contain 'in bondage' or 'in villeinage', and seldom deviated from 'holds to him and his heirs at the will of the lord for services and customs'. The only variation occurred in the 1410s, when the phrase 'by the rod' was added for a few years, but then dropped.

Almost every recorded transfer of customary land was a hereditary tenure, including disposals of land stuck in the lord's hands. Just a single grant for the tenure of a term is documented, when Edward Cook acquired one grange '*de bondagio domini*' for the term of his life '*per legem Anglie*'.[46] Similarly, a single grant at leasehold is recorded, when in 1408 two acres of land in the lord's hands were granted at farm for five years.[47] The court remained sharply watchful of the acquisition of any free land by its serfs, actively seizing such lands until the tenant enrolled the transaction in the court and formalized its conversion to 'soiled land'.[48]

In 1438 43 'free and native' tenants, and six serfs by blood, performed fealty

---

[45] This case study is based upon c.210 extant courts between 1401 and 1500, CUL Vanneck Mss, box 3, and 9 accounts dating from the period 1282 and 1302, TNA SC6/995/2 to 11.

[46] CUL Vanneck Mss, box 3, court held October 1435.

[47] CUL Vanneck Mss, box 3, court held October 1408.

[48] For example, CUL Vanneck Mss, box 3, courts held January 1421, June 1423, and June 1427.

to John Mowbray, but serfs were not distinguished in subsequent fealty lists.[49] In 1489 the court reminded its customary tenants that they must not pursue actions against other tenants of the manor in any court other than that of Cratfield.[50]

Incidents of villeinage

Tallage and capitage were both levied in the early fourteenth century, but there is no subsequent record of either.[51] After 1401 there are no references to heriot, childwite or millsuit see (table 11.1). In the early fourteenth century the lord could call upon 1,451 week, and 992 harvest, works for his demesne each year, although most of the week works were routinely sold.[52] Labour services are not mentioned in the extant court rolls, which indicates that by c.1400 they must have been fully and permanently commuted. Variable entry fines were charged throughout the fifteenth century, and elections to the offices of reeve and messor continued to be held.

Thus, by the time the court series begins in 1401 all the incidents of villein tenure had decayed, although merchet and chevage continued to be levied on the personally servile. Both males and females were liable to merchet, until the last male merchet was charged in 1410.[53] In 1429 the court noted that William Howe had married and so it sought the lord's advice on what action to take, but nothing ever happened.[54] The frequency of merchets fell dramatically after 1420, as did the level of fine after 1450 (see table 11.10). The dramatic rise in the mean charge in the last quarter of the fifteenth century was due solely to an exceptional 20s. merchet imposed upon Agnes Alson.[55]

Neither chevage nor presentments for absence are recorded at all between 1400 and 1416, despite a good series of court rolls (see table 11.12). Thereafter chevage became a regular feature, although the number of cases each year never exceeded four, and the level of fine was seldom high, with 4d. the modal charge (table 11.11). The court's interest in fugitives increased on three occasions during the fifteenth century. The first occurred during the late 1420s, when the number of chevage payers rose from one in 1427 to four in 1430, and the level of fine imposed upon three of them jumped from a few

49 CUL Vanneck Mss, box 3, court held March 1438. In fact, John Mowbray had succeeded his father as Duke in 1432, but, on this evidence, Cratfield was not restored to him until 1438.

50 CUL Vanneck Mss, box 3, court held October 1489.

51 TNA SC6/995/11.

52 TNA SC6/995/6 to 11.

53 CUL Vanneck Mss, box 3, court held June 1410.

54 CUL Vanneck Mss, box 3, court held October 1429. Howe did continue to render chevage.

55 CUL Vanneck Mss, box 3, court held December 1485.

11.9　Frequency of merchet, heriot, childwite and millsuit
at Cratfield, 1400 to 1499

Period	Merchet	Heriot	Childwite	Millsuit
1400–24	12	0	0	0
1425–49	2	0	0	0
1450–74	3	0	0	0
1475–99	2	0	0	0

11.10　Incidence of merchet, and mean size of levy,
at Cratfield, 1400 to 1499

Period	Number of merchets	Mean levy	Number of marriages without licence	Mean levy
1400–1424	12	38d.	0	0
1425–1449	2	60d.	0	0
1450–1474	3	24d.	0	0
1475–1499	2	132d.	0	0

pennies to 6s. 8d. (John and Henry Fuller), and 3s. 4d. (William Spink). Spink was an absentee landholder, who was also accused of allowing his tenement to fall into disrepair, for which he was amerced a further 3s. 4d.[56] Similarly, in 1427 the court threatened William Howe, who held land in Cratfield but lived in nearby Walpole, with a £5 penalty if he failed to rebuild and reoccupy the ruinous house on his holding.[57] A year later, the homage was ordered to attach John Fuller of Hoxne (Suffolk) and bring him bodily to the next court, with a penalty of 6s. 8d. for non-compliance, and then the lord's advice was sought when Henry Fuller failed to pay chevage.[58] The increased interest in chevage and the state of houses on customary holdings between 1427 and 1430 was followed by a sudden reduction of interest in both (see table 11.12). This pattern is unlikely to have reflected a genuine surge of emigration – it is more likely to reflect either an attempt to improve land occupancy by officials of a new lord, who had acceded to the manor in 1425, or a deliberate tactic by some emigrants opting voluntarily to register their existence to a new manorial regime through the payment of chevage.

Another surge of interest in absentees occurred after 1438, coinciding with John Mowbray's acquisition of the manor. The performance of fealty at his first court generated a list of serfs by blood, which provided the basis for

---

[56]　CUL Vanneck Mss, box 3, court held October 1430.
[57]　CUL Vanneck Mss, box 3, court held June 1427.
[58]　CUL Vanneck Mss, box 3, courts held November 1428 and October 1431.

chasing absentees.[59] The final wave of enforcement occurred in the late 1460s and early 1470s, when the manor targeted two families, the Fullers and the Howes. By the 1480s, just one family – the Howes – paid chevage.

11.11 Incidence of chevage, and mean size of levy,
at Cratfield, 1400 to 1499

Period	Number of chevage cases	Mean fine per case
1400–1424	10	3.6d.
1425–1449	43	11.7d.
1450–1474	43	4.1d.
1475–1499	35	3.7d.

11.12 Recorded flight of serfs from Cratfield, 1416 to 1497

Year	Number of people presented for absence	Number of people charged for chevage
1416	0	1
1417	0	1
1419	0	1
1421	0	3
1422	0	2
1423	0	2
1425	0	2
1426	0	2
1427	0	1
1428	0	1
1429	0	3
1430	0	4
1431	0	2
1432	1	1
1433	1	2
1434	0	1
1435	0	1
1436	1	2
1438	3	1
1439	1	4
1440	1	4
1441	1	2
1442	1	2
1443	1	2

59 CUL Vanneck Mss, box 3, court held March 1438.

1444	0	2
1446	1	1
1447	1	1
1448	1	1
1449	1	1
1450	1	1
1451	1	1
1453	1	1
1455	3	0
1456	1	0
1457	1	0
1459	1	2
1460	1	2
1461	1	2
1462	1	0
1463	2	2
1464	1	2
1465	2	2
1466	2	2
1467	2	2
1468	2	3
1469	0	4
1470	2	4
1471	2	4
1472	0	4
1473	2	3
1474	3	2
1475	0	3
1476	0	4
1479	0	3
1480	0	4
1481	0	3
1482	0	2
1486	0	2
1488	0	2
1489	0	2
1492	0	2
1493	0	2
1494	0	2
1496	0	2
1497	0	2

Attitudes to serfdom

No serfs paid fines for permission to enter holy orders or to be educated. In 1420 William Howe paid 4d. as a licence to learn the art of a 'weaver of linen or woollen cloth' for three years in nearby Walpole (Suffolk), on condition that he returned to Cratfield each year. He duly paid chevage for the next two years, and then moved back to live on the manor.[60] In 1458 a list of serfs was drawn up at the same time as the Dunningworth list, detailing the existence of five families but the progeny of just two of them. There are no recorded claims to be free, and a single manumission (for William Ales) is recorded.[61] The only case of documented peasant resistance occurred late in 1492, when Andrew and Ralph Howe – the last two serfs to pay chevage at Cratfield – both 'refused to pay their chevage'. Both were aggrieved because they were living in Framlingham castle, and therefore presumably in the service of their lord, but they must have quickly reconsidered their position, because they duly recommenced payments at the next court.[62]

The heightened sensitivity about fugitives in the late 1420s, and then again in the late 1430s, was associated with other aggressive tactics against serfs. The orders to return to the manor and to rebuild houses, under the threat of financial penalties, in the late 1420s were novel, and, as the cases of the two Fullers and William Spink demonstrate, they were coupled with a temporary but sharp increase in the fines for chevage. The same happened in the late 1430s. For example, John Eyr had routinely paid 3d. chevage in the early 1420s to live in Trimley (Suffolk), but returned to Cratfield around 1427 and stayed, performing fealty to the new lord in March 1438. However, he left soon afterwards, abandoning his holding, for which he had to pay a large chevage fine of 3s. 4d. He died away from the manor in 1441.[63]

A sudden rise in the number and/or size of chevage payments, and the unexpected appearance of a long-departed serf in the court records paying chevage or merchet, is usually indicative of a seigniorial crackdown. Yet, occasionally, the explanation is rather different. In 1441 an estate official negotiated a merchet of 8s. from Richard Spink, a serf whose family had left Cratfield in the 1390s and who had long since settled in west Suffolk. Four years later Spink travelled to Cratfield to pay chevage for the first time and to perform servile fealty in full court.[64] No explanation is provided for this

---

[60] CUL Vanneck Mss, box 3, courts held January 1421, December 1422 and June 1424.

[61] CUL Vanneck Mss, box 3, court held December 1453, but no sum is given.

[62] CUL Vanneck Mss, box 3, courts held June and December 1493.

[63] CUL Vanneck Mss, box 3, courts held March 1438, February 1439, October 1439, October 1440 and October 1441.

[64] Bailey, 'Blowing up bubbles', p. 351; CUL Vanneck Mss box 3, court held June 1445.

sudden flurry of activity, which could be interpreted as an example of the aggressive pursuit for profit of a wealthy but long-departed serf. However, in 1443 Christina Spink, a widow, died seized of 12¼ acres in Cratfield, but her two closest heirs had recently pre-deceased her. The land was granted to Margaret Cottingham as the daughter of Christina's husband. Margaret acquired another acre of land in 1445 after the death of one Alice Spink.[65] The active involvement of members of the extended Spink family in the land market, at the same time as the long-departed Richard Spink submitted to servile status on his home manor, may be a coincidence, but it seems unlikely. It is more likely that Richard was willingly and actively taking these steps in order to register an interest in a possible inheritance. If this interpretation is correct, then it provides support for Yates' observation that the survival of serfdom in the fifteenth century involved an element of choice on the part of the serf.[66] It also adds credibility to the suggestion that some long-departed serfs chose to pay chevage for the first few years after the arrival of a new lord of the manor as a precautionary measure, in case of an inheritance or the desire to seek some patronage or protection from the lord.

Summary of chronology and key indicators
By the time the Cratfield court roll series begins in 1401 almost all customary land was held on a hereditary villein tenure, although the main pecuniary incidents associated with villeinage had been dropped, and the phrase 'in villeinage' does not appear in any conveyance.

In the first decade of the fifteenth century personal servility was still being enforced upon a handful of serf families through the single incident of merchet, although from 1410 it was no longer charged upon males and from the 1420s its frequency on females declined. As merchet declined, so chevage increased in importance and significance. It first appeared in 1416, then towards the end of the 1420s it increased in frequency. It is still recorded at the very end of the fifteenth century, albeit on a single serf family. There are no signs of any serious fall in the number of tenants in the fifteenth century, hardly any peasant resistance, and no manumissions.

---

[65] CUL Vanneck Mss, box 3, courts held October 1443 and October 1445.
[66] Yates, *Town and countryside*, p. 212.

Staverton[67]

Customary land tenures

It is not possible to establish the original extent of customary land at Staverton, although it was large judging by the high volume of unfree land transactions recorded in the manorial courts. Most holdings were fragmented and individual transactions were small. Before 1349 all were occupied. Customary land owed merchet, millsuit, heriot (but not tallage), entry fine and a wide range of labour services, from winter and summer works, to harvest, harrowing and ploughing services.[68]

The Black Death badly disrupted the land market, with many holdings lying abandoned throughout 1349 and the early part of 1350, but thereafter it picked up steadily as many heirs claimed their inheritances. The language of servility was quickly dropped from the formula for conveyances of customary land. Before 1350 villein tenure had usually been described as held by the tenant 'and his brood...in bondage for services'.[69] Immediately after the Black Death each parcel was still described as 'customary' or 'native', but references to 'bondage' and 'brood' in conveyances disappeared. From 1351 land was consistently described as 'held by him and his heirs at the will of the lord for services', a formula that hardly changed for the next century.[70]

Most customary land was therefore gradually re-occupied on hereditary villein tenure. Some of the land that still lay unoccupied was granted instead to new tenants 'at the will of the lord', with no further tenurial details provided: these were literally held at the lord's will as temporary grants, which could be rescinded immediately if the heir appeared or, indeed, if anyone stepped forward to take the land on the old terms. They seldom did. For example, at some stage in 1350 Stephen atte Wall had obtained two roods of abandoned customary land lying in nearby Wantisden 'at the will of the lord', but, in the absence of any subsequent claim from the rightful heir, he

---

[67] This case study is based upon 292 courts between 1350–1364, 1367–8, 1374–6, 1400–12 and 1422–1484, SROI HD1538/357/3 to 6. There are 15 extant accounts between 1268 and 1307, TNA SC6/1005/7 to 21, and nine from 1399 to 1474, SROI HD1538/256/2 to 10.

[68] See the works' account of 1306–7, TNA SC6/1005/21, where, for example, 1,633 winter works, 448 summer, 730 harvest, 110 harvest boon and 57 harvest carriage works were due from customary holdings.

[69] For the formula, see, for example, SROI HD1538/357/1, court held March 1331. In 1306–7 all customary land was held on villein tenure, TNA SC6/1005/21.

[70] See, for example, the grant in 1351 of one 'native' messuage in Stratford granted to John Oxe, a serf by blood, 'to hold to him and his heirs at the will of the lord for services', court held May 1351, SROI HD1538/357/3, m. 18. Between 1400 and the 1440s 'to hold to him and his heirs at the will of the lord for services and customs' appears regularly and consistently, SROI HD1538/357/4 and 5.

sought to obtain a more secure grip on the land. In March 1351 he formally surrendered the land in the manor court, only to be immediately re-admitted on new terms: 'to hold for the term of his life and, after his death, [the two roods] will remain with John his son and heir at the will of the lord'.[71]

Hence after 1349 most customary land was reoccupied on villein tenure, while a minority was granted to new tenants on a temporary tenure (at the arbitrary will of the lord). There was little conversion of customary land to leasehold. These general developments are reflected in the contents of the first manorial account extant after the Black Death, dating from 1400–1, when 90% of labour services were still notionally available, and 91% of rents of assize were paid, both of which reflect the high level of occupancy of customary land on hereditary villein tenure. The conversion of some land to tenancy at will is reflected in the 70s. 6d. received from 'the issues of diverse lands and tenements in the hands of the lord after the death of their tenants'; a modest 4s. 4d. was received from the lease of customary lands, reflecting the relative absence of grants of leasehold in the court rolls.[72] So, at the opening of the fifteenth century, around 90% of the original customary land continued to be held on a form of villein tenure, and the remainder was held on either insecure tenures or leases or lay untenanted.

Hereditary tenure continued to dominate the transfers of customary land in fifteenth-century courts. The practice of issuing a separate copy of the court roll entry of admission was certainly well-established by 1400, because the remarkable yet chance survival of 40 of the landlord's copies of these admissions to customary landholdings have survived from the fifteenth century, the earliest of which dates from 27th January 1400.[73] These are exceptionally rare survivals, because landlords seldom kept their separate copy of the land transaction (instead, they relied upon the record of the court itself), but their existence proves that the practice of issuing copies was already firmly established here by 1400.

The formula for conveyances established in the 1350s remained stable and consistent until the 1460s, when the formula was altered slightly to 'him, his heirs and assignees by the rod at the will of the lord rendering services and customs', and by the 1500s the standard format had changed again to 'him, his heirs and assignees by the rod at the will of the lord according to the custom of the manor'.[74] The removal of 'rendering services and customs' reflected the fact that labour services were no longer liable from these holdings (see below).

[71] SROI HD1538/357/3, court held March 1351.
[72] SROI HD1538/357/2 (1400–1).
[73] SROI HD1538/357/13 to 29, and 36 to 59.
[74] See, for example, SROI HD1538/357/6, m. 1 (courts held in 1461), and HD1538/357/7, m. 1 (courts held in 1509).

There is no evidence after 1400 for any change in the area of customary land converted to leasehold. Only three new leases are recorded in the first decade of the fifteenth century, and barely a dozen throughout the rest of the century. Most of these leases were used to attract tenants for land lying abandoned in the lord's hands, all of whom paid small entry fines upon admission.[75] Thereafter, some were converted back to hereditary tenure upon expiry of the lease.[76] The remainder were eventually converted to fee farms. For example, in May 1424 John Haukswode of Ufford was granted one pightle of pasture for the term of his life, paying 12d. at farm per annum and a 12d. entry fine, but John surrendered the lease in September 1425 and was immediately re-admitted: 'the lord grants and leases at farm ... to hold to him and his heirs, rendering 12d. per annum', and the marginal note states unequivocally 'fee farm'.[77] After the 1420s fee farms were preferred to conventional leases to attract tenants for abandoned land.[78] They were held 'for him, his heirs and assignees at the will of the lord according to the custom of the manor ... at fee farm'.[79] Yet fee farms still comprised a small minority of all land grants: only 17 are recorded at Staverton between 1425 and 1475, and none thereafter. The terms of the last grant at fee farm in 1475 are virtually indistinguishable from those of the conventional hereditary tenures.

Hence customary land in c.1500 was overwhelmingly held on hereditary tenure at Staverton. Even the demesne warren was granted in this form, rather than leased by copy of contract, which would have been the more conventional route.[80] In 1425 48 free and customary tenants swore fealty to the new lord of the manor, together with 14 serfs by blood. In December 1436 there were 68 free and native tenants, and just five serfs by blood. In 1462, when 57 performed fealty, serfs were no longer distinguished.[81]

Incidents of villeinage

Millsuit was regularly imposed before 1350, and in the 1350s five men were amerced an average of 4d. for failure to mill at the lord's mill (see table 11.13). Millsuit disappeared after 1357 (see table 11.1). A demesne mill continued in existence for the whole of the fifteenth century, with the exception of the early 1450s when fire partially destroyed it; it was repaired and operational

---

75 In 1440 Thomas Parchant was granted the lease of 2½ acres in Wantisden 'which Alex Andrew lately abandoned', SROI HD1538/357/5, m. 64.

76 Such as those expiring in 1442, SROI HD1538/357/5, mm. 70–1.

77 SROI HD1538/357/5, mm. 7, 12.

78 SROI HD1538/357/5, mm. 83 (1446), 97 (1451); HD1538/357/6, m. 12 (1471).

79 SROI HD1538/357/6, m. 15 (court held in 1475).

80 SROI HD1538/357/7, m. 6. The warren was granted to Nicholas Talle of Framlingham 'to hold to him, his heirs, assignees' etc.

81 SROI HD1538/357/5, mm. 12 and 52 (1425 and 1436); HD1538/357/6, m. 4 (1462).

again by 1455.[82] Before the Black Death a collective charge of 4s. was made for capitage, which continued to be paid annually until its disappearance sometime between 1406 and 1431.[83] Tallage is not recorded before the Black Death, despite a good series of extant accounts, which is unusual for a manor on this estate. Recognition was collected upon the accession of a new lord to the manor in 1319, which suggests that, for some reason, this manor paid recognition rather than tallage.[84] Neither were imposed after 1348–9 (see table 11.1).

11.13 Frequency of merchet, heriot, childwite and millsuit at Staverton, 1338 to 1499

Period	Merchet	Heriot	Childwite	Millsuit
1338–42*	/	/	X	/
1350–74	35	2	0	5
1375–99	2	0	0	0
1400–24	19	0	0	0
1425–49	20	0	0	0
1450–74	3	0	0	0
1475–99	5	0	0	0

* / = recorded, X = not recorded, SROI HD1538/357/1

Heriot was charged occasionally before 1350, although it was always a cash payment rendered by heirs admitted to the holding of a deceased tenant, and so it was scarcely distinguishable from an entry fine. The last heriot was recorded in 1351 (see table 11.1). Heirs continued to pay a cash sum for their admittance to the holding, but thereafter it was simply called an entry fine. Conventional entry fines were routinely charged on all admittances to customary land. Unfortunately, the proliferation of grants of small slivers of land, with pightles, buildings and 'pieces' of undisclosed area attached to them, prevents the construction of any meaningful series of land values per acre for Staverton. In general, fines were high and variable, although they fell

[82] SROI HD1538/357/5, mm. 98, 106.

[83] TNA SC6/1005/7 to 20. No account survives between 1406 and 1431, SROI HD1538/356/4 and 5. The latter records 'nothing for capitagium, because the fine is made in the court rolls', but nothing is recorded in the courts, HD1538/356/5.

[84] TNA SC6/1005/7 to 20 does not record tallage: the payment of 20s. recognition at the accession of Edward de Monte in 1319 is documented in SROI HD1538/357/1, m. 12.

11.14 Utilization of Main Labour Services
at Staverton, 1306–7 and 1400–1

Year	Winter Works Decayed/Sold/Used			Summer works Decayed/Sold/Used			Harvest Works Decayed/Sold/Used			Harvest Boon works Decayed/Sold/Used		
1306–7	8%	76%	16%	8%	54%	38%	9%	15%	76%	4%	96%	0%
1400–1	18%	82%	0%	16%	74%	10%	21%	79%	0%	6%	94%	0%

across the later Middle Ages, from around 28d. per acre in the 1350s to c.10d. per acre in the early 1480s.[85]

A high proportion of labour services was routinely sold before the Black Death (see table 11.14). In 1306–7, for example, over one half of all winter, summer and harvest boon works were commuted on an *ad hoc* basis, and only harvest works were actively used on the demesne. By 1400–1 more than three quarters of all works were sold each year, and only a few summer works were actually used: they were all deployed to repair the manorial mill. The account notes that some of these sales, totalling 27s. 8d., had been agreed and recorded twelve years previously (in 1388), which indicates a negotiated commutation.[86] Unfortunately no court rolls survive from the late 1370s and 1380s when these agreements had been struck, although one such agreement survives from 1352, when the five co-tenants of a nine-acre landholding paid 12d. to be exonerated their labour services for the year.[87] Eventually, by the early 1440s, all the remaining labour services had been formally negotiated into long term commutations, and the works' section disappears from the manorial account.[88] Thus in the early fourteenth century a minority of labour services had been used on the demesne each year, and the majority commuted at will; by 1400 around 15% of labour services were decayed, a few were used, and the rest were commuted through a combination of at will and negotiated agreements; and by 1440 all had either disappeared, decayed or had been formally negotiated into permanent commutations.

Each year customary landholders were required to provide four manorial offices (reeve, ploughreeve, park keeper and capitage officer) through a system of rotating 'elections', for which the office holders enjoyed relief

[85] SROI HD1538/357/3, mm. 19 to 53, and HD1538/357/6, mm. 25 to 33, calculated from admissions to arable land only where the area is clearly stated.

[86] SROI HD1538/356/2.

[87] SROI HD1538/357/3, m. 25.

[88] The last extant works' section dates from the 1439–40 account, whose contents are almost identical to the works' accounts of the 1400s, see SROI HD1538/356/2 to 6. In 1445–6 all remaining works are recorded as sold in the revenue section of the account, and the works' section disappears, HD1538/356/7. 1,229 winter works generated 34s. 1d., 403 summer works fetched 16s., and 610 harvest works 56s. 3d.

from their labour services for the year of office. In the 1330s and 1340s those elected as reeve could opt to pay 30s. to evade office, and after 1350 this option was taken in most years.[89] The latter is partly explained by the unpopularity of such a demanding job, but also by the split of liable holdings into the hands of three or four tenants, who would rather share the cost of exoneration between them than determine which one would perform the office. Elections to all four offices continued until the 1440s, then lapsed in the 1450s; payments to exonerate then disappear completely. In the 1460s a revised system had emerged, whereby the customary tenants had to elect three people to the offices of reeve, messor and collector, although by 1478 just the collector was being elected.[90] In the early sixteenth century all elections had been discontinued.[91]

In 1355 the court ordered an inquiry to establish which serfs had bought free land, but had not registered the purchase formally within the court rolls.[92] It continued to monitor and enforce the regulations about soiled land throughout the fifteenth century.

11.15 Incidence of merchet, and mean size of levy,
at Staverton, 1350 to 1499

Period	Number of merchets	Mean levy	Number of marriages without licence	Mean levy
1350–74	29	26d.	6	57d.
1375–99	0	0	2	40d.
1400–24	17	22d.	2	27d.
1425–49	20	20d.	0	0
1450–74	3	19d.	0	0
1475–99	5	26d.	0	0

Childwite was not levied at Staverton either before or after 1349 (see table 11.13). Merchet remained a regular levy upon male and female serfs until the mid-fifteenth century – for example, 29 cases are recorded in the period 1350–74 and 20 in 1425–49 (see table 11.15).[93] Presentments for marrying

---

[89] For an example before 1350, see SROI HD1358/357/2, court held March 1346.

[90] SROI HD1538/357/5, m. 78 for elections in the 1440s; mm. 103–6 for the absence of any elections in the 1450s; HD1538/357/6, mm. 4, 8,14 for elections in the 1460s, and m. 22 for the election of the collector alone.

[91] SROI HD1538/357/7.

[92] SROI HD1538/357/3, m. 41.

[93] The absence of merchets between 1375 and 1399 reflects the sizeable gap in the court-roll series.

without licence were much less frequent, and the last such entry occurred in 1408. The frequency of merchet remained consistent until the late 1430s, after which it dropped sharply. The last male merchet was levied in 1460, and thereafter merchet was mainly levied upon the female offspring of just two families.[94] It was still charged in the early sixteenth century.[95]

The average charge for merchet was never particularly high, varying between 19d. and 26d. (see table 11.15), a level which remained remarkably constant between 1350 and 1450. The charges for male merchets were generally lower (ranging between 6d. and 8s., and averaging 18d.) than those for females (between 6d. and 6s. 8d., averaging 27d.). The disappearance of the lower value male merchets after 1460 helps to explain the slight rise in the mean value of merchets from 20d. (1425–49) to 26d. (1475–99, see table 11.15). Very occasionally the level of fine in an individual case attracts a short, explanatory, comment: a female marrying a freeman (a higher rate), marriage to another resident serf (lower), or some relief due to poverty.[96] Marriages without licence attracted higher fines than merchets (see table 11.15), especially in the generation after the Black Death (averaging 57d. in 1350–74 compared to the 26d. for merchet), implying that officials wished to reward the proactive and open reporting of marriages.

11.16 Incidence of chevage, and mean size of levy,
at Staverton, 1350 to 1499

Period	Number of chevage cases	Mean fine per case
1350–74	0	0
1375–99	0	0
1400–24	90	12.8d.
1425–49	26	5.3d.
1450–74	77	3.8d.
1475–99	59	4.0d.

Migrant serfs were managed loosely in the two decades after the Black Death at Staverton. Not a single serf paid chevage in the immediate aftermath of the Black Death (see table 11.16). Presentments for absence were made in most years in the 1350s, but then ceased after 1358 (see table 11.17).

---

94 See, for example, the 3s. 4d. rendered by Joanna Oxe in 1515, and the same paid by her sister Matilda in 1518, SROI HD1538/357/7, mm. 7, 10.

95 SROI HD1538/357/7, mm. 7, 10.

96 For example, Walter Baldwyn paid 12d. and 'no more because he has no goods', and Katherine Town 2s. 'and no more because a pauper', SROI HD1538/357/1, m. 16 (Baldwyn) and /5, m. 32 (Town).

11.17 Recorded flight of serfs from Staverton, 1350 to 1484

Year	Number of people presented for absence	Number of people charged for chevage
1350	4	0
1351	4	0
1354	4	0
1356	2	0
1357	8	0
1400	3	3
1401	3	4
1402	1	6
1403	0	5
1404	0	8
1405	0	5
1406	0	7
1407	0	8
1408	2	6
1409	0	8
1410	0	8
1411	1	7
1422	0	6
1423	1	4
1424	0	5
1425	1	4
1426	2	4
1427	4	11
1428	7	9
1429	5	10
1430	10	9
1431	11	11
1433	11	12
1434	11	12
1435	11	12
1436	11	12
1438	11	11
1439	11	8
1440	11	9
1441	11	10
1442	11	8
1443	11	7
1444	0	8
1446	0	8

1447	2	9
1448	6	10
1449	6	10
1450	6	10
1451	6	7
1453	0	7
1454	6	6
1455	6	6
1456	0	6
1457	0	5
1459	0	5
1460	11	5
1461	11	5
1464	1	6
1470	2	9
1475	0	8
1476	0	5
1477	7	5
1478	0	7
1479	0	7
1480	0	6
1481	0	6
1482	0	6
1483	0	5
1484	0	4

However, this indifference had completely evaporated by the very end of the century, when chevage payments had become frequent. In 1400 three serfs paid chevage and three more were absent. Until 1403 chevage payers were reported twice a year, and they paid in two instalments, although in 1404 this cumbersome system was dropped and chevage was recorded and paid once a year, usually in the first court after Michaelmas (29 September). The absence of interest in flown serfs before c.1400 is striking, and it implies that the manorial administration only became really interested in flown serfs when faced with a chronic shortage of tenants. However, it may be that the development of chevage as a regular payment to live off the manor only became properly established when the use of *capitagium* waned. Whatever the reason, the average charge for chevage peaked at the beginning of the fifteenth century at 13d. (see table 11.16), but then fell to 5d. in the second quarter of the century. After 1450 the level settled to around 4d. per person per annum.

The combined numbers paying chevage and presented for absence held steady at around six per annum during the first quarter of the fifteenth century, but then rose markedly in the second quarter (see table 11.17): for example, between the mid-1420s and the early 1430s the number rose from five to 22. This looks like an administrative crackdown following the accession of a new lord in 1425, rather than a sudden exodus of serfs. There is little doubt that the administration at this time was determined to be well-informed about departed serfs. In the November court of 1430 ten fugitives were presented for their absence, and, 'by the advice of the lord', each was threatened with a 6s. 8d. penalty unless they appeared at the next court.[97] The number of chevage payers was maintained at around a dozen throughout the 1430s before falling to around six in the 1450s. After 1443 presentments for absence were no longer made consistently, and they finally disappear after a short enforcement wave in the early 1470s. Four people were still paying chevage in 1484, after which the court-roll series is disrupted, but there are no payments of chevage when the series resumes in 1509.[98]

Attitudes to serfdom

No servile genealogies have survived from Staverton, and there are no payments for permission to be educated, apprenticed or to enter holy orders. A single manumission is recorded in 1455, when Matthew Oxe paid 6d. to have its details formally entered into the proceedings of the manor court, a case which contains three points of interest. First, it was granted for devoted service in the household of the Duke of Norfolk, and Matthew does not appear to have purchased the charter. Second, Matthew had changed his name from Oxe to Groom, presumably because Oxe was a well-known servile surname in those parts. Third, the manumission grant explicitly extended to all his progeny, land and chattels, a clause designed to remove any legal ambiguity about their status.[99]

The introduction and enforcement of chevage from c.1400, and the heightened interest in formally identifying and monitoring serfs, provoked dissent from two of them. Early in 1404 estate officials physically seized Richard Speyr for undisclosed reasons, and only released him upon the deposit of £10 16s. 8d. as security for his good behaviour. Yet he fled the manor that summer, and so the pledge was forfeit. In 1410 he was reported as marrying without licence. Similarly, in 1407 Alex King of Campsey Ash was forced to swear servile fealty in front of the whole court, presumably after disputing

---

97 For example, John Haconn, shearman, 'and all his brood' were ordered to return from 'Wodestrete in the parish of St Alban' in London, SROI HD1538/357/5, m. 31.

98 SROI HD1538/357/6 and 7.

99 See Chapter 2; SROI HD1538/357/5 m. 106.

his status, and within a year he too had left the manor.[100] There is no record of other such disputes.

11.18   Incidence of recorded non-performance of labour services
at Staverton, 1351 to 1458

Year	Non-Performance of Labour Services
1351	1 withholds
1352	9 withhold
1353	1 withholds
1355	3 withhold hay works, 26 withhold harvest boon works, 6 withhold weeding works
1356	6 withhold harvest works, 3 withhold works, 6 withhold hay works, 1 mows badly
1360	2 withhold harvest
1458	3 withhold hay works

These are recorded amercements (including pardons), not presentments.

Refusals to perform labour services were rare, occurring in a total of seven years (see table 11.18). Most were minor and isolated incidents. Resistance was concentrated in the 1350s, culminating in a collective protest against harvest works in the summer of 1355. This was part of a wider testing of the bounds of the relationship between customary landholders and the lord in the immediate aftermath of the Black Death. In 1352 Alex Blanchflower had openly refused to take up the office of plough reeve, for which contempt he was fined 13s. 4d., and in 1357 all lands of Richard de Upgate were ordered to be seized after he had refused to serve as reeve.[101] Thereafter, overt refusals and even passive resistance were unusual. Just three cases merit attention. In 1402 the homage was sharply warned for its failure to elect the three lesser manorial officials: annual elections to all four quickly resumed.[102] In 1481 Richard Cutting bluntly refused to perform the office of collector. The outcome is not recorded in subsequent courts, and the series is disrupted after 1484, but when it resumes in 1509 all elections had ceased.[103]

The final recorded act of resistance was an odd affair, drawn out over 20 years. In 1427 those attending the manorial court (the 'homage') were ordered to compile a new rental, under a penalty of 40s. for non-compliance.

---

[100]   SROI HD1538/357/4, courts held March 1404, July 1404, November 1407, and December 1408.

[101]   SROI HD1538/357/3, mm. 22, 40.

[102]   SROI HD1538/357/4, court held December 1402.

[103]   SROI HD1538/357/6, m. 28.

The order was repeated regularly until 1430, when a collective fine of 6s. 8d. was imposed and a further 40s. penalty threatened. The order continued to be issued in the early 1430s, but no more penalties were imposed and even the threat of punishment for non-compliance disappeared.[104] In 1447 the call for a new rental was repeated, with a fresh penalty of 20s.[105] It is not clear if the rental was ever produced, although it is clear that it was not produced within the manorial administration's preferred timeframe. It seems highly unlikely that the lord's administration would have been wholly dependent upon the tenantry for the information essential to the production of a rental – after all, officials had court and account rolls, and earlier rentals, full of relevant information. In which case, the officials may have been deliberately making pointed and symbolic demands upon the tenants, which were duly resisted.

Summary of chronology and key indicators
The vast majority of customary land at Staverton was reoccupied on heredi-tary villein tenure during the 1350s, although the phrase 'in villeinage' was dropped from conveyances immediately. Likewise, the key servile incidents attached to these tenures largely disappeared in the 1350s: heriot and millsuit were recorded for the last time in this decade, recognition was paid before 1349 but not at all afterwards, and most week works were commuted at will. By 1400 copies were routinely made of the court-roll entry describing the land transaction and issued to tenants. Thus certainly by the end of the fourteenth century, and probably earlier, villein tenure had evolved into a less onerous hereditary tenure. Merchet was the main incident of personal servility, and it was routinely enforced throughout the period. Chevage was introduced around 1400, and it was enforced regularly and routinely until its disappearance at the end of the fifteenth century.

From these chronologies, it is evident that neither migration nor manu-mission contributed much to the decline of villeinage. Resistance against servile burdens was limited, confined mainly to the 1350s and focused upon elections to office and labour services. The timing of this resistance correlates well with the chronology of the decline of the tenurial aspects of villeinage, and it sent discouraging messages to the landlord about continuing with personal services, but its scale and duration were limited. There is no evidence for a seigniorial reaction in the 1350s and 1360s. The imposition of chevage provoked some individual dissent in the 1400s. The major changes to villein tenure correlate closely with the massive reduction in population in 1349.

[104]   SROI HD1538/357/5, mm. 19, 20, 26, 28, 31, 32, 34, 41.
[105]   SROI HD1538/357/5, m. 86.

Forncett[106]

Forncett (Norfolk) possessed a classic manorial structure, with a sizeable demesne and a majority of peasant land held in villeinage.[107] The latter is still identified as *terra nativa* in fifteenth-century documents. No early court rolls have survived to establish the tenurial formula used in earlier conveyances. Free tenants and sokemen owed few labour services. Customary holdings were organized into two categories, 5-acre tenures owing heavy week and harvest works, and 2½-acre tenures with lighter labour services. There was some variation in the exact rent package, but many 5-acre tenures paid 6d. cash each year, 1¾d. as 'saltpenny', one quarter of oats, four hens, and owed 70 winter works, 10 summer and 24 harvest works.[108]

The population of Forncett probably halved between the early fourteenth century and the mid-1370s, mainly attributable to the Black Death and subsequent epidemics.[109] There are no courts or accounts to track the immediate response to the Black Death, but the survival of accounts from the mid-1370s provides a clear indication of the scale and nature of tenurial change. In the 1270s no demesne or peasant land had been leased, yet in the 1370s around 70% of all customary land was now leased for c.£18 per annum, and much of the demesne was also leased separately. Between the 1370s and 1406 most of the remaining customary land was converted to leases for terms of years.[110]

The leases of former customary land were granted for a cash rent, suit of court, and the vast majority were for the term of seven years. By the 1420s 10-year leases were most common, and by the 1440s 20-year leases dominated. Grants of new leases peaked in the 1430s, and thereafter both the number of grants, and the area under leasehold, declined. As leases expired they were converted instead to a fee farm 'at the will of the lord according to the custom of the manor', which Davenport equates with a copyhold.[111] They first appeared in the 1420s, increased markedly in the 1460s, and by the end of the fifteenth century they dominated landholding in Forncett. A

106   This section on Forncett is entirely dependent upon Frances Davenport's classic study. She does not provide last dates for servile incidents, or provide information about their size and frequency, and so no such information is presented here for this manor.

107   Davenport, *Economic development*, p. 16.

108   Davenport, *Economic development*, pp. 60–1, 63, 68.

109   Davenport, *Economic development*, p. 105.

110   Davenport, *Economic development*, pp. 52, 58, 67, 70–1, Appendix VIII, Appendix IX, pp. xxx, xxxi, xlix.

111   Davenport describes all hereditary customary land after c.1400 as 'copyhold', *Economic development*, pp. 57 and 69, which is a very liberal use of the term at this early stage.

total of 103 separate grants at fee farm were made between 1422 and 1500. Even parcels of demesne arable, initially at leasehold for terms of years, were gradually converted to fee farms.[112] The amount of free land acquired by serfs (which manorial officials categorized as 'soiled land') increased in the later fourteenth century, peaking at around 100 acres.[113] The legal status of serfs did not prevent them from acquiring sizeable holdings or enjoying a high level of material comfort.[114]

In 1400 the 67 people performing fealty to the new lord in the manorial court were categorized either as free tenants (30%), customary tenants (37%) or serfs by blood (33%), the latter being the descendants of the villein landholders of the early fourteenth century. By 1565 only three bond families remained.[115] Davenport attributed the decline in serfs to their migration from the manor and to a lack of male heirs. The scale of recorded migration between 1400 and 1575 was large: 126 serfs had left the manor, mainly to neighbouring villages within ten miles (53%), but also to Norwich (17%) and towns along the East Anglian coast (11%).

The most striking element of the management of personal servility at Forncett is its persistence deep into the sixteenth century, even though villein tenure had disappeared well before the end of the fourteenth century. Customary tenants had been originally compelled to grind their corn at the lord's windmill, which was still operational in the 1370s, but by 1406 it had dilapidated and fallen out of use.[116] Heriot had never been levied. Tallage and *capitagium* were prominent in the early fourteenth century, annually charged at around £9 13s. 4d. and 8s. respectively, but both had disappeared by the 1370s.[117] Similarly, in c.1300 virtually all of the week and harvest works owed by villein tenants were available to the demesne each year, and most were actively employed. The proportion commuted at will from year to year varied markedly, but averaged around 30%.[118] By the mid-1370s the majority of these works were no longer available to the demesne, because the lands owing the services were either untenanted or had been converted to leasehold. For example, in 1376–7 just 10% of all winter works were used, 20% were sold, and the remainder were 'decayed' because the land was no longer held on villein tenure. By 1408 the whole manor was leased, most works had decayed, although a handful had been commuted – none were used.[119] All

[112] Davenport, *Economic development*, pp. 57, 76–7.

[113] Davenport, *Economic development*, pp. 16, 74–5.

[114] Davenport, *Economic development*, pp. 86–96.

[115] Davenport, *Economic development*, pp. 83–4, 96.

[116] Davenport, *Economic development*, pp. 36, 59, lv.

[117] Davenport, *Economic development*, pp. 37–43, 54, and Appendix IX.

[118] Davenport, *Economic development*, pp. 47, Appendix VIII, pp. xxxiii, xxxix, xl.

[119] Davenport, *Economic development*, pp. 51–2, 58, Appendix IX, pp. lxii–lxiii.

holders of customary land were liable to be elected to serve as reeve and messor, and some reluctance to discharge both offices is recorded in the third quarter of the fourteenth century. Many tenants paid 40s. to be exonerated from the office of reeve until the end of the fourteenth century, after which the charge was dropped.[120]

By the mid-1370s many of the tenurial aspects of villeinage had greatly diminished, and by 1400 they had disappeared entirely. All that then remained were two elements of personal servility, merchet and chevage, both of which continued to be enforced for nearly two more centuries.[121] Few court rolls survive before 1400, but one from 1373 contains a presentment for the absence of eight serfs, and others contain evidence for the payment of chevage for licence to live off the manor (as opposed to capitage). In the 1370s absence and chevage were being managed more closely and rigorously at Forncett than at Dunningworth, although the charge for chevage is comparable (ranging from 3d. to 3s. 4d. per annum).[122] The last record of merchet occurred in 1563, and of chevage in 1573.[123]

The number of serfs who paid chevage was not especially large, reckoned at just ten individuals between 1404 and 1527. Hence the majority of emigrants did not pay chevage, and the charges were low for those who did. Yet the persistent recording of serfs throughout the fifteenth century eventually paid financial dividends in the sixteenth, when the lord was able to raise money from serfs who had withdrawn their chattels from the manor without permission, from the seized chattels of bondsmen convicted of felonies, and, finally, from the sale of manumissions, five of which are recorded in the court rolls. The sums received are not usually disclosed, but John Doyes may have paid the huge sum of £120 for his manumission.[124] In 1527–8 undisclosed 'fines' obtained from two bondmen generated £10, or 13% of total receipts from the manor that year.[125]

Summary of chronology and key indicators

By the 1370s over two thirds of the former customary land at Forncett, and by the early fifteenth century nearly all of it, had been converted to leases for years. Between the 1430s and 1470s many of these leases were converted upon expiry to perpetual fee farms, which restored hereditary tenure for a straight money rent and no servile incidents. Seigniorial interest in personal servility was active in the 1370s, especially relating to emigrant serfs.

---

[120] Davenport, *Economic development*, pp. 50–1, 75n, li.
[121] Davenport, *Economic development*, p. 96.
[122] Davenport, *Economic development*, pp. 72–4.
[123] Davenport, *Economic development*, pp. 92, 96.
[124] Davenport, *Economic development*, pp. 88–95.
[125] Davenport, *Economic development*, p. 58.

11.2 Values of customary arable land at Forncett 1340s to 1490s (d. per acre)

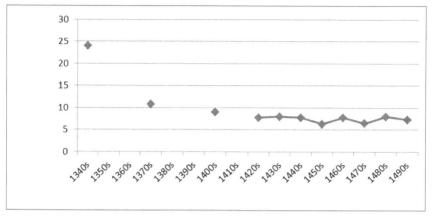

The fragmentary nature of the evidence from Forncett in the third quarter of the fourteenth century prevents any close analysis of peasant resistance or migration during the period when leasehold displaced villein tenure. However, the level of recorded flight in the 1370s is much higher than at Dunningworth in the same decade (no comparable evidence for the 1370s exists from Cratfield or Staverton), which must reflect real differences in the extent of out-migration. Peasant migration must have exacerbated the difficulties in finding tenants at Forncett in the generation after the Black Death, and these difficulties are the most likely explanation for the widespread conversions to leasehold there.

The data for land values are patchy before the 1420s, although the mean value of a customary acre at lease fell 55% between the 1340s and 1370s, then fell by 17% between the 1370s and 1400s, and by a further 13% between the 1400s and 1420s (see graph 11.2).[126] The significant fall in value between the 1340s and 1370s corresponds with the major conversion of former customary land to leasehold. The value then remained steady for the rest of the fifteenth century at around 8d. per acre, with the exception of two sharp falls in the 1450s and 1470s, both of which were followed by swift recovery. The recovery in the 1460s coincides with a surge in grants at fee farm, which suggests that tenants were able to obtain more concessions from their lord – shifting from fixed term tenancies to secure inheritances – during the dire conditions of the 'Great Slump'. Manumission was unimportant in the decline of serfdom until the sixteenth century, when it became the principal means of eradicating personal servility at Forncett.

---

[126] Davenport calculates the rental value of customary land in the 1340s at 24d. per acre, then provides leasehold values per acre for the same from the 1370s (10.75d. per acre), Davenport, *Economic development*, pp. 71–2, 78.

Conclusion

In the second half of the fourteenth century customary land continued to be granted on hereditary villein tenure at Cratfield, Dunningworth and Staverton, which underlines the preference of estate officials to preserve this tenurial form wherever local circumstances allowed. However, villein tenure after the Black Death was different from that which had existed before. Millsuit, tallage/recognition and heriot were all recorded before 1349, but then disappeared almost immediately afterwards, week works were extensively commuted, and in the 1360s the use of the powerfully servile phrase 'in villeinage' was dropped from conveyances at both Dunningworth and Staverton, and it is likely that the same had happened at Cratfield. In contrast, customary land at Forncett was extensively converted to leasehold soon after the Black Death, which is strongly indicative of a shortage of tenants there, a problem exacerbated by a stream of emigrants from the manor. The departures continued even after most of the customary land had been converted to leases, which seems to indicate that Forncett was not an especially attractive place to make a living.

The shedding of most of the incidents of villein tenure in the 1350s at Dunningworth and Staverton was clearly a deliberate policy, as estate officials endeavoured to attract tenants in unprecedented conditions. As such, they responded pro-actively and pragmatically to a monumental shortage of tenants in the land market. There is no evidence for any kind of 'seigniorial reaction' in the third quarter of the fourteenth century, and very little peasant resistance to servility. Indeed, the management of personal servility during this period was loose and inconsistent. By 1380 the most onerous incidents of villein tenure had been shed on three, and probably all four, manors, and the enforcement of personal servility was lax on at least two.

There is a stark contrast between the rapid decline of villein tenure on the Norfolk estate in the immediate aftermath of the Black Death, and the aggressive management of its surviving bondmen in the sixteenth century. A distinct change in managerial approach on the estate is discernible between c.1380 and c.1420, when greater attention was paid to personal servility. This was manifest in the targeting of individual serfs, in challenges to personal status, and in the transformation of chevage from a high value, but low frequency, exaction before c.1400 to one characterized by a lower value, but much higher frequency, thereafter. This crackdown triggered direct conflict with those who were targeted, some of whom left their home manor.

Similarities in the management of both tenures and servility across these four manors, especially in the fifteenth century, are indicative of the emergence of more consistent and coordinated administrative policies across the East Anglian manors of the Norfolk estate. For example, the identification and control of 'soiled land' (free tenures acquired by serfs) is consistent across all four manors, as is the introduction and development of fee farms from the mid-1420s. The extent to which fee farms were deployed on individual manors largely reflected the extent to which leases had emerged in the second half of the fourteenth century, just as the extent of leasehold had in turn depended upon the degree of difficulty experienced in re-tenanting customary lands in the immediate aftermath of the Black Death. Leases already dominated at Forncett by the 1370s, and thereafter fee farms were used extensively to convert these leases back to a hereditary tenure. Officials at Cratfield must have had little difficulty filling holdings in the fourteenth century, and as a consequence leases were very rare and fee farms were non-existent – furthermore, the manor was temporarily held by another lord in the 1420s, when fee farms were first introduced on the Norfolk estate. Leases had been used to some degree at both Dunningworth and Staverton, and hence fee farms appeared on a limited scale in the mid-fifteenth century as a device to convert them back to hereditary tenure.

The emergence of a strong sense of direction from the centre of the Norfolk estate around 1400 is also apparent in the move to impose and manage chevage consistently.[127] It would appear that each manor was required to identify and record all serfs, and to monitor each of them assiduously thereafter, and lists of serfs and their progeny were produced to aid this process. Thus chevage became the defining incident of personal servility on the estate, the means by which the dukes of Norfolk tagged and tracked their serfs throughout the fifteenth, and well into the sixteenth, centuries. Thereafter, the arrival of a new lord of the manor usually coincided with a temporary surge in chevage payments, as the new regime sought to take stock of its assets, and as some flown serfs opted to register their presence with the new lord. The correlation between new lords and surges of interest in emigrants is evident in 1400, the late 1420s, 1448 and 1477 at Dunningworth and Staverton.

The single exception to this pattern proves the rule. The administration of chevage was *not* tightened at Cratfield around c.1400, although its officials made some attempt to make up lost ground in the late 1430s. The failure to tag all surviving serfs at the beginning of the fifteenth century made it much more difficult to preserve servility at Cratfield thereafter, and consequently the manor had only one recorded serf family by the end of the fifteenth century. The explanation for this laxness is that Cratfield was not held as part of the main Norfolk inheritance in the early fifteenth century, when instead it was temporarily alienated to other lords until it returned to the estate in

---

[127]   Tighter management of serfs is also apparent on the manor of Walton (Suffolk) on the same estate, see SROI HA119/50/3/17.

1438. In contrast, Dunningworth, Forncett and Staverton remained part of the core inheritance throughout.[128] Because the management of serfdom had slipped at Cratfield in the early fifteenth century, it proved very difficult to restore once the manor was eventually returned to the Norfolk portfolio, although the surge in recorded serf migrants upon its return in the late 1430s indicates that some attempt was made.

During the fifteenth century the persistent tracking of serfs through chevage was embedded within the management culture of the estate. However, the size of the fines, and indeed the size of those for merchet, were not large, which indicates that the estate had not yet settled upon the policy of pursuing its bondmen aggressively for financial profit, for which it was notorious in the sixteenth century. The precise reason for this softer approach in the fifteenth century is unclear. It could have been simply a function of the chronic shortages of cash that dogged the economy, which would have inhibited the ability of serfs to pay; in contrast, the greatly improved liquidity within the economy, and rising agrarian profits, in the sixteenth century would have increased the cash flow of well-to-do bondmen, and made them richer pickings. It could also have had something to do with the personal disposition toward servility of successive dukes. This changed decisively with the accession of the Howard dukes of Norfolk, who acquired the estates in 1483, and whose identification and pursuit of serfs was immediately more aggressive than their predecessors. The Howards viewed their serfs with an eye for profit bordering on extortion, but their policy of squeezing of serfs in the sixteenth century did not draw upon a long-established tradition: as we have seen, in the late fourteenth century the imposition of personal servility was slight on two of the manors. The Howards were therefore indebted to estate officials during the 1390s and 1400s, who had arrested the drift of personal servility on the estate by energetically recording all the remaining serfs they could identify. They had effectively created an inventory of serfs on each manor in the early fifteenth century, thus providing their successors with a clear baseline from which to track and pursue serfs subsequently through chevage and serf genealogies. The Howards cashed in on this good fortune. Their actions provide the best example of the way in which a lord's personal disposition towards serfdom could alter the course of its history locally.

The final point to emerge from this case study is the changing significance of manumission in the decline of serfdom. Local manorial documents are

---

[128]   The devolution of the manor offered in Copinger, *Manors of Suffolk*, volume 2, pp. 48–50 is incorrect. Fealty lists contained within the court rolls of Cratfield reveal that in 1406 the manor was in the hands of Constance, Countess Marshall, and in 1413 it was still with Constance but now held jointly with John Grey. It was restored to the Mowbrays in March 1438, CUL Vanneck Mss, box 3.

not ideal for tracking trends in the scale of manumission, but the evidence from these four manors is that it hardly featured before 1500, with just a half dozen recorded cases. Manumission became more important in the sixteenth century, when it was established as the mechanism for formally releasing the remaining bondmen from their condition, and as a source of seigniorial profit.

12

Miscellaneous manors

The final chapter of Part II considers the evidence for the decline of serfdom on 23 manors distributed across Buckinghamshire, Norfolk, Oxfordshire and Suffolk, i.e. the Category B manors described in Chapter Five. This category is mainly comprised of small- and medium-sized manors held by lower-status landlords. These were the most common types of manor in medieval England, but they rarely feature in academic studies, because their archives have seldom survived. The assessment of the decline of villeinage across a sample of such ubiquitous, but under-researched, manorial forms is essential if a balanced and representative picture of the processes of that decline is to be formed.

The individual manors included in this sample have all left a run of court rolls sufficiently informative to take a reliable snapshot of the profile of villeinage, and its management, over at least two decades. In some cases, the court rolls are supplemented with a handful of manorial accounts or rentals.[1] In each case the body of documents is smaller than for each of the individual case studies in chapters Six to Eleven, which means that it is not possible to apply the detailed methodology used there. The information relating to the management of the incidents of villeinage, and to land values and patterns of peasant resistance, is either too fragmentary or limited to warrant separate analysis and presentation for each manor. However, there is still much to be gleaned from the general patterns that emerge from the sample.

The sample of 23 manors also contains sub-groupings which offer other features of interest. Beeston, Runton and Beeston Felbriggs, and Runton Hayes comprise the main manorial units in two contiguous parishes on the north Norfolk coast, and so offer the opportunity to view the evolution of villeinage in a tight geographical area across manorial boundaries. A group of manors in west Suffolk (Badwell Ash, Drinkstone, Harleston, Higham, Lackford, Lidgate, Norton, Thorpe Morieux and Withersfield), and another group from east Suffolk (Debach, Harkstead, Holbrook, Iken and Winston), provide a useful contrast with another from the south Midlands (Akeley, Hardwick Russells and Weedon Vale all in Buckinghamshire, and Radclive in Oxfordshire). Finally, two manors in close proximity (Barton Magna and Fornham St Martin) were selected because they were held by the same land-

---

[1] See Appendix for the profile of each manor, and the nature, number and whereabouts of the surviving sources for each.

lord, and thus enable some assessment of the continuity of administration of villeinage on the same estate, but also because they have left sufficient archives to track tenurial developments there in detail.

In order to organize, present and analyze this diverse information in a coherent and meaningful way, this chapter first considers the development of villein tenures on all of the manors after 1349; it then explores the chronology of decline and the management of the key incidents of villeinage; and, finally, it assesses the evidence for attitudes to serfdom.

Customary land tenures

Throughout the late fourteenth and fifteenth centuries customary land on most of the manors within the sample continued to be labelled as such in court- and account-roll entries. Whether the land was held as a large and integral holding, or as a smaller, standalone parcel, manorial courts continued to identify its unfree origins, irrespective of the form of tenure on which it was held. The most common description was 'native land', and sometimes the name of the original villein *tenementum* was also included – for example, 'one acre of native land formerly of Smith's tenement'. Hence even at the end of the fifteenth century administrators and tenants could still identify and distinguish the ancient villein land from freehold and demesne land, and the fact that they went to such effort is itself significant. However, the description of land was less important than the tenure on which it was held after 1349. The evolution of villein tenure on each of the 23 manors in the sample falls into one of four distinct groups, which, for clarity and simplicity, are analyzed in turn.

Type 1 manors: evolving hereditary tenure

The principal characteristic of a Type 1 manor is that after 1349 either all or the majority of its customary land continued to be held on a hereditary tenure, albeit one which shed its servile incidents over time. A small minority of the customary land on each manor may have been converted to fixed-term tenures. There are 15 manors in this category.[2]

On Type 1 manors where court rolls are extant from the period immediately after the Black Death, the use of 'in villeinage/bondage' disappeared quickly from conveyances. In the 1340s customary land at Runton Hayes had been 'held in bondage for him and his heirs', but in the 1350s the use of

---

[2] Beeston, Debach, Drinkstone, Hardwick Russells, Harkstead, Harleston, Higham, Holbrook, Norton, Radclive, Runton and Beeston Felbrigg, Runton Hayes, Thorpe Morieux, Weedon Vale, Withersfield. The Norfolk manors studied by Whittle also fall into this category, see *Agrarian capitalism*, p. 82.

'bondage' was dropped, while at Debach the use of 'holds in bondage for him and his for services and customs' ceased immediately after 1349.[3] At Drinkstone the use of 'in villeinage' had disappeared by the early 1370s.[4] After the 1370s such phrases are no longer found on any Type 1 manor.

The formulae which had replaced these phrases by c.1370 usually remained settled thereafter, and their content and structure are remarkably similar from one manor to another. On almost every Type 1 manor they contained the key phrases 'to hold to him and his heirs' and 'at the will of the lord', the former establishing the principle of inheritance, and the latter reiterating that the title to the land could only be defended in the lord's manorial court. On ten of the 15 manors the formula comprised a minor variation upon 'to him and his at the will of the lord for customs and services'.[5] On the remaining five manors the formulae were broadly the same, although the phrase 'according to the custom of the manor' was included.[6]

References within the conveyance to holding 'by copy' are exceptionally rare. However, the rarity of written examples should not be taken to imply

---

3   Runton Hayes grants from the early 1350s were usually 'to hold for him and his at the will of the lord making services and customs', and only once – in the court of 1367 – did the language revert to 'in bondage', NRO WKC 2/167 398 x 8. At Debach 'in bondage' was common in the 1340s, but had disappeared completely by the time the court-roll series resumes in the 1360s, SROI HD230/1/1.

4   SROB E7/10/1.3.

5   'Seisin to hold to him and his at the will of the lord for services and customs' (Beeston) TNA DL30/102/1402; 'holds to him and his heirs at the will of the lord for services and customs' (Debach) SROI HD230/1/1; 'to hold to him and his heirs by the rod at the will of the lord for services and customs' (Drinkstone) SROB E7/10/1.3; 'holds from the lord of this manor for services' (Harkstead) SROI S1/10/6.1; 'seisin for him and his heirs by the rod at the will of the lord for services' (Harleston) SROB E3/15.7/1.1; 'to hold to him and his heirs and assignees for services' (Higham) SROI HA246/A/2; 'seisin to hold to him and his heirs making services and customs' (Holbrook) SROI S1/10/9.1; 'to hold to him and his heirs at the will of the lord for services and customs' (Runton and Beeston Felbrigg) NRO WKC 2/166 398 x 7; 'to him and his heirs at the will of the lord for services and customs' (Runton Hayes) NRO WKC 2/167 398 x 8; and 'seisin, for him and his heirs by the rod at the will of the lord for services and customs' (Thorpe Morieux) SROB 1700/1/1 to 4.

6   The formulae are: 'to hold to him and his according to the custom of the manor for rents and services' (Hardwick Russells) New College, Oxford, 3847; 'seisin to hold to him and his heirs, and his assignees, by the rod at the will of the lord for services and customs according to the custom of the manor' (Norton) SROB 553/1; 'him and his heirs according to the custom of the manor rendering and making rents and customs' (Radclive) New College, Oxford, 4106, although see courts in 1429 where 'at the will of the lord' was also added, and June 1477 when reference is made to a copy; 'to him and his according to the custom of the manor for rents and services' (Weedon Vale) New College, Oxford, 3847 ; 'to him, his heirs and assignees at the will of the lord according to the custom of the manor' (Withersfield) SROB E3/15.16/1.2.

the infrequency of their use, if one documented example from Hardwick Russells is indicative of wider practice. In 1398 Alice Henne appeared in the manorial court to assert her reversionary interest in one customary virgate as the widow of its recently deceased tenant. The court-roll entry states clearly that 'she claims to hold the said messuage and the said virgate of land through a certain copy [*per quandam copiam*]': in other words, the copy of the original grant to her husband was the proof of her title to the land, and the court accepted it as such.[7]

Transfers of hereditary tenures dominated the customary land market on Type 1 manors. The general patterns can be illustrated using the example of Norton. Customary landholdings here were mainly small and non-standardized, and there were no large and integral holdings. Throughout the 1380s and 1390s Norton manorial accounts reveal hardly any decays of customary rents, and the availability of 97% of all labour services from customary holdings.[8] Thus the level of occupation of customary land on villein tenure was high, which is confirmed by the dominance of hereditary grants in the court rolls when the extant series begins in 1422. This situation changed a little between the 1420s and 1450s, when the court rolls record a small, but distinct, rise in the area of customary land converted to leasehold, although after the 1450s new leases dried up completely.[9] This development is also reflected in a small rise in the 'decays' of the basic rents of assize, which had been negligible in the 1390s, but rose to 9% of due rents in the 1420s, and to 20% in the late 1440s.[10] Some of these non-payments were due to the abandonment of customary land, and the rest reflect the conversions to leasehold.[11] The majority of the customary land, though, remained on hereditary tenure.

Thus the extent of customary land converted to fixed-term tenures on

---

7   New College, Oxford, 3847, court held March 1398.

8   SROB 553/21 to 26.

9   SROB 553/1 and 2. Very occasionally, a lease was granted for the term of a life. In 1397–8 Amicia Birchard leased the eight-acre *tenementum* Birchard for 7s. per annum for the time of her life, and in 1420–1 the parson of Tostock church leased an acre of arable for the term of his life, SROB 553/24 and 25.

10 SROB 553/21 to 35.

11 These courts also tended to be active in identifying and controlling the market in 'soiled' land, i.e. freehold tenures which had been acquired by serfs. Norton provides a good example of this practice. The court remained vigilant concerning the purchase of free land by its serfs, insisting that such acquisitions were recorded and the land was formally classified as 'soiled'. It also guarded zealously against the possibility of 'soiled land' subsequently reverting back to freehold. For example, when in 1465 it was reported that Nicholas Seriant had purchased 3 acres of soiled land without registering the acquisition in the manorial court, the lord's officials pursued the matter relentlessly until it was resolved that Seriant had subsequently sold the land to Adam Mullay, who in 1467 was formally admitted to it but charged an inflated entry fine of 9s., SROB 553/2.

Type I manors was limited.[12] Where it did occur, the area involved was small, just a few acres here and there, and there were seldom more than a couple of such grants in any one year, and none at all in many years.[13] Grants for terms of lives were seldom granted on the East Anglian manors. A rare example is recorded at Debach in 1364, when John and Matilda del Hel surrendered their hereditary smallholding to the lord and immediately received it back again to hold for the term of their lives.[14] The vast majority of fixed-term grants were at leasehold, which was used to shift land lying abandoned in the lord's hands because it could not be tenanted on the old terms. Many of the grants at lease were a feature of the period c.1380 to c.1420. They tended to disappear thereafter, when expiring leases were usually re-granted as hereditary tenures.[15] On a few East Anglian manors after mid-century leases were replaced with fee farms. For example, leases at Harleston died out in the 1440s, to be replaced in the 1450s and 1460s by some grants at fee farm.[16] At Holbrook in the 1460s a spate of fee farms is recorded, although in some cases these were conversions of hereditary tenures as well as re-grants of leases: in other words, a fee farm was sometimes used as a permanent, negotiated, commutation for all servile incidents on hereditary villein tenure, and at other times it was used as a device for persuading people to take on vacant land.[17] Both practices are recorded at Drinkstone, where between the 1430s and 1460s a small number of hereditary tenures whose services were formally replaced with a commercial money rent were labelled 'fee farms'. All the other grants at fee farm were used to entice tenants for land lying in the lord's hands: both practices ceased after the 1470s.[18] At Beeston from

---

[12]   For the avoidance of doubt, these are leases of former customary land, *not* grants of small parcels of demesne land. The insistence in the court-roll entries on identifying the original status of the land at lease usually makes this distinction easy to draw, although, just occasionally, it is not clear whether the land being leased is customary or demesne. Some good examples of such uncertainty are recorded at Beeston in the 1460s, TNA DL30/102/1404.

[13]   For example, at Runton and Beeston a total of seven leases – none for more than ten acres – were granted in seven courts held between 1418 and 1426, NRO WKC 2/166 398 x 7. For other examples, see SROB E3/15.7/1.1 (Harleston), and TNA DL30/102/1403 and 1404 (Beeston).

[14]   SROI HD230/1/1.

[15]   See, for example, the disappearance of life tenancies by the 1430s at Hardwick Russells and Weedon Vale, New College, Oxford, 3848.

[16]   SROB E3/15.7/1.1. The formula for hereditary tenures was 'seisin to hold for him and his heirs by the rod at the will of the lord for services'.

[17]   The formula for fee farms at Holbrook was 'to hold to him and his heirs and assignees by the rod at the will of the lord for a rent', compared with the standard and still dominant hereditary tenures that were held '...at the will of the lord making services and customs', SROI S1/10/9.2.

[18]   For example, in October 1432 a cottage and 2 acres were granted at fee farm 'to him, his heirs and assignees at the will of the lord'; and conversions of holdings

the 1470s some vacant land was granted on a hereditary tenure for straight money rent with no servile incidents, although these grants were not labelled as a fee farm.[19]

Conventional leases of customary land were rare on the three south Midland manors, although all of them experimented with fixed-term tenancies between c.1380 and c.1420. The developments at Radclive are curious. During the 1380s some customary cottages were granted on fixed-term tenancies for years, although the court-roll entries studiously avoided the use of words such as 'leasing' or 'farm' in the conveyance. For example, a cottage and one acre were granted for the term of 11 years 'at the will of the lord rendering ancient services, and if [the tenant] does not perform works then he will render 2s. per annum to the lord'; another cottage was so granted for 12 years.[20] These are leaseholds in all but name. Such grants had disappeared completely when the court-roll series resumes in the 1420s, and again in the 1460s, when all land transfers were hereditary tenures.[21] Hardwick Russells and Weedon Vale record some conversions to life tenancies in the 1390s and 1400s for a money rent – most were for a single life, although in 1398 a customary toft and dovecote lying in the lord's hands were granted for three lives to John Toursey, his wife and son.[22] The absence of leaseholds at Hardwick was explained in one court because the custom of the manor

held by services to a straight cash rent, entry fine but no services are documented in the courts held in October 1462 and March 1463, SROB E7/10/1.3.

[19] The best example of this device is the case of Thomas Burslete of East Runton, who had relinquished a tenement and five customary acres sometime in the late 1450s. However, no alternative tenants could be found, and so in 1464 the holding was re-granted to Thomas 'and his heirs by the rod at the will of the lord for services, and for 6d. per annum and suit of court'. The standard hereditary tenures never stipulate the annual cash rent in the court record of the transfer, and so the inclusion of this information, plus the marginal note that this was a 'new rent', indicates that something about the tenure had changed – most likely the formal removal of liability for labour services, TNA DL30/102/1404, m. 3.

[20] New College, Oxford, 4106, court held July 1389.

[21] New College, Oxford, 6715 to 6735. This short dalliance with grants for a term is not readily explained, although it occurred at a time when the manor itself was being was leased in its entirety to a third party. It may be that when, from c.1400, the collection of rents and the running of the manorial court became the responsibility of the lord once more, the experiment with grants for a term ceased.

[22] Hardwick court held June 1398; see also Weedon court held July 1399, when a half virgate was granted to Thomas Colyns, his wife and son for the term of their lives for rents and services (i.e. not for a money rent), New College, Oxford, 3847. A couple of the conversions to single life tenancies for money were probably small parcels of demesne, rather than customary, land, see courts held September 1392, February 1393, and May 1393.

prohibited leasing (for terms of years).[23] By the mid-fifteenth century all grants were heritable.

Type 2 manors: combination of hereditary tenures and leases

The principal characteristic of Type 2 manors is that a large propor-tion (between one third and two thirds) of the customary land was held on a hereditary tenure, just as on Type 1 manors, while the remainder was converted to leases for years. The shift to leasehold occurred at various times between the c.1350s and the c.1420s, but thereafter fewer and fewer leases were renewed upon expiry – instead, the customary land was re-granted on a hereditary tenure. Hence, by 1500 hereditary tenure was once again the dominant, if not the only, form of customary tenure on these manors. There-fore the tenurial profile of Type 2 manors in 1500 was identical to that on Type 1 manors, but the pathway was subtly different. There are five manors in this category.[24]

The use of 'in villeinage/bondage' quickly and permanently disappeared from the formulae of conveyances of all customary tenures on those manors where court rolls survive from the third quarter of the fourteenth century. For example, the format before 1349 at Winston usually included 'held in villeinage', but in the 1350s the phrase was dropped completely.[25] In the 1340s land at Iken was held 'in villeinage', but not after the 1350s.[26] At Lackford the phrase 'in villeinage for customs and services' was still commonly used in the 1360s, but it had disappeared when the court-roll series resumes in the 1390s.[27]

By the last quarter of the fourteenth century the formulae for convey-ances of hereditary tenures had largely settled into a consistent format. The formulae were very similar to those found on Type 1 manors, and those on all five Type 2 manors included the key phrase 'to hold to him and his'; four manors also included 'at the will of the lord'.[28] The fifth, Lidgate, had

---

23 Richard Mower, Mariota his wife and Simon his son held two tofts and half a virgate of customary land, but had leased them to one Robert Hogges 'against the custom of the manor without the licence of the court'. The lands were seized and the three were then readmitted after paying a 20s. entry fine, although the rent package had been converted to a straight money rent of 11s. per annum, New College, Oxford, 3847, court held April 1392.

24 Badwell Ash, Iken, Lackford, Lidgate, and Winston.

25 The formula sometimes appeared as 'to him and his heirs for services and customs', or 'to him according to the custom of the manor for services', CUL EDC 7/19/2, 8 and 12. After 1350 on one single occasion the word 'brood [*sequela*]' was preferred to 'heirs', CUL EDC 7/19/15.

26 SROI HD32/293/388, mm. 7, 11.

27 SROB E3/15.12/1.2(b) and E3/15.12/1.13.

28 For example, 'to him and his heirs by the rod at the will of the lord for services and customs' (Badwell Ash), SROB 1825/1 to 4; 'holds to him and his heirs for

a settled format when its court series begins in 1391, which changed little thereafter: 'to him, his heirs and assignees according to the custom of the manor for services and customs'.[29] The relative unimportance of the phrase 'according to the custom of the manor' within the formulae of conveyances on both Type 1 and 2 manors is striking: just six out of the 18 manors included the phrase, most of them in the south Midlands.[30] However, the sample does provide unequivocal evidence that its use was spreading towards the end of the fifteenth century among the East Anglian manors, usually as a direct replacement for the phrase 'for services and customs'. The specific examples of Badwell Ash and Winston are discussed below, and the change also occurred at Lackford.[31]

Not only were conversions of customary land to leases much more common on Type 2 than Type 1 manors, but the process also started earlier. At Iken and Winston leaseholds spread rapidly within a generation of the Black Death. At Winston a few parcels of customary land had been granted at lease before 1349, usually for the term of a life.[32] In the early 1350s customary land was re-granted on the old terms whenever possible but, from the mid-1350s, that which still lay untenanted was converted to leasehold for a term of years, based upon a money rent, but with no entry fine. These were granted to the tenant 'and his assignees', signifying the right to transfer the lease during its term to a nominated third party.[33] Odd parcels of customary land were leased at Iken in the 1350s, but then after the second outbreak of the Black Death in 1361 the number of grants increased dramatically, many of which were used to dispose of land abandoned in the lord's hands.[34] Most were for terms of four to six years, with no entry fine. It is impossible to

---

customs and works at the will of the lord' (Iken), SROI HD32/293/388, mm. 11ff; and 'to hold for him and his heirs by the rod at the will of the lord for services and customs' (Winston), CUL EDC 7/19/20 to 30. At Lackford the formula was still a little unsettled in the 1390s, sometimes appearing as 'to him and his heirs according to the custom of the manor', then, on other occasions, as 'to him and his heirs holding the same by the rod' – by the mid-fifteenth century it had settled upon 'seisin for him his heirs and assignees by the rod at the will of the lord for customs and services', SROB E3/15.12/1.7 and 1.13.

[29] SROB E3/11/1.1 to 1.5.

[30] Hardwick Russells, Lidgate, Norton, Radclive, Weedon Vale and Withersfield.

[31] The phrase 'for customs and services' was routinely included in mid-fifteenth-century grants at Lackford, but by the early sixteenth century it had been omitted and replaced with 'according to the custom of the manor': compare SROB E3/15.12/1.7 with 1.9.

[32] For example, in 1307 John Wymark died seized of one acre of land leased for the term of his life, and his son was immediately admitted on the same terms, CUL EDC 7/19/20.

[33] See, for example, CUL EDC 7/19/18, 21 and 33.

[34] SROI HD32/293/388, mm. 32, 34–64.

calculate the exact balance between hereditary tenures and leases at Iken and Winston with any precision, due to the absence of any manorial accounts, but between c.1360 and c.1400 the number of grants of each form of tenure in the court rolls was roughly even.

The shift to leases gathered momentum much later on the other three manors. At Lackford hardly any farms of customary land were granted in the 1350s and 1360s, when income from leases was negligible, yet it exceeded £20 per annum by the mid-1390s, when numerous short-term leases of two and three years are recorded.[35] At Lidgate between 1391 and 1409 not a single lease of customary land is recorded in the extant court rolls, but the death of three tenants in the autumn of 1410 exposed difficulties finding replacements for the large, standardized, 'full-lands', which prompted a strong swing to leases over the next two decades.[36] Full-lands were increasingly granted as integral holdings at farm for a term of years (ranging between three years and 20) for cash rent only, with a small entry fine and suit of court.[37] As the difficulties finding tenants persisted into the 1420s, so longer 20-year leases became more popular.[38] The number of leases also increased in the 1420s at Badwell Ash from very occasional grants to around three per court, although it is not always clear from the description of the land parcels whether the demesne or customary land was being leased – it was probably both. They continued to be granted at a similar rate for the next four decades.[39]

During the fifteenth century leases for terms of years gradually disappeared from all five manors. In the 1440s expiring leases at Iken began to be re-granted as hereditary tenures and described as fee farms; tenants must have preferred the greater security of fee farms, and were in a stronger position to press for them during the recession of mid-century, although very occasionally the lord squeezed a higher rent in return.[40] However, by the beginning of the sixteenth century the phrase 'fee farm' was no longer used

---

35 The absence of leases in the 1360s is evident in both the fragmentary court rolls that survive from that decade, and in a partial account of 1364, SROB E3/15.12/1.2(b), and E3/15.12/2.1. The growth of rental income from leases is evident in the two surviving accounts from the 1390s, SROB E3/15.12/2.2 and 2.3.

36 The court-roll series does not start until 1391, SROB E3/11/1.1.

37 They were usually 'leased at farm', although one full-land granted to William Wellys at farm was also 'by the rod at the will of the lord', SROB E3/11/1.2, court held September 1411. One exception to the trend for a straight cash rent was the *tenementum* and full-land granted to Robert Yemanry for a reduced cash rent of 10s. and some light works, SROB E3/11/1.3, court held July 1418.

38 See, for example, SROB E3/11/1.3, April 1421, and SROB E3/11/1.4, mm. 2, 5.

39 SROB 1825/1 to 14.

40 SROI HD32/293/395, mm. 44–70. For example, in 1472 Alan Page's lease of 'certain lands' for 9s. per annum expired and instead it was re-granted to John Barker on a fee farm at 19s. per annum.

at Iken.[41] The surge in leases at Lackford during the 1390s lost momentum thereafter, when re-grants were mainly on hereditary tenure; indeed, mid-fifteenth-century court rolls note explicitly that some such grants had been 'lately held at farm [*nuper ad firmam*]'.[42] Similarly, at Lidgate from the 1430s expired leases tended to be re-granted as a hereditary tenure for a money rent, so that the latter gradually became the sole form of tenure for customary land.[43] The use of the copy also became established as proof of title in the manorial court. In 1440 William Yardley died seized holding a full virgate '*per copiam*', and in 1455 Ralph Verse held a *tenementum* in Lidgate 'from the lord by copy'.[44]

Badwell Ash and Winston also conform to the fashion for converting leases back into hereditary tenure during the course of the fifteenth century, although in both places the phrase 'fee farm' was conspicuously avoided in the conveyance. Instead, the word 'farm' was written in the margin of the court-roll entry. At Badwell between the 1420s and 1460s leases for years were granted according to a conventional format, but then in 1473 William Cross received the 'farm' of 10 acres for 14s. 4d. per annum 'to hold to him, his heirs and assignees by the rod at the will of the lord according to the custom of the manor'. Thereafter, this form of grant, which converted the lease into a hereditary tenure, displaced leases completely.[45] At Winston this device was also used to negotiate permanent commutations of labour services for some tenants holding hereditary tenure. For example, in 1413 John Gren-emere surrendered a messuage and four acres, which he had held for ancient services, only to be readmitted immediately to the same holding for 8s. 8d. per annum in lieu of the services: the grant was to 'him and his heirs by the rod at the will of the lord according to the custom of the manor', yet the marginal note stated 'farm, annually 8s. 8d.'[46] Hence, in the 1480s, the evolved hereditary tenure at Winston was held 'for him, his heirs, his assignees by the rod at the will of the lord *for services*' (my italics); in contrast, hereditary tenures that were either former leases or negotiated commutations were held 'for him, his heirs, his assignees by the rod at the will of the lord *according to*

---

[41] SROI HD32/293/395, mm. 87–99.

[42] SROB E3/15.12/1.9.

[43] For example, a former leased cottage was granted to John More in 1455 'in perpetuity by the rod at the will of the lord' for 20d. rent per annum, SROB E3/11/1.4 m. 19.

[44] SROB E3/11/1.4, mm. 17, 19.

[45] See also the subsequent courts in the mid-1470s where many such conversions were formally enrolled, SROB 1825/1/14.

[46] CUL EDC 7/19/40, m. 1. Similarly, John Newman had held at leasehold a messuage, 20 acres of customary land and ten acres on diverse tenures, and in May 1414 he transferred to the same form of tenure, in his case rendering 30s. '*pro firma*' each year.

the custom of the manor, and it was clearly described as a 'farm' in the margin of the roll.[47] Both paid an entry fine upon admission and an annual cash rent only, but the latter was higher upon the hereditary 'fee farm'.

Type 3 manors: tenure for the term of a life or lives

The principal characteristic of Type 3 manors is that the majority or all of the original customary holdings were converted to tenure for the term of a life or lives. Leases for years were either absent or rare.

One manor, Akeley in Buckinghamshire, falls into this category, whose court-roll series begins in 1382. In the 1380s conveyances of customary land did not contain the phrase 'in villeinage/bondage', although most were still held on hereditary villein tenure; for example, Richard Hawkins was admitted to a messuage and half virgate 'for him and his according to the custom of the manor rendering rent, services and customs'.[48] However, not all the formulae used in the transfer of villein land in the 1380s are as clear as this example: sometimes the court-roll entry is inscrutable about the exact terms of the tenure, and, at other times, reveals the existence of terms of lives.[49] Yet during the 1390s the majority of grants shift decisively to tenures for the term of lives, coinciding exactly with a sharp fall in land values.[50] By 1400 the formula for conveyances had settled upon 'for the term of a life according to the custom of the manor for ancient services'.[51] Labour services were still notionally available at Akeley in the 1390s, although it is unlikely that they were used (see below, p. 257). Tenure for life was the main form of tenure after 1400. The extant court-roll series ceases in 1422, so it is not possible to follow subsequent developments. Akeley is located on the frontier of the west and midland zone identified by Hoyle, where in the sixteenth century copyholds for lives dominated.[52]

---

47 CUL EDC 7/19/74, mm. 4, 5, 15, 18, 21, 23, 24.

48 New College, Oxford, 4084, court held October 1392. See also the grant of a cottage in April 1390 'to hold to him and his according to the custom of the manor for rents and services as anciently owed'.

49 For example, admission to a cottage in June 1383 contains no details about rent or conditions, except that it was held for the term of the life of the tenant and rendered a 40d. entry fine. In September 1392 Walter Dawes died seized of a messuage, half virgate and a cotland, and his son William was admitted according to the same formula, except 'for the term of a life' was inserted after 'to hold for him and his heirs'; John Parkyn was admitted to another half virgate in the same court, and the phrase 'for the term of a life' was included within the main body of the formula, New College, Oxford, 4084.

50 The mean level of entry fine into the standard half virgate at Akeley was 7s. 9d. in 1380–9; 2s. 8d. in 1390–9; 2s. 10d. in 1400–9; 4s. 5d. in 1410–19; and 1s. 8d. in 1420–9.

51 New College, Oxford, 4085, court held March 1400.

52 Hoyle, 'Tenure and the land market', p. 6.

Type 4 manors: leases

The principal characteristic of Type 4 manors is that villein tenure was substantially or completely replaced by leasehold after 1350, but, unlike Type 2 manors, few of these leases were converted to fee farms, or re-converted to hereditary tenures, before 1500. Two of the 23 manors fall into this category.[53]

Before 1349 the majority of the customary land at Barton Magna and Fornham St Martin was organized into standardized holdings of eight- or sixteen-*acreware*, few of which were re-occupied in the aftermath of the Black Death. In 1354 over one half of the customary land at Fornham St Martin was still unoccupied, judging from the decay of 51% of week works and over 60% of rents of assize, a situation which did not improve for another decade.[54] In 1364 at Barton Magna 80% of all week works were decayed.[55] Thus, in both cases, the majority of the standardized customary holdings remained abandoned and untenanted for at least a decade after the Black Death.

The seigniorial solution to this severe and sustained problem was to offer customary land on leasehold instead, usually as complete holdings but sometimes broken up into smaller parcels of land, a combination which proved successful in increasing the level of occupancy. Court sessions from the mid-1350s at Fornham St Martin were dominated by a succession of leases of customary land, so that rental income from this source rose rapidly from 36s. 3d. in 1355–6, to £5 13s. 4d. in 1358–9, and to £6 7s. 7d. in 1365–6.[56] As a consequence, annual rental income from peasant land rose from around £5 12s. in the 1330s to £7 12s. in the mid-1360s.[57] Repeated grants and re-grants of leases dominate the court rolls of the 1380s and 1390s, which contain few references to land transactions in villeinage.[58] Leases soon came to dominate landholdings at Barton Magna too. By the 1380s its manorial accounts contain long lists of individual leases, each documented in great detail. In the 1380s and 1390s the rental income from the lease of customary lands oscillated between £14 and £17 per annum, and each year the list of rents was

[53]   Barton Magna and Fornham St Martin.

[54]   SROB E3/15.6/2.23a, 2.24, 2.31.

[55]   SROB E18/155/2.

[56]   Income from cash leases fluctuated around 30s. per annum for the first half of the 1350s, see E3/15.6/2.24 and 2.25. The court grants are detailed in E3/15.6/1.3, mm. 6–8, 15, 22–3; the rise in leased income after 1356 is detailed in E3/15.6/2.25, 2.26 and 2.31.

[57]   In the 1330s rents of assize raised 65s. 2d. per annum, plus around 47s. of various leases and negligible decays of rent, SROB E3/15.6/2.10 to 2.13. In 1365–6 rents of assize were still nominally the same, although decays of rent had risen to 43s., while leases of customary land now fetched £6 7s. 7d., SROB E3/15.6/2.31.

[58]   SROB E3/15.9/1.5.

extended by a sizeable section entitled 'new leases', as old leases expired and new ones were created.[59]

The landlord managed the handful of holdings that remained on villein tenure at Fornham aggressively, which must have underlined their unattractiveness to tenants. In 1382 Robert Black was required to render an extraordinarily high entry fine of £5 upon acquisition of a cottage in villeinage, and the vocabulary of the grant is striking: 'to hold for him and his brood in bondage for services and customs'. Similarly, a heriot was demanded from the estate of a freeman who had died holding customary land.[60]

Leases continued to dominate at Barton Magna for the whole of the fifteenth century. Grants and re-grants of expired leases of customary land litter its extant manorial courts from the 1420s and 1430s, where hardly any grants in villeinage are recorded.[61] Income from leases of customary land held steady at around £16 per annum from the 1390s to the early 1440s, during which time around 550 acres of former customary land were at lease.[62] Thereafter, the land market contracted during the Great Slump of the mid-fifteenth century. In 1454–5 the income from leases, and the area under lease, had dropped sharply to £9 15s. 3d. and around 330 acres.[63] A fall in the area under cultivation is also suggested by the increase in the decays of rents of assize, from around 40% of the total in the 1430s to 65% in the mid-1450s.[64] Signs of recovery in the land market only emerge at the very end of the century. For example, in 1490–1 around 330 customary acres were still leased, but, compared with the 1460s, their rental yield had now increased by 15% to £11 7s. 10d.[65]

Why did leases replace villeinage so comprehensively after the Black Death on these two manors? The answer probably lies in their three, shared, characteristics: first, most of the customary land on both manors was organized into large, standardized, holdings; second, the manors were geographically close (four miles) to each other; and, finally, they both formed part of the estate of the cellarer of Bury St Edmunds abbey. Their tenurial history has much in common with Chevington and Fornham All Saints (Chapter Ten). The shift to leases is also strongly evident on two other manors on the cellarer's estate, Risby (Suffolk) and Mildenhall (Suffolk), and so this tenurial development appears to have been an estate-wide policy. For example,

59   SROB E18/151/1; E18/155/3.
60   SROB E3/15.9/1.5, courts held August 1382 and November 1393.
61   SROB E18/151/1.
62   SROB E18/155/3 (1380s and 1390s); E18/155/5 for 1419–20; and E18/155/8, see accounts for 1431–2 and 1441–2.
63   SROB E18/155/8.
64   SROB E18/155/4 and 8.
65   SROB A6/1/14.

in 1351 three customary holdings had been converted to life leases at Risby, although by 1361 two of them had returned to villein tenure.[66] Thereafter, the area of customary land at lease each year rose, from c.40 acres in the mid-1360s to c.80 acres in the 1380s, peaking in the 1410s at c.140 acres. From the 1390s labour services ceased to be used, because most had decayed through conversions to leasehold.[67] The Mildenhall account rolls contain a huge section of leases of customary land. A sizeable area – 330 acres – was already leased in the 1320s, which then increased to 725 acres in the 1380s, rising to a peak of c.1,110 acres in the 1410s. This level held steady into the early sixteenth century, although the financial yield from the farms declined during the mid-fifteenth century.[68] Around half of the original customary land in Mildenhall was still held on villein tenure in the 1390s, judging by the availability of around one half of all labour services to the demesne each year, although over the next 30 years the proportion of available works fell as the area of customary land at lease expanded.[69] The few remaining labour services disappeared through negotiated commutations in the 1430s when the demesne was finally leased.[70] Perhaps the experience of leasing customary land well before the Black Death at Mildenhall convinced the cellarer's officials to extend its use in response to the crisis of occupancy on the estate after 1349.

The structure of leases at both Fornham St Martin and Barton was the same: cash rent, small entry fine and granted through the court roll for a stipulated term of years. At the end of the fourteenth century six-year leases were common, whereas in the 1420s ten-year terms had become popular at Barton, and by the 1450s most were between seven and 12 years. A few 30- and 40-year leases were granted, and even one 99-year lease is recorded in 1491.[71] The growing length of the terms of leases reflects the preference for greater security of tenure, as does the tendency for the lessee to obtain the right to assign the lease to a third party in a few leases from the 1450s at Barton. Both these developments are exemplified in a lease granted in 1482 to Thomas Edward, who obtained a sizeable package of land in Fornham St Martin 'leased at farm' for 40 years, held 'to his heirs and assignees by the

---

[66] SROB E3/15.13/2.10 and 2.16.

[67] Bailey, *Marginal economy*, pp. 228, 269; for labour services, see SROB E3/15.13/2.21.

[68] Bailey, *Marginal economy*, pp. 228, 268–9.

[69] SROB E18/455/1 and BL, Additional Rolls, 53120 to 53134.

[70] See SROB E18/455/1 and BL Add. Rolls 53135 (1425–6) and BL Add. Rolls 53136 (1439–40).

[71] See SROB E18/155/8 for the emergence of 30- and 40-year leases, and see A6/1/14 for the 99-year lease.

rod and at the will of the lord'.[72] The use of a copy of the court-roll entry of the lease also spread as proof of title. As early as 1394 the Fornham court ordered all its tenants 'whether free or native' to 'show a copy of their charter and copies of all their tenures at the next court, under penalty of 40d'.[73] In 1491 John Fyson of Barton was in the 28th year of a 30-year lease of 18 acres of land 'at farm by copy'.[74] The increasing attractiveness of leases to a wider cross section of fifteenth-century society is demonstrated by one entry in the same account, which reveals that one 'Thomas Cook, knight' had recently leased 5 acres of customary land.[75]

What became of these leases in the late fifteenth century? No Barton court rolls are extant after the 1450s, although all the evidence from its account rolls indicates that long-term leases continued to dominate tenures on the manor, and that customary land held at farm was simply re-granted upon expiry of the lease.[76] Interestingly, a subtly different picture emerges at Fornham, where some late fifteenth-century court rolls, but no accounts, have survived. In the 1480s the courts reveal some difficulties finding new tenants after the expiry of leases for customary land, and consequently some parcels were successfully re-granted on hereditary tenures. By the second quarter of the sixteenth century most new grants recorded in the Fornham court rolls were now hereditary tenures by copy.[77] It is a striking contrast that a shortage of tenants in the 1360s resulted in the conversion of hereditary villein tenures to leasehold, but that another period of shortage in the 1480s resulted in the re-conversion of some leases back to hereditary tenure. Overall, however, in c.1500 leases remained the main form of tenure for the original customary lands on Type 4 manors.

[72] SROB E18/155/8 and E3/15.9/1.8. This 40-year lease, protected by the right of heirs to inherit or for assignees to acquire it within the term of the lease, is similar in many respects to a grant for the term of a number of lives.

[73] SROB E3/15.9/1.5, m. 5, court held June 1395.

[74] SROB E18/155/8 and A6/1/14.

[75] SROB A6/1/14.

[76] SROB E18/155/8 and A6/1/14.

[77] SROB E3/15.9/1.8 and 1.9. The dominance of hereditary grants in the Fornham courts of the 1520s and 1530s does not necessarily mean that leases were quickly disappearing; it may be that new leases were now simply enrolled directly onto the account, rather than recorded in the court roll. Unfortunately, no accounts have survived to test this hypothesis.

Incidents of villeinage

Labour services

The selection of manors for this sample was influenced by the availability of an adequate series of court rolls, which are the best source of information about the management of the overwhelming majority of villein incidents. They provide less information about the management of labour services, which are best studied through a series of manorial accounts. Unfortunately, few manorial accounts are extant from the manors in the sample, so it is often difficult to reconstruct the chronology of the disappearance of week works.[78] There is, however, sufficient evidence for a number of general patterns to be observable.

One pattern is that on the eve of the Black Death a heavy burden of week works is most characteristic of manors held by higher-status landlords, such as Barton Magna, Fornham St Martin and Lidgate. They were less common on gentry manors. Norton is probably typical of the latter category, where only seasonal labour services of various kinds, and no week works, were owed.[79]

Another pattern is that, irrespective of the composition of labour services, they tended to survive longer on those manors where villein tenures endured, i.e. Type 1 and Type 2 manors. Unfortunately, the relative absence of accounts from the sample means that we cannot know the extent to which these services were actually used or commuted at will. It is probable that the majority of Type 1 and Type 2 manors retained the option of using them each year, but seldom took up the option and instead commuted them for cash. In fact, this had been the standard practice before the Black Death on a number of these manors. For example, at Lidgate in 1346–7 over £9 was received from the commutation at will of most of the available works, and at Harkstead in 1341–2 every single labour service was commuted under 'sale of works'.[80] On the rare occasions after 1350 where lords did choose to deploy labour services, their focus was exclusively upon seasonal and – especially – harvest services. As late as the 1390s around 80% of all seasonal labour services at Norton were still employed, only 10% were sold on an *ad hoc* basis, and the rest were either allowed to office holders or decayed.[81] Harvest services were the last

---

[78] See Appendix. The manors with the best series of accounts are Barton Magna, Fornham St Martin, Hardwick Russells, Norton and Radclive.

[79] SROB 553/25.

[80] TNA SC6/1002/16 (Lidgate), where there is no works' account, implying that all labour services were commuted at will that year; SROI S1/10/6.6 (Harkstead), where 'all customary works sold, 20s; all harvest works sold, 12s.'

[81] Although the labour services at Norton were largely seasonal, with no onerous week works, SROB 553/21 to 23.

to go, and even in the 1420s nearly 80% of its harvest and ploughing services were still directly employed each year.[82]

The administrative device of retaining the option to use week works but, in practice, commuting them all at will year after year was cumbersome, although at least it meant that the tenants were regularly reminded of the lord's theoretical right to deploy them. Sooner or later, however, officials recognized that the option would never realistically be exercised again, and so they pro-actively entered into negotiated commutations. Some of these were for a fixed term, as in 1382 when the lord of Holbrook entered into separate agreements with 19 customary tenants to commute all labour services due from their landholdings for an annual cash payment for a fixed term of seven years.[83] Other negotiated commutations were piecemeal rather than collective. For example, in 1421 a single tenant of a messuage and four customary acres at Winston paid 9s. 6d. to commute all winter, summer and harvest services attached to his holding, and in 1440 a toft and virgate in Weedon Vale was granted on an hereditary tenure for an annual rent of 14s. instead of the ancient rents and services (with the exception of a heriot).[84] Finally, a permanent negotiated commutation might be reached with all tenants, based on the customary monetary valuation of the labour services. The 1445–6 account roll for Harkstead noted that nothing had been received from 'sales of works' this year, but, instead, a fixed cash sum had been permanently added to the rents of assize 'with the assent of the lord and tenants'.[85] This signified the shift from repeated annual commutations at will to a formal and permanent negotiated commutation.

Another pattern is that week works disappeared earliest on Type 3 and 4 manors, because the conversion of hereditary villein tenure to fixed-term tenures always involved the substitution of labour services for cash. The huge swing to leases at Barton Magna from the late 1350s meant that by 1363–4 only 20% of all week works were still available to the demesne; its accounts dating from the 1370s contain no works' section, and no mention of commutations, because all labour services had now disappeared.[86] Similarly, in the mid-1360s 60% of all week works had decayed at Fornham St Martin, and the remainder disappeared in the 1370s when the manor was leased in its entirety.[87] The conversion of a large area of customary land to leases on Type

[82] SROB 553/25 to 27.

[83] SROI S1/10/9.1, court held December 1382. The sums for each holding varied between 5s. and 12s., with 8s. the most common, totalling £7 7s. 0d. each year.

[84] CUL EDC 7/19/44, court held October 1421; New College, Oxford, court held May 1440.

[85] SROI S1/10/6.6.

[86] SROB E18/155/2 and 3.

[87] SROB, E3/15.6/2.23a; E3/15.6/2.31; Bailey, *Marginal economy*, p. 235.

2 manors also reduced the quantity of works available to the demesne, and further reduced the incentive to utilize the remaining services. The court rolls of Lackford contain few references to labour services, and a stray manorial account from 1440–1 contains no income from the sale of works, and no works' account, signifying both their disappearance and the absorption of payments for negotiated commutations into the fixed rent structure.[88]

The decision to lease the demesne on a longer-term contract was usually accompanied by a decision to commute all labour services permanently. When the Norton demesne was finally leased in the 1440s, most of the labour services were commuted at will each year – in 1444–5, for example, 83% were sold at a set rate of 1¼d. each. In addition, some of the manor's customary tenants now negotiated permanent commutations, payments for which were formally enrolled in the manorial account.[89] Demesne lessees either had no desire to employ labour services or lacked the power to coerce reluctant tenants into performing them. The latter is suggested by an unusual example from Radclive, where in 1382 the lessee received official remission of £30 13s. 11d. from his rent charge to reflect the reality that he had been unable for a number of years to raise the labour services included as part of the lease.[90] Virgaters at Akeley carried a heavy burden of labour services, which created an interesting situation after 1398 when the manorial demesne was leased to the tenants of the manor as a collective body for 24 years, including access to all remaining labour services. The tenants were thus able to determine themselves whether to cease performing the services or not. Whatever they decided, the overall package proved attractive because they renewed the lease in 1421.[91]

Evidence for resistance to labour services is very limited, although this may simply reflect that fact that few were actually deployed rather than any lack of hostility. Neither collective nor personal refusals to perform were commonplace, and those that occurred are usually restricted to the period immediately after the Black Death. For example, two men detained a total of 22 works at Drinkstone in the later 1350s, but no detentions are recorded subsequently.[92] The only exception to this general rule is Beeston, a Type 1 manor where various aspects of villeinage were a source of tension around

---

[88] SROB E3/15.12/2.3.

[89] SROB 553/27 to 34.

[90] New College, Oxford, 6715.

[91] Each virgate owed a cash rent of 18d. per annum and 300 works. New College, Oxford, 4084, court held May 1398; 4085, court held November 1421.

[92] SROB E7/10/1.2, John de Sproutone detained nine harvest works and Peter Waryn detained 13 works, attracting a retrospective commutation charge of 3s. 3d., and an amercement of 3d.

c.1400. Collective refusals to perform services were recorded here in 1390, 1392 and 1412, before disappearing completely.[93]

Heriot

Heriot is recorded on 14 of the 23 manors in the sample (see table 12.1). The render of the best beast was widespread in the later fourteenth century, but thereafter cash heriots became increasingly common. At Akeley and Radclive heriot was payable whenever a holding was surrendered, and an entry fine was also due from the incoming tenant. Elsewhere heriot was only payable upon the death of the tenant, although on some East Anglian manors the render of a heriot released the incoming heir from paying an entry fine.

Heriot was present on each of the Buckinghamshire manors, where it was routinely collected. By the mid-fifteenth century the size of the heriot to be paid was often stipulated in advance, i.e. when the tenant was admitted to the holding. In contrast, heriot is not recorded at all on nine of the 19 East Anglian manors. For example, there is no render of heriot in any of the extant sources from Harkstead, and in 1417 a court-roll entry noted explicitly that it was not owed by the estate of a deceased customary tenant.[94] Heriot probably survived the fifteenth century on seven of the 23 manors, including all of those in Buckinghamshire.[95]

In East Anglia heriot disappeared quickly from those manors which underwent a substantial shift to leasehold, because it was not charged on leases. The last heriots at Barton Magna were collected during the epidemic of 1349, and only two are recorded after 1349 at Fornham St Martin, the last in 1393.[96] Similarly, the frequency of heriot was severely reduced on Type 2 manors, where its disappearance from customary land converted to leases exerted pressure to remove it from hereditary tenures too. For example, just two heriots are recorded at Badwell Ash between 1419 and 1443.[97] At Winston a total of ten heriots are recorded between 1350 and its disappearance in 1449, and it was very rare post-1420.[98] When Richard Moyse died holding a

---

[93] The most serious being in 1392, with substantial fines being recorded in both the January and April courts: TNA DL30/102/1395, court held November 1390; DL30/102/1396, courts held January and April 1392; DL30/102/1401, m.5, court held March 1412.

[94] SROI S1/10/6.1.

[95] The manors where heriot probably survived after 1500 are Akeley, Beeston, Hardwick Russells, Iken, Radclive, Runton Hayes, and Weedon Vale.

[96] In July 1387 the Barton court noted that no heriot was due from a customary *tenementum* after the death of its tenant, SROB E18/151/1; for Fornham, see SROB E3/15.9/1.5 to 1.7.

[97] SROB 1825/1/1 and 11.

[98] CUL EDC 7/19/56, court held June 1449.

12.1 Last recorded date of the key incidents of villeinage on 23 manors

The dates under the name of each manor refer to the range
of extant court rolls.

TYPE 1 MANORS

Manor	Chev.	Pres. abs.*	Child.	Heriot	Merchet	Millsuit	Recog.	Tallage
Beeston 1384–1492	1476	1409	1402	1475	1426	1390	None	None
Debach 1365–1403	None	None	None	None	1387	None	None	None
Drinkstone 1352–1483	None	1377	None	None	None	1352	None	None
Harkstead 1415–22	None	None	None	None	None	None	None	None
Hardwick Russells 1398–1471	None	None	None	1460	None	None	None	None
Harleston 1413–99	1458	1459	None	None	1424	None	None	None
Higham 1431–47	None	None	None	None	None	None	None	None
Holbrook 1378–1484	1394	1484	1397	1483	1396	None	None	None
Norton 1422–1500	1443	1495	None	1492	1467*	None	None	None
Radclive 1378–1495	None	None	None	1477	None	None	None	None
Runton/ Beeston Felbrigg 1381–1509	1408	None	None	None	1398	None	None	None
Runton Hayes 1349–1480	None	None	None	1477	None	None	1349	None
Thorpe Morieux 1359–1450	1409	None	None	None	1403	None	None	None
Weedon Vale	1439	1441	None	1460	1454	1471*	None	None
Withersfield 1388–1432	None	None	None	None	None	None	None	None

* presentment only

Type 2 Manors

Manor	Chev.	Pres. Abs.	Child.	Heriot	Merchet	Millsuit	Recog.	Tallage
Badwell Ash 1419–95	None	None	None	1443	None	None	None	None
Iken 1349–1490	1487	1472	1373	1492	1474	None	None	None
Lackford 1366–1487	1398	1411	None	None	1398	None	None	None
Lidgate 1394–1490	1490	1490	None	1439	1440	None	None	None
Winston 1350–1499	1426	1424	1383	1449	1421	1356	1432	None

Type 3 Manors

Manor	Chev.	Pres. Abs.	Child.	Heriot	Merchet	Millsuit	Recogn.	Tallage
Akeley 1382–1422	1393	1404	None	1422	1382	None	None	None

Type 4 Manors

Manor	Chev.	Pres. Abs.	Child.	Heriot	Merchet	Millsuit	Recog.	Tallage
Barton Mga 1349–1456	1423	1456	None	1349	1439	None	None	None
Fornham St Martin 1351–1510	None	1399	None	1393	None	None	1389*	None

* presentment only

hereditary tenure in 1427, his estate was ordered 'to satisfy the lord as to the best beast to be rendered after the death of the said Richard, as is the custom of the manor'. Yet nothing happened, despite reminders, until 1432 when the court was ordered to pronounce upon the matter. The jurors confirmed that Richard's best beast had been a horse worth 24s., which had still not been rendered as heriot, and so his widow and executors were ordered to attend the next court. There is no record that they ever did so, despite a good series of court rolls.[99] Soon afterwards, however, the relatives of other deceased customary tenants did not pay heriot.[100] Nor was heriot restored when leases

---

99   CUL EDC 7/19/47, court held May 1427; see 7/19/48 for the reminders; and 7/19/50, court held October 1432 for the valuation by the homage, and the subsequent inactivity.

100   See, for example, CUL EDC 7/19/55, court held October 1446.

were eventually restored to hereditary tenures during the second half of the fifteenth century on the East Anglian manors.

Even on Type 1 manors, where hereditary villein tenure continued to dominate landholdings, the late dates of the last recorded incidence of heriot disguise the fact that its frequency had been in sharp decline. For example, at Runton Hayes seven heriots were collected between 1350 and 1399, and four between 1400 and 1480.[101] The number of heriots at Norton remained broadly constant between 1425 and 1475, but then fell markedly in the last quarter of the fifteenth century.[102] At Beeston no heriots were paid between the 1380s and 1410s, mainly due to a profusion of death-bed transfers, but none were charged even when tenants died in possession of customary land.[103] Then four cash heriots were paid between 1467 and 1475, after which the incident disappeared completely.[104]

On two manors, Iken and Lidgate, a heriot was levied upon serfs, irrespective of whether they held land or not, but not upon customary tenants.[105] For example, Alan Barker of Iken did not hold any land when he died in 1460, but his estate was ordered to render half of his best beast, and in 1473 Olivia Barker rendered a cow as heriot after her death.[106] The manorial court of Lidgate collected heriot from deceased serfs, such as the landless William Grigg and Robert Wenge who lived in nearby Ousden (Suffolk), although it was unsuccessful in its attempts to do so from the estate of the long-departed Hugh Gille, who had died holding lands in Kedington (Suffolk).[107]

---

[101] NRO WKC 2/167 398 x 8.

[102] The court-roll series across the whole of this period is largely complete, and yields evidence of eight heriots between 1422 and 1449, seven between 1450 and 1474, and three between 1475 and 1499, with the last recorded in October 1492, SROB 553/5.

[103] The frequency of death-bed transfers, and the failure to charge heriot upon the death in possession of Adam Frost, are documented at TNA DL30/102/1401 mm. 1 to 5.

[104] The sudden appearance of heriot is hard to explain, TNA DL30/102/1404 mm. 8, 14, 23. In all four cases an heir succeeded a deceased tenant, and no entry fine was charged, so it may be that a new scribe, unfamiliar with the East Anglian custom of paying an entry fine in lieu of heriot, misnamed the payment as heriot. All four were cash heriots.

[105] For example, compare the heriot rendered on the death of an Iken serf in September 1408 with the non-payment of heriot upon the deaths of other tenants around the same time, SROI HD32/293/395, mm. 7 to 25.

[106] SROI HD32/293/388, m. 61 court held April 1460, and m. 69, March 1473.

[107] SROB E3/11/1.1, court held June 1393; and E3/11/1.4, courts held in 1430 (Wenge) and April 1435 (Grigg).

Millsuit

Millsuit is recorded on three manors in the sample, a surprisingly low number. This might reflect its patchiness before 1350 in East Anglia.[108] However, there is no doubt that it was deliberately discarded on some manors soon after the Black Death. For example, millsuit had been regularly imposed in the early fourteenth century upon the unfree tenants of Fornham St Martin, but it is not recorded at all after 1349.[109] Likewise, it disappeared in the 1350s at both Drinkstone and Winston.[110] Millsuit was only routinely imposed on one manor in the sample, Beeston, where six men were amerced a total of 18d. in April 1385, and five a total of 10d. in August 1390. In November 1390 six men were amerced for possessing mill stones to the prejudice of the lord's mill.[111] All references to millsuit ceased thereafter, although in 1412 the recent lessee of the manor was amerced for allowing the lord's mill to become dilapidated and thus preventing his tenants from using the mill. Irrespective of the presence or not of millsuit, milling activity was still subject to some regulation by manorial authorities. At Weedon Vale in 1471 all tenants were warned not to mill barley malt on hand mills, under a penalty of 6s. 8d., and the lessee of the demesne mill at Lidgate was fined for charging excessive tolls in May 1439.[112]

Tallage and recognition

Recognition was imposed on three out of 23 manors in the sample, and tallage not at all.[113] Both had been much more widespread before 1349.[114] It is possible that after 1350 these payments were recorded only in the manorial account, in which case the reliance upon court rolls as the main source of information for our sample might lead to its under-representation. However, the evidence from Chevington, Fornham All Saints and Walsham, discussed in chapters 6 and 10, shows that the collection of tallage and recognition attracted some mention in court rolls, usually through the election of assessors or collectors. Thus it is reasonable to suppose that the evidence from the

---

[108]   Bailey, 'Villeinage in England', pp. 446–7.

[109]   For millsuit before 1349 at Fornham, see SROB E3/15.9/1.1, mm. 11, 20; E3/15.6/1.3, mm. 18–19.

[110]   For example, the only reference post-1350 at Winston was the 3d. amercement on John Tailor in August 1356 for not milling at mill of lord, CUL EDC 7/19/15; Drinkstone SROB E7/10/1.1. Millsuit had featured regularly in the 1330s and 1340s on both manors.

[111]   TNA DL30/102/1392 and 1395.

[112]   New College, Oxford, 3847, court held January 1471; SROB E3/11/1.4, m. 17.

[113]   Fornham St Martin, Runton Hayes and Winston.

[114]   In 1346–7 40s. tallage was paid at Lidgate, TNA SC6/1002/16; Hervey, ed., *Pinchbeck Register*, II, p. 468 for recognition at Barton.

sample is reliable, and that tallage was an insignificant feature of villeinage after 1350.

Robert de Repps, the lord of Runton Hayes, perished in the Black Death of 1349 and his wife, Alice, received 2s. recognition from 'all native and villein tenants' at her first court in November 1349. Yet in 1368, when John de Repps succeeded her as lord of the manor, recognition was neither requested nor paid, and it never featured again.[115] The tenants of Winston paid 33s. 4d. in 1366 as recognition upon the election of a new prior of Ely, and again in 1425. In 1432 the sum was reduced to 20s. 'by special grace', but it was never levied again.[116]

Recognition was due from all customary tenants at both Fornham St Martin and Winston, both manors held by ecclesiastical landlords. In 1383 those at Fornham St Martin were instructed to render 10s. in recognition of the new abbot of Bury St Edmunds, John de Timworth, and three tenants were appointed to 'assess and collect' the due. Yet they did not do so at any point during the next six years, despite repeated reminders, and despite incurring penalties totalling 32s. in successive courts. After 1389 references to either the recognition fine or to its non-collection cease, although we cannot know whether the lord had relented or the tenants had finally paid.[117] Yet, regardless of who won this stand-off, it is remarkable that the appointed assessors were prepared to incur such heavy cumulative fines rather than render (a much less expensive) recognition. They were adopting a considered and determined stance of passive resistance, presumably with the support – moral and financial – of the rest of the customary tenants and leaseholders. The absence of any record in 1389 of the collection of recognition upon the election of abbot William Cratfield – which caused such ill-feeling at Chevington and Fornham All Saints – is probably significant: it seems likely that the earlier resistance at Fornham St Martin had convinced the abbey's administration of the futility of trying to collect recognition for abbatial elections from manors located on the estate of the cellarer. The absence of any evidence for recognition at Barton Magna, which was part of the same estate, strengthens this argument.

The passive but determined resistance of the customary tenants of Fornham St Martin also characterized their response to instructions to draw up a new rental and to compile a new roll of those owing suit to the court.

[115]   NRO WKC 2/167 398 x 8.

[116]   CUL EDC 7/19/20, court held January 1366; 7/9/46, court held October 1425; 7/19/49, court held October 1432; and see 7/9/62, court held June 1462, when a new prior was elected but no recognition charged.

[117]   SROB E3/15.9/1.5, courts held September 1383, September 1384, August 1385, August 1386, August 1387, September 1389. Similarly, it is possible that the assessors did not pay all or some of the 32s. imposed upon them, but we cannot known definitively in the absence of any contemporary accounts.

Estate officials had first ordered these tasks in 1385, and the failure of the tenants to respond triggered a succession of petty collective fines, comprising a few pennies every year, until August 1395, when the lord's patience finally snapped and a sizeable punishment of 6s. 8d. was imposed upon the whole homage. Yet the heavier fine had no impact – nothing was done, and the annual penalty for non-compliance quickly returned to 6d. per annum. As late as 1406 neither the rental nor the roll of suitors had been completed.[118]

Personal servility

Leyrwite/childwite

Childwite quickly diminished in frequency and importance after 1348–9. We can prove that it had been levied before 1348–9, but not thereafter, at Barton Magna, Drinkstone and Fornham St Martin.[119] Childwite is recorded on four of the 23 manors after 1349.[120] It had disappeared by the 1380s on three of them, and its late survival (until 1402) at Beeston is very unusual.[121] However, on all four manors its frequency was exceptionally low. For example, child-wite survived until 1383 at Winston, but there were just two recorded cases between 1349 and 1383. In 1378 its manorial court ordered three servile women to appear at the next court and provide security that they would not marry without licence. Within 18 months one of them had paid a marriage fine, while the other two were amerced for childwite. The women then disappear from the record, and childwite was never levied again.[122]

While the frequency of childwite was very low, the fines charged for it were generally fixed and relatively high. Before the Black Death the fine for childwite on manor after manor in East Anglia had been standardized at a rate of 2s. 8d., which was high compared with the level of fine in many parts of England.[123] The high and standardized fine had emerged as a deter-rent to fornication during a period when many East Anglian communities were straining under severe demographic pressure. The easing of that pres-sure after the Black Death removed this economic justification, but there is little evidence that the fine was reduced. The standard charge was 2s. 6d. at

[118]   SROB E3/15.9/1.5 and 1.6.
[119]   SROB E18/151/1 (Barton Magna); SROB E7/10/1.1 to 1.3 (Drinkstone); SROB E3/15.9/1.1 and 1.2 (Fornham)
[120]   Beeston, Holbrook, Iken and Winston.
[121]   TNA DL30/102/1399.
[122]   CUL EDC 7/19/25, courts held January 1378 and July 1379; 7/19/26, court held October 1379; and 7/19/28, court held October 1383.
[123]   Bailey, 'Villeinage in England', pp. 440–1.

Holbrook and Winston, and 2s. 8d. at Beeston and Iken.[124] The only evidence for a reduction in its level comes from Beeston in 1402, when it dropped to 12d.[125] The persistence of a high fine was probably due to a combination of custom and the difficulty of opposing it – pregnant, single, women were vulnerable and exposed, and their cause was unlikely to attract a groundswell of support from other serfs. The combination of high fines and very low frequency suggests that childwite had lost its general relevance after 1350, but also that it continued to be deployed selectively. The lord may have insisted upon it as part of a wider policy of enforcing personal servility, which seems to have been the case at Beeston. In contrast, at Winston it seems to have been a device to bring pressure to bear on two particular women for reasons that are not fully apparent.

Merchet

Merchet is one of the most ubiquitous incidents of personal servility, recorded on 14 of the 23 manors after 1349. It had been even more widespread before 1349.[126] However, by the 1390s only nine manors still imposed merchet, and by the 1450s the number had shrunk to three (see table 12.1).

The fines ranged from 12d. to 20s., with most around 4s., although the evidence is too fragmentary to identify meaningful trends in their average level.[127] Servile women paid merchet on most manors, although at Beeston, Debach, Iken and Winston males were also liable. Fines for male merchet tended to be lower; for example, the mean fine at Beeston was 80d., while the average for males was 30d.

The most striking aspect of merchet is that, despite its relative ubiquity and longevity as a servile incident, its frequency was low on most manors. The last record of merchet at Akeley in 1382 is actually the *only* recorded merchet there after 1349, and even that appears to have had a very particular explanation: Joanna Beyham paid an enormous 20s. licence to marry wher-

---

[124] SROB S1/10/9.1; CUL EDC 7/19/25; TNA DL30/102/1392.

[125] TNA DL30/102/1399.

[126] Merchet was the most widespread incident of villeinage before 1349 in Suffolk, Bailey, 'Villeinage in England', p. 439. Nine manors within our sample do not provide any record of merchet after 1349, and manorial sources dating from before 1349 are extant from four of them: in all four cases, merchet had been collected prior to the Black Death. Hence we can be certain that merchet was being deliberately discarded in the wake of the epidemic. The four manors are Debach (SROI HD230/1/1, merchet recorded in the only court of 1347); Drinkstone (SROB E7/10/1.1, numerous examples); Fornham St Martin (SROB E3/15.9/1.1, 1.2 and 1.3, numerous examples); and Runton Hayes (NRO WKC 2/167 308 x 8, merchet recorded in court held February 1343).

[127] For example, after 1349 the 13 merchets recorded at Winston averaged 38d., the six at Lidgate averaged 47d., and the five at Norton averaged 48d.

ever she wished, which looks like the remarriage of a widow.[128] Similarly, just one merchet is recorded at Runton Felbrigg before the last recorded incident in 1398. On the handful of manors where merchet continued to be levied after c.1400, its frequency diminished rapidly. 16 merchets and four marriages without licence are recorded at Beeston between 1384 and 1407, but none at all between 1407 and 1413, and only one thereafter (in 1426).[129] Just six merchets are recorded in fifteenth-century Lidgate, four at Norton, and five at Iken.[130] In the 1470s, when merchet finally disappeared at Iken, just one serf family was being targeted.[131]

The regularity of merchet at Beeston before 1407, followed by its sudden and dramatic decline, indicates that, at certain times and places, its management was more a reflection of managerial policy than of the frequency of servile marriages. A similar impression emerges from Norton, where not a single merchet was levied between 1427 and 1439, but then in 1440 four were imposed simultaneously at a standard rate of 3s. 4d. each. It then disappeared again until a stray presentment in 1467, when Katherine Souter was ordered to be attached by body after marrying William Howes of Weston (either Coney or Market Weston, Suffolk).[132] This pattern most likely reflects the selective use of merchet by landlords for a particular (unknown) purpose.

Chevage

Presentments for absence or chevage payments are recorded on 15 of the 23 manors in the sample, which meant that it was the most common incident of personal servility after 1349. The management of flown serfs was the most widespread and energetic aspect of the management of personal servility in the late fourteenth and fifteenth centuries, generating much illuminating information about serfs and their migratory patterns. Chevage or presentments for absence survived into the fifteenth century on 13 of those 15 manors, and beyond 1450 on eight of them. However, a slightly different picture emerges if we consider chevage alone, which survived beyond 1400 on ten of the 15 manors, and on just five after 1450.

The size of fines tended to be large and variable in the second half of the fourteenth century, when chevage was imposed less frequently. As chevage became levied more frequently from around the beginning of the fifteenth century, so the level of fine fell and settled to between 3d. and 10d. For example, between 1384 and 1406 just six licences to live away from the manor

[128]   New College, Oxford, 4084, court held October 1382.

[129]   TNA DL30/102/1395 to 1408.

[130]   SROB E3/11/1.1 to 1.5 (Lidgate); SROB 553/1 to 4 (Norton).

[131]   The merchets at Iken are recorded in SROI HD32/293/395, mm. 6, 23, 42, 48 and 70. The Barkers were the targeted family.

[132]   SROB 553/4.

were paid at Beeston, averaging 28.3d., yet after 1407 it became a more regular payment at the much lower rate of 6d. The average fine at Harleston in the 1420s was 8d., dropping to 6d. in the 1440s.[133] Chevage at Lidgate averaged 10d. Two manors, Akeley and Barton Magna, persisted with the traditional render of a capon. In June 1381 Henry Anetel of Barton obtained a licence to live off the manor for ten years in exchange for four capons per annum, and in 1387 Alicia Pach of Akeley agreed to render one capon per annum to live in Morton (Buckinghamshire) for the rest of her life.[134]

Although an interest in flown serfs often persisted until well into the fifteenth century, the bald statement of the last year in which chevage was charged upon a given manor often disguises both a dramatic fall in its frequency before that final disappearance, and the small number of serfs involved. At Runton and Beeston Felbrigg the last chevage payment in 1408 was in fact the only such payment after the arrival of plague.[135] At Beeston between 1413 and the final appearance of chevage in 1474, just two people paid chevage, with no charges at all between 1413 and 1470.[136] Chevage at Barton Magna was paid by just a single serf in the years leading up to its final disappearance in 1423, while between 1382 and 1399 a grand total of three people paid chevage at Akeley and four were presented for absence.[137] Similarly, only three serf families remained at Iken after 1421, one of whom, Alan Barker, was the only person to pay chevage throughout the middle decades of the fifteenth century until his death in 1460; the final record of chevage there in 1487 was an isolated payment by one Robert Barker.[138] Just eight different individuals are identified as flown in the whole of the long court series for Holbrook, eight people in that for Norton, five at Harleston, and four (all from the same family) at Winston.[139]

The management of chevage and of presentments for absence shows much variation across the sample, but, in general, the evidence reinforces the argument that its frequency was determined as much – if not more – by administrative changes, and by the willingness of serfs to pay it, than by real

---

[133] SROB E3/15.7/1.1.

[134] SROB E18/151/1; New College, Oxford, 4084.

[135] NRO WKC 2/166 398 x 7.

[136] TNA DL30/102/1402 to 1406.

[137] SROB E18/151/1; New College, Oxford, 4084.

[138] SROI HD32/293/395, m. 25 for the three serf families in 1421; m. 61, court held April 1460, and m. 79, court held May 1487. The largest number of different people recorded as either absent or paying chevage within the sample was 28 at Lidgate between 1397 and 1490, which still falls a long way short of the >50 emigrants recorded on most of the Ramsey abbey manors in the first half of the fifteenth century see p. 77 above.

[139] In c.67 courts for Holbrook, SROI S1/10/9.1 and 9.2, and c.55 for Harleston, SROB E3/15.17/1.1.

fluctuations in migration. Often, no cases are recorded for a number of years, followed by a sudden surge of activity. For example, no presentments for absence or chevage payments were made in any of the courts held between 1379 and 1391 at Weedon Vale, but over the next decade around three people each year were presented for absence.[140] In the 1410s the same manor court rolls once again fall completely silent on the matter, until 1435 when seven people were suddenly presented for absence, and Thomas Green rendered the first recorded chevage payment. There followed an intense interest in absentees every year until 1441, after which all record of departures ceased abruptly and permanently.[141] Similarly, chevage appeared in just one court of Runton and Beeston Felbrigg (in 1408, when brothers Richard and Thomas Hoddesdon paid a combined total of 10s.), which cannot reflect the real pattern of migration from the manor.[142]

There are a number of explanations for such variations in the management of absence. One is that manorial officials were relaxed about out-migration until they experienced serious difficulties in finding tenants for landholdings. Hence a sudden spate of abandonment of holdings, and a shortage of replacement tenants, triggered an interest in departed serfs, some of whom might have been absent for several years. This seems to have occurred at Holbrook, where one serf had paid chevage in 1378, but no other cases were recorded in any courts in the 1380s. Then in 1389 a small number of leases of abandoned customary land were granted, and in May 1390 William Anly refused to be admitted to a messuage and a 15-*acreware* holding after the death of his father, both of which hint at a shortage of willing tenants for customary land. In 1392 presentments for absence and chevage re-appeared after an absence of 14 years, and officials also adopted a more aggressive approach: the fines were much higher, and absentees were additionally charged 1d. capitage for not holding land from the manor.[143] Similar concerns surfaced at exactly the same time at Akeley, and triggered a similar response. A sudden slump in the land market is suggested by a collapse in the average entry fine paid for the standard half virgate from 7s. 9d. in the 1380s to 2s. 8d. in the 1390s. Then in April 1391 William Wotton abandoned a half virgate of land and fled the manor, leaving his goods and chattels within his house, and in July John Parkyn abandoned his house and holding

---

[140]   New College, Oxford, 3847.

[141]   New College, Oxford, 3848.

[142]   NRO WKC 2/166 398 x 7.

[143]   Alan Barry had been charged 6d. to be off the domain in November 1378, then no presentments were made in the 1380s: it is hard to believe that no serf migrations occurred at all for over a decade. In May 1392 Matthew de Alton was amerced 3s. 4d. to live at Walberswick, and Richard le Man 2s. to live in Harwich, both attracting 1d. capitage in addition, SROI S1/10/9.1.

to move to nearby Buckingham. After a decade of indifference to recording migrants, manorial officials ordered his return and the seizure of all his land and goods. John immediately undertook to pay the rent and services, and to live there in the near future.[144]

A second explanation for a change in the management of absence was a change in landlord, as the regular flurry of activity that often accompanied the arrival of a new lord of the manor testifies. The requirement to perform fealty to a new lord invariably flushed out the names of absent serfs, and, in any case, a new administration was usually keen to establish its authority. In addition, a particular lord might have had a strong personal commitment to upholding servility, whether for the profit that might eventually accrue or out of a belief that this was part of the natural order of things. Lords who were also professional lawyers usually had a sharp eye for such matters. The disposition of the lord would also help to explain differences between and within manors in the use of presentments for absence or of chevage, and the balance between them. During a flurry of interest in flown serfs in the 1430s at Weedon, after years of inactivity, manorial officials 'sought the counsel of the lord' on what to do next.[145] There is also the possibility that a surge in chevage payments after the accession of a new lord of the manor reflected a desire among some long-flown serfs to register their existence with the new administration, in case the association might prove useful to them in the future.

Iken, Lidgate and Norton provide three good examples of these phenomena. In the first two decades of the fifteenth century presentments for absence were recorded at Iken, but the first chevage payment did not appear until 1423, which coincided with the accession of a new lord to the manor.[146] A similar pattern is observable at Lidgate, where presentments for absence are regularly recorded at the turn of the fourteenth century, but chevage is not charged until 1420. Presentments for absence then dwindled, while chevage became established as a regular and lucrative charge, with the number of cases often rising after the accession of a new lord of the manor.[147] At Norton chevage was charged on a couple of people every year between 1422 and 1431, but then stopped for the next six years. It recommenced in 1437, after which the same three people paid an average of 45d. chevage every year until 1443, when it disappeared permanently. Its disappearance between 1431 and 1437 is difficult to explain, although it was probably due to lax manage-

---

[144]   New College, Oxford, 4084, courts held April, July and September 1392.

[145]   New College, Oxford, 3848, court held June 1435.

[146]   SROI HD32/293/395, m. 27, court held May 1423.

[147]   Such as in 1435 when the performance of fealty revealed absences and thus provided a basis for increased presentments and interest in flown serfs over the next couple of years, SROB E3/11/1.4 mm. 15, 16, 17.

ment during the twilight years of the lord of the manor, Sir William de Bardewell, who died in 1434.[148] The renewal of chevage after 1437 was part of a general tightening of the administration of the manor, as the new lord finally got a grip upon his estate – for example, the number of court orders to officials increased around the same time, and in 1440 four isolated merchets were levied. There was another change in lordship in 1444, and a change in approach probably explains the altercations between successive bailiffs of the manor and one William Martin, the first in late 1444 and the second in November 1445.[149] The exact cause of the dispute is not recorded, but William's angry response – which is recorded – indicates that he was being pressurized about his servility. The court roll notes that William had shouted '*in Anglicis verbis* 'I wele never ben the lordys bonde cherll'. The new administration then backed off – chevage was never again levied at Norton.[150]

The importance of regarding chevage as a servile incident rather than as an invariable index of migration is underlined by the changes to the ways in which it was managed at Beeston Regis. In the 1380s and 1390s chevage here was charged upon all '*nativi et anlepymen*' who did not hold any land from the lord, which included resident but landless serfs, at a standard rate of 1d. per person: in other words, the *capitagium* variant of chevage. Between 1384 and 1406 around ten people paid this levy each year, while a grand total of six people paid an additional sum expressly to live off the manor.[151] Licences to live off the manor were more costly than capitage; in 1397 Clarissa Swetman paid the largest such licence, 3s. 4d., as a lump sum to cover her departure from the manor to live in the house of the lessee of the demesne, presumably in domestic service.[152] In 1407 the practice of charging separate licences for not holding land, and for living off the manor, ceased abruptly. The 1d. capitage payment disappeared, and chevage assumed the conventional form of an annual, and variable, payment for licence to live off the manor (from 1d. to 12d. per person).[153]

Does the evidence from our sample support the contention that peasant

148   Copinger, *Manors of Suffolk*, vol. 1, p. 350.

149   Copinger does not record this change in lordship, but the Norton court of October 1444 recorded the first court of Hugh Bokenham, armiger, and Walter Gerard, clerk, SROB 553/1.

150   The outburst is recorded in the November court, 1445, SROB 553/1 .

151   Confusingly, the manor called the 1d. levy for landless serfs *chevagium* rather than *capitagium*, but there is no doubt about its usage: the court held November 1389 refers to '*nativi and anlepymen*', TNA DL30/102/1395, and that of December 1392 states explicitly that these people paid *chevagium* because they 'hold nothing from the lord', TNA DL30/102/1396. Payments for living off the manor were called just that.

152   TNA DL30/102/1398.

153   TNA DL30/102/1400.

migration rose markedly after 1400? Of those manors with a good series of records at this date, only two (Lidgate and Winston) record any rise in recorded presentments for absence and chevage, although the increase was small when compared to the 'veritable tide' of emigrants leaving the manors of Ramsey abbey around this time (see p. 77). For example, at Lidgate in the 1390s four serfs were routinely presented for absence, which rose to six in 1397 and 1402, then fell back to four in the 1410s.[154] At Winston between 1350 and 1399 there had been no chevage payments and just four presentments for absence (for the same person).[155] Then in 1400 two flown serfs rendered the first chevage payments, and a third was presented for absence. There is no obvious explanation for the sudden appearance of chevage, but it was then levied on four individuals on 35 occasions between 1400 and 1426 at an average charge of 18d. The highest number of payments in any one year was four, in 1411, and presentments for absence virtually disappeared once chevage appeared. However, after 1426 both chevage and presentments were abandoned simultaneously and permanently.[156] Of the remaining manors with records extant around 1400 there is no evidence for an increase in emigration. On the contrary, all recorded interest in migrants disappeared completely during the 1390s and 1400s at Akeley, Fornham St Martin, Lackford, Runton and Beeston Felbrigg, and Thorpe Morieux.

The reasons why flown serfs continued to pay chevage to their home manor are not stated, and so remain obscure. In some cases, the demands of a powerful lord were difficult – perhaps unwise – to resist. In most cases, there are grounds for arguing that serfs were opting to pay chevage as a voluntary tax. There were some benefits to the serf in these circumstances: chevage was a public acknowledgement and reinforcement of the bond between lord and serf, which nominally provided the latter with some protection against the actions of other predatory lords. The 'protection' would mainly have taken the form of deterrence, in the sense that anyone interfering with the affairs of the bondman of another lord would risk retribution from that lord. Such a deterrent may have been worth having during the political turbulence and disorder of Henry VI's adult reign. Occasionally, the protection could be tangible. In 1387 the Beeston court amerced an outsider, James atte Hekere, 40d. for the unjust harassment of one of its serfs, Margaret Shelle, in a Christian court, and one Margaret Tolly was also amerced 6d. for beating one of the lord's serfs.[157]

---

[154] SROB E3/11/1.1 to 1.3.

[155] CUL EDC 7/19/14 to 35. The presentments were for Margaret White between 1382 and 1384. The Winston court had only recorded four chevage payments before the Black Death, Bailey, 'Villeinage in England', pp. 448–9.

[156] CUL EDC 7/19/36 to 47.

[157] TNA DL30/102/1394.

The main motivation for paying chevage was the prospect of obtaining some direct personal benefit, such as maintaining an interest in a landed inheritance. Occasionally, though, the reasons could be more complex and personal, as revealed by the case of the Langhaugh family of Winston (Suffolk). In 1371 Thomas de Langhaugh paid a merchet of 6s. 8d. and the court was ordered to seize him 'whom the lord claims for his serf by blood': curiously, the entry in the court roll does not state that Thomas was absent. The call was repeated in 1374, and in both 1377 and 1378 the bailiff was amerced for failing to act upon the order. The punishments had the desired effect, because in January 1379 Thomas came into court to receive a messuage and eleven acres of customary land that was lying abandoned in the lord's hands.[158] An explanation for this rather unusual series of events is suggested by a much later court entry, which noted that Thomas lived 'on the fee of John Framlingham within the leet of Winston'. So Thomas had always lived within the parish of Winston, but before 1379 he did not hold land from the lord of Winston, whose bondman he was.[159] Between the acquisition of that land in 1379 and his death in 1417, Thomas appears regularly in the Winston court rolls going about his daily affairs. In 1395 he was amerced 6s. 8d. for marrying a second time without licence. In the early 1400s three sons (Thomas junior, Alexander and William) from his first marriage began to pay chevage routinely, and in 1405 his daughter Margaret paid a 2s. merchet to marry Walter Clerk.[160] Thomas was often on the presentment jury which reported the absences and activities of his fugitive children.[161] His sons paid chevage in most years, although they occasionally missed and were presented for absence instead.

One suspects that the Langhaugh boys paid their chevage at the behest of the patriarch, who actively negotiated better deals with the lord's officials on their behalf. For example, Alex Langhaugh first paid chevage (2s.) in 1400, but in 1410 the fine was reduced to 12d. 'on condition that he returns during the harvest to serve the lessee of the manor'. Alex's reluctance is suggested by his breach of these terms in 1414, for which he was fined by the court.[162] His brother William had been presented for absence at various times in the 1400s, until in 1410 it was established that he was residing with a butcher in Bramford (Suffolk). In June 1411 he appeared at the court 'and acknowledged his status in front of brother Thomas Ramsey, steward' and agreed to pay 3s. 4d. for chevage that year, but 12d. thereafter on condition that he returned

158   CUL EDC 7/19/23, mm. 1, 2; 7/9/25 mm. 1, 4, 5.
159   CUL 7/19/41, court held June 1417, see also 7/9/40a, court held October 1410.
160   CUL EDC 7/19/33, court held May 1395, and 7/9/39, court held October 1405.
161   See, for example, CUL EDC 7/19/38, court held October 1404; 7/19/40a, court held October 1411; and 7/19/40, court held October 1413.
162   CUL EDC 7/19/40, mm. 2, 3, and 7/9/40a.

to the manor once a year.[163] Again, paternal persuasion, and the incentive of a reduced rate, probably convinced William that the demeaning appearance was worthwhile. The events after Thomas's death in 1417 are also suggestive of this interpretation, because the court immediately ordered seizure of Thomas's chattels and the attachment 'by body' of all his progeny, as if the lord's officials knew that the essential link had been severed. They were right. By this date two of his sons, and a married daughter, lived in London, and thereafter only one of them – Alex, who for a while lived in nearby Framsden – paid chevage or returned to Winston.[164] The influence of their father, and the option to inherit his landholding, had convinced the Langhaugh boys to pay chevage; once father had died, and the boys' future lay in London not Winston, they stopped doing so. The case of the Langhaughs reveals that some serfs willingly paid chevage for personal or tactical reasons, so that they – and not necessarily the lord's officials – determined when it disappeared.

Attitudes to serfdom

Special licences

The frequency with which special licences were sought or granted is exceptionally low in the sample. There are no examples of serfs obtaining licences for permission to educate themselves. On two occasions interest is shown in serfs who had entered holy orders, but no licences were charged. After 1380 John Oldars was routinely presented for absence from Fornham St Martin, until in 1393 it was reported that he had taken holy orders. His absence continued to be recorded until 1399, but he never returned and paid neither a licence nor chevage.[165] Likewise, there is no evidence that Walter Aneley, a Weedon Vale serf who fled to become vicar of Siston parish near Bristol, ever paid a licence.

Two licences to pursue a trade are recorded. The afore-mentioned Alex Langhaugh of Winston paid chevage regularly after 1400, and for a while was domiciled with a butcher in Bramford (Suffolk), until 1415 when he paid 2s. 'for licence to have the trade of a shearman [*articium sissoris*]'.[166] In 1393

---

[163]   CUL EDC 7/19/40 and 40a.

[164]   CUL EDC 7/19/41, court held June 1417 records the death of Thomas and the presentment to seize Thomas junior, William, Alex and Margaret. Another daughter Margaret (probably from his second marriage in 1395) lived with her mother, Thomas's widow, in Winston until her marriage in 1421 (7/9/44, court held October 1421). See fn 166 below.

[165]   SROB E3/15.9/1.5, courts held August 1380, August 1393, and December 1398.

[166]   CUL EDC 7/19/41 to 47. Alex was the last person to pay chevage at Winston, rendering 6d. in 1426 to live in nearby Framsden (Suffolk) see fn 164 above.

Walter Hankyn of Akeley paid 12d. to live in Buckingham with William Cook, a butcher, in order to establish his art – he pledged to maintain his landholding in Akeley, and swore not to leave the lordship without licence.[167]

Claims to be free

Disputes between serfs and their lords over personal status were rare. When they occurred, manorial courts were always careful to handle them with procedural correctness.

The handful of disputes over status that did occur within the sample usually arose in one of two sets of circumstances. The first was when the seigniorial administration was pressing to impose personal servility at some stage during the second half of the fourteenth century, as the severance of the close link between tenurial and hereditary servility after the Black Death led to an increase in the practice of labelling explicitly 'serfs by blood' in the manorial court rolls. It was inevitable that some of those so labelled would have overtly disputed their status, although only four such cases are recorded within the sample. Peter Waryn claimed to be free in the Drinkstone court in 1354, and so was ordered to attend a later court to present his case. When he did so in October 1356 the jury confirmed that, although Waryn had recently bought free land, his family had paid merchet in 1322, and so they confirmed his servility. Peter then had to swear an oath of recognition of his servile status.[168] John Peke of Lackford was another who was forced to recognize his servility in front of the whole court after an unsuccessful claim to be free.[169] When John Wenge of Lidgate denied his servility, the court ordered that all his land, goods and chattels be seized.[170] Finally, a jury at Iken declared Richard de More to be servile, following a dispute that had run for many years.[171]

The second set of circumstances in which disputes over status were likely to arise was through the ignorance of the landlord's officials, which might have been due to incompetence or, more likely, due to administrative disruption or discontinuity following a change in manorial lordship. In the 1360s and 1370s there was confusion at Debach about the status of two serfs. Augustus son of Hugh claimed to a new lord that he had purchased a charter of manumission from the previous lord of the manor, and so he was asked to present the charter at a later court. Unfortunately the outcome is not known.[172] The same lord was uncertain whether Nicholas del Cherche, who had recently

---

[167]   New College, Oxford, 4084, court held January 1393.
[168]   SROB E7/10/1.2.
[169]   SROB E3/15.12/1.14, court held February 1404.
[170]   SROB E3/11/1.3, court held November 1418. The outcome is not recorded.
[171]   Dyer, *Everyday life*, p. 229.
[172]   SROI HD230/1/1, court held May 1372.

died, was a bastard or a serf, and so asked the court jurors to determine the matter: 12 years later, they still had not answered the question.[173] In contrast, the lady of Lidgate intervened decisively to resolve similar uncertainty, issuing explicit instructions that an inquisition jury of 18 tenants should be sworn in at the manor court held in August 1435 to establish whether John Batchelor of Fordham (Cambridgeshire) was her serf. The jury concluded that Batchelor, and his ancestors, were all free.[174] There are strong similarities between this Lidgate case and the inquisitions into servile status at Aldham (see Chapter Eight), where the evidence in the court rolls suggests that the verdicts were unsafe. The Lidgate court rolls reveal that in 1397 one John Batchelor had illegally flown the manor, and in 1418 he was recorded as living in Fordham.[175] In the inquiries at both Lidgate and Aldham, the lords were at pains to trial the defendants properly in their own manorial courts, and they abided by the decisions of their own inquisition juries.

Novel forms of servitude
Just four examples of the imposition of demeaning or novel forms of service are recorded in the whole of the sample, one of which was the case of Alex Langhaugh of Winston, described above. In the other three cases: the court of Beeston Regis charged Nicholas Picket 2s. for the right to employ one of the lord's serfs, Thomas Skylman, in his service between 11 November 1390 and 29 September 1391;[176] at Lidgate Richard Reveson was forcibly elected in 1394 to serve the lord in the office of ploughman as a punishment for his deficiencies as reeve the previous year, when he had failed 'to ordain any servant to serve the lord in that office';[177] and Roger Wisman of Iken took a holding in 1378 and promised 'to serve the lord as a labourer, taking for his wage what is just'.[178] These are extreme, novel and demeaning forms of servitude. In each case it is likely that the lord was seeking to make an example of particular individuals for very specific reasons, as in the Reveson case. The dating of the Beeston and Lidgate cases to the 1390s is significant, because the administrators on both manors were active in their enforcement of the incidents of personal servility at precisely that time.

Manorial officials did adopt a few simple tactics to pressurize relatives to bring about the return of emigrants, although such measures were still uncommon. In 1377 Robert atte Churche was ordered to bring

---

[173] SROI HD230/1/1, courts held March 1365 and November 1377.
[174] SROB E3/11/1.4 m. 14.
[175] SROB E3/11/1.2, 1.3.
[176] TNA DL30/102/1395, court held November 1390.
[177] SROB E3/11/1.1, court held July 1394.
[178] SROI HD32/293/388, cited by Dyer, 'Economic and social background', pp. 25–6.

his two departed sons to the next manorial court of Drinkstone, but he refused outright and was punished with a 20s. fine.[179] This is an extreme and rare example, and usually a fine was threatened rather than collected. In September 1392 Adam and Thomas Gille of Lidgate were given until the next court to return three flown members of their family under the threat of a penalty of 13s. 4d., and, similarly, William and John Wenge were ordered to effect the return of Thomas Wenge under a 6s. 8d. penalty. Both penalties were incurred at the next court for their failure to do so, and the penalties then further increased to 20s. and 10s. respectively. However, the matter was then dropped.[180] At Weedon Vale in 1392 all attendees at the manor court were held responsible for the return of two flown serfs under collective penalties of 6s. 8d. for one man and 3s. 4d. for the other. A third serf, Thomas Stacey, was forced in his absence to find security of £5 from three specified residents. The threats were repeated over each of the next four courts, but the penalties were not forfeited and the men never returned.[181] At Akeley in 1388, and again in 1392, the closest blood relatives of flown serfs were personally obligated to return them; when nothing happened, the whole homage was fined 2d., and the lord's advice sought on what to do next.[182] The matter was then quietly dropped. Finally, William Palle of Beeston was forced to pledge that he would not leave the manor, and was forced to find 100s. security.[183] Once again, these tactics were rare, they were not sustained, and they were adopted for specific purposes in local circumstances.

Serf genealogies

There are no recorded serf genealogies of the type found at Dunningworth and Cratfield, or on the Spalding priory estate. Furthermore, court officials seldom sought details about the progeny of existing serfs. Only four manors showed any interest in such details, and in every case the interest was episodic and fleeting. The manorial court of Iken paid very little attention to serfs between 1386 and 1394, when the accession of John Russell as lord of the manor resulted in a sharp change in policy. His first court in May 1394 exposed little official knowledge of the manor's servile population, which triggered an immediate inquiry into the matter. The outcome was a list of

179   SROB E7/10/1.2, cited by Dyer, 'Economic and social background', p. 24. This is the only such example from Drinkstone.
180   Although in 1394 William and Richard Reveson were fined 3d. each for not seizing Thomas when he returned briefly to the village, SROB E3/11/1.1, courts held September 1392, February 1393, and July 1394.
181   New College, Oxford, 3847, courts held April and September 1392, and February and May 1393.
182   New College, Oxford, 4084, courts held April 1388 and July 1392.
183   TNA DL30/102/1392, court held December 1384.

five departed serfs and details of their progeny – for example, it was found that Richard Collys lived at Letheringham (Suffolk), but had no progeny, while William Conele had flown with a son and three daughters.[184] However, this list did not result in any returnees or chevage payments. In April 1407 the lord's officials ordered the compilation of a definitive list of serfs living on and off the manor, but nothing ever materialized.[185] At Holbrook in 1477 the details of the progeny of three serf families were carefully recorded for the first time, all of whom had left the manor, but no further action was taken and chevage was not levied.[186] In May 1436 six serf families swore servile fealty to the new lord of the manor of Lidgate, Sir Edward Neville, and details of their progeny were included; in contrast, just two serfs swore servile fealty in 1477, when no further details were given.[187] Finally, in 1398 the court of Lackford ordered an inquiry into the whereabouts of John atte Hylle 'and his brood [*sequela*]', although nothing further is recorded.[188]

Extortion of flown serfs

There are no examples of extorting wealthy, long-flown, serfs through either enormous fines for chevage and/or entry fines or heavy demands for the purchase of manumission. There are, however, two cases where lords appear to be positioning themselves to make such demands. In 1393 the court of Beeston ordered the executors of the will of Thomas atte Hallegate, serf by blood, to produce an inventory of his goods and chattels for inspection at the next court. No details are recorded in the following court, although his son paid 6s. 8d. to live off the manor in Northrepps (Norfolk) for the year.[189] In March 1398 the Weedon Vale court noted that Walter Anelye had recently abandoned a messuage and calculated the cost of its repair at 20s. Officials therefore ordered the seizure of goods and chattels to that value. At the very next court, in June, it was reported that Walter was now vicar of Siston parish near Bristol, which suggests that the lord was positioning to extract a sizeable chevage or manumission from a well-to-do serf; unfortunately, the outcome of this case is not known.[190]

References to, and examples of, manumission are exceptionally rare, hardly featuring at all within the sample.[191]

---

[184] SROI HD32/293/388, mm. 3, 5, courts held May 1394 and September 1395.
[185] SROI HD32/293/395, mm. 7 to 14.
[186] SROI S1/10/9.2.
[187] SROB E3/11/1.4, m. 15; and E3/11/1.5, court held September 1477.
[188] SROB E3/15.12/1.13.
[189] TNA DL30/102/1397, courts held June and December 1393.
[190] New College, Oxford, 3847.
[191] The only recorded grant is to William del Hel of Debach, John and Thomas his sons, and all their brood and chattels – no sum is mentioned, court held 1373

Reaction and resistance

In the generation after the Black Death there is no evidence for a 'seignio-rial reaction', i.e. no sense in which landlords acted with the intention of re-imposing villeinage aggressively. On the contrary, the incidence of key incidents such as week works, millsuit, tallage, and leyrwite diminished rapidly during this period, the use of 'in villeinage' disappeared from convey-ances, and on some manors fixed-term tenancies displaced villein tenure. Chevage was surprisingly uncommon, although it attracted large fines where it was charged. The decline of villein tenure in the third quarter of the fourteenth century, and the associated failure of a seigniorial reaction to materialize, largely explains the scarcity of peasant resistance to, and action against, the main incidents of villeinage. The only evidence for coordinated and collective resistance was the refusal to pay recognition at Fornham St Martin in the 1380s and 1390s. Merchet was the only servile incident to be widely upheld at this time, albeit as a personal incident upon serfs rather than upon tenants of customary land.

Just one manor within the sample yields evidence of involvement in the Peasants' Revolt of 1381. The manorial 'court rolls and other memoranda of the lord' of Runton and Beeston Felbriggs were burned 'by the commons of the countryside'.[192] The burning of court rolls is usually regarded as evidence of overt opposition to villeinage, which would imply that the seigniorial management of serfdom on this manor in the run up to 1381 had been suffi-ciently aggressive and novel to provoke direct action. Alternatively, it is possible that there had been no seigniorial reaction at Runton (there was certainly nothing at Runton Hayes in the 1360s and 1370s), and the rolls just happened to be accessible to a band of marauding rebels, who burnt them in a symbolic and copycat gesture of defiance towards 'bad lordship' in general.[193] Of course, the destruction of the rolls means that we will never know. In general, the absence of conflict over villeinage on every one of the manors in the sample where records have survived from the 1360s and 1370s is striking. Yet this is at odds with the violence and severity of the Revolt in East Anglia, unless the latter is better explained more in terms of discontent with the quality of royal justice, with the Crown's fiscal policies, and with political weakness, rather than more narrowly with serfdom.[194]

SROI HD230/1/1. There is an incidental reference to an earlier manumission at Norton, SROB 553/1, court held February 1456.

[192]   NRO WKC 2/166 398 x 7, court held October 1381.

[193]   H. Eiden, 'Joint action against "bad" lordship: the Peasants' Revolt in Essex and Norfolk', *History*, 83 (1998), p. 22, notes this area of Norfolk was a hotspot for the burning of manorial court rolls, which might be indicative of copycat action – it is perhaps significant that the court described the arsonists as 'the commons of the countryside' rather than as local tenants.

[194]   Eiden, 'Joint action', pp. 5–30.

Most evidence for tension between lords and peasants is confined to the period from the mid-1380s to the mid-1410s, when it swirled around the management of personal servility. During this period many landlords made some efforts to enforce chevage or merchet, or to pressurize tenants to hold customary land, although such efforts were neither sustained nor persistent. The single exception was the manor of Beeston, where during this period the lord's officials pressed consistently to uphold many elements of villeinage, provoking isolated instances of collective and personal resistance.[195] After c.1410 aggressive seigniorial tactics are hardly found anywhere, including Beeston. After this date, the numbers of serfs on individual manors were so small that collective resistance was unlikely, although individual serfs might take exception to over-zealous officialdom, as the redoubtable William Martin of Norton showed.[196]

Conclusion

This chapter has drawn upon a sample of 23 manors, many of them small- or medium-sized and held by lower-status landlords. These were the most numerous types of manor in England around c.1300, where villeinage tended to be less prominent, but they have been overlooked in most published studies of the subject. This study is the first to attempt to reconstruct the chronology of decline on such a large sample of this type of manor.

On 15 out of the 23 manors villein tenure evolved into a hereditary tenure whose servile incidents had lapsed or had been commuted (Type 1 manors). Most customary holdings were small and non-standardized, and demand for them in the aftermath of the Black Death remained steady. The use of 'in villeinage/bondage' disappeared from their conveyances soon after the Black Death, and the formulae which then came to be used on each manor remained fairly settled and consistent thereafter. The package of incidents rendered by these holdings after 1348–9 was not very onerous. Labour services were due on all of the 15 manors, although week works were less common and tended to be commuted at will rather than performed in person. The notional liability of these holdings for labour services persisted long after the Black Death, until they were removed by negotiated commutations. Villein land on the majority of these manors owed no other incidents: only three of the 15 manors carried liability for millsuit after 1348–9, none for recognition or tallage, and only seven for heriot. Where heriot did exist, it tended to endure deep into the fifteenth century or beyond, although the corollary of its endurance was its decreasing frequency. On 9 of the 15 manors either

---

[195]   TNA DL30/102/1395 to 1401.
[196]   See p. 270.

personal servility was not recorded and/or its incidents had entirely disappeared by 1400.[197] Childwite appeared on two of the 15 manors, chevage on seven and merchet on eight (see table 12.1). By the end of the fourteenth century childwite was extremely rare, and merchet was severely weakened – it disappeared between 1397 and 1403 on four of the seven manors where it featured, and soon afterwards on the remaining three. Chevage lasted longest, but after 1410 even it featured on just four manors.

Five of the 23 manors are categorized as Type 2 manors, where around half of the customary land on each manor evolved into a hereditary tenure without servile incidents, and the remainder was converted to leasehold. Once again, 'in villeinage' disappeared from the conveyances of the hereditary tenures in the generation after the Black Death, and the new formulae were settled and similar. On two of the five manors, the conversions to leases occurred mainly in the 1350s and 1360s, while on the other three they mostly took place between the 1390s and 1420s. Whatever the timing, the motivation was usually the same: seigniorial desperation to acquire tenants for land which could not be tenanted on the old terms. Yet from the middle of the fifteenth century these leases were gradually converted back to a secure hereditary tenure for money rent, with the result that by the early sixteenth century the tenurial profile of all five manors was very similar to that of Type 1 manors. Labour services declined quickly on these manors after 1348–9, while millsuit and recognition were recorded on just one manor. Heriot was the most durable incident, recorded on four of the five manors, but after 1400 it became increasingly infrequent. Personal servility had disappeared by the early fifteenth century on two of the five manors, but persisted on the other three through the sole incident of chevage.

Villein tenure was converted to tenure for the term of a life or lives (Type 3 manors) on one manor, Akeley in Buckinghamshire. The amount of detail contained in its court rolls about the exact terms of tenancy is variable, but there is decisive evidence in the 1390s for a widespread conversion from hereditary villein tenure to life tenancies. This always involved the replacement of all the main incidents of villeinage with a cash rent, leaving just liability for heriot and an entry fine. Personal servility had disappeared soon after c.1400.

At Barton Magna and Fornham St Martin villein tenure was almost entirely replaced with leaseholds by the mid-1360s (Type 4 manors). Customary holdings here were large and standardized, and carried a heavy weight of week works, but in the 1350s few of these could be tenanted on the old terms. Converting them to leasehold proved very successful at increasing occupancy rates. The length of leases increased during the fifteenth century,

---

[197] Debach, Drinkstone, Hardwick Russells, Harkstead, Higham, Holbrook, Radclive, Runton Hayes, and Withersfield.

and lessees acquired the right to assign the lease to others during its term. Leases continued to dominate customary landholdings for the whole of the fifteenth century, although towards the end of the century a few began to be converted back into a hereditary tenure at Fornham St Martin. All labour services, millsuit and heriot disappeared with the shift to leases, and in the 1380s leaseholders successfully resisted attempts to collect a recognition payment. Personal servility persisted at Barton Magna until the mid-fifteenth century, albeit imposed upon just a handful of people. On both manors, childwite was unknown after 1348–9, and the imposition of both chevage and merchet was infrequent and low key.

Across the whole sample of 23 manors, the aggressive seigniorial management of serfdom was unusual. Evidence is rare for those forms of behaviour which signify contempt for serfs, such as the imposition of novel forms of service, disputes over status, pressurizing relatives to return flown serfs, the use of special licences, the creation of serf genealogies, the compilation of details about the progeny of serfs, and, finally, the financial extortion of flown serfs. Where evidence does exist for this type of behaviour, it usually dates from the period c.1380 to c.1410 then quickly subsides. There is no evidence for a seigniorial reaction between the 1350s and the 1380s, and hardly any evidence for either direct peasant action or even passive resistance against the incidents of serfdom.

Thus villein tenure effectively disappeared within a generation of the Black Death on the overwhelming majority of manors within this sample. In a minority of places, it was swept away by the conversion of customary land to tenures for a term or to leasehold. In the majority of places, villein tenure appears superficially to have continued just as before, but, upon closer inspection, it had altered radically: in the 1350s and 1360s the use of 'in villeinage' lapsed, and the key incidents of villeinage melted away. After 1348–9 week works were widely commuted, tallage scarcely featured anywhere, and millsuit was rare. Only heriot showed any durability, although on many East Anglian manors even its frequency declined sharply in the fifteenth century. After the collapse of villein tenure during the third quarter of the fourteenth century, some landlords then focused their attention upon identifying and regulating personal servility. They did so through the incidents of merchet and chevage, although merchet – the main test of villeinage in the common law – was in terminal decline by 1400, and chevage was imposed upon very few people. Personal servility was rare after 1400.

Thus villein tenure largely disappeared between 1350 and 1380, and personal servility between 1380 and 1400. The consistency of this chronology across the sample is striking, and the timing is markedly earlier, and slightly shorter, than the c.1380 to c.1450 timeframe promoted by many historians (see Chapter 2). It means that by the end of the 1370s hereditary tenures rendering little more than a cash rent, entry fine and perhaps heriot were widely established in East Anglia, a rent package readily identifiable with the heritable copyholds of the sixteenth century. Similarly, by the end of the fourteenth century, and perhaps a little earlier, tenures for the term of a live or lives were also established on one Buckinghamshire manor. The significance of these developments will be considered in the final, concluding, section of the book.

PART III

Conclusions

13

The Chronology of the Decline of Serfdom

Issues, methods and sources

Chapter 1 sketched how historians have come to regard serfdom as central to an understanding of the economy and society of late medieval England. Its decline is also regarded as central to an understanding of how and why England became the world's first industrial society, because this was an essential prerequisite for the development of a free market in wage labour and the creation of capitalist farming. Yet, despite the subject's importance, the issue of exactly when serfdom disappeared during the fourteenth and fifteenth centuries, and why, has not been re-assessed for decades.

There were two basic elements of villeinage in England, namely unfree tenure and personal (hereditary) unfreedom. Villein tenure is assumed to have shed its main servile incidents – tallage, week works, millsuit and heriot – between c.1370 and c.1410, and then evolved through a variety of rather indistinct tenurial forms before emerging during the sixteenth century as copyhold tenure (Chapter 2). Hereditary personal servility – characterized by liability to leyrwite, merchet and chevage – lingered a little longer, but by the middle of the fifteenth century it had dwindled to the point of irrelevance, after which the numbers of serf families in England could be counted in their hundreds rather than tens of thousands (Chapter 3). Serfdom just withered away during the fifteenth century and its last vestiges were finally eradicated during the sixteenth century.

Chapter 4 considered how historians have debated the causes of decline without reaching a clear conclusion. All agree that manumission – the formal purchase and grant of freedom – was not a significant factor. It is also agreed that after the Black Death serfdom was undermined by demographic decline and associated economic pressures, peasant resistance to seigniorial attempts to reinforce serfdom, and the migration of serfs from their birthplace in search of opportunities elsewhere. However, the relative importance of each of these forces, and the interplay between them, remain matters of conjecture and dispute.[1] Furthermore, it remains uncertain how exactly these forces shaped the different pace of decline from place to place, or the ways

---

[1]   Dyer, 'New serfdom in England', pp. 428, 433.

in which copyholds for lives emerged in some parts of England whereas hereditary copyholds became established in others.

Finding answers to these difficult and elusive questions requires new research based upon a more precise methodology. Many studies have tended to lack precision about how serfdom should be defined and about the exact chronology of its decline, and so here the approach has been to define villeinage explicitly and unambiguously; to construct a careful chronology of decline for each component of villeinage on an individual manor; and then to correlate that chronology with any local evidence for fluctuations in manumissions, resistance and migration, and for changes in land values (see Chapter 5).

Villeinage in late medieval England is defined as comprising three main elements: a person holding villein tenure; a person required to render to his or her lord some or all of a range of key servile incidents; and, finally, a condition regarded as inferior and subordinate. The first objective of each of the various case studies (chapters 6 to 12) was to trace the evolution of villein tenure on each manor, based upon either the shedding of servile incidents and the disappearance of the phrase 'in villeinage' from conveyances, or the scale of conversions of villein land to other forms of customary tenancy. The second objective was to establish a precise chronology for the disappearance from each manor of the key incidents of villeinage, that is tallage, week works, heriot, merchet, millsuit, chevage, and leyrwite: this involves charting their declining frequency and the date when each was levied for the last time. The third objective was to explore social attitudes towards villeinage, based upon the ways in which lords managed the relationship with their serfs. Having reconstructed the chronology of decline of villeinage on an individual manor, the fourth objective was to establish whether it correlated with observable changes in land values, recorded migration, peasant resistance or grants of manumission. The focus is upon identifying and establishing such links empirically, not simply assuming or asserting them.

The history of villeinage has been largely written from the perspective of the largest manors, many of them situated within the estates of noble or major ecclesiastical landlords. This is because such places have left the most substantial archives, whereas few records survive from the smaller manors of lesser lords. However, the latter were numerically the most important types of manors and landlords in late medieval England, so their absence from most academic studies of villeinage is a serious shortcoming. There are strong grounds for supposing that the nature and chronology of villeinage's decline might have been rather different in such places. On the one hand, it is possible that lesser landlords, with their closer and more personal involvement in the management of their estates, upheld villeinage for longer. On the other hand, it is much more likely that their limited political power, and the propensity for such estates to change ownership frequently, meant that they were incapable of preserving serfdom, which consequently disappeared earlier or quicker than on the estates of the great landlords. Certainly, more studies of villeinage on gentry manors would throw new light on MacCulloch's observation that continuity of ownership was an important element in determining where serfdom did persist into the sixteenth century.[2]

The sample of 38 manors chosen for this study is drawn from a variety of seigniorial estates, including the classic manors of aristocratic landlords, but it focuses particularly on lesser landlords to widen its typicality. The sample was selected to provide a contrast between manors located in the south and east Midlands, principally Buckinghamshire and Oxfordshire (and also Leicestershire), and those from East Anglia, principally Suffolk (and also Norfolk). It is further subdivided into two categories: Category A contains 15 manors with a long and full series of court rolls, and some manorial accounts, capable of sustaining an in-depth analysis of the decline of serfdom over a lengthy period; and Category B contains 23 manors, each with a good set of court rolls but less detailed than those for Category A (and perhaps a few account rolls), sufficient to reveal the main contours of the decline. Manorial court rolls are essential for the record and management of merchet, leyrwite, recognition and millsuit, and they are usually reliable sources of information about tallage and chevage. Account rolls are essential for reconstructing the utilization of labour services, and are sometimes important sources of information about chevage and tallage.

The chronology of the decline of villein tenure

The evidence from the sample of 38 manors challenges the traditional view that villein tenure decayed between c.1370 and c.1410. The experience of smaller gentry manors, and, indeed, the experience of many large manors held by great lords, shows that villein tenures were, in fact, in headlong retreat from the 1350s, and had largely decayed by the 1380s, on all types of manors. Villein tenure can be judged to have decayed on a manor when either a majority of the main tenurial incidents of villeinage ceased to be collected, or when a majority of the original customary land had been converted to fixed-term tenancies for money rent. Using these criteria, villein tenure decayed between 1350 and 1380 on ten of the 15 best-documented (i.e. Category A) manors in the sample.[3]

---

2 MacCulloch, 'Bondmen', pp. 95–7.
3 Villein tenure had substantially decayed between these dates at Aldham, Chevington, Cuxham, Dunningworth, Forncett, Fornham All Saints, Staverton, Tingewick and Upper Heyford. It survived after 1380 on just three manors:

The rapid and widespread decline during this period of the main incidents attached to villein tenure is striking, especially the very low frequency of tallage/recognition. Tallage had been a ubiquitous and important servile incident in the thirteenth and early fourteenth centuries, to the extent that it was regarded as one of the two most reliable indicators of villeinage under the common law. Despite its importance, after 1350 it was recorded on just five out of the 38 manors, and it had been demonstrably dropped after the Black Death on nine manors.[4] After 1400 it survived on just two manors (Chevington and Winston), where its collection was the subject of sustained resistance from all customary tenants. The collapse of millsuit is less surprising, but it is still striking. It is not recorded on 29 of the 38 manors after 1348–9. After 1360 it is recorded on just five manors, and it survived into the fifteenth century on just two.[5] Millsuit, like tallage, was simply being dropped after the Black Death on a number of manors.

Historians have long been aware of the widespread commutation of week works before c.1350, and our evidence reinforces the widely held belief that they were scarcely used after 1380 – only seasonal, mainly harvest, labour services survived into the fifteenth century. At most, three of the 38 manors yield evidence of week works being used after 1400.[6] On 12 manors week works were dismantled formally and completely by c.1380 through the conversion of villein tenure to fixed-term tenancies for cash only, i.e. through decayed commutations.[7] On a few manors all or most week works were commuted at the will of the lord every year, which simply continued a practice established well before the arrival of plague.[8] On some others, the proportion of week works commuted at will rose after 1350.[9] The case studies have highlighted

Kibworth Harcourt (to the 1420s), Walsham (1390s) and Walsham High Hall (1390s). The incidents of villeinage were not prominent at Holywell before c.1350. We cannot know the date of disappearance at Cratfield and Walsham Churchhouse, due to a lack of sources, but it had demonstrably disappeared when extant sources commence at both places in the first decade of the fifteenth century.

4   Tallage or recognition was collected before 1349, but not afterwards, at Barton Magna, Cratfield, Cuxham, Dunningworth, Forncett, Lidgate, Runton Hayes, Upper Heyford and Walsham High Hall. It survived after 1350 at Chevington, Fornham All Saints, Fornham St Martin, Walsham and Winston.

5   Millsuit demonstrably disappeared during the course of the 1350s at Aldham, Drinkstone, Staverton and Winston, and, at places such as Dunningworth and the Fornhams, it had been levied before 1348–9 but not afterwards.

6   Certainly at Walsham, and possibly at Akeley and Beeston.

7   The 12 manors are Aldham, Barton Magna, Chevington, Cuxham, Dunningworth, Forncett, Fornham All Saints, Fornham St Martin, Iken, Lackford, Upper Heyford and Winston.

8   Such as at Harkstead, Lidgate and Kibworth Harcourt.

9   Such as at Dunningworth and Staverton.

the importance of negotiated commutations, in which landlords entered formal agreements with individuals or groups to replace labour services with cash rents either for a fixed term or indefinitely.[10] Whether negotiated or at will, the income from commutations was absorbed, sooner or later, into the fixed rental income of the manor: the 'sale' of labour rent was thus ossified as money rent. In the middle of the fifteenth century some hereditary tenures were converted to fee farms, which effectively meant that commutation at the will of the lord was replaced with a permanent, negotiated, settlement.[11] After 1350 there are few refusals to perform labour services, or instances of performing them badly, within the sample, which indicates that resistance was not a major factor in their disappearance, or that, in many cases, they had already disappeared. However, the cases of resistance that *are* recorded tend to be concentrated in the 1350s, and these were often collective actions. Thus peasant resistance could serve to discourage any thoughts that some lords might have entertained about utilizing, or reviving, week works to solve the post-plague problem of acute labour shortages.[12]

Heriot was the only one of the main tenurial incidents of villeinage to survive the transformation into copyholds. It is recorded on 26 of the 38 manors after 1348–9, 19 after 1400, and 13 after 1450. There is a marked regional contrast in the use of heriots. In the south Midlands heriot was often charged on all land transfers, not just *post mortem*, and, unlike other servile incidents, it was charged on life tenancies. In East Anglia heriot was due only on *post mortem* transfers, but it was routinely evaded through the use of death-bed transfers and the payment of an entry fine in lieu by an incoming heir. It was not charged on leaseholds. These contrasts explain why heriot remained a strong feature of customary tenures in the south Midlands at the end of the fifteenth century, whereas it had widely disappeared in East Anglia.[13] However, even in the south Midlands its frequency declined during the fifteenth century, mainly because a tenant who died holding multiple customary holdings was permitted to render just one heriot to cover them all. Its survival into the sixteenth century partly reflects the fact that the payment of a death duty was a common element of all types of landholding, and therefore not deemed to be especially demeaning or associated exclusively with servility.

---

[10] See, for example, at Aldham, Beeston, Holbrook and Upper Heyford,

[11] Such as at Badwell Ash, Drinkstone, Walsham Churchhouse and Winston.

[12] For example, at Aldham, Chevington, Drinkstone, Dunningworth, Staverton, Upper Heyford and Walsham.

[13] A similar pattern has been identified in fifteenth-century Norfolk (where heriot was rare) and west Berkshire (where heriot was common), J. Whittle and M. Yates, '*Pays reel or pays legal*: contrasting patterns of land tenure and social structure in eastern Norfolk and western Berkshire, 1450–1600', *Agricultural History Review*, 48 (2000), pp. 13–14.

In the thirteenth century merchet was regarded as the main test of villeinage in the common law, and it was usually payable by both tenants of villein land (irrespective of whether the tenant was personally free or unfree) and landless serfs. After the Black Death it became concentrated upon hereditary serfs by blood and ceased to be a liability on villein land-holders. Court-roll entries emphasized explicitly that the named individual eligible for merchet was *nativus/nativa domini de sanguine*, and there is no evidence that villein tenants were required to pay. The halving of the number of merchets levied after the Black Death at Walsham certainly owed much to a shift from charging it upon villein landholders to just hereditary *nativi*. Likewise, the dip in the frequency of merchets in the third quarter of the fourteenth century on manors such as Aldham and Dunningworth is sugges-tive of a period of readjustment during which villein landholders ceased paying merchet, but officials were not yet imposing it rigorously upon serfs.

The final strand of evidence for the rapid decay of tenurial elements of villeinage in the 1350s and 1360s is the extent to which villein land was converted to contractual tenancies. Large-scale conversions of customary land to fixed-term tenancies in these two decades were characteristic of at least ten of the 38 manors in the sample.[14] Many of these manors contained large, standardized and integral holdings, such as full-lands and virgates, which had been abandoned during the epidemic of 1348–9 and continued to lie vacant for a number of years afterwards. The only way in which land-lords could entice tenants to take up these customary holdings was to convert them to money rent, largely free of servile incidents, on a fixed-term contract. Although these tenancies gave the landlord the option to reconvert the holding to the original villein tenure upon expiry of the term, in practice the vast majority were simply re-granted to the same or to a different tenant on another fixed-term contract. There is no doubt that tenants preferred the large holdings on fixed-term tenures for a money rent, despite the loss of inheritance rights and heavier cash burden. By contrast landlords were initially reluctant to make these conversions, judging by the length of time during the 1350s that they were prepared to sit on vacant holdings in the hope of finding tenants on the old villein tenure.

How does this earlier chronology of decline compare with the evidence for changes in the language of conveyances and in the use of copies? The correlation with the disappearance of 'in villeinage/in bondage' is remarkably strong. These phrases were used routinely before the Black Death on every manor for which documentation survives, but they had fallen out of use by

---

[14] Aldham, Barton Magna, Chevington, Cuxham, Forncett, Fornham All Saints, Fornham St Martin, Iken, Upper Heyford and Winston.

1380 on almost every one.[15] Hitherto, historians have been uncertain about whether to attribute any significance to short-term changes in the use of such language, and, in any event, they had not noticed much change before c.1390. The evidence from the case studies is compelling and significant. In the generation after the Black Death 'in villeinage' disappeared from the conveyances of villein tenure at precisely the time when many key tenurial incidents of villeinage were in full retreat, and when contractual tenures were spreading rapidly.[16] Thus the use of 'in villeinage' and 'in bondage' must have been associated specifically with a rent package based primarily on servile services and incidents, and, as that package fell away, so these phrases were discarded.

This study has also shown that at precisely the time when the use of 'in villeinage' declined, so the phrase 'at the will of the lord [*ad voluntatem domini*]' came to be inserted routinely and consistently into the formulae of conveyances on many manors. The expression 'at the will of the lord' was used occasionally in customary conveyances before 1348–9, but afterwards it became the norm rather than the exception.[17] This did *not* mean that all land held 'at the will of the lord' was vulnerable to seizure and eviction on the landlord's whim, as some authorities have implied.[18] The express purpose of the term was to emphasize that the transfer of the land, and any claims to its title, were matters to be handled exclusively in the lord's own manorial court.[19] Land thus held which included a qualifying statement that the tenant held the land heritably, or for a stipulated term, enjoyed protection in that respect in the manorial court; in contrast, land held 'at the will of lord' with no qualifying term *could* be terminated literally at the arbitrary will of

---

[15] Servile phraseology survived until the 1420s at Kibworth Harcourt, and into the 1380s (just) at Fornham St Martin. It demonstrably disappeared between 1349 and 1380 from 19 manors: Akeley, Aldham, Barton Magna, Chevington, Cuxham, Debach, Drinkstone, Dunningworth, Forncett, Fornham All Saints, Iken, Lackford, Runton Hayes, Staverton, Tingewick, Upper Heyford, Walsham, Walsham High Hall and Winston.

[16] The key distinction is that the language used to describe villein *tenure* changed decisively, although the language used to describe villein *land* did not. The land parcels themselves continued to be labelled as 'native' or 'customary', to distinguish their origins from the fragmenting demesne land or from free holdings.

[17] 'At the will of the lord' was not frequently used before 1348–9, but then became common afterwards, at Aldham during the 1350s, Chevington (1360s), Debach (1360s), Drinkstone (1370s), Dunningworth (1370s), Fornham All Saints (1370s), Iken (1360s), Runton Hayes (1350s), Walsham (1380s), Walsham High Hall (1370s) and Winston (1350s).

[18] See P.L. Larson, 'Peasant opportunities in rural Durham: land, vills and mills, 1400–1500', in B. Dodds and C.D. Liddy, eds., *Commercial activity, markets and entrepreneurs in the Middle Ages. Essays in honour of Richard Britnell* (Woodbridge, 2011), p. 151; Harvey, 'Aspects of the peasant land market', p. 331.

[19] A subtle but important point, and one made by Smith, 'Peasantry', p. 353.

the lord.[20] The phrase 'at the will of the lord' occurs more often in the sample than the phrase 'according to the custom of the manor': the latter appears frequently and early on the south Midlands manors, but it was much less common in East Anglia.[21] However, during the second half of the fifteenth century its use began to spread slowly in East Anglia.[22]

It is highly likely that the practice of issuing a 'copy' to the tenant as proof of title also spread rapidly after c.1350. It was known but rare in the early fourteenth century, and widespread in the mid-fifteenth. Little is known about its rate of diffusion between those dates, although Faith suspected that the use of the copy was more widespread before c.1450 than many historians have supposed.[23] The lack of knowledge is mainly a function of the very low survival rate of such copies – much lower than for other types of sources – because landlords had little incentive to retain their copy for archival purposes (they relied on the entry in the court roll instead) and because hardly any documents held by medieval peasants are extant. Yet this study has added weight to Faith's suspicions by unearthing some fragments of evidence which prove that the use of the copy was well established by the later fourteenth century on some manors: the chance survival of a remarkable collection of seigniorial 'copies' from Staverton, which show unequivocally that by 1400 they were already in common usage; the explicit confirmation in 1398 of the use of the copy as proof of title in the manor court of Hardwick Russells; and the issuing of instructions to tenants on some manors in the 1390s to produce their 'copies' for scrutiny.[24] If the copy was indeed common at the end of the fourteenth century, then it is plausible to argue that it had

---

[20]   Thus 'x acres held at the will of the lord' were liable to random seizure, whereas 'x acres held for him and his heirs at the will of the lord', or 'x acres held at the will of the lord for the term of a life', or 'x acres held at farm for seven years at the will of the lord' were not.

[21]   'According to the custom of the manor' featured regularly in conveyances at Akeley, Cuxham, Hardwick Russells, Holywell, Kibworth Harcourt, Radclive, Tingewick, Upper Heyford, and Weedon Vale among the south Midlands manors, and at Norton, Lidgate and Withersfield on the East Anglian manors. It was also common in fifteenth-century Wiltshire, see J. Hare, *A prospering society. Wiltshire in the later Middle Ages* (Hatfield, 2011), p. 117.

[22]   The phrase began to be inserted into conveyances at Badwell Ash, Lackford, Staverton and Winston.

[23]   See, for example, Faith, 'Berkshire', pp. 125, 130, 140 and 151. In 1377 a customary holding at Woolstone had become 'a copyhold in fact if not in name', and in the 1370s Englefield tenants had to show whether they held their lands 'for life, for years, by copy or by charter'.

[24]   See pp. 105, 122, 221, 243, 254. Staverton; Fornham All Saints; Cuxham; Walsham. See also Larson, 'Peasant opportunities', p. 151 n. 44.

spread rapidly in the wake of the Black Death.[25] Its growing use makes good sense in a period when turnover in the customary land market was high, because it aided the task of keeping track of tenants and tenancies. As the differences between villein tenure and free tenure narrowed, and as countless new tenants of varying status acquired various forms of customary tenure, the copy served as the reliable reference point for lord and tenant alike: it provided both with a handy and reliable proof of title, while reminding everyone that the title to the property was only defensible in the lord's own manorial court.[26]

Tenurial and personal unfreedom had largely overlapped before the Black Death, and so estate administrators did not bother much to maintain a clear distinction between them. This situation altered dramatically in the 1350s and 1360s. The catastrophic levels of mortality during the first and second outbreaks of plague forced some landlords to make significant and immediate tenurial concessions in order to avert damaging levels of vacant holdings. Others could no longer rely upon their indigenous servile population to fill all or most of their customary land, but had to attract a new kind of tenant with an improved package without the overt incidents of villeinage. The changes to villein tenure increased the gap with hereditary servility, which rendered the use of phrases implying the existence of such a link – such as 'in bondage' and 'in villeinage' – especially unwelcome and inappropriate. Estate administrators now moved to establish a much clearer distinction between the two. Serfs came to be described routinely as 'serfs of the lord by blood' in manorial documents. In contrast, 'in villeinage' was quickly dropped from villein tenure and replaced with expressions such as 'holds at the will of the lord' and 'according to the custom of the manor', which were more narrowly and obviously concerned with the status of land. They were also tighter legal formulae, which asserted the land's unfree status unequivocally without implying the existence of labour services and other servile incidents as a relevant criterion of that unfreedom, and without implying anything about the tenant's personal status.

[25] Thus adding significance to Faith's discovery of references to copies in the 1370s, and to the existence of copies in a rental of the Berkeley estate in 1378, Wells-Furby, *Berkeley estate*, p. 106. Copies also spread in the later fourteenth century on the estate of the bishopric of Durham, Larson, *Conflict and compromise*, p. 195.

[26] In the wake of the Black Death the influx of new tenants to various manors has been documented by Schofield, 'Tenurial developments', pp. 261–4; Raftis, *Peasant economic development*, pp. 76–8, 110–13.

The chronology of the decline of personal servility

It is widely contended that landlords reacted to their weakened position after the Black Death by coercing serfs to hold land on disadvantaged tenures and binding them in novel ways to work on the manor, until the shock waves from the Peasants' Revolt in 1381 forced them to moderate such conduct.[27] The incidents of personal servility are assumed to have been tightly enforced and widely resented in the three decades after the Black Death. Thereafter, they were gradually relaxed. By the 1390s leyrwite/childwite had largely disappeared, and it is widely supposed that during the first half of the fifteenth century merchet faded away. Serfs streamed away from their home manors after the Peasants' Revolt, and recorded migration through chevage and presentments for absence rose to a peak around 1400. After that date, only a few lords maintained track of their remaining serfs through the devices of annual chevage payments and detailed genealogies. Landlords who persisted with such policies were still able to identify, and profit from, their last remaining bondsmen in the sixteenth century. However, such survivals were rare. After c.1380 personal servility is assumed to have faded across much of England, and to have largely gone by c.1450 (see Chapter 3).

The precise chronologies constructed as part of this study suggest a rather different story. Childwite was fairly common in the early fourteenth century, but after the Black Death it was unusual. It was actively dropped after the first epidemic on a minimum of four manors.[28] After 1348–9 it was still found on 18 of the 38 manors in the sample, but, after 1400, on just two. Even where it did survive, it was levied very infrequently. At Chevington it was not imposed at all between 1361 and 1381, but then was reintroduced during the next six years as part of a heightened interest in personal servility before quickly disappearing. Just two cases are recorded at Winston after 1349, and at Walsham its frequency fell sharply in the 1350s, and then again in the 1370s. It is highly unlikely that any of these patterns mirrored genuine trends in illegitimacy or sexual misconduct among female serfs. The levy of childwite was determined mainly by managerial policy, and after 1348–9 the policy of the vast majority of lords and manors was to abandon it.

Merchet was a more frequent and ubiquitous incident than leyrwite/childwite, as befits one of the two main tests of villeinage under the common law. Before 1348–9 it had been levied on nearly every manor within the sample; we can be certain that it appeared on at least 31 of them. It was usually imposed on females who married, although on a handful of manors it was

---

[27] See pp. 70–3.
[28] Barton Magna, Drinkstone, Fornham St Martin and Walsham High Hall.

imposed on males as well.[29] Overall, the level of fine charged was modest, around 4s., and tended to decline gently over time. Merchet disappeared completely after the epidemic of 1348–9 on five of those 31 manors, and its frequency declined on the remaining 26, mainly due to the reduced population and the shift from charging all villein landholders to just serfs.[30] In many places it disappeared at some point in the second half of the fourteenth century: after 1400 24 of the 38 manors provide no record of merchet, and after 1450 31 manors no longer imposed it.[31] Even these stark figures conceal the scale of the decline in the late fourteenth century, because its frequency usually diminished markedly in the years leading up to its final disappearance.[32] Only at Beeston and Walsham was it maintained consistently, before disappearing suddenly around c.1400.[33] Such patterns are more indicative of changes in the seigniorial approach to merchet rather than reflecting the base level of servile marriages. On the 14 manors where merchet continued to be recorded after 1400, its frequency fell sharply in the second quarter of the fifteenth century.[34]

Historians have not normally distinguished carefully between presentments for absence and chevage, despite the subtle difference between the two. The presentment was the reporting mechanism to the court, undertaken by jurors and/or the landlord's officials, whereas chevage was a formal

[29] Charging both males and females for merchet was unusual, and confined to the East Anglian manors: it was a feature at Beeston, Cratfield, Dunningworth, Staverton, Walsham High Hall and Winston.

[30] The five manors where merchet disappeared after 1348–9 are Cuxham, Debach, Drinkstone, Fornham St Martin and Runton Hayes.

[31] The disappearance of merchet can be illustrated more closely by considering just the evidence for the best-documented sample of Category A manors. On these, merchet was recorded after 1348–9 on 12 of the 15 manors, on seven after 1400, and on just four after 1450. It disappeared between 1348–9 and 1399 from Aldham, Fornham All Saints, Upper Heyford, Walsham and Walsham High Hall; between 1400 and 1449 from Kibworth Harcourt, Chevington and Tingewick; and continued after 1450 on the four manors on the duke of Norfolk's estate, Dunningworth, Cratfield, Staverton and Forncett. It was not recorded at Holywell, and it had already disappeared by the time Walsham Churchhouse courts commence in the 1400s.

[32] For example, eight merchets were recorded in 1375–99 at Chevington, before the last one in 1420; seven at Fornham All Saints in 1375–99 before the last one in 1399; and a mere six at Aldham in the whole of the period after the Black Death and its disappearance in 1392. At Akeley and Runton Felbrigg just one post-Black Death merchet is recorded in good runs of court rolls.

[33] Also 13 merchets were recorded at Tingewick between 1400 and 1426, when it suddenly disappeared.

[34] In addition, male merchets disappeared on the duke of Norfolk's manors, although female merchets survived here until the sixteenth century; male merchets disappeared in 1410 at Cratfield, 1431 at Dunningworth, and 1460 at Staverton.

payment from the serf. Presentments were therefore easier to make, and so, unsurprisingly, they were more numerous than chevage payments, and, on some manors, they also continued to be recorded long after chevage had gone. Taken together chevage and presentments for absence represent the most ubiquitous incident of personal servility after 1348–9, recorded on 28 of the 38 manors in the sample. The number of annual chevage payments on any individual manor within the sample ranges from zero to 12, and it is rare for more than five cases to be recorded annually. When it was charged, the level of fine could be high (between c.9d. and c.6s.). From the 1380s the frequency of chevage began to rise on many of those manors where it was recorded, but, as it did so, the level of fine declined (eventually settling at around 4d.).[35]

During the late fourteenth century presentments for absence and chevage were regular features of personal servility, although they seldom related to more than half a dozen serfs each year on any given manor. The tendency on a few manors for the frequency of chevage to increase after c.1380, and for its average fine to fall, is paralleled by other adjustments to its use. In the thirteenth century chevage had assumed a number of forms from manor to manor, one of which was 'capitage', a charge upon any serfs who did not hold land on the manor. Capitage is not common within our sample, but, on those manors where it did exist, it disappeared around c.1400, in one case mutating into the conventional form of chevage, i.e. as a licence to live off the manor.[36] It is possible to interpret these patterns as evidence for increased migration from some manors in the decades either side of 1400, but another, more convincing, interpretation is likely. At this time the nature of chevage was changing from a variety of forms and uses into a single consistent format. It became a low-value payment for permission to reside off the manor, albeit one paid more frequently, and it settled into this format on a number of estates around c.1400. By this date, chevage had displaced merchet and tallage as the main incident of servility, and, in practice, as its primary test.

After c.1400 presentments for absence were effectively being deployed as flags for serfs about whom estate officials had some information, but insufficient to convert it into any financial return. The reasons why some flown serfs continued to pay chevage, while others simply ignored seigniorial pressure to do so and instead were either presented as absent or disappeared from the record, are never stated. It is difficult to see how landlords could

---

[35] For example, just two chevage payments were made at Dunningworth between 1350 and 1374, averaging 5s., seven between 1375 and 1399 (2s.), and 99 between 1475 and 1499 (4d.). Eight were made between 1350 and 1374 at Chevington, 66 between 1375 and 1399. Three are recorded between 1350 and 1399 at Aldham, 13 between 1400 and 1424.

[36] The specific case is Beeston. Capitage disappeared from Dunningworth, Forncett, Holbrook and Staverton around this time.

readily enforce annual chevage payments from departed serfs, unless the payee had his or her own reasons for doing so. Most serfs paid to keep a toehold in their manor of origin, probably to retain an interest in a land-holding or inheritance like Richard Spink of Cratfield; some may have been under familial pressure to pay, such as the Langhaughs of Winston; a few, such as the Crembells of Aldham, may even have paid to ensure the protec-tion of a powerful lord in periods of disorder and political turbulence.[37]

Chevage and presentments for absence are not recorded after 1348–9 on ten of the 38 manors, and after 1400 they are not recorded on 15. The most severe period of decline occurred in the first half of the fifteenth century, which meant that after 1450 25 out of 38 manors contain no record of either. Chevage disappeared faster than presentments for absence – after 1410 chevage is not recorded on 24 of the 38 manors. Yet the close focus upon the last date on which chevage was charged can be very misleading, because, like merchet, it became very infrequent on many manors, and applied to small numbers of serfs, long before its final disappearance. For example, chevage was finally abandoned around c.1440 at Cuxham, Kibworth, Tingewick and Walsham, yet, in each case, its last appearance was an isolated occur-rence, appearing briefly after decades in which it had not been levied at all.[38] Indeed, in a humorous act of defiance in 1439, the manorial jurors of Tinge-wick presented as absent the names of six serfs who had actually left in the 1390s and who had long since died.[39]

By 1400 childwite and merchet were no longer levied on a majority of the 38 manors within the sample, and by 1410 the same was true of chevage. On the minority of manors which did preserve personal serfdom after c.1400, the number of recorded serfs was low and the demands upon the majority of them – merchet and chevage – were few, inexpensive and infrequent. Five manors, belonging to the dukes of Norfolk and the earls of Oxford, had been successful in identifying a pool of serfs around c.1400 and establishing effective control mechanisms over them, and consequently they were able to preserve personal servility well into the fifteenth century; it even survived into the sixteenth century on the four manors held by the dukes of Norfolk. However, this remarkable late survival must be placed in its proper perspec-tive. After the first decade of the fifteenth century either personal servility was no longer enforced on the majority of the manors, or it had largely

---

[37] See pp. 143–4, 218–19, 272–3.

[38] For example, chevage was paid in 1399 and again in 1416 at Tingewick, but nothing else until a number of presentments for absence between 1439 and 1445. Chevage was not recorded at all at Walsham for decades, until one person paid each year between 1423 and 1439. The Kibworth jurors refused to present migrants after 1407, and they had rarely been recorded at all at Cuxham after 1349, until a sharp enforcement wave at the end of the 1430s.

[39] See p. 155.

been reduced to a few serfs and a single incident. This conclusion supports the belief that serfdom had become virtually irrelevant in fifteenth-century England.[40]

Attitudes to serfdom

Contemporary attitudes towards villeinage, especially a seigniorial belief in the serf's baseness and inferiority, are another characteristic of the condition. Reconstructing beliefs and attitudes from manorial records is a difficult task, because they seldom record what people thought. However, it seems plausible to suppose that landlords who imposed unusual or demeaning incidents upon their serfs, or who extracted sizeable fines for the standard incidents, are likely to have held very conservative views of serfdom. A number of practices which might reflect such attitudes were sketched in Chapter 5: charging special licences to leave the manor; forcing individual serfs to swear an oath recognizing their status in front of other tenants in the manorial court; physically seizing migrant serfs; imposing novel and restrictive conditions of service; constructing genealogies of serf families and ordering jurors to enquire of progeny; and pursuing and extorting the descendants of long-departed villeins.

The insistence that serfs obtain special licences from their lord for permission to receive training that would enhance their knowledge and skill base – i.e. to be educated, to enter holy orders, or to enter a trade – is recorded on some English estates, and it was a particularly demeaning restriction, because it raised barriers to personal advancement, and because the necessary absence from the manor could easily have been permitted through the payment of chevage. The evidence from the sample underlines the rarity of these licences: it yielded not a single case of a licence to educate or to enter holy orders.[41] However, it has produced an interesting new perspective on licences to pursue a trade, of which five cases are recorded in the sample.[42] The earliest dates from 1393, but they were manifestly unusual and attracted nominal charges of just a few pence each. It is tempting to suggest that this was a novel levy introduced by some landlords in response to one of the provisions of the Statute of Cambridge in 1388, which required children who had worked in agriculture to remain in that sector thereafter rather than train for a trade.[43]

[40] Whittle, *Agrarian capitalism*, p. 46; Hare, *A prospering society*, pp. 125, 130.
[41] Two cases of serfs entering holy orders are recorded, at Fornham St Martin and Weedon Vale, but no licences were charged.
[42] Licences to pursue a trade are recorded at Akeley (1393), Winston (1415), Cratfield (1420), and two at Dunningworth (1451, 1470).
[43] Farmer, 'Prices and wages', pp. 486–7.

If this interpretation is correct, it would add to a small but coherent body of evidence which highlights c.1385 to c.1410 as a period when personal servility was managed more aggressively and tightly on nine manors, all held by high-status landlords.[44] Chevage and presentments for absence were recorded more frequently, targeted serfs were threatened with sizeable penalties, claims to be free increased, and other tensions over the status of serfs are documented. The impositions of special licences to trade and to enter holy orders are concentrated in this period. There are parallels here with a changing approach nationally to the problem of labour shortages. Complaints about villeins in parliamentary petitions and legislation are all concentrated between 1376 and 1402, when they were castigated for evading the obligations of their tenure, and migrating to towns. Such complaints correlate with a slump in agrarian profits and land values during this period, which would have heightened seigniorial sensitivity to such losses. Yet the national debate on labour was also shifting in the 1380s and 1390s, away from an idealistic desire to return to the conditions of the 1340s towards managing specific issues, such as vagrancy, mobility and contracts of service. The coincidence between these developments and the concerns about the mobility of serfs on some of our manors is striking. Equally striking is that after 1402 all references to serfdom disappear from parliamentary petitions: around the time that it had disappeared from most of our manors.[45]

This is the only compelling evidence for the existence of any kind of seigniorial reaction. The case studies provide little support for the argument that landlords created and imposed novel forms of servitude as part of a wider move to re-impose serfdom. A total of 12 people within the whole sample were subject to unusual restrictions on their mobility or their place of work, whose cases are all confined to the period 1350 to 1410. Of these, three Chevington serfs, and one each from Beeston and Staverton, were shackled with the threat of hefty financial penalties, and forced to find pledges as security, because their lord suspected them of preparing to flee the manor.[46] In 1368 Agnes Heyward was required to swear an oath in court that neither she nor her children would leave Upper Heyford. Two serfs had restrictions placed on their employment.[47] Four serfs were made to swear oaths in the court of their manorial lord that they would return to their home

---

[44] Heightened interest in serfs in the 1380s and 1390s is evident at Akeley, Beeston, Chevington, Dunningworth Fornham All Saints, Iken, Lidgate, Staverton and Tingewick.

[45] Given-Wilson, 'Service, serfdom', pp. 23–4, 28–36.

[46] John Prochet, Joanna Goding and Richard le Maister of Chevington (1362–4); William Palle of Beeston (1384), and Richard Speyr of Staverton (1404).

[47] Thomas Skylman of Beeston (1391), and Robert Reveson of Lidgate (1394).

manor to work for him, probably during the harvest, if required.[48] There is no doubt that these restrictions were novel, very public and demeaning: to these must be added the five cases of licences to pursue a trade. Yet a grand total of 17 cases from 38 manors, nearly 3,500 manorial court sessions, and 150 years does not represent a movement of any significance. They were rare and exceptional occurrences, and a very particular set of personal circumstances usually applied in each case. For example, the four forced oaths, promising to return to work for the lord if required, look like bargains struck between the serfs and officials over chevage.

Disputes over personal status, and claims by serfs to be free, were very uncommon, and usually occurred when a landlord was attempting to tighten the management of the servile population. The determination of officials on the estate of the duke of Norfolk to tighten their control over personal servility in the 1390s and 1400s after a period of lax administration provoked denials from three individuals, one of whom was eventually confirmed as a freeman after a formal manorial inquiry.[49] Similarly, officials at Aldham and Lidgate conducted four separate inquiries into the status of long-departed serfs, all of whom were declared free.[50] Just nine other claims to be free are recorded in the sample.[51]

Historians have tended to draw attention to the eye-catching and demeaning ways in which some landlords managed personal servility during the fifteenth century, such as the compilation of serf genealogies, the extortion of wealthy emigrants, and slurs about the servile origins of the nouveau riche. The case studies reveal that such behaviour was extremely rare. Only two separate lists of serfs and their families have survived from the manors in the sample, both from the estate of the dukes of Norfolk. The production of updated lists seems to have been a feature of this particular estate in the fifteenth century, and helps to explain how it managed to maintain track of small numbers of bond families into the sixteenth century.[52] A few other

---

[48] John Page of Chevington (1358); Nicholas Mervyn of Aldham (1369); Roger Miller of Aldham (1371); and Alex Langhaugh of Winston (1410).

[49] Two at Dunningworth, one at Staverton.

[50] The cases of John Batchelor of Lidgate (1435); of John Skylman and William Dedewall of Aldham (1436); and the Mervyn brothers of Aldham (1459).

[51] Peter Waryn of Drinkstone, confirmed as servile (1356); Alicia Maisterjohan of Upper Heyford, confirmed as servile (1362); Richard de More of Iken (1364), confirmed as servile; Augustus son of Hugh, and Nicholas del Churche, of Debach, outcome unknown (1370s); Elias Typetot of Walsham, confirmed as free (1385); John Prochet of Chevington, confirmed as servile (1388); John Peke of Lackford, confirmed as servile (1404); and John Wenge of Lidgate, confirmed as servile (1418).

[52] The 1458 listings from Cratfield and Dunningworth have survived, and the preamble to both indicates that they were updates to earlier lists.

manors directed their manorial juries to produce detailed information about the progeny of serfs, but the number of occasions was small and the interest was fleeting.[53]

Evidence for the extortion of wealthy serfs is also thin. The best examples are from Forncett in the early sixteenth century, when in one year the fines charged upon two bondmen comprised 13% of manorial income, and, on another occasion, a manumission raised a remarkable £120. Otherwise manumissions are seldom mentioned or recorded in the manorial court rolls.[54] The courts of Beeston and Weedon Vale collected background information about two serfs, in a manner which suggests that the lord was positioning to extract a sizeable fine from them. The only other unequivocal evidence for the extortion of serfs comes from the manor of Aldham, whose officials increased the level of chevage charged annually upon the two Cremball brothers for a short period in the 1430s and early 1440s: the charge escalated from 12d. each per annum in 1436 to 10s. each in 1442, before falling back to its original level.

There is no doubt that some of the landlords within our sample did restrict, demean and/or profit from serfs in various ways, and that, by extension, they must have regarded serfdom as a base condition. Yet the number of such examples is extremely small, given the size of the sample and its chronological range. The creation of serf genealogies, and disputes over status, were very rare. The creative imposition of novel forms of service was most unusual, and, when it occurred, it had a very specific explanation. Landlords did not routinely extort large sums of money from their serfs, at least not before the sixteenth century: the squeezing of bondmen for one-off fines, and for expensive manumissions, during the sixteenth century indicates that the dukes of Norfolk – or their lawyers – had determined to manipulate and exploit this legal loophole, although the number of serfs left to extort was very small. Thus, even if late-medieval landlords *were* contemptuous of serfs, they seldom resorted to extreme, novel or overtly demeaning tactics in their management of them. Indeed, the management of serfdom tended to be pragmatic and generally low key; it followed customary expectations and processes. The battery of weapons at the disposal of landlords to exploit personal servility was small and lacking firepower – it was effectively confined to merchet, chevage and one-off windfalls through manumission. After c.1400 personal servility was largely irrelevant, and its survival as the

---

[53] Tingewick in 1368; Chevington in the 1380s and 1390s; Lackford in 1398; Iken in the 1390s; Lidgate in 1436; and Holbrook in 1477.

[54] Five manumissions are mentioned in the court rolls of Forncett, and one each at Debach, Norton, Cratfield, and Staverton.

relic of an earlier system on a few manors was more about upholding an arcane social theory than profit.[55]

Correlating the chronology of decline with the causes of decline

How well does the chronology for the decline of villein tenure between c.1350 and c.1380, and of personal servility between c.1350 and c.1400, correlate with observed movements in those social and economic forces deemed to have caused their decline: namely, manumission; economic and demographic decline; peasant resistance; and migration?[56] The evidence for manumission is extremely limited, just nine documented cases across the whole sample that do not conform to any obvious timeframe. This confirms the widely held view that manumission did not contribute importantly to the decline of serfdom in the late fourteenth and fifteenth centuries. However, manumission does feature more prominently in the sixteenth century as the means of removing serfdom formally, when landlords and lawyers used it systematically to squeeze financial windfalls from the few remaining servile families on their estates.

The changing value of arable land is regarded as the best indicator of underlying shifts in economic conditions in pre-industrial societies, although evidence for it in late medieval England is difficult to win from the sources, mainly due to the fixed nature of rents. From fragmentary data, historians have argued that the money value of land rose a little between the 1350s and the 1370s, fell by 20% over the next two decades, then stabilized before another c.20% fall in the early fifteenth century; the lowest values are recorded during the Great Slump of c.1440 to c.1470. Information about prices and wages in agriculture is much more reliable and abundant (see table 4.1) than for land values, and broadly reinforces this chronology. These data have encouraged the widely held view that the period c.1355 to c.1375 represents an 'Indian Summer' of the English economy, in which the agricultural sector enjoyed a period of unexpected buoyancy.

The argument for an 'Indian Summer', followed by the downward trend in prices after the mid-1370s, corresponds well with the traditional view that villein tenure declined from the 1380s, but it is starkly at odds with the evidence from our sample that villein tenure was disintegrating in the 1350s and 1360s. However, the data for land values previously deployed all commence in or after the 1350s, which means that historians have not been

---

able to make direct comparisons with values from the pre-plague era.[57] Fortunately, and exceptionally, the most reliable data from six of our manors provide reference points from the 1340s, and so enable values for customary arable land to be tracked across the period of the Black Death. On all six, the value of land fell dramatically between the 1340s and the 1360s: the smallest fall was 15%, the largest was 53%, and the mean was 35%.[58] This represents the greatest contraction in land values across any 20-year period in the later Middle Ages. It corresponds closely with the period when villein tenure was retreating fastest on our sample of manors.

There is little evidence for direct peasant resistance from the sample. Where it did occur, resistance was directed at week works and tallage/recognition. Opposition to week works was mainly concentrated in the 1350s, when concerted action is recorded on six manors.[59] The experience must have sent a warning about the difficulty of enforcing week works and maintaining villein tenure at a pivotal moment, and the response of the affected landlords to this warning was usually pragmatic and conciliatory, as evidenced at Aldham and Walsham. Likewise, on those manors where tallage/recognition survived beyond c.1370, its subsequent decline was also precipitated by active opposition, as the examples of Chevington, Fornham All Saints, Kibworth Harcourt and Upper Heyford reveal.

If our sample is typical – and it includes classic manors held by major institutional landlords as well as smaller manors held by minor lords – then the argument that overt peasant resistance undermined serfdom is exaggerated. Of course, the retreat of villein tenure so soon after the Black Death meant that the targets for opposition were smaller, and shrinking faster, than historians had once supposed. Yet the evidence does point to one clear conclusion: where active resistance *was* recorded, it was usually targeted at labour services and tallage. It is not really surprising that collective dues should provoke collective resistance, because they were demanded from a large number of people at the same time, and there was some safety in

---

57 The data series are derived from leasehold values of either customary land and/ or demesne land per acre, which become much more common after 1349 as both forms of land were increasingly leased.

58 Chevington (mean leasehold value of customary arable per acre, -15%), Cuxham (mean value of a half virgate granted for money rent, -45%), Dunningworth (mean entry fine value of customary arable land per acre, -53%), Fornham All Saints (mean leasehold value of customary arable per acre, -19%), Walsham (mean entry fine value of customary arable per acre, -40%), Upper Heyford (mean value of a virgate granted for money rent , -38%). All percentage falls comparing 1340–9 with 1360–9 decennial averages, except Cuxham which is 1340–9 and 1350–9. The value of customary land fell by 55% between the 1340s and late 1370s at Forncett, see graph 11.2.

59 Aldham, Chevington, Dunningworth, Staverton, Walsham and Upper Heyford.

numbers when resisting. Resistance to the imposition of personal incidents occurred less frequently, because their personal nature and timing isolated the individual, and so were not conducive to collective action. Single, as opposed to collective, acts of resistance are mainly confined to the period c.1380 to c.1410, when some individuals reacted to attempts to tighten the management of personal servility.

Patterns of recorded migration from the sample do not correlate closely with the decline of villein tenure. Serfs certainly left their home manor around the time of the Black Death, and landlords were sensitive to such departures, but the scale of recorded migration in the 1350s and 1360s on most manors was simply not large enough to be regarded as a major contributor to the local shortage of tenants and, by extension, a significant factor in triggering tenurial change. In the third quarter of the fourteenth century villein tenure declined on manor after manor, while recorded departures were minimal. Only at Cuxham, and to a lesser extent Aldham, did the scale of departures in the early 1350s demonstrably exacerbate the losses in the pestilence itself, therefore adding to the shortage of tenants and eventually forcing significant changes to villein tenure in order to attract outsiders. Two other observable surges of recorded migration occurred between c.1385 and c.1410 in some places, and in the 1430s and 1440s. The latter post-dates the main phase in the decline of serfdom, and so is irrelevant to it. The former corresponds with another fall in land values, and chronic seigniorial difficulties in finding tenants, even after earlier concessions on villein tenure. This provides a context for understanding the attempts of some lords to tighten their management of serfs, in order to stem the flow of potential tenants, during this period, but few were successful and consequently personal servility decayed in most places. The scale of departures is nothing like those recorded on the estates of Ramsey abbey around c.1400.

The character and volume of recorded migration within the sample creates doubts about just how accurately it reflects the actual level of serf migration from the manor. Historians have tended to assume that annual presentments for absence and chevage payments do provide a reliable indicator, while acknowledging that we cannot know the absolute levels of migration from any given manor. Yet the quirkiness of the record on many manors – presentments for absence one year, chevage the next, then neither for a few years – points to fluctuations in administrative efficiency in either recording the information or extracting it from the juries sitting in session in the manor court. On occasions, an increase in the number of annual chevage cases was a function of a wider attempt to enforce personal servility on the manor;[60]

---

[60] See the rise of chevage payments to a peak between 1388 and 1396 at Chevington, as part of a wider interest in personal status, childwite and merchet, and then the sudden withdrawal of interest after 1403, pp. 179–83.

on others, it was directly linked to a sudden seigniorial concern about vacant holdings.[61] On some manors, the accession of a new lord of the manor often triggered a short period in which chevage and presentments increased, as the requirement of all tenants and serfs to swear fealty to a new lord revealed the names of absentees, and as incoming lords zealously sought to tighten the manor's administration. Serfs also volunteered to pay chevage on these occasions, as a means of registering their existence with the new lord in case it became useful to them in the future.

Summary

The adoption of a precise and quantitative method for dating the decline of villeinage on a given manor, and the study of a more representative sample of English manors, has generated a very different picture of the decline of serfdom to the one previously sketched by historians. It reveals that by the time of the Peasants' Revolt in 1381 villein tenure had effectively decayed on a sizeable majority of manors, whether small gentry manors or large manors held by bureaucratic landlords. Tallage/recognition – one of the key tests of villeinage in the courts of common law – was actively dropped after the Black Death on at least nine manors, and it was uncommon across the sample. Leyrwite/childwite was hardly known after the Black Death, and even the key test of personal servility, merchet, fell in frequency in the last quarter of the fourteenth century almost everywhere, and did not survive the fourteenth century on a sizeable majority of manors. Similarly, after 1348–9 chevage does not feature on a sizeable minority of manors, and was largely maintained as a voluntary 'tax' payable by emigrant serfs who wished to retain an interest in their home manor for some reason. Some manors continued to label some people as *nativi* for a while after the lapse of the last servile incident, but the practice did not last long. Most manors did not persist with such labelling. From this evidence, it can be confidently argued that by 1400 personal servility was already in terminal decline. Its restricted survival thereafter is eye-catching but, when judged from the perspective of wider society, irrelevant.

It might be tempting to conclude from the eye-catching examples of the extortion of wealthy villeins, and of the construction of regular or elaborate serf genealogies, that serfdom was still prominent in fifteenth-century England, and that many serfs were still a source of profit to their lord. Such a conclusion would be highly misleading. In reality, these practices are rare:

---

[61] See, for example, at Chevington and Cuxham in the 1350s; at Upper Heyford in the 1360s and early 1370s; in the 1390s at Akeley and Holbrook; and the 1420s at Cratfield.

most are drawn from the estates of a small number of high status and/or monastic landlords, and they are atypical of the vast majority of English manors and estates. After c.1400 the courts of most manors had ceased to impose servile incidents upon 'serfs by blood' or even to continue identifying them as such. Some courts listed or labelled serfs without charging them for any incidents. Personal servility was much diminished on the minority of manors where it was still maintained: it now involved little more than the imposition of chevage and merchet, at reduced rates, upon a small and shrinking pool of serfs.

The principal reason for persisting with listing or labelling serfs in the fifteenth century was to maintain track of them, even though the attendant profits rarely justified the administrative effort. There are three likely explanations for this behaviour. A few landlords kept tabs upon their dwindling servile population in the hope that, one day in the distant future, significant profits might accrue. Others persisted with the archaic belief that some symbol of customary overlordship ought to be maintained: what else explains the abbot of Bury St Edmunds' fruitless pursuit of recognition deep into the fifteenth century, long after all other incidents of servility had gone on his estate, and long after recognition itself had been abandoned on the sister estate of the Cellarer? Monastic houses dominated the list of landlords who listed serfs, because their bureaucratic administrators were doggedly committed to preserving the ancient rights and endowment of their institution, even if those rights no longer possessed any relevance: to do otherwise would be to dishonour their founder or saint, and to neglect their inheritance. They recorded serfs dutifully until it was axiomatic that there would be no loss in ceasing the practice, because of their dogmatic understanding of the obligations of their stewardship, and, perhaps, because of an inherent social conservatism. They did not record serfs because they were actively exploiting them for profit.

These revised chronologies of c.1350 to c.1380 (tenures) and c.1350 to c.1400 (personal servility), are significantly different from the traditional timeframes of c.1370 to c.1410 (tenures) and c.1380 to c.1450 (personal servility). The implications of this earlier chronology of the decline of serfdom for our understanding of the economic and social history of late medieval England are considerable. The next, and final, chapter of the book will explore those implications for the transformation of villen tenure and the emergence of copyholds; for the nature of relations between lords and peasants in the postplague era; for our understanding of the causes of the decline of serfdom; and, indeed, for the very nature of serfdom itself in later medieval England.

14

From Bondage to Freedom:
Towards a Reassessment

A 'seigniorial reaction' and an 'Indian Summer', c.1350 to c.1380

The Black Death posed huge economic and social challenges as it moved across Europe between 1347 and 1353, but national and regional responses to it varied. It is widely held that plague had little impact initially on English society, due to two mutually reinforcing developments in the third quarter of the fourteenth century. First, landlords are assumed to have reacted to the shortages of tenants and labourers by re-imposing serfdom through a widespread 'seigniorial reaction'. Second, landlords also benefited from the unexpected buoyancy of grain prices and rental incomes between c.1355 and c.1375, an 'Indian Summer' in which life on the manor continued much as before. As a consequence of both of these developments, the Black Death is considered to have been 'purgative not toxic', and real signs of change only become evident from the mid-1370s.[1]

This interpretation fits well with the traditional dating of the decline of serfdom from the 1370s, and it also conforms to an established academic tradition of downplaying the direct and immediate impact of the Black Death.[2] However, neither this chronology nor this interpretation fit the findings of the case studies explored within this book, which point unequivocally to the 1350s and 1360s as the period when villein tenure, and some elements of personal servility, began to retreat decisively. The clear implications of the case studies run contrary to the orthodoxy, and indicate that the Black Death constituted a profound economic shock of direct and lasting impact, which neither a seigniorial reaction nor an Indian Summer could offset. Reconciling such different perspectives is not straightforward, but neither is it impossible.

The 'seigniorial reaction' c.1350 to c.1381
Freedman summarizes the views of many historians when arguing that between 1350 and the Peasants' Revolt in 1381 'in many instances [peasants'] social condition was lowered as lords either imposed servitude on those

---

[1] A.R. Bridbury, 'The Black Death', *Economic History Review*, 26 (1973), p. 591.
[2] Horrox, *Black Death*, pp. 229–36.

previously considered free or coerced those who had been allowed to escape supervision…marriage fines increased in frequency and amount … its effect was to sharpen the resentment of tenants against servitude'.[3] However, the case studies yield very little evidence for such a 'seigniorial reaction'. On the contrary, they provide secure grounds for revaluating many of the main lines of argument used to support the case for it. One of the most prominent arguments has been that rental incomes were remarkably buoyant in the third quarter of the fourteenth century when compared to the second quarter, which, given the catastrophic loss of population in 1348–9, has been taken as reliable evidence that landlords were manipulating customary rents in their favour, and 'seizing a larger proportion of the decreasing product … than before'.[4] However, the case studies have shown that buoyant rental income after 1350 is more likely to reflect the *disappearance* of villein tenure rather than its resuscitation and manipulation by landlords. Those manors whose rental income from customary land was higher in the 1370s than in the 1340s were those which had, in fact, converted a large proportion of their customary land from villein tenure to fixed-term tenancies for a commercial money rent. Far from proving the existence of a seigniorial reaction, the rise in rental income actually reflects radical changes in tenurial structure in favour of tenants and supported by landlords.

Another key element in the case for a seigniorial reaction is the belief that after 1348–9 serfs were subject to the introduction of novel and restrictive forms of service, and that the existing incidents of servility were imposed aggressively. However, our case studies show that new forms of servitude were extremely rare, and that the isolated examples usually had a very specific explanation. Certainly, a heightened interest in flown serfs is widely discernible in the early 1350s, but in most places neither chevage, nor merchet nor leyrwite were especially common or frequent. Indeed, on a number of manors between the 1340s and the 1370s servile incidents such as tallage, millsuit, week works, leyrwite and merchet were deliberately and demonstrably abandoned.

The case studies have also exposed the dangers of cherry-picking colourful examples of the aggressive management of serfs, then presenting them as indicative of behaviour which was commonplace. For example, the restrictions placed upon four serfs from Aldham and Upper Heyford in the 1360s and early 1370s appear to be strongly indicative of a harsh seigniorial reaction, but when placed within the secure context of the management of tenures and servility on those manors over three decades, and within the context of a wider sample of manors, they are exposed as exceptional. This

3   Freedman, *Images of medieval peasants*, p. 262.

4   G.A. Holmes, *The estates of the higher nobility in the fourteenth century* (Cambridge, 1957), pp. 114–16.

is not to deny the desire of serfs to be free of servile incidents, nor to deny the existence of tension and conflict between landlords and serfs during this period, including breaking the bounds of customary norms, some physical seizure and restraint of serfs, and opposition to servile incidents. But there is no evidence that this occurred with any persistence on any individual manor, or on any scale across a number of manors, in the sample. On the contrary, when the management of villeinage is considered carefully within its local context, and across the whole of the period c.1350 to c.1380, it was pragmatic, accommodating and diminishing on the vast majority of manors. Even a powerful and conservative landlord, such as the abbey of Bury St Edmunds, capitulated on villein tenure and paid little attention to its serfs in the third quarter of the fourteenth century. Other conservative landlords, such as Merton College, were unable to maintain a uniform policy towards villeinage on their estates.

The most compelling evidence from the case studies for any sort of 'seigniorial reaction' is the attempt on ten of the 38 manors to tighten the management of serfs by blood in the two to three decades *after* the Peasants' Revolt.[5] Landlords are supposed to have been in headlong retreat on issues relating to villeinage between 1381 and c.1410, and serfs are assumed to have streamed away from the manor rather than resisting.[6] In fact, as soon as the tensions from the Revolt had subsided, a handful of high-status landlords heightened their interest in the servile status of a few, targeted, individuals and in the way in chevage was managed.[7] These aggressive policies coincided with difficulties from c.1390 in filling landholdings, but they also appear to have been linked with a shift in the nature of the national debate on the problem of labour, which involved new policies focusing upon employment contracts and the perceived problem of workers drifting from agriculture to trade.[8] The introduction of licences upon some serfs wishing to pursue a trade was almost certainly linked to the provisions of the Statute of Cambridge in 1388, and reflects a new intensity on some estates toward the management of serfs. Some serfs resisted these aggressive policies; some left their manor. Most of these landlords soon decided that the effort was not sustainable, although a few were more tenacious. As a result, personal servility was found

---

[5]   The tightening of the management of personal servility in the three decades after 1381 is recorded at Akeley, Beeston, Chevington, Dunningworth, Forncett, Fornham All Saints, Iken, Lidgate, Staverton and Tingewick.

[6]   Brenner, 'Property and progress', p. 97; Razi, 'Serfdom and freedom', p. 187.

[7]   The landlords were the earls of Arundel at Beeston; New College, Oxford, at Akeley and Tingewick; the dukes of Norfolk at Dunningworth, Forncett and Staverton; a gentry lord at Iken; and the abbot of Bury St Edmunds at Chevington and Fornham All Saints.

[8]   Given-Wilson, 'Service, serfdom', pp. 24–36.

on few manors after c.1410, and it was not especially prominent or onerous where it was maintained.

The refinement of the management of servile absences from the manor is the main feature of personal servility between c.1385 and c.1410. Variant forms of chevage disappeared, and it became exclusively a licence to live off the manor: everywhere, it became a more frequent, low-value, levy, rather than an occasional, high-value, charge. The evolution of chevage was complemented by the use of presentments for absence as a rudimentary tracking device for those serfs whom the lord's officials could identify as having left the manor but not paying chevage. There are grounds for arguing that many serfs who paid chevage *chose* to do so, as a voluntary tax paid to maintain links with their home manor for undisclosed reasons. Whatever, after c.1400 chevage – not merchet or tallage – became *the* defining incident of personal servility.

The absence of any 'seigniorial reaction' between c.1350 and c.1380 on the majority of manors within the sample is not proof of its absence from England at large. The final judgement upon its existence or not will require a proper and careful balancing of those places where it did not occur against those where it did. At the very least, though, our findings should encourage a more critical, perhaps even more sceptical, re-evaluation of the concept. They also reveal the importance of considering any evidence for novel or aggressive seigniorial behaviour carefully and securely within its local context, in order to establish its exact scale, duration, and whether it had a specific explanation.

If there was no real attempt to re-impose serfdom after the Black Death on many manors in the Home Counties and East Anglia, as our case studies suggest, then how can the Peasants' Revolt of 1381 be explained in terms of opposition to tenurial or servile conditions on the manor?[9] One way would be to explain it terms of relative deprivation, in the sense that rebels were stirred into action in 1381 on those manors where villeinage had changed little, such as the estates of St Alban's abbey, where the anger at such intransigence would have been heightened by the knowledge that rapid change was happening all around them.[10] Another way would be to argue that rebels were responding to specific acts of provocation. Once the spark of revolt had ignited the social tinderbox of May 1381, local conflict over serfdom – or, indeed, other issues associated with local lordship – fanned the flames of discontent even further. The example of the abbey of Bury St Edmunds illustrates this point admirably. Historians (including this one) had assumed that the ferocity of the attack on the abbey, and the murder of a number of

9   See M. Bailey, 'Was there a seigniorial reaction in England between 1350 and 1380?' (forthcoming).

10   Freedman, *Images of medieval peasants*, pp. 260–1.

its monks, in June 1381 must have been provoked by the harsh management of its villeins in the third quarter of the fourteenth century. However, this assumption is not supported by the discovery that in the 1350s and 1360s the abbey largely abandoned villein tenure, and showed limited interest in personal servility, on every one of the four Bury manors included in this study.[11] The long-standing antipathy between the abbey and the townsfolk of Bury St Edmunds provides a better context for understanding the explosion of violence.[12] But there is also no doubt that the irksome personal campaign against serfs on the abbatial estate in the spring of 1381 conducted by one of its senior monks, John de Lakenheath, did contribute to the targeting of the abbey during June.[13] Nevertheless, our case studies have revealed that the abbot showed more interest in imposing personal servility *after* the Revolt than before.

Serfdom was a factor in the Revolt of 1381. Yet, with villein tenure already in retreat and little evidence of a seigniorial reaction on many manors, its contribution to the Revolt merits some reassessment, and probably downplaying. This is not as radical a suggestion as it might initially appear, because historians have often acknowledged that there was much more to the Revolt than villeinage: as Dyer has remarked, 'to interpret the revolt solely in terms of lord-tenant relationships is to take far too narrow a view of the events in 1381 ... it is not possible to attribute any single aim to a very heterogeneous group of rebels'.[14] If the role of serfdom *is* to be downplayed, then frustration with the fiscal policies of the Crown, failure in war, concerns about official corruption, the quality of justice, the labour legislation, and heightened frustrations from the mid-1370s caused by the slump in grain prices all loom larger in explanations of the Revolt.[15]

The 'Indian Summer' c.1355 to c.1375

At first glance, in the 1350s and 1360s neither the land market nor grain prices nor wage rates behaved in a manner commensurate with the loss of nearly one half of the population of England. Grain prices were around 50% higher in these decades than they had been in the 1330s and 1340s, and wage rates rose rather than soared.[16] 'The statistics of wages and prices do not indicate ... that there was any change in the relative scarcities of land

---

[11] Barton Magna, Chevington and the two Fornhams.

[12] See Bailey, *Medieval Suffolk*, pp. 184–93.

[13] See above, p. 182.

[14] Dyer, *Everyday life*, pp. 214, 217; see also A.R. Bridbury, *The English economy from Bede to the Reformation* (Woodbridge, 1990), pp. 209–10.

[15] Bridbury, 'The Black Death', p. 585.

[16] Bridbury, 'The Black Death', pp. 578–81; J. Hatcher, 'England in the aftermath of the Black Death', *Past and Present*, 144 (1994), pp. 6–9.

and labour.'[17] These conditions were likely to result in burgeoning profits for grain producers, encouraging the full re-occupation of landholdings and the charging of competitive rents despite the terrible mortality. Indeed, it is generally held that replacement tenants were found with 'relative ease', such that 'holdings were soon all filled'.[18] Bridbury attributes this phenomenon to the 'submerged and pullulating throng' of people ready to step into the gaps in landholding, and so argues that the Black Death had 'little effect … on the social and economic life of the country'; hence the third quarter of the fourteenth century has been dubbed an 'Indian Summer' of the economy.[19] This enabled manorial lords 'to carry on after the Black Death as they had before', until prices collapsed in the late 1370s.[20]

These contentions do not sit easily with the evidence from our sample for the rapid decline of villein tenure in the third quarter of the fourteenth century, and the difficulties on many manors of finding tenants for some customary holdings during the 1350s. If the underlying economic conditions were so favourable, why did some landlords experience sluggishness in filling holdings and why did many concede so widely on villein tenure? The answer must lay in the wide variations from manor to manor in the extent of overpopulation before the Black Death and also in the risk and uncertainty that lurked just below the surface. The higher grain prices were mainly due to a severe climatic anomaly, in which cool and wet summers severely depressed grain yields between 1352 and 1375, and bullion flows added to the inflationary pressures.[21] Hindsight vision can produce blind spots, in the sense that the survivors of the Black Death would have perceived greater unpredictability and volatility in the agrarian conditions of the 1350s than is immediately obvious to modern historians. The Indian Summer was not uniformly hot and cloudless: Stone comments that although 'a useful and memorable metaphor, some of its implications are misleading', and even its finest advocate, Bridbury, admitted that it was not 'untroubled'.[22] Peasant farmers, lacking the capital and continuity of seigniorial demesnes and

---

[17]   Bridbury, 'Black Death', p. 578.

[18]   Schofield, 'Tenurial developments', p. 251; Bolton, *Medieval English economy*, p. 62.

[19]   Bridbury, 'The Black Death', pp. 588, 591.

[20]   Allen, *Enclosure and the yeoman*, p. 65.

[21]   B.M.S. Campbell, 'Grain yields on English demesnes after the Black Death', in Bailey and Rigby, eds., *Town and countryside in the age of the Black Death*, pp. 147–9; J. Munro, 'Before and after the Black Death: money prices, and wages in fourteenth century England', in T. Dahlerup and P. Ingesman, eds., *New approaches to the history of late medieval and early modern Europe* (Copenhagen, 2009), pp. 335–64.

[22]   Stone, *Decision-making*, p. 120; Bridbury, 'Black Death', p. 584. See also Hatcher, 'England in the aftermath', p. 8.

anxious about the risks they faced, may have felt the troubles more keenly than landlords. Certainly, we have underestimated the extent and scale of concessions on villein tenure required to achieve such remarkable levels of re-occupation of customary land, and, in particular, we have underestimated the length of time the process of re-occupation took in some places (i.e. until the early 1360s).[23]

The difficulties of finding tenants in the 1350s and early 1360s were most pronounced on those manors in the sample characterized by large, standardized, landholdings.[24] Why should these prove most difficult to tenant? An initial aversion to acquiring large holdings on villein tenure may be explained by the rank inexperience of many survivors of the Black Death, who had not previously possessed significant landholdings, and who lacked the capital, the equipment and the knowledge to take on a large arable holding in such uncertain times. They also faced the problem of acquiring a holding that had not been ploughed, weeded or maintained for a period of time, which therefore required a major effort to restore it to tillage. Many prospective tenants were unlikely to have access to a reliable supply of labour to help them in their task, because of the deaths of many friends and relatives in the epidemic.[25] Their own problems in finding enough labour were exacerbated by the requirement upon them to perform regular week works and other labour services off the holding as part of the rent package of villein tenure. Tenants genuinely struggled to perform them. The real and opportunity costs of week works jumped after 1348–9, which made large customary holdings on villein tenure particularly unattractive. Finally, the heir to one of these large customary holdings, or anyone seeking to purchase the title to it from the existing landholder or heir, was required to find a sizeable amount of capital to cover both the entry fine and the purchase price, but the outlay of such capital must have appeared risky in the wake of the Black Death, especially when the weather was so poor in the early 1350s.[26] All these reasons

---

[23] These points are implicit in the authoritative discussion of the post-Black Death land market in Schofield, 'Tenurial developments', pp. 255–6. See Horrox, *Black Death*, pp. 238–9, 283–7, for examples of concessions offered in the 1350s to retain and attract tenants.

[24] For example, Aldham, Barton Magna, Chevington, Cuxham, Fornham All Saints, Fornham St Martin and Upper Heyford. It was not, however, true of all manors with large standardized holdings: see, for example, good rates of re-occupation at Kibworth Harcourt and Tingewick. See also some difficulties recorded on the estate of the bishopric of Winchester in the 1360s and 1370s, M. Page, 'William Wykeham and the management of the Winchester estate, 1366–1404', in W.M. Ormrod, ed., *Fourteenth-century England, III* (Woodbridge, 2004), pp. 117–18.

[25] Stone, *Decision-making*, pp. 102–3, 251–2.

[26] The agrarian difficulties caused by poor weather in 1349–52, and again the late 1350s and early 1360s, are discussed in Campbell, 'Grain yields on English demesnes', pp. 144–6.

help to explain why these holdings sometimes proved to be the most difficult to re-tenant on the old terms.[27] Offering them for a straight money rent on a fixed-term tenancy greatly increased their attractiveness to newcomers to the land market in the conditions of the 1360s and 1370s.

Rethinking the third quarter of the fourteenth century

The discovery that villein tenure underwent dramatic change in many places soon after the Black Death is significantly at odds with the traditional view that 'the Black Death … did not bring a swift end to villeinage'.[28] It is possible that the case studies are atypical, of course, but other historians have uncovered similar experiences elsewhere. Larson discovered that the greatest changes in the land market on the estates of both the bishopric and priory of Durham occurred between 1355 and 1380, which provided opportunities for enterprising peasants to accumulate land.[29] Wells-Furby documents a huge swing to life tenancies for money, and the effective disappearance of labour services, after the epidemics of 1348–9 and 1361 on the Berkeley estate in Gloucestershire, while Muller has documented a major shift from villein tenure to leasehold at Brandon (Suffolk) by the 1360s.[30] Future studies might well generate further examples – if so, the pressure to reassess the traditional interpretation of the economy in the third quarter of the fourteenth century will grow.

There is also the possibility that previously published studies may have inadvertently overlooked the real extent of tenurial change in the third quarter of the fourteenth century. Hardly any of the published estate and regional studies conducts a forensic assessment of the frequency of servile incidents and the language of conveyances, which is essential to reveal what was really happening to villein tenure. In addition, they tend to skim over the drift of the large customary landholdings to money rents, whose significance may therefore have been overlooked. It is possible that historians have been so distracted by the buoyancy of grain prices, and by the orthodoxy that

---

[27] Labour services were also the sticking point to the re-occupation of large, standardized, villein holdings elsewhere in Oxfordshire during the 1350s. At Crawley many holdings remained unoccupied until the second plague outbreak in 1361, after which all labour services were commuted at 6s. 8d. per yardland annually 'on account of the poverty and scarcity of the homage', and the same tactic had to be employed at Curbridge and Haily to jump start the customary land market, see *VCH Oxfordshire*, volume 14 (Woodbridge, 2004), pp. 180, 211, 241.

[28] Hatcher, 'England in the aftermath of the Black Death', p. 33: see also Page, *Crowland abbey*, pp. 120–5; DeWindt, *Holywell-cum Needingworth*, pp. 64–5; Schofield, 'Tenurial developments', p. 251.

[29] Larson, *Conflict and compromise*, p. 238; Larson, 'Peasant opportunities', pp. 145–56.

[30] Wells-Furby, *Berkeley estate*, pp. 105–7; Muller, 'Peasants, lords', pp. 163–5.

the Black Death had no immediate impact, that they have not really looked for signs of change in the third quarter of the fourteenth century.

The potential of this line of argument can be illustrated by revisiting Raftis' classic study of the estates of Ramsey abbey. This identifies the 1390s as the tipping point in the decline of villein tenure, although it offers no analysis of the changing frequency of millsuit, tallage, merchet, leyrwite or heriot after the Black Death; indeed, Raftis scarcely mentions these incidents, so we cannot ascertain whether they were still being collected after 1350 and with what frequency.[31] However, a detailed appendix to the book reveals that the frequency of week works was unquestionably declining at this time, because their use halved on most manors between the 1340s and 1360s due to the spread of commutation of various sorts.[32] Close scrutiny of another statistical appendix reveals that by c.1380 a surprisingly large minority of the customary virgates on the manors studied by Raftis had already been either converted to money rent or could not be tenanted on the old terms.[33] Hence there are symptoms of real tenurial change on the Ramsey estates in the third quarter of the fourteenth century, which Raftis himself appears to have sensed without grasping their full significance: he comments in passing that 'the real economic disturbances over these troubled years' are hidden, and elsewhere observes that 'from the mid fourteenth century the structure of villein holdings changed considerably'.[34] Only detailed research into the changing frequency of servile incidents on every Ramsey manor will establish the real extent of change, but there are sufficient grounds for supposing that the apparent resilience of villein tenure here between 1350 and 1390 may prove to be illusory.

If one accepts that the Indian Summer was more troubled than it once appeared, and that a seigniorial reaction did not materialize in many places, then the argument that villein tenure was in rapid retreat between the 1350s and the 1370s on many manors becomes much more credible and plausible. Grain prices were unquestionably buoyant in the 1350s and 1360s, but persistently high prices for grain in the wake of such a demographic catastrophe

---

[31] Raftis, *Ramsey abbey*, pp. 251–80.

[32] Raftis, *Ramsey abbey*, pp. 278–9.

[33] At Slepe in 1381 31% of virgates were either held for money rent or untenanted, 43% at Houghton (1372), 37% at Upwood (1371), 32% at Warboys (1379), and 19% at Abbots Ripton (1388), Raftis, *Ramsey abbey*, pp. 268–72. On its more distant manors, a higher proportion of virgates had been converted to money rents, see Raftis' own evidence for Elton (1380) within the same appendix, and Lawshall, where a partial account for 1364–5 shows a shift to leasing of the main customary holdings, SROB E7/17/10 and Bailey, *Medieval Suffolk*, p. 199. The spread of money rents and fixed-term tenancies in the 1370s on the Ramsey estates is discussed in Raftis, *Tenure and mobility*, pp. 65–6, and Jones, 'Bedfordshire', p. 192.

[34] Raftis, *Ramsey abbey*, pp. 253, 281.

are less a sign of economic recovery than of significant disruption to the supply of grain, and of shortages and risks in grain production and marketing.[35] The extent to which the Black Death severely disrupted the supply of grain, and also its marketing, is an area requiring further exploration, as are the hidden difficulties within the labour force. The uncertainty plaguing the market for land is revealed by the mean value of customary land, which, on the evidence of six manors within our sample, fell by a dramatic 35% between the 1340s and 1360s. Hitherto the scale and consistency of this fall has not been properly recognized. If c.1355 to c.1375 really was an 'Indian Summer' for the English economy, then it was punctuated by turbulence and characterized by storms. The unusual combination of reduced customary land values and high grain prices is indicative of short-term volatility and disequilibrium, and of considerable risk and uncertainty, in a world where there was suddenly plenty of land but not quite enough grain.

The transformation of villein tenure into copyholds, c.1300 to c.1550

The transformation of villein tenure into copyholds between the fourteenth and sixteenth centuries is one of the most important developments in the agricultural history of England. It represented a rationalization and reconfiguration of the terms on which around one half of the land was made available to the peasantry, and created a cradle in which agrarian capitalism grew. Hence Whittle's justifiable claim that 'forms of land tenure were the most significant legacy of the [medieval] manorial system to the sixteenth century and beyond'.[36] Although the importance of this transformation is widely understood, a detailed understanding of its dynamics during the later Middle Ages has proved elusive, partly because customary tenures during this transitional period have been regarded as a muddle. Furthermore, the reasons why particular variants of copyhold came to be distributed along distinctive regional lines in sixteenth-century England remain unknown.[37]

The case studies have shed important new light upon both of these issues. Primarily, they have shown that the third quarter of the fourteenth century represented a watershed in the development of customary tenures in many places. In the 1340s the overwhelming majority of customary land was held 'in villeinage' on a hereditary tenure for servile incidents, while a very small minority was held on fixed-term tenures, either for servile incidents or for a

---

[35] Campbell, 'Grain yields on English demesnes', pp. 137–8, 144–9. See also M. Mate, 'Agrarian economy after the Black Death: the manors of Canterbury Cathedral priory 1348–91', *Economic History Review*, 37 (1984), pp. 342–3.

[36] Whittle, *Agrarian Capitalism*, p. 64.

[37] Smith, 'English peasantry', p. 368.

money rent. The Black Death delivered a profound shock to the land market, with widespread vacancies throughout 1348–9. Where holdings were filled relatively quickly and completely, then hereditary tenure continued to be dominant, although the servile incidents attached to it either lapsed and/or were commuted at varying speeds over the next few decades. Wherever and whenever customary holdings could not be filled on the old villein tenure, then landlords were forced to convert them to one of three forms of fixed-term tenures (life tenancy, lease for years, or at will without any stipulated term), in which a money rent replaced most, if not all, of the old servile incidents. The extent to which these fixed-term tenures had spread, and the extent to which servile incidents had declined on hereditary villein tenure, by c.1380 has been seriously underestimated.

Hereditary customary tenure c.1350 to c.1500

Hereditary villein tenure remained the most common form of tenancy throughout the fourteenth and fifteenth centuries on our sample: it dominated on 29 of the 38 manors (Type 1 and Type 2 manors).[38] All these manors experienced a relatively quick and full re-occupation of customary land after the high mortalities in 1348–9 and 1361–2, indicating that sufficient numbers of replacement tenants were available locally and were willing to step into the vacancies. Such manors were usually characterized by a degree of overpopulation on the eve of the Black Death, an active market in customary land, and a relatively high proportion of smallholdings. These combined to create a deeper pool of prospective tenants, many of them seeking to augment their meagre holdings, and an established culture of absorbing newcomers to the property market. Therefore they were better equipped to cope with the shock of the mortalities and to fill the vacancies that followed.[39]

The case studies have also revealed that the impressive pace and completeness of the re-occupation on heritable villein tenure was, in reality, aided through a reduction in the servile incidents attached to its rent package.

---

[38] The manors dominated by hereditary tenures were categorized in Chapter 12 as 'Type 1 and Type 2'. The Type 1 manors are Beeston, Cratfield, Debach, Drinkstone, Hardwick Russells, Harkstead, Harleston, Higham, Holbrook, Kibworth Harcourt, Norton, Radclive, Runton and Beeston Felbrigg, Runton Hayes, Staverton, Thorpe Morieux, Tingewick, Walsham, Walsham High Hall, Weedon Vale and Withersfield. Type 2 manors experienced some significant conversion to some form of fixed-term tenure between c.1350 and c.1420, although these were then reconverted to hereditary tenures by copy by the beginning of the sixteenth century. Type 2 manors are Aldham, Badwell Ash, Dunningworth, Iken, Lackford, Lidgate, Walsham Churchhouse and Winston.

[39] Whittle and Yates, '*Pays reel* or *pays legal?*', p. 17, observe that the Norfolk manors in their sample, dominated by smallholdings and an active customary land market, tended to be more densely tenanted than those in west Berkshire, characterized by larger landholdings.

However, these concessions are only apparent through the careful reconstruction of the management and frequency of each of them. The shedding
of servile incidents after 1348–9 was especially a feature of manors belonging
to lesser lords (e.g. Debach, Drinkstone, Runton Hayes, Walsham High
Hall, Withersfield), but it was also true of some manors belonging to greater
landlords (e.g. Aldham, Winston). In the three decades after the arrival of
the Black Death the frequency of tallage, merchet and millsuit fell sharply,
or even disappeared entirely, from the rent package of many customary lands
held on hereditary tenure, and, as Page and Cheney recognized long ago,
week works were also extensively commuted.

The shedding and/or monetarization of these servile incidents corresponded with other subtle changes to the dignity of villein tenure during the
same period. The phrase 'held in villeinage' disappeared from conveyances of
customary land almost everywhere, and instead it was commonly replaced
by the phrase 'at the will of the lord'. The latter was a tighter, more legalistic
expression, whose purpose was to emphasize that the title to the land could
only be defended in the manorial court of the landlord. Its use and spread
reflected the narrowing of the differences between villein and free tenures as
the former shed some servile incidents. It also reflected the greater presence
of freemen, incomers and non-serfs among the tenants of customary land,
to whom it signalled the landlord's good faith with respect to the title. The
symbolism of all of these changes was clear: villein tenure was no longer
immutable, but it could be altered through negotiation, non-cooperation or
rebellion.

Servile incidents that had lapsed, or were commuted at will each year,
could still in theory be re-instated one day. The case studies have also shown
that some fifteenth-century tenants of hereditary customary land sought to
protect themselves against this possibility. The disappearance after c.1450 of
the phrase 'services and customs' from conveyances on five manors, and its
replacement with 'according to the custom of the manor', is highly suggestive of this process.[40] The omission of 'services' signified the removal of the
one word within the conveyance that still maintained a formal link with the
old servile incidents, and its replacement with the phrase 'according to the
custom of the manor' acknowledged, from the perspective of the tenant, that
for decades the custom had been not to impose them.[41] Other tenants nego-

---

[40] A trend documented at Tingewick, Winston, Lackford, Badwell Ash and
Staverton. At Walsham the use of 'services and customs' was dropped in the
fifteenth century, although the phrase was not replaced with 'according to the
custom of the manor'.

[41] As we noted earlier, the phrase 'according to the custom of the manor' is
non-specific, because the precise nature of custom varied from manor to manor.
The deployment of this imprecise phrase provided some scope to all parties to

tiated permanent commutations of all servile incidents; although this was a more expensive option than simply allowing them to lapse, the payment of a fixed annual sum of money eradicated the prospect of their future restoration.[42] Most of these developments occurred when the land market was most depressed between the 1420s and 1470s, i.e. when landlords most feared losing tenants if they did not accede to pressure to renegotiate. Similarly, during the same period, some hereditary tenants entered into collective agreements with their lords to reduce and standardize the level of money rents and/or entry fines, such as at Kibworth Harcourt.[43] Landlords had little option but to cooperate, although the nature of their concessions served to hinder their successors, and to protect tenants, in the very different economic circumstances of the sixteenth century.

Fixed-term tenures, c.1350 to c.1500

On nine out of 38 manors in the sample, after 1350 the overwhelming majority of customary land was converted into fixed-term tenures. Tenure for the term of a life or (usually three) lives was the dominant form of fixed-term tenancy on four of these nine (Type 3 manors), all located in Oxfordshire or west Buckinghamshire.[44] Leases for years were the dominant form of fixed-term tenure on five of the nine, all in East Anglia (Type 4 manors).[45] Furthermore, on eight manors within the 29 where hereditary tenure dominated, a sizeable *minority* of the customary land was also converted to leases for years between the 1350s and 1450s ('Type 2' manors).[46] In all cases, conversions of customary land to fixed-term tenures involved the replacement of most or all of the original servile incidents with a money rent at market rates.

challenge its meaning, which is perhaps why some landlords were willing to agree to this particular change in the language of conveyances. Indeed, during the very different legal and economic circumstances of the sixteenth century, its precise meaning came to manipulated and challenged.

[42] For example at Aldham, Badwell Ash, Beeston, Drinkstone, Holbrook and Winston.

[43] Not a feature of any other manors in our sample, but such agreements are recorded elsewhere, see Jones, 'Bedfordshire', pp. 203–4.

[44] Type 3 manors were described in Chapter 12. The four manors in this category are: Akeley, Cuxham, Holywell and Upper Heyford.

[45] Manors where leases dominated were described in Chapter 12 as 'Type 4'. The five manors in this category are: Barton Magna, Chevington, Forncett, Fornham All Saints and Fornham St Martin. By the second half of the fifteenth century, the leases at Chevington, Forncett and Fornham All Saints were being replaced by hereditary fee farms.

[46] Some leases for years are evident between c.1350 and c.1420 at Aldham, Badwell Ash, Iken, Lackford, Lidgate, Walsham Churchhouse and Winston, but were then reconverted to hereditary tenures. At Dunningworth tenure at will without a stipulated term was prominent, until it, too, was replaced with hereditary tenure during the course of the fifteenth century.

Conversions to fixed-term tenures invariably occurred whenever tenants were unwilling to hold customary land on hereditary villein tenure. The case studies have shown that this unwillingness tended to be greatest on manors dominated by large, standardized holdings, and held by higher-status land-lords, where many such holdings often lay unoccupied for years after the first outbreak of plague. As we have seen, large holdings posed greatest oper-ational risk to prospective tenants in the immediate aftermath of plague. Furthermore, manors with such holdings, where the land market had been relatively inactive and subletting had been restricted or prohibited on the eve of the Black Death, did not tend to possess a pool of reserve tenants, and they also lacked an established means or culture of attracting immigrant tenants.[47] Consequently, they struggled to find replacement tenants from the immediate locality in the aftermath of the Black Death, and so conver-sions to fixed-term tenures were designed to attract newcomers, as Schofield recognized.[48]

The case studies have also provided a deeper understanding of the way in which the two main types of fixed-term tenure (leases for years and life tenancies) developed after 1350. Both expanded rapidly in two distinct phases, the first between c.1350 and c.1370, and the second between c.1390 and c.1420. Time and again, a tenant came forward to take on customary land lying abandoned in the lord's hands once it was converted to one of these fixed-term tenancies. Tenants certainly liked the absence of servile incidents, while the option of relinquishing the land or renegotiating its rent package at the end of the term was reassuring given the prevailing uncertainties in the land market. Landlords tolerated – perhaps even promoted – fixed-term tenancies, because they boosted occupancy rates of customary land without representing a permanent concession on villein tenure: after all, there was always the possibility of renegotiating a fixed-term tenancy in the landlord's favour, or even of restoring villein tenure, upon expiry of the term.

For all the similarities between leases for years and life tenancies, their pathways of development during the course of the fifteenth century were significantly different. The main difference is that life tenancies continued to spread, while the interest in leases for years waned. On manors where life tenancies had first gained a toehold after the Black Death, they went from strength to strength, gradually displacing the remaining hereditary tenures during the course of the late-fourteenth and fifteenth centuries and eventu-ally evolving into fully-fledged copyholds for lives in the sixteenth century.[49] They also spread to other manors. For example, in the late fifteenth century

---

47   Schofield, 'Tenurial developments', p. 264.

48   Schofield, 'Tenurial developments', p. 251.

49   Tenures for lives displaced hereditary tenures by the early fifteenth century at Akeley, Cuxham and Upper Heyford. They gained a toehold in the land market

tenants on the estate of the bishopric of Worcester voluntarily surrendered holdings held heritably in order to be immediately readmitted on tenures for lives instead.[50] In contrast, leases for years were popular between the 1350s and the 1420s, but declined thereafter. At first the average length of leases tended to increase, and clauses allowing a lessee to assign a lease to a third party were introduced, both of which are indicative of a desire among tenants for greater security.[51] Yet from the second quarter of the fifteenth century the area under leases then contracted almost everywhere, and the land was increasingly converted back into heritable tenure upon expiry of the lease.[52]

Answering the question 'why did leases for years wither?' in the fifteenth century is more straightforward than answering the question 'why did life tenancies endure?' The growing popularity of holding customary land on leaseholds between the 1350s and the 1420s coincided exactly with the period when it was most volatile. The data for land values presented in this study reveal phases of rising values (the 1360s, 1380s and 1410s) alternating sharply with those of falling values (the 1370s, 1390s and 1420s). In such volatile and uncertain conditions, short-term leases for years were fit for purpose because they maintained flexibility and reduced risk for the tenant. When this volatility diminished after the 1420s, and land values stabilized within a deep trough, leases lost some of their popularity. Tenants now sought greater protection against the possibility that servile incidents might be restored by either entering into much longer leases or converting leases back into a hereditary tenure, now paying just an entry fine and a fixed cash rent. The conversion of leases back into a hereditary tenure, permanently released from servile incidents, represented a major seigniorial concession, but it was still preferable to the alternative of tenants abandoning their holdings during the Great Slump of the mid-fifteenth century.

The waning of leases in the fifteenth century runs contrary to Brenner's hypothesis that abandoned customary land was removed from peasant proprietorship in England, which in turn enabled sixteenth-century landlords to re-package the land into large leasehold farms on commercial

after 1350, but subsequently disappeared, at Hardwick Russells, Tingewick and Weedon Vale.

[50] This estate lay in the west Midlands, where copyholds for lives were commonplace in the sixteenth century, Dyer, *Lords and peasants*, p. 294. A similar trend is identifiable on the Gloucestershire manors of Westminster abbey, Harvey, *Westminster abbey*, p. 280.

[51] A trend noted by Harvey, *Westminster abbey*, pp. 276–7, 281.

[52] For example, Aldham, Badwell Ash, Chevington, Dunningworth, Iken, Lackford, Lidgate and Winston. The only manors where leases did survive to any great extent until the sixteenth century were Barton Magna and Fornham St Martin.

rents.[53] The return of many leases to hereditary tenures from mid-century reinforces the argument that customary tenants came to enjoy a good deal more security of tenure than Brenner had supposed.[54] The decision to sanction these conversions made sense to mid-fifteenth-century landlords, although, by removing the opportunity to renegotiate rent levels when the land changed hands, it would prove to be a severe impediment to their late-sixteenth-century successors. The reality was that late-medieval landlords did not always promote leaseholds; it was the peasants themselves who were the main force behind their initial spread and subsequent contraction.[55]

The regional distribution of copyholds in the sixteenth century

One of the great unanswered questions relating to the agrarian history of early modern England is why did copyholds for lives dominate in the southern and western areas of England, and copyholds of inheritance dominate across the rest of the country? Historians have not succeeded in constructing any sort of credible answer to this question, while recognizing that the answer lies shrouded in the tenurial mists of the later Middle Ages. Those mists have now begun to lift.

As we have seen, in c.1300 hereditary villein tenure dominated peasant landholding across England. After 1350 tenures for a term increased markedly in usage and popularity, but did so along lines which were novel and regionally distinctive. By the 1370s conversions of customary land to life tenancies had become firmly established in pockets of Oxfordshire, the western fringes of Buckinghamshire and elsewhere in south and west England, although they were not yet widespread.[56] Thereafter they spread gradually, displacing hereditary villein tenure as they did so. In some places, long leases for years may also have been converted into life tenancies. There is little doubt that, slowly but surely, tenants in these parts of England were developing a preference for life tenancies. They were effectively relinquishing permanent rights of inheritance and liability for all the old servile incidents, in return for a simpler and more dignified rent package comprising an annual money rent, entry fine and heriot.

Thus, through a slow process of emulation and diffusion, did life tenancies displace hereditary villein tenure in much of southern and western England.

---

53 Brenner, 'Agrarian class structure', pp. 33, 48–9; French and Hoyle, *English rural society*, pp. 5–6.

54 Whittle, *Agrarian capitalism*, pp. 308–9, 315.

55 Mate, 'East Sussex land market', pp. 53, 65.

56 For example, tenures for lives were not established in all parts of late fourteenth-century Oxfordshire, where hereditary tenures continued to dominate, see, for example, *VCH Oxfordshire*, volume 14 (Woodbridge, 2004), pp. 180–1, 211–12, 241–2.

Meanwhile, in eastern England and the Home Counties some hereditary customary land was converted to leases for years, whereas life tenancies were uncommon. Why was leasehold for years the fixed-term tenure of choice in East Anglia, whereas life tenancies were preferred in Oxfordshire? Part of the answer to this question lies in the particular steps taken to fill vacant holdings from the 1350s, when the decision about *which* fixed-term tenancy to deploy was informed by local knowledge and experience. East Anglian folk turned to leases for years, partly because small quantities of customary land had already been converted to leases for years prior to the Black Death and so were known to, and trusted by, lords and tenants alike.[57] Further-more, the practice of sub-letting parcels of villein land for short periods was also well established here in the early fourteenth century.[58] Both practices derived from the commercialized and precocious nature of the region's land market, and sub-letting also enabled the owner to retain rights of inher-itance and thus preserve the re-sale value of customary land. Converting vacant customary holdings to short-term leases also made good sense in the uncertain and commercially sensitive land market of the post-plague era, because it presented frequent and formal opportunities to relinquish the land or to renegotiate its terms in response to fluctuating conditions.

In contrast, short-term leases of customary land were much less common in early fourteenth-century Oxfordshire and Buckinghamshire, partly because the local land market was less active or commercialized, and they remained rare thereafter.[59] Life tenancies were already better established in this part of the country – for example, in c.1300 villein cottages at Cuxham were all held for terms for lives, and life tenancies are recorded before the Black Death on some manors in western counties such as Shropshire and Gloucestershire.[60] The willingness to relinquish permanent rights of inherit-ance may well have been due to the relatively inactive land market in such regions, which limited the re-sale value of customary land.

---

57 See the examples at Aldham, Chevington and Fornham All Saints. The practice was known elsewhere in East Anglia: Bailey, *Marginal economy*, p. 228 (Mildenhall, Lakenheath); Bailey, 'Ely and Lakenheath', p. 8.

58 Licensed sub-letting of customary land in the late thirteenth- and early fourteenth-centuries is a strong feature of those East Anglian manors characterized by large, standardized holdings, Bailey, 'Villeinage in England', p. 442.

59 A point made by Faith for Berkshire, where leases and sub-leases of customary land scarcely appear before the mid-fifteenth century, Faith, 'Berkshire', pp. 125–7, and by Tompkins for Great Horwood in Buckinghamshire, Tompkins, 'Great Horwood', p. 174.

60 See, for example, Wenlock in Shropshire, where in the 1320s most villein holdings were held for three lives – this area was also characterized by life leases and copyholds for lives in the sixteenth century, rather than copyholds by inheritance, *VCH Shropshire*, volume 4, pp. 110–11, 138; Wells-Furby, *Berkeley estate*, pp. 96–7.

Thus, when faced with chaotic and unprecedented circumstances in the wake of the Black Death, landlords turned to the type of flexible, fixed-term, tenancy with which they and their prospective tenants were already more familiar. The initial success of that form of tenure in attracting tenants to vacant holdings would have then encouraged the wider spread of the local 'good practice', as one manor emulated the example of its neighbour, and perhaps as lords and administrators serving on the councils of other local lords advised and promoted its adoption across the estate.[61] The process of emulation then reinforced and sharpened the differences in regional practice, of leases for years in East Anglia, and of life tenancies in Oxfordshire. Very occasionally, a manor experimented with both forms of fixed-term tenancy during the late fourteenth century before settling upon one: Aldham experimented with life grants before settling on leases for years; Upper Heyford upon leases for years before settling upon life tenancies; and Hardwick Russells and Weedon Vale even granted life tenancies before returning to hereditary tenure.[62]

The preference for, and the persistence of, life tenancies in the western area of our sample also offers an insight into how local differences in the buoyancy of land markets influenced tenant attitudes to inheritance rights. Faith has shown how peasant families valued rights of inheritance highly during periods when land was scarce and expensive (such as the thirteenth and sixteenth centuries), but much less so when it was abundant and cheap (late fourteenth and fifteenth). Similarly, Whittle has observed that the precise nature of inheritance rights mattered more in those areas of the country where the local land market was relatively inactive, on the grounds that tenants thus had limited opportunities to pick up land by other means.[63] Both of these observations make good sense, although, in the light of them, the preference for hereditary tenures in East Anglia, where localized land markets were active, and the preference for life tenancies in Oxfordshire, where they were relatively inactive, seems perverse: surely, inalienable rights of inheritance should be least valued where tenants could readily access an active market for land, and *vice versa*? Yet it would appear that hereditary rights continued to be valued in East Anglia, where the land market had caused holdings to fragment, because they enhanced the saleable value of those slivers of land, rather than because they secured access to land. Life tenancies spread in places where the land market was inactive, because the

---

[61] The importance of councils in gentry households, comprised of professionals, supporters and friends, is emphasized in R.H. Britnell, 'The Pastons and their Norfolk', *Agricultural History Review*, 36 (1988), p. 135.

[62] See above, pp. 136, 157, 245. Also Jones, 'Bedfordshire', p. 203; Lomas, 'South-east Durham', p. 311.

[63] Faith, 'Peasant families', pp. 88–92; Whittle, *Agrarian capitalism*, p. 91.

resale value of customary holdings was low and because land was readily available from the lord for anyone who wanted it in the depressed conditions of the fifteenth century.

Thus the regional distribution of copyholds for lives in sixteenth-century England broadly follows the emerging distribution of tenures for lives in the fifteenth century, which in turn owes much to decisions which can be securely dated to the 1350s and 1360s. Those decisions were a direct response to local shortages of tenants after the Black Death, because fixed-term tenancies for customary land were unusual before 1348–9. By c.1400 western Buckinghamshire already represented a transitional zone between the area of hereditary tenure to the east, and the emerging area of life tenancies to the west.[64]

Historians of the early modern period are best placed to evaluate the economic and social significance of the presence of different types of copyhold tenures by the sixteenth century, and the structure of the rent packages attached to them. French and Hoyle observe that the 'variegated patterns of tenancy imply very different structures of power within the [early-modern] countryside', which in turn 'imply very different experiences' from place to place.[65] Expressed in its crudest form, copyholds for lives and leaseholds exposed tenants to some insecurity and greater expense, and provided the landlord with more legitimate openings to auction the holdings to the highest bidder. If commercially re-negotiable tenancies dominated the local land market, then the balance of power shifted towards landlords in times of rising land values, who had more opportunities to displace peasant land-holders and to re-package the land into sizeable capitalist farms paying commercial rents. In contrast, in places dominated by copyholds of inheritance landlords had much less scope to intervene in the customary land market, and as a consequence their tenants enjoyed greater security.[66]

There is also a clear sense that different types of tenure are associated with different pathways of regional development; for example, a broad correlation has been established between the distribution of insecure copyholds

---

[64] Hereditary tenures dominated at Hardwick Russells, Weedon Vale, Tingewick and Great Horwood, whereas to the west life tenancies emerged at Akeley, Cuxham, and Upper Heyford. Life tenancies were also spreading through Berkshire and Wiltshire during the course of the fifteenth century, Whittle and Yates, '*Pays reel* or *pays legal*?', p. 12; Yates, *Town and countryside*, p. 142; Hare, *A prospering society*, pp. 117–18. For the geographical distribution of hereditary copyholds, and those for lives, in the sixteenth century and later, see French and Hoyle, *English rural society*, p. 3; J.V. Beckett and M.E. Turner, 'Freehold from copyhold and leasehold: tenurial transition in England between the sixteenth and nineteenth centuries', in B.J.P. Bavel and P. Hoppenbrouwers, eds., *Landholding and land transfer in the North Sea area* (Turnhout, 2004), p. 289.

[65] French and Hoyle, *English rural society*, pp. 8, 30, 32.

[66] French and Hoyle, *English rural society*, pp. 294–5.

and the arable heartlands of England on the one hand, and between copyholds of inheritance and regions of wood pasture on the other. However, none of these observations are meant to imply the existence of a direct, predictable and invariable relationship between tenurial forms and regional development. Local circumstances, such as farm-size, the degree of agrarian specialization, the mentality of the lord, social attitudes to land acquisition and exploitation, and agrarian class structure all influenced regional social and economic development. The isolation of a single unifying explanation for patterns of change across Europe does not, and cannot, do justice to the complexity of historical experience.[67]

Chronology and causation

What caused serfdom to decline in late medieval England? The method here has been to approach this simple but challenging question by ascertaining whether any correlation exists between the chronology of decline and specific aspects of social and economic change. The case studies have shown clearly that manumission was unimportant before c.1500. Its prominence rose after c.1500 in eradicating the last vestiges of serfdom, probably spurred by the rising wealth of serfs who had profited from improving agrarian conditions and profitability.

The correlation between recorded peasant resistance to serfdom, or recorded migration, and observable changes to villeinage is not strong overall. The correlation is strongest during two short periods: in the 1350s, when evidence for some tenurial change occurred alongside a rise in both emigration and resistance to labour services; and around 1400, when some increase in conflict over personal servility occurred at the same time as its decline on a few manors. Yet the strongest demonstrable correlation is between the decline of villeinage and the trend of customary land values, which fell sharply between the 1340s and the 1360s, the very period when villein tenure underwent lasting change. They fell again between the 1380s and c.1410, which again correlates well with the chronology of decline of personal servility on most manors.

These findings support Britnell's conclusion that 'class conflict is an unconvincing prime mover of economic and social development [and] the development and decline of villeinage'.[68] However, this does *not* mean that economic forces are a convincing prime mover. Declining land values provide the best general context for understanding the decline of serfdom,

---

[67] Rigby, *English society*, pp. 141–4; French and Hoyle, *English rural society*, pp. 23–38.

[68] R.H. Britnell, 'Agriculture, marketing and rural change, 1000–1500', in J. Broad, ed., *A common agricultural heritage? Revising French and British rural divergence* (The Agricultural History Review Supplement Series, 5, 2009), p. 114.

but they do not offer anything like a complete explanation, because their exact local impact was mediated through the complex interplay of other forces. For example, although the value of customary land fell c.40% between the 1340s and the 1360s at each of Cuxham, Upper Heyford and Walsham, the trajectory of villeinage was different: hereditary villein tenure survived at Walsham, albeit with some watering down of its servile incidents, whereas it virtually disappeared at Cuxham and Upper Heyford. Likewise, a general fall in land values between the 1380s and c.1410 corresponded with the abandonment of personal servility on many manors within the sample, but its more strenuous imposition on a few. Clearly, the same economic trend could and did produce different responses. What the case studies illuminate more than anything is the economic and social turbulence of the 1350s and 1360s, caused by successive outbreaks of the Black Death and exceptional climatic volatility, which created conditions that fatally weakened the foundations of villeinage in England. There are powerful grounds for revisiting and challenging the long-held belief that the Black Death did not trigger direct and immediate economic and social change.[69]

The pursuit of a single prime mover of socio-economic change is the pursuit of alchemist's gold. Broad economic shifts, and conflict in social relationships, both provide powerful generic contexts for understanding serfdom's decline in England, but an explanation for its disappearance from any one locality requires an appreciation of the complex interplay of various forces. To varying degrees, the case studies have revealed how the particular trajectory of decline after the Black Death in the localities was shaped by the pre-existing profile of servile incidents (light or heavy); the structure of landholding (large, standardized holdings or smallholdings); the depth of the pool of available tenants; the availability, or not, of alternative land locally, and its tenurial characteristics; the attractiveness of a particular locality as a place to make a living; the disposition and power of the landlord; and the attitude of, and degree of unity between, serfs and tenants.

The inter-relationship between local landholding structures, the availability of tenants immediately after the Black Death, and the decline of villeinage have been explored above (pp. 312–20). The case studies also highlight that the personal disposition and status of the landlord could influence the local trajectory of decline. Serfdom was more likely to be maintained on the manors of high-status landlords than those of gentry lords, partly because there was usually a greater continuity of management of the former, which better enabled them to sustain a consistent policy towards serfs and to preserve the manorial court rolls which documented servile liability.[70]

---

[69] The establishment of this orthodoxy is expertly summarized in Hatcher, 'England after the Black Death', pp. 3–8, and Horrox, *Black Death*, pp. 229–36.

[70] Gentry lords who bucked this trend were often lawyers.

MacCulloch was correct on this point. However, even a powerful, perpetual landlord could not uphold serfdom if the mix of local forces was sufficiently adverse, as Merton College discovered at Cuxham. Similarly, New College acquired its estate at the end of the fourteenth century, but proved incapable of restoring villeinage on those manors where it had already declined. The personal disposition of a particular landlord towards servility could also be influential in determining whether or not serfdom continued on an estate, although the ability of the estate's administration to implement such a policy might have informed that thinking. For example, both the duke of Norfolk and the abbot of Bury St Edmunds adopted a hard line towards serfs in the 1390s, but then the abbot decided to abandon serfdom while the duke determined to maintain it on a small, but clearly identified, pool of serfs. The ability of the abbot to enforce serfdom was further diminished in the late 1390s by the shift away from the direct exploitation of his demesnes on many manors, which involved some reduction in the apparatus of estate management.

The case studies have also highlighted how the options and alternatives available locally to villeins could influence the pace at which serfdom declined. For example, the nature and chronology of its decline on two small manors in Walsham followed that on the main manor closely, indicating that lords were heavily influenced by developments around them. The earls of Arundel were committed to upholding serfdom at Beeston in the 1380s and 1390s, but their failure to do so thereafter cannot have been aided by the early collapse of villeinage on local manors such as Runton and Beeston Felbriggs, and Runton Hayes, which meant that the earls' tenants had ready access to more attractive options nearby. Landlords competed with each other for tenants and labourers, and the latter shopped around for the best terms. In the 1360s Alice de Mauro of Upper Heyford even competed with Sir William Shareshull – the architect of the Statute of Labourers – for the labour of two of her serfs. Manors were not islands, especially in East Anglia where a settlement could often be split between a number of manorial units, and consequently lords had to reckon with the options locally available to their own serfs.

It would be facile and trite to conclude from these observations that serfdom was in a state of flux in the second half of the fourteenth century, and that its decline locally was a function of a complex mix of variables, even though this would be an accurate statement. It is arguably more interesting to show how these multiple variables interacted, an approach also bearing fruit in early modern studies.[71] The method of separating out and isolating the main causes of change – popular among historians in the 1970s and

---

[71]   French and Hoyle, *English rural society*, pp. 23–41.

1980s – certainly aids an initial understanding of these complex processes, but it can impede deeper analysis if it subsequently discourages or diverts the exploration of their interaction. After all, the geographical mobility of serfs was often a function of both pull factors (e.g. economic opportunity, family links) and push factors (e.g. social discontent, desire for personal betterment). Rents, too, were determined by a variable combination of custom, law and the relative bargaining power of different social groups, as well as the forces of supply and demand in the land market. Likewise, manumission may be regarded as a mechanism, not a cause, whose use depended upon the shifting realities of social relations between lords and serfs, the asset base of serfs, and a particular lord's need for ready cash. As the example of Aldham in the 1350s shows, the causes of the decline of serfdom at key moments were sometimes tightly intertwined, and cannot be easily or plausibly segregated. Hence the importance of exploring the dynamic interplay between the various contributing factors, rather than trying to isolate and rank linear causation.

Care when handling causation is usefully complemented by taking care to avoid the temptation of making subjective judgements about historical events and attitudes. Historians may reasonably judge a particular landlord's treatment of his serfs to be harsh or aggressive on the basis of a direct comparison with either the same lord's previous policy and/or the norms on other estates, but who are we to judge whether the treatment is 'exploitative' or 'oppressive' when the lord thought one thing and the serf thought another?[72] Similarly, who are we to judge if serfdom was a 'bad', or a 'good', thing? Serfdom bestowed both advantages and disadvantages, which shifted over time, and what matters is how the villein or the lord – not the historian – judged the balance between the two.[73] The dramatic decline of serfdom in the second half of the fourteenth century, and its complete disappearance during the sixteenth, indicates that villeins came to judge it to be disadvantageous to them, and that landlords were unable to defend it; or, alternatively, that landlords themselves did not regard serfdom as sufficiently advantageous to be worth fighting for.

From bondage to freedom

The final questions are, without doubt, the most difficult to answer, but they strike at the heart of the nature of serfdom in late medieval England, and why it declined. From what type of bondage had English serfs been released? What type of freedom had they obtained, and how did it contribute to the 'transition' from feudalism to capitalism?

---

[72]   Rigby, 'Historical causation', pp. 233–41.
[73]   Hatcher, 'Serfdom and villeinage', p. 5.

From what type of bondage had around half of the English population been released over the course of the fourteenth and fifteenth centuries? As we noted at the very beginning of this book, serfdom assumed very different forms throughout medieval Europe, although in general terms it refers to a system in which some people were bonded to a lord or a particular piece of land, and were therefore placed under the jurisdiction of a lord. Villeinage in England in c.1300 certainly fitted this generic definition, but it did not provide landlords with significant or arbitrary powers of 'extra-economic' compulsion, enabling them to extract from peasants rent above the economic level.[74] A combination of custom and the common law limited the seigniorial scope for arbitrary action within villeinage, which by c.1300 was character- ized mainly by financial disabilities rather than physical restraint on move- ment or action.[75] This explains Dyer's assessment that English lordship was largely ineffective and why tenants were treated 'gingerly'.[76] It also explains why the rents paid for many customary lands at this date were sub-economic, which meant that the system *protected* many villein tenants against the worst excesses of the market.[77] Villeinage in England in c.1300 was also uneven, in the sense that both its burdens and its implementation varied from manor to manor, and some lords did not bother to enforce all of their codified rights over villeins.[78] To what extent do our case studies support these perspectives?

The nature and operation of villeinage *before* 1348–9 on the 38 manors used in this study is not easy to reconstruct, because of an absence of extant sources from the pre-plague period – after all, the manors were principally chosen on the basis of the quality of their *post*-1348–9 records. However, the evidence from those which have left a pre-1348–9 archive reinforces how unevenly some of these servile incidents had been imposed before the Black Death. For example, tallage was collected infrequently at Upper Heyford; it was not collected at all at Staverton, even though it was common on other nearby manors belonging to the same lord. Chevage was extremely rare at both Upper Heyford and Walsham. There is even an example of one manor, Holywell, where customary land existed, but there is no record of the collec-

---

74   Freedman and Bourin, 'Introduction', p. 1; Rigby, *English society*, pp. 25–34.

75   Hatcher, 'Serfdom and villeinage', p. 14; Dyer, 'Ineffectiveness of lordship', pp. 73–9.

76   Dyer, 'The ineffectiveness of lordship in England', p. 79; and Rigby, *English society*, pp. 127–38 summarizes some of the shortcomings of the 'extra-economic compulsion' argument.

77   Hatcher, 'English serfdom and villeinage', pp. 3–39; Kanzaka, 'Villein rents', pp. 593–618; Campbell, 'Agrarian problem', p. 69. See also Wells-Furby, *Berkeley estate*, pp. 107–11.

78   Campbell, 'Agrarian problem', pp. 37–8, 40–2; Bailey, 'Villeinage in England', pp. 430–57.

tion of servile dues before 1348–9.[79] Hence this study has reinforced just how uneven was villeinage before the Black Death, both in terms of the variations in the liability for servile incidents from manor to manor, and in the frequency with which they were actually collected.[80] There was a multitude of unfreedom in early fourteenth-century England.

The unevenness of English villeinage before 1348–9, and its failure to provide lords with powers of extra-economic compulsion, does not mean that it was irrelevant to the lives of serfs. The evidence from those manors in the sample with a pre-1348–9 archive also shows very clearly that servile incidents, present in the first half of the fourteenth century, were being discarded in the second half.[81] This, together with the rapidity with which villein tenure retreated after 1348–9, is proof of the unpopularity of villeinage, and the resentment felt towards its burdens. Freedman has observed shrewdly that 'servile status was felt to be onerous, unjust and worth sacrifice to cast off or resist, even in places [such as England] where there was little if any short-term gain in moving out of villeinage'.[82] Contemporaries regarded villeinage in England as socially and economically disadvantageous, irrespective of whether modern historians judge it to have been neither an especially onerous nor exploitative form of serfdom.

What type of freedom had been obtained, defining 'freedom' as being 'free from' certain restrictions? Customary land comprised around half of all peasant land in the early fourteenth century, and by the sixteenth century it had gained freedom from its former dependence upon the jurisdiction of the landlord's own court for all matters pertaining to proprietorial rights, because its title could now be defended in the common law courts. The tenant enjoyed access to a higher, more equitable, reliable and consistent (if more expensive) source of justice, which, in effect, meant access to a court of appeal in the case of dispute over proprietary rights within the seigniorial court. Customary land had also broken free from the dominance of a rent package based upon incidents that had been unpredictable, personal and demeaning, and by c.1500 its rent package was overwhelmingly monetarized. The disappearance of theoretical restrictions upon the dispersal of chattels, and of liability to various fines at key moments of the life cycle whose size was uncertain, eradicated vulnerability to seizure of personal assets, which

---

[79] See pp. 129–30.

[80] See also the discussion in Hatcher, 'Serfdom and Villeinage', pp. 19–21. In the early fourteenth century the Berkeley lords in Gloucestershire were 'not wedded to the concept of villeinage' and their attitude was 'generally benevolent or pragmatic', Wells-Furby, *Berkeley estate*, p. 115.

[81] As evidenced at Aldham, Barton Magna, Cuxham, Chevington, Drinkstone, Forncett, Fornham All Saints, Fornham St Martin, Kibworth Harcourt, Runton Hayes, Upper Heyford, Walsham, Walsham High Hall, and Winston.

[82] Freedman, *Images of medieval peasants*, p. 262.

meant that people were now freer to accumulate capital securely. These developments removed a source of social stigma and prejudice against the tenants of customary land, and they also removed the sense of capricious domination and injustice felt by serfs. Partly as a result of these freedoms, ordinary rural dwellers were generally wealthier in c.1500 than they had been in c.1300.[83] There were some countervailing developments, although they had nothing to do with serfdom: for example, all labourers – whether descended from freemen or serfs – had become subject to the regulation of their work habits through an emerging body of labour legislation.[84]

How did the acquisition of these various freedoms contribute to the transition from feudalism to capitalism in England? The answer lies in the ways in which the loosening of the labour market, and the changes to customary tenures, created a new paradigm in which substantial changes to the structure of English farms, and by extension their productivity, became easier and more likely. Campbell has argued convincingly that the proliferation of smallholdings with pitifully low labour productivity created a severe 'agrarian problem' in early fourteenth-century England, largely due to the way in which the peculiar and tangled structure of land rents 'bred farm fragmentation, rural congestion and indebtedness'. Only substantial structural reform – involving the introduction of contractual tenancies, competitive rents, exchanges of land parcels, and larger farms – could remove the bottleneck, although the tangle of tenures and the pressure on resources had become so great on the eve of the Black Death that the process of reform would take centuries, not decades, to complete properly.[85]

Britnell, Dyer and Schofield have argued independently that the spread of leasehold tenure, whether for demesne or customary land, was an important feature of tenurial change during the fourteenth and fifteenth centuries.[86] Leases provided agriculturalists with more flexibility to acquire individual parcels of land to create larger, more compact and more rational farming units, which in turn rendered farm improvements, such as proper hedging and ditching, more likely.[87] As an economic contract rather than a feudal tenure, leases were also more likely to attract new money and talent into the

[83] Whittle, *Agrarian capitalism*, p. 306; Hare, *Prospering society*, p. 115.

[84] Whittle, *Agrarian capitalism*, pp. 275–301; M.K. McIntosh, *Controlling misbehaviour in England, 1370–1600* (Cambridge, 1998), pp. 1–45.

[85] Campbell, 'Agrarian problem', pp. 69–70.

[86] Britnell, *Commercialisation*, pp. 197–203; Britnell, *Britain and Ireland*, pp. 436–7; and Britnell, 'Agriculture, marketing and rural change', pp. 113–14. C. Dyer, *Making a living in the Middle Ages: the people of Britain 850–1520* (London, 2002), pp. 346–52; Schofield, 'Tenurial developments', pp. 256–61; Hare, *Prospering society*, pp. 99–116.

[87] C. Dyer, *An age of transition? Economy and society in the later Middle Ages* (Oxford, 2005), pp. 206–7.

customary land market, and promoted entrepreneurship among wealthier agriculturalists, both of which were likely to promote greater polarization of land ownership within rural communities. Indeed, during the second half of the fourteenth century the gap between the larger and smaller peasant land-holders demonstrably increased in England, and the former were especially enterprising in their use of labour.[88] Leases charging commercial rents also forced farmers to use land and labour more efficiently. Thus the expansion of leasehold represented a qualitative break with feudal relations of production.[89] Leases also attracted new tenants and immigrants, providing them with a niche within the village community.[90]

Britnell, Campbell, Dyer and Schofield's lines of argument can now be integrated and developed further. This study has shown that the conversion of customary land to fixed-term tenures for a money rent occurred earlier, and on a larger scale, than has been previously recognized.[91] These forms of tenure had been rarely used for customary land before 1350, but they spread quickly thereafter. The discovery that life tenancies were firmly established by the 1370s, and that they usually involved the conversion of servile incidents to a monetarized rent package, is novel. The extent of conversions to leasehold by the 1370s has also been underestimated. The significance of these changes is that they constituted exactly the type of tenurial reform necessary to unravel the tangled and inefficient structure of rent which had characterized the 'agrarian problem' of the early fourteenth century.

The tactic of enticing new tenants to take on abandoned customary land in the 1350s and 1360s by converting it to either leases for years or life tenancies was invariably successful, and it also drew new entrants to the land market; some were opportunist migrants of limited means and servile origins, but others came from social groups – freemen, townsfolk, artisans, even lesser lords – which had previously exhibited little interest in entering the customary land market.[92] Before 1348–9 the demeaning rent package

---

[88] For the general trend towards engrossment and larger farm size in the fifteenth century, see Razi, 'Family, land and the village community ', pp. 31–4; Dyer, *Making a living*, pp. 357–62; Dyer, *Age of transition*, pp. 206–7; Hare, *A prospering county*, pp. 137–9. For the trend towards engrossment on the manors within our sample, see Bailey, *Medieval Suffolk*, pp. 246–9; Dyer, 'Suffolk farmer', pp. 7–11, 19–22 (Chevington); Davenport, *Development of a Norfolk manor*, pp. 81–3; and p. 157 for Upper Heyford.

[89] Hybel, *Crisis or change?*, p. 207; Dyer, *Age of transition*, p. 199 notes that the lessee 'developed a relationship with the lord on the basis of the mutual advantages of the contract', rather than some other feudal-based relationship.

[90] Schofield, 'Tenurial developments', pp. 251, 260–64.

[91] Recorded on Type 2 to Type 4 manors, a total of 17 out of 38 of the sample.

[92] For the influx of new tenants after 1350, see Raftis, *Ramsey abbey*, p. 251; Mate, 'East Sussex land market', pp. 56–7; Schofield, 'Tenurial developments', pp. 252, 260–2; Hare, *A prospering society*, pp. 115, 122.

attached to villein tenure and the eagerness of villein heirs to inherit ensured that the customary land market was effectively closed to the wealthiest sections of society. Thereafter the failure or reluctance of some heirs, and the improved dignity of customary land that had been converted to money rents, combined to reduce the barriers to entry significantly, and enticed new tenants with capital and an eye for an opportunity. Attention has often been drawn to the extraordinary mobility of labourers in the second half of the fourteenth century, yet the mobility and turnover of tenants was also exceptional as they sought out new and better opportunities.[93]

The rapidity and the scale with which fixed-term tenures spread after 1350 suddenly increased the degree of choice and variety in the customary land market. In the 1340s a solid line of hereditary villein tenure had existed across England, but by the 1360s this line had been repeatedly broken by a rising tide of tenurial variety. This variety created competition and mocked the power of landlords, many of whom cut deals in their desperation to find tenants.[94] It also created a dynamic for further change, by signalling starkly to customary tenants and landlords everywhere that hereditary villein tenure was not immutable, but susceptible to alteration through bargaining, negotiation or resistance. Villein tenure had dominated customary landholding before 1350, although its precise terms and burdens were uneven. After 1350 the rapid increase in tenurial variety exacerbated that unevenness, and sharpened the edge of competition for tenants of customary land, with adverse implications for landlords.

These developments also created pressure upon those landlords who were still maintaining hereditary villein tenure to remove some or all its servile incidents in order to retain their own tenants. This explains the subtle (and easily overlooked) changes to the rent packages of hereditary tenure in the third quarter of the fourteenth century identified in our case studies. The drastically reduced frequency, or even the lapse, of servile incidents such as millsuit and tallage, the widespread commutation of week works and the dropping of 'in villeinage' from land transfers make most sense when viewed as attempts to improve the dignity, security and attractiveness of villein tenure in the teeth of sharpened competition. Similarly, the provision of a copy of the land transfer mimicked the freeman's possession of a charter, and, although the copy could not be pleaded in any court other than that of the issuing lord, it symbolized the lord's good faith in respect of the title

---

[93]   R.H. Britnell, 'Land and lordship: common themes and regional variations', in B. Dodds and R.H. Britnell, eds., *Agriculture and rural society after the Black Death* (Hatfield, 2008), pp. 158, 161; J. Mullan, 'Accumulation and polarization in two bailiwicks of the Winchester bishopric estates, 1350–1410: regional similarities and contrasts', in Dodds and Britnell, eds., *Agriculture and rural society*, pp. 186–7.

[94]   Larson, 'Peasant opportunities', p. 147.

to new tenants who were not serfs themselves. Landlords often introduced such improvements voluntarily and proactively, because they recognized rapidly and pragmatically that the demeaning and burdensome elements of villeinage had to be diluted if widespread vacancies were to be avoided. The recruitment and retention of tenants for customary land in the 1350s and 1360s depended on competing in a buyer's market, which in turn depended upon widespread seigniorial concessions, not coercion.

Not all landlords made concessions on villein tenure in the immediate aftermath of the Black Death. On some conservative estates, such as those of St Alban's and Westminster abbeys, there appears to be little sign of change before the 1390s. There, and elsewhere, landlords targeted established servile families with vested interests and large landholdings, who were least likely to leave their home manor and could therefore be milked for servile incidents. Landlords whose initial inclination was not to make concessions faced either a shortage of tenants or increasing tension with those tenants who remained, and they may have suffered for their obstinacy during the Peasants' Revolt as their tenants expressed anger at their *relative* deprivation. Their experience has hitherto dominated our thinking about the chronology of decline of villein tenure, but the typicality of such policies is open to serious challenge when the experience of lesser lords, and other great landlords, is considered. It is apparent that after the Black Death the extent of tenurial choices in the customary land market, and the speed at which they became available, has been underestimated. The speed and extent of change, and the social profile of the people entering this land market, were such that by c.1380 a wholesale return to the old villein tenures was no longer possible, and the long-term viability of those that still survived was severely threatened. Increased choice and competition provides a major explanation for the decline of serfdom in England, and, indeed, the particular pace at which it declined in a given locality.[95]

Even if villein tenure had changed dramatically by c.1380, it did not mean that England was now hurtling inexorably towards agrarian capitalism. The nature and extent of tenurial change meant that substantial progress had been made to removing a major structural impediment to the emergence of larger and more commercial farms. However, the extent to which such farms actually emerged, and the extent to which they raised productivity and profitability, depended also upon market conditions, which remained stubbornly unfavourable for the next century. The depressed demand for agrarian produce between the mid-1370s and the mid-1460s, exacerbated by sustained shortages of coin and the general conditions of over-supply, posed severe operational difficulties for commercial producers. Simply creating a

---

[95] Whittle, *Agrarian capitalism*, p. 310; Britnell, 'Agriculture, marketing and rural change', pp. 118–20.

larger farm in late medieval England was not in itself a guarantee of success, because enhanced exposure to the market could result in problems of capitalization and of recruiting sufficient labour to run the farm.[96] Nor does it follow that a leaseholder was automatically a more commercial or precocious farmer.[97] It was not until the sixteenth century that a sustained improvement in market and monetary conditions created sufficient incentive for the creation of larger, more efficient, farms on a grander scale. When they did improve, English producers were in a better position to exploit them than their counterparts in other European countries, because of those structural and tenurial changes to the customary land market which had begun immediately after 1348–9. Those changes to the late-medieval customary land market also helped to determine whether tenants or landlords most benefited from the improved conditions in the sixteenth century. The manifold outcomes of the myriad negotiations over tenure between c.1350 and c.1480 – whether variable entry fines were retained, or cash rents were fixed, or hereditary rights were removed – had a significant but largely unforeseeable impact on where the balance of future benefit was to rest in each locality. Agrarian conditions were broadly and persistently unfavourable to landlords in this period, which meant that landlords were likely to be making more concessions over tenure than tenants: and it is logical to suppose that concessions which were less favourable to a mid-fifteenth-century landlord than to his tenant would continue to be so in the late sixteenth century. While this observation holds in general terms, it is not invariable. Tenants who preferred fixed-term tenures in the aftermath of the Black Death and continued to opt for them thereafter, and tenants who sought to replace their hereditary tenures with life tenancies, were making decisions which worked to the great disadvantage of their sixteenth-century successors.

The Black Death caused a precipitous fall in customary land values, and triggered, to varying degrees, resistance to labour services, migration and non-cooperation. During the 1350s and 1360s these mutually reinforcing trends promoted the dilution of many servile obligations, improvements to the dignity of customary land, the spread of fixed-term tenures, and the multiplication of money-based forms of tenure. These developments caused multiple breaches in the ubiquitous line of hereditary villein tenure, and through the breaches poured new tenants of varying social status. The social stigma attached to customary land, and the myth of the immutability of hereditary villein tenure, had been broken. Historians have stressed the heightened competition for *labour* after 1348–9, but tenurial change reflects the sharpened competition between landlords for *tenants*.

---

[96]   Faith, 'Berkshire', pp. 139–43; Larson, 'Peasant opportunities', pp. 151, 156.
[97]   Britnell, 'Land and lordship', p. 166.

The choices available to serfs and villein tenants in England increased markedly as a consequence of the social and economic turbulence caused by the Black Death. Many landlords quickly diluted villein tenure in various ways in order to preserve the attractiveness of customary land, and they also recognized the difficulties of enforcing personal servility when work and land was widely and competitively available. These decisions and actions inflicted a terminal wound at the heart of villeinage. By c.1380 serfdom in England could be neither revived nor restored. The edifice of obstacles and legal threats that it had once presented to personal mobility, and to the secure accumulation of capital, was now ruined beyond repair. This did not mean that agrarian capitalism had been built in its place. It did mean that the wide-ranging and complex structural reform of tenancies and rents, which was essential to the alleviation of Campbell's 'agrarian problem' and to laying the foundations for commercialized farms, lurched irrevocably forward between c.1350 and c.1380. Put another way, it meant that money-based and competitive tenures – the first decisive step towards the 'democratization of property ownership' which Allen regarded as the basis for the development of yeoman agriculture in early modern England – were already an irreversible component of the customary land market.

This study challenges the historiography of late medieval England by arguing that English serfdom, while disagreeable and irksome enough to be worth shedding, was nevertheless not as terrible a condition as it has conventionally been perceived or portrayed, either in its first or second phases. English serfdom was not economically disadvantageous to serfs, nor did it provide landlords with a legal weapon with which to exploit and to extort them systematically or arbitrarily. Its principal disadvantage to serfs was social, because of their inferior position in the common law, and because their status and dignity were diminished by its characteristic incidents. Thus, if its subsequent decline is to occupy a position of central importance in the 'transition debate' and in the history of succeeding centuries, then its significance lies less in what caused its decline, and more in what it had been, what emerged from its detritus, and how quickly it emerged. The real issue is how did the timing and manner of serfdom's decline first promote then sustain the creation of larger, commercial farms in England between 1300 and 1800, especially when compared with other parts of Europe? The question is not unfamiliar, but the answers are now more surprising, nuanced, complex and fascinating.

Appendix
List of original sources used in this study

The classification of each manor as large, medium or small follows the definitions established in Chapter Five (p. 97). The range of years given for court rolls is continuous whenever court sessions survive from two consecutive years: hence a statement 'courts 1350–76, 1379–85, 1450' means that there is no gap in extant court sessions greater than two consecutive years in the periods 1350 to 1376, and 1379 to 1385; no courts survive from 1377 or 1378; and none survive after 1386, with the single exception of one or more courts from 1450.

The approximate number of surviving court sessions and accounts is a reliable and accurate indication of those which are extant and which are capable of yielding usable information about villeinage for that manor. An exact enumeration is meaningless for three reasons. First, an account may have survived, but upon inspection it proved to be partial, damaged or a duplicate. Second, some record of a court session may have survived, but it too proved to be damaged, illegible or incomplete. Third, the enumeration of leet courts is problematic for the purposes of this study. Not all manors in the sample held leets. Others held separate leets earlier in the period, but later merged the leet with the manorial court baron due to dwindling business. On some manors the leet court contained no business relating to the management of villeinage.

Akeley, Buckinghamshire
Medium manor held by Longueville priory, Normandy, until 1441 when it was transferred to New College, Oxford: *VCH Buckinghamshire*, volume 4 (London, 1969), p. 145.
c.67 courts 1382–1422, New College, Oxford, 4084 and 4085.
2 accounts, 1442–6, New College, Oxford, 5805 and 5806.

Aldham, Suffolk
Large manor held by the de Vere, earls of Oxford: Bailey, *Medieval Suffolk*, p. 17.
c.165 courts 1350–71, 1377–1408, 1415–59, 1468–76, 1486–8, 1504, CUL Vanneck Mss, box 1, SROI HA68/484/135, HA68/484/315.
5 accounts, 1328–9, 1413–14, 1415–16, 1431–2, 1527–8, two rentals, 1442, 1477, CUL Vanneck Mss, box 2.

Badwell Ash, Suffolk

Medium manor held by a single gentry family until 1354, when it was acquired by Ixworth priory (Suffolk): W.A. Copinger, *Manors of Suffolk*, volume 1 (London, 1905), p. 260.

c.36 courts 1419–43, 1446–51, 1460–5, 1468–75, 1480, 1495, SROI 1825/1/1 to 15.

Barton Magna, Suffolk

Large manor held by the cellarer of Bury St Edmunds abbey: Bailey, *Medieval Suffolk*, p. 17.

c.60 courts 1349, 1355, 1363, 1368, 1377–81, 1397–1409, 1419–56, SROB E18/151/1 and 2.

26 accounts 1364 to 1494, SROB E18/155/2 to 8, A6/1/14 and 15.

Beeston Regis, Norfolk

Medium manor held by the earls of Arundel until 1464, then by the Crown: F. Blomefield, *History of the county of Norfolk*, volume 8 (London, 1808), pp. 87–8.

c.159 courts 1384–1413, 1425–6, 1462–77, 1481–92, TNA DL30/102/1392 to 1407.

Chevington, Suffolk

Large manor held by the abbot of Bury St Edmunds.

c.220 courts 1352–1500, SROB E3/15.3/1.1a to 1.40(b).

40 accounts 1351 to 1461, SROB E3/15.3/2.9 to 2.42.

2 rentals 1389, 1478–9, SROB E3/15.3/3.1 and 3.2.

Cratfield, Suffolk

Medium manor held by the earls (from 1397, dukes) of Norfolk: W.A. Copinger, *Manors of Suffolk*, volume 2 (Manchester, 1908), pp. 48–50.

c.210 courts 1401–1500, CUL Vanneck Mss, box 3.

9 accounts 1282 to 1302, TNA SC6/995/2 to 11.

Cuxham, Oxfordshire

Medium manor held by Merton College, Oxford.

c.59 courts 1351–63, 1377–1411, 1436–48, 1458, 1466, 1474–89, Merton College, Oxford, 5916 to 5941.

9 accounts 1350–9, c.60 farmers' accounts 1395–1495, Merton College, Oxford, 5875, 5879 to 5887, 5888 to 5891.

Debach, Suffolk

Small manor held by a succession of gentry lords: Copinger, *Manors of Suffolk*, volume 6, pp. 263–4.

c.22 courts 1365–74, 1380, 1387–1403, SROI HD230/1/1.

Drinkstone, Suffolk
Small manor held by a succession of gentry lords: Copinger, *Manors of Suffolk*, volume 6, pp. 262–4.
c.65 courts, 1351–77, 1428–32, 1445–7, 1461–83, 1499, SROB E7/10/1.2 and 1.3.
1 account 1474–5, SROB E7/10/1.4.

Dunningworth, Suffolk
Medium manor held by the earls (dukes, from 1397) of Norfolk: Bailey, *Medieval Suffolk*, p. 17.
c.280 courts 1353–67, 1375–1489, and 1496–1500, SROI HD1538/207/2 to 9.
3 accounts 1390–1, 1397–8, 1475–6, TNA SC6/995/15 and SROI HD1538/206/6 and 7.

Fornham All Saints, Suffolk
Large manor held by the abbot of Bury St Edmunds.
c.65 courts 1350–5, 1366–76, 1381–7, 1391–1400, 1415–23, SROB E3/15.6/1.7 to 1.17 and E3/15.7/1.7 to 1.15.
52 accounts 1338 to 1476, SROB E3/15.6/2.21 to 2.63 and E3/15.7/2.5 to 2.15.
3 rentals 1302 and 1441, BL Add. Ms 34689; 1458–9 SROB HA528, Hengrave Hall deposit 114.

Fornham St Martin, Suffolk
Medium manor held by the cellarer of Bury St Edmunds abbey: Bailey, *Medieval Suffolk*, p. 17.
c.77 courts 1351–9, 1363, 1369–73, 1377–99, 1406, 1419–21, 1482–1510, SROB E3/15.6/1.3; E3/15.9/1.5 to 1.8.
19 accounts 1322 to 1366, SROB E3/15.6/2.5 to 2.20, 2.23a, 2.24 to 2.27, 2.30a, 2.31.

Hardwick Russells, Buckinghamshire
Small manor held by a succession of minor gentry lords until New College acquired it in 1385: *VCH Buckinghamshire*, volume 3 (London, 1969), p. 364.
c.20 courts 1397–1403, 1419–23, 1435–41, 1450–4, 1459–60, 1471, New College, Oxford, 3847 to 3849.
8 accounts 1388–1402, New College, Oxford, 6082 to 6090.

Harkstead, Suffolk
Small manor held continuously by a single gentry family: Copinger, *Manors of Suffolk*, volume 6, pp. 43–5.
c.38 courts (one court held per annum) 1415–22, 1464–9, 1474–8, 1483–5, SROI S1/10/6.1 and 6.2.
4 accounts 1341–2, 1418–19, 1445–6, 1448–9, SROI S1/10/6.6.

Harleston, Suffolk
Medium manor held by Butley priory (Suffolk).
c.55 courts 1415–16, 1420–6, 1433–46, 1450–64, 1469–79, SROB E3/15.17/1.1.

Higham, Suffolk
Small manor held by a succession of different gentry lords: Copinger, *Manors of Suffolk*, volume 6, p. 48.
c.19 courts 1431–47 (one court held per annum), SROI HA246/A2/2.

Holbrook, Suffolk
Medium manor held by a succession of different gentry lords: Copinger, *Manors of Suffolk*, volume 6, pp. 64–5.
c.67 courts 1378–1399, 1463–70, 1473–85, SROI S1/10/9.1 and 9.2.

Holywell, Oxfordshire
Small manor held by Merton College, Oxford.
c.50 courts 1349–66, 1377–89, 1438–62, 1474, 1485–8, 1496, Merton College, Oxford, 4549 to 4559.
c.60 accounts 1372–1473, Merton College, Oxford, 4523 to 4536.

Iken, Suffolk
Medium manor held continuously by a gentry family: Copinger, *Manors of Suffolk*, volume 5, pp. 144–5.
c.135 courts 1349–74, 1377–1497, SROI HD32/293/387, 388, 390, 392, and 395.

Lackford, Suffolk
Medium manor held continuously by a gentry family: Copinger, *Manors of Suffolk*, volume 7, pp. 43–5.
c.44 courts held 1354, 1361–5, 1391–8, 1402–12, 1438, 1454–9, 1462–4, 1467, 1486–7, 1503, 1508, SROB E3/15.12/1.1 to 1.15.
3 accounts 1368–9, 1396–7, 1400–1, SROB E3/15.12/2.1 to 2.3.
4 rentals 1396–7, 1399, 1402, 1487, SROB E3/15.12/3.1 to 3.3, 3.8.

Lidgate, Suffolk
Large manor held by the Beauchamps, Lords Bergavenny: Copinger, *Manors of Suffolk*, volume 3, p. 79.
c.98 courts 1392–7, 1411–40, 1455–90, SROB E3/11/1.1 to 1.5.
1 account 1346–7, TNA SC6/1002/16.

Norton, Suffolk
Medium manor held by a succession of gentry lords: Copinger, *Manors of Suffolk*, volume 1, pp. 353–4.
c.198 courts 1422–1501, SROB 553/1 to 5.
11 accounts 1383 to 1439, SROB 553/21 to 31.

Radclive, Buckinghamshire

Small manor held by a succession of gentry lords until 1379 when it was acquired by New College, Oxford: *VCH Buckinghamshire*, volume 4 , p. 221.
c.20 courts 1384–9, 1418–30, 1464–77, 1499, New College Oxford, 4106, 4107.
c.100 accounts 1378–1495, New College, Oxford, 7087 to 7188.

Runton and Beeston Felbriggs, Norfolk

Two small manors were held by the Felbrigg family (gentry lords); Blomefield, *History of the county of Norfolk*, volume 8, pp. 88–9, 159. The courts were usually held in Runton, and 12 extant courts were held in Beeston-iuxta-Mare, but never in the same year as a court held in Runton. The personnel and business of the Runton and Beeston courts are very similar. This indicates that a single court was held to cover both manors.
c.66 courts 1381–1412, 1417–29, 1452–9, 1490, 1495–1509, NRO WKC 2/166 398 x 7.

Runton Hayes, Norfolk

Small manor held by a succession of gentry lords: Blomefield, *History of the county of Norfolk*, volume 8, p. 160.
c.105 courts 1349–51, 1354–67, 1379–1423, 1429–33, 1438–9, 1447–50, 1460, 1469, 1477, 1480, NRO WKC 2/167 398 x 8.

Staverton, Suffolk

Medium manor held by the earls (dukes, from 1397) of Norfolk: Bailey, *Medieval Suffolk*, p. 17.
c.292 courts 1350–1364, 1367–8, 1374–6, 1400–12 and 1422–1484, SROI HD1538/357/3 to 6. 15 accounts 1268–1307, TNA SC6/1005/7 to 21, and 9 accounts between 1399 and 1474, SROI HD1538/256/2 to 10.

Thorpe Morieux, Suffolk

Small manor held continuously by a gentry family: Copinger, *Manors of Suffolk*, volume 3, pp. 204–5.
c.46 courts 1350, 1359–65, 1372, 1379–80, 1383–4, 1388–91, 1403–12, 1438–54, SROB 1700/1/1 to 4.

Tingewick, Buckinghamshire

Large manor held by Harmondsworth priory until 1391, when it was acquired by New College, Oxford: *VCH Buckinghamshire*, volume 4, pp. 240–50.
c.100 courts 1382–1457, 1477, 1489–1500, New College, Oxford, 4133 to 4139.

Upper Heyford, Oxfordshire

Large manor held by a succession of gentry lords, until its purchase in 1380, then acquisition in 1382, by New College, Oxford: *VCH Oxfordshire*, volume 6 (London, 1959), pp. 197–8.

c.23 courts 1316–18, 1327–9, 1333–4, 1340–7; c.55 courts 1350–80, 1436, 1443, 1463–75, 1485–96, New College, Oxford, 3821 to 3825.

c.23 accounts 1342 to 1396, New College, Oxford, 6272 to 6295.

Walsham, Suffolk

Medium manor held by a succession of different gentry lords: Lock, *Court rolls of Walsham, volume 2*, pp. 10–11.

c.235 courts 1351–4, 1359–1400, 1404, 1407–14, 1423–64, 1467–1500, Lock, *Court rolls of Walsham, volume 2*; SROB HA504/1/10.1 to 10.12; HA504/1/11.1; HA504/1/12.1 to 12.25; HA504/1/13.1 to 13.30; HA504/1/14.1 to 14.13; HA504/1/15.1 to 15.20; HA504/1/16.1 to 16.13; HA504/1/17.1 to 17.22.

25 accounts 1373 to 1455, SROB HA504/3/1 to 15.12.

Walsham Church House, Suffolk

Small manor held by Ixworth priory (Suffolk).

c.32 courts 1409, 1413–14, 1417, 1421, 1424–5, 1429, 1446–7, 1452, 1456–7, 1463, 1468–72, 1476, 1480–6, 1488–93, 1497–9, SROB HA504/1/13.23, and HA504/1/21 to 22.8.

Walsham High Hall, Suffolk

Small manor held by a succession of minor gentry lords until 1379 when it was absorbed within Walsham manor: Lock, *Court rolls of Walsham, volume 2*, p. 12.

c.13 courts 1351–5, 1359, 1365–6, 1371–4, 1379, 1381, Lock, *Court rolls of Walsham, volume 2*.

Weedon Vale, Buckinghamshire

Small manor held by a succession of minor gentry lords, although William Wykeham attempted, but failed, to secure it for New College, Oxford: *VCH Buckinghamshire*, volume 3, p. 365.

c.32 courts 1379, 1386–93, 1397–1403, 1419–23, 1435–41, 1450–4, 1459–60 and 1471, New College, Oxford, 3847 to 3849.

Winston, Suffolk

Medium manor held by the prior and convent of Ely: Bailey, *Medieval Suffolk*, p. 17.

c.260 courts 1350–1484, CUL EDC 7/19/14 to 73.

Withersfield, Suffolk

Small manor held by a succession of gentry lords: Copinger, *Manors of Suffolk*, volume 5, pp. 309–10.

c.7 courts 1388, 1402, 1433, 1462–4, 1486, 1501, SROB E3/15.16/1.1 to 1.3.

Chronology

1348–9 The first great plague epidemic, the Black Death, rages through England

1351 The Statute of Labourers is passed, seeking to cap wages, restrict mobility and promote annual contracts of employment

c.1351 to c.1375 The 'Indian Summer' of the English economy

1360 Treaty of Brétigny confirms English military gains in France and cessation of hostilities

1361–2 Second visitation of plague

1363 Sumptuary laws attempt to regulate consumption patterns, especially through commodity prices and the dress of the lower orders

1369 Third visitation of plague; resumption of war with France

c.1376 to c.1400 The 'Chaucerian Climate Anomaly' contributes to generous harvests and a sustained fall in grain prices

1377 Death of Edward III; accession of Richard II; first Poll Tax

1381 The Peasants' Revolt, centred on London, the Home Counties and East Anglia

1388 Statute of Cambridge refines earlier labour legislation, including provisions to restrict agricultural workers from moving into trades

1399 Capture and deposition of Richard II; accession of Henry IV

1402 Last petition to House of Commons discussing serfdom

1413 Death of Henry IV; accession of Henry V

1415 Henry V's invasion of France

1422 Death of Henry V; accession of Henry VI

1431 Henry VI crowned king of France in Paris

c.1440 to c.1470 The 'Great Slump' of the English economy

1450 Cade's Rebellion

1453 Loss of France

1461 Deposition of Henry VI; accession of Edward IV

1470 Restoration of Henry VI; flight overseas of Edward IV

1471 Restoration of Edward IV; execution of Henry VI

1483 Death of Edward IV; deposition of Edward V; accession of Richard III

1485 Death of Richard III; accession of Henry VII

1509 Death of Henry VII; accession of Henry VIII

1536 Petition to House of Lords to abolish serfdom rejected

Bibliography

Aberth, J., *The Black Death. The Great Mortality of 1348–50* (New York, 2005).

Allen, R.C., *Enclosure and the yeoman. The agricultural development of the south Midlands 1450–1850* (Oxford, 1992).

Aston, T.H., and C.H.E. Philpin, eds., *The Brenner Debate. Agrarian class structure and economic development in pre-industrial Europe* (Cambridge, 1985).

Bailey, M., *A marginal economy? East Anglian Breckland in the later Middle Ages* (Cambridge, 1989).

Bailey, M., 'Blowing up bubbles: some new demographic evidence for the fifteenth century', *Journal of Medieval History*, 15 (1989).

Bailey, M., 'The Prior and Convent of Ely and the management of their manor of Lakenheath', in Franklin and Harper-Bill, eds., *Ecclesiastical studies*.

Bailey, M., 'Rural society', in Horrox, ed., *Fifteenth-century attitudes*.

Bailey, M., ed., *The English manor c.1200 to c.1500* (Manchester, 2002).

Bailey, M., *Medieval Suffolk. An economic and social history 1200 to 1500* (Woodbridge, 2007).

Bailey, M., 'Villeinage in England: a regional case study c.1250–c.1349', *Economic History Review*, 62 (2009).

Bailey, M., 'Was there a seigniorial reaction in England between 1350 and 1381?' (forthcoming).

Bailey, M., and S.H. Rigby, eds., *England in the age of the Black Death. Essays in honour of John Hatcher* (Turnhout, 2012).

van Bavel, B.J.P., and P. Hoppenbrouwers, eds., *Landholding and land transfer in the North Sea area* (Turnhout, 2004).

van Bavel, B.J.P., and P.R. Schofield, eds., *The development of leasehold in north western Europe c.1200–1600* (Turnhout, 2008).

van Bavel, B.J.P., and P.R. Schofield, 'Introduction', in van Bavel and Schofield, eds., *Development of leasehold*.

Beckett, J.V., and M.E. Turner, 'Freehold from copyhold and leasehold: tenurial transition in England between the sixteenth and nineteenth centuries', in van Bavel and Hoppenbrouwers, eds., *Landholding and land transfer*.

Benedictow, O., *The Black Death, 1346–1353. The complete history* (Woodbridge, 2004).

Bennett, J.M., 'Medieval peasant marriage: an examination of marriage licence fines in the *Liber Gersumarum*', in Raftis, ed., *Pathways to medieval peasants*.

Bennett, J.M., 'Writing fornication: medieval leyrwite and its historians', *Transactions of the Royal Historical Society*, sixth series, XIII (2003).

Bloch, M., *Land and work in medieval Europe* (London, 1967).

Bolton, J.L., *The medieval English economy 1150–1500* (London, 1980).

Bonfield, L., and L. Poos, 'The development of deathbed transfers in medieval English manor courts', in Razi and Smith, eds., *Medieval society*.

Bothwell, J., P.J.P. Goldberg and W.M. Ormrod, eds., *The problem of labour in fourteenth-century England* (York, 2000).

Brand, P., and P.R. Hyams, 'Seigneurial control of women's marriage', *Past and Present*, 99 (1983).

Brenner, R., 'Agrarian class structure and economic development in pre-industrial Europe', in Aston and Philpin, eds., *The Brenner Debate*.

Brenner, R., 'The agrarian roots of European capitalism', in Aston and Philpin, eds., *The Brenner Debate*.

Brenner, R., 'Property and progress: where Adam Smith went wrong', in Wickham, ed., *Marxist history-writing*.

Bridbury, A.R., 'The Black Death', *Economic History Review*, 26 (1973).

Bridbury, A.R., *The English economy from Bede to the Reformation* (Woodbridge, 1990).

Britnell, R.H., 'The Pastons and their Norfolk', *Agricultural History Review*, 36 (1988).

Britnell, R.H., 'Tenant farming and tenant farmers: Eastern England', in Miller, ed., *AgHEW, III*.

Britnell, R.H., 'Feudal reaction after the Black Death in the Palatinate of Durham', *Past and Present*, 128 (1990).

Britnell, R.H., *The commercialisation of English society, 1000–1500* (Cambridge, 1993).

Britnell, R.H., ed., *Daily life in the Middle Ages* (Stroud, 1998).

Britnell, R.H., *Britain and Ireland, 1050–1530* (Oxford, 2004).

Britnell, R.H., 'Land and lordship: common themes and regional variations', in Dodds and Britnell, eds., *Agriculture and rural society*.

Britnell, R.H., 'Agriculture, marketing and rural change, 1000–1500', in Broad, ed., *A common agricultural heritage?*

Britnell, R.H., and J. Hatcher, eds., *Progress and problems in medieval England. Essays in honour of Edward Miller* (Cambridge, 1996).

Broad, J., *Transforming English rural society. The Verneys and Claydons 1600–1820* (Cambridge, 2004).

Broad, J., ed., *A common agricultural heritage? Revising French and British rural divergence* (The Agricultural History Review Supplement Series, 5, 2009).

Byrne, J.P., *The Black Death* (Santa Barbara, 2004).

Campbell, B.M.S., 'Population pressure, inheritance and the land market in a fourteenth century peasant community', in Smith, ed., *Land, kinship and life-cycle*.

Campbell, B.M.S., 'Land and people in the Middle Ages, 1066–1500', in Dodgshon and Butlin, eds., *An historical geography of England and Wales*.

Campbell, B.M.S., 'The agrarian problem in the early fourteenth century', *Past and Present*, 188 (2005).

Campbell, B.M.S., 'The Land', in Horrox and Ormrod, *A social history of England 1200–1500*.

Campbell, B.M.S., 'Grain yields on English demesnes after the Black Death', in Bailey and Rigby, eds., *Town and countryside in the age of the Black Death*.

Campbell, B.M.S., and K. Bartley, *England on the eve of the Black Death. An atlas of lay lordship, land and wealth* (Manchester, 2006).

Cantor, N.F., *In the wake of plague: the Black Death and the world it made* (New York, 2001).

Carus-Wilson, E.M., ed., *Essays in economic history*, volume two (London, 1962).

Carus-Wilson, E.M., 'Evidence for industrial growth on some fifteenth-century manors', in Carus-Wilson, ed., *Essays in economic history*, II.

Castor, H., *Blood and Roses. The Paston family and the War of the Roses* (London, 2004).

Cheyney, E.P., 'The disappearance of English serfdom', *English Historical Review*, XV (1900).

Cohn, S.K., *The Black Death Transformed. Disease and culture in early renaissance Europe* (London, 2002).

Copinger, W.A., *The manors of Suffolk*, 7 vols (London and Manchester, 1905–11).

Coss, P.R., 'Age of deference', in Horrox and Ormrod, eds., *Social history*.

Cross, C., D. Loades and J.J. Scarisbrick, eds., *Law and government under the Tudors. Essays presented to Geoffrey Elton* (Cambridge, 1988).

Cunningham, W., *The growth of English industry and commerce* (Cambridge, 1890).

Curry, A., and E. Matthew, eds., *Concepts and patterns of service in the later Middle Ages* (Woodbridge, 2000).

Dahlerup, T., and Ingesman, eds., *New approaches to the history of late medieval and early modern Europe* (Copenhagen, 2009).

Darbyshire, H.S., and G.D. Lumb, eds., *The history of Methley*, Publications of the Thoresby Society, 35 (1934).

Davenport, F.G., 'The decay of villeinage in East Anglia', *Transactions of the Royal Historical Society*, XIV (1900).

Davenport, F.G., *The economic development of a Norfolk manor* (Cambridge, 1906).

Denney, A.H., ed., *The Sibton abbey estates. Select documents 1325–1509*, Suffolk Records Society, volume 2 (1960).

Dewindt, E.B., *Land and people in Holywell-cum-Needingworth* (Toronto, 1972).

Dobson, R.B., ed., *The Peasants' Revolt of 1381* (second edition, Basingstoke, 1983).

Dodds, B., and R.H. Britnell, eds., *Agriculture and rural society after the Black Death* (Hatfield, 2008).

Dodds, B., and C.D. Liddy, eds., *Commercial activity, markets and entrepreneurs in the Middle Ages. Essays in honour of Richard Britnell* (Woodbridge, 2011).

Dodgshon, R.A., and R.A. Butlin, eds., *An historical geography of England and Wales* (second edition, London, 1990).

Douglas, D.C., *The social structure of medieval East Anglia* (Oxford, 1927).

Du Boulay, F.R.H., *The England of Piers Plowman. William Langland and his vision of the fourteenth century* (Woodbridge, 1991).

Du Boulay, F.R.H., and C.M. Barron, eds., *The reign of Richard II: essays in honour of May McKisack* (London, 1971).

Dyer, C., *Lords and peasants in a changing society. The estates of the Bishopric of Worcester 680 to 1540* (Cambridge, 1980).

Dyer, C., 'Peasant holdings in west Midland villages 1400–1540', in Smith, ed., *Land, life cycle*.

Dyer, C., 'The social and economic background to the rural revolt of 1381', in Hilton and Aston, eds., *The English Rising of 1381*.

Dyer, C., *Everyday life in medieval England* (London, 1994).

Dyer, C., *Making a living in the Middle Ages: the people of Britain 850–1520* (London, 2002).

Dyer, C., *An age of transition? Economy and society in the later Middle Ages* (Oxford, 2005).

Dyer, C., 'Villeins, bondsmen, neifs and serfs: new serfdom in England, c.1200–c.1600', in Freedman and Bourin, eds., *Forms of servitude*.

Dyer, C., 'The ineffectiveness of lordship in England 1200–1400', in C. Dyer, P. Coss and C. Wickham, eds., *Rodney Hilton's Middle Ages*.

Dyer, C., 'A Suffolk farmer in the fifteenth century', *Agricultural History Review*, 55 (2007).

Dyer, C., P. Coss and C. Wickham, eds., *Rodney Hilton's Middle Ages: an exploration of historical themes* (Past and Present Supplement, 2007).

Eiden, H., 'Joint action against "bad" lordship: the Peasants' Revolt in Essex and Norfolk', *History*, 83 (1998).

Epstein, S.A., *An economic and social history of later medieval Europe, 1000–1500* (Cambridge, 2009).

Evans, R., 'Merton College's control of the tenants at Thorncroft 1270–1349', in Razi and Smith, *Medieval society*.

Faith, R.J., 'Peasant families and inheritance customs in medieval England', *Agricultural History Review*, 14 (1967).

Faith, R.J., 'Berkshire: the fourteenth and fifteenth centuries', in Harvey, ed., *Peasant land market*.

Faith, R.J., *The English peasantry and the growth of lordship* (Leicester, 1997).

Farmer, D.L., 'Prices and wages 1350–1500', in Miller, ed., *AgHEW, III*.

Field, R.K., 'Migration in the later Middle Ages: the case of some Hampton Lovell villeins', *Midland History*, 8 (1983).

Finberg, H.P.R., *Tavistock abbey* (Cambridge, 1951).

Fisher, M., '"A thing without rights, a mere chattel of their lord". The escape from villeinage of a Suffolk family', *Proceedings of the Suffolk Institute of Archaeology and History*, 42 (2009).

Fox, H.S.A., 'The exploitation of the landless by lords and tenants in early medieval England', in Razi and Smith, eds., *Manor court in medieval England*.

Fox, H.S.A., and O.J. Padel, eds., *The Cornish lands of the Arundells of Lanherne, fourteenth to sixteenth centuries*, Devon and Cornwall Record Society, 41 (2000).

Franklin, M., and C. Harper-Bill, eds., *Ecclesiastical studies in honour of Dorothy M. Owen* (Woodbridge, 1995).

Freedman, P., *The origins of peasant servitude in medieval Catalonia* (Cambridge, 1991).

Freedman, P., *Images of medieval peasants* (Stanford, 1999).

Freedman, P., 'Rural society', in M. Jones, ed., *The new Cambridge medieval history* (Cambridge, 2000).

Freedman, P., and M. Bourin, eds., *Forms of servitude in northern and central Europe. Decline, resistance and expansion* (Turnhout, 2005).

Freedman, P., and M. Bourin, 'Introduction', in Freedman and Bourin, eds., *Forms of servitude.*

French, H.R., and R.W. Hoyle, *The character of English rural society. Earls Colne, 1550–1750* (Manchester, 2007).

Fryde, E.B., 'Peasant rebellion and peasant discontents', in E. Miller, ed., *AgHEW, III.*

Fryde, E.B., *Peasants and landlords in later medieval England c.1380 to c.1525* (Stroud, 1996).

Galbraith, V.H., 'Thoughts about the Peasants' Revolt', in Du Boulay and Barron, eds., *The reign of Richard II.*

Given-Wilson, C., 'The problem of labour in the context of English government, c.1350–1450', in Bothwell, Goldberg and Ormrod, eds., *The problem of labour.*

Given-Wilson, C., 'Service, serfdom and English labour legislation 1350–1500', in Curry and Matthew, eds., *Concepts and patterns of service.*

Goldberg, P.J.P., *Medieval England. A social history 1250–1550* (London, 2004).

Goody, J., J. Thirsk and E.P. Thompson, eds., *Family and inheritance. Rural society in western Europe 1200 to 1800* (Cambridge, 1986).

Gottfried, R.S., *Bury St Edmunds and the urban crisis: 1290–1539* (Princeton, 1982).

Gray, C.M., *Copyhold, equity and the common law* (Cambridge, Mass., 1963).

Gray, H.L., 'The commutation of villein services in England before the Black Death', *English Historical Review*, XXIX (1914).

Gummer, B., *The Scourging Angel. The Black Death in the British Isles* (London, 2009).

Hagen, W.W., 'Village life in east-Elbian Germany and Poland 1400–1800: subjection, self-defence, survival', in Scott, ed., *Peasantries of Europe.*

Hare, J.N., 'The lords and their tenants: conflict and stability in fifteenth-century Wiltshire', in Stapleton, ed., *Conflict and community.*

Hare, J.N., *A prospering society. Wiltshire in the later Middle Ages* (Hatfield, 2011).

Hargreaves, P., 'Seigniorial reaction and peasant responses', *Midland History*, 24 (1999).

Harriss, G., *Shaping the Nation. England 1360 to 1461* (Oxford, 2005).

Harvey, B., *The estates of Westminster abbey in the later Middle Ages* (Oxford, 1977).

Harvey, P.D.A., *A medieval Oxfordshire village. Cuxham 1240 to 1400* (Oxford, 1965).

Harvey, P.D.A., ed., *Manorial records of Cuxham, Oxfordshire, c.1200–1359*, Oxfordshire Record Society, 50 (1976).

Harvey, P.D.A., ed., *The peasant land market in England* (Oxford, 1984).

Harvey, P.D.A., 'Aspects of the peasant land market in medieval England', in. Harvey, ed., *The peasant land market in England*.

Harvey, P.D.A., 'Tenant farming and tenant farmers: the Home Counties', in Miller, ed., *AgHEW, III*.

Harvey, P.D.A., 'The peasant land market in medieval England and beyond', in Razi and Smith, eds., *The medieval manor court*.

Hatcher, J., *Rural economy and society in the Duchy of Cornwall 1300–1500* (Cambridge, 1970).

Hatcher, J., 'English serfdom and villeinage: towards a reassessment', *Past and Present*, 90 (1981).

Hatcher, J., 'The great slump of the mid-fifteenth century', in Britnell and Hatcher, eds., *Progress and problems*.

Hatcher, J., 'England in the aftermath of the Black Death', *Past and Present*, 144 (1994).

Hatcher, J., *The Black Death. An Intimate History* (London, 2007).

Hatcher, J., and M. Bailey, *Modelling the Middle Ages. The theory and practice of England's economic development* (Oxford, 2000).

Hervey, F., ed., *Pinchbeck Register of the abbey of Bury St Edmunds and related documents*, volume 2, (Brighton, 1925).

Highfield, J.R.L., ed., *The early rolls of Merton College, Oxford*, Oxford Historical Society, 18 (1964).

Hilton, R.H., 'Kibworth Harcourt. A Merton College manor in the thirteenth and fourteenth centuries', in Hoskins, ed., *Studies in Leicestershire agrarian history*.

Hilton, R.H., *The English peasantry in the later Middle Ages* (Oxford, 1976).

Hilton, R.H., *Bondmen made free* (London, 1977).

Hilton, R.H., *The decline of serfdom in late-medieval England* (second edition, London, 1983).

Hilton, R.H., *Class conflict and the crisis of feudalism. Essays in medieval social history* (second edition, London, 1990).

Hilton, R.H., 'Feudalism and the origins of capitalism', in Hilton, *Class conflict and the crisis of feudalism*.

Hilton, R.H., and T.S. Aston, eds., *The English Rising of 1381* (Cambridge, 1984).

Holmes, G.A., *The estates of the higher nobility in the fourteenth century* (Cambridge, 1957).

Holt, R., 'Whose were the profits of corn milling? The abbots of Glastonbury and their tenants 1086–1350', *Past and Present*, 116 (1987).

Holt, R., *The mills of medieval England* (Oxford, 1988).

Horrox, R.E., ed., *The Black Death* (Manchester, 1994).

Horrox, R.E., ed., *Fifteenth-century attitudes* (Cambridge, 1995).

Horrox, R.E., and W.M. Ormrod, eds., *A social history of England 1200–1500* (Cambridge, 2006).

Hoskins, W.G., ed., *Studies in Leicestershire agrarian history*, Transactions of the Leicestershire Archaeological Society, 24 (1949).

Howell, C., 'Inheritance customs in the Midlands, 1280–1700, in Goody, Thirsk and Thompson, eds., *Family and inheritance.*

Howell, C., *Land, family and inheritance in transition. Kibworth Harcourt 1280–1700* (Cambridge, 1983).

Hoyle, R.W., 'An ancient and laudable custom. The definition and development of tenant right in north-west England in the sixteenth century', *Past and Present*, 116 (1987).

Hoyle, R.W., 'Monastic leasing before the Dissolution: the evidence of Fountains abbey and Bolton priory', *Yorkshire Archaeological Journal*, 61 (1989).

Hoyle, R.W., 'Tenure and the land market in early modern England: or a late contribution to the Brenner debate', *Economic History Review*, 43 (1990).

Hyams, P.R., *King, lords and peasants in medieval England* (Oxford, 1980).

Hybell, N., *Crisis and change. The concept of crisis in the light of agrarian structural reorganisation in late-medieval England* (Aarhus, 1989).

Jones, A., 'Bedfordshire: the fifteenth century', in Harvey, ed., *Peasant land market.*

Jones, E.D., 'Going round in circles: some new evidence for population in the later Middle Ages', *Journal of Medieval History*, 15 (1989).

Jones, E.D., 'The medieval leyrwite: a historical note upon fornication', *English Historical Review*, 107 (1992).

Kanaza, J., 'Villein rents in thirteenth-century England: an analysis of the Hundred Rolls of 1279–80', *Economic History Review*, 55 (2002).

Kaye, J.M., *Medieval English conveyances* (Cambridge, 2009).

Kelly, J., *The great mortality. An intimate history of the Black Death* (London, 2005).

King, E., *England 1175–1425* (London, 1979).

King, E., 'Tenant farming and tenant farmers: the East Midlands', in Miller, ed., *AgHEW, III.*

Kitsikopoulos, H., ed., *Agrarian change and crisis in Europe, 1200–1500* (Abingdon, 2012).

Kitsikopoulos, H., 'England', in Kitsikopoulos, ed., *Agrarian change and crisis.*

Kitsikopoulos, H., 'Epilogue', in Kitsikopoulos, ed., *Agrarian change and crisis.*

Klima, A., 'Agrarian class structure and economic development in pre-industrial Bohemia', in Aston and Philpin, eds., *The Brenner Debate.*

Kosminsky, E.A., *Studies in the agrarian history of England in the thirteenth century* (Oxford, 1956).

Kula, W., *An economic theory of the feudal system* (London, 1976).

Langdon, J., 'Lordship and peasant consumerism in the milling industry of early fourteenth-century England', *Past and Present*, 145 (1994).

Langdon, J., *Mills in the medieval economy. England, 1300–1540* (Oxford, 2004).

Langton, J., 'The historical geography of European peasantries', in Scott, ed., *Peasantries of Europe.*

Larson, P.L., *Conflict and compromise in the late medieval countryside. Lords and peasants in Durham, 1349–1400* (London, 2006).

Larson, P.L., 'Peasant opportunities in rural Durham: land, vills and mills, 1400–

1500', in Dodds and Liddy, eds., *Commercial activity, markets and entrepreneurs.*

Latham, R.E., 'Minor enigmas from medieval records', *English Historical Review*, 76 (1961).

Levett, A.E., *Studies in manorial history* (Oxford, 1938).

Lobel, M.D., 'The 1327 rising at Bury St Edmunds and the subsequent trial', *Proceedings of the Suffolk Institute of Archaeology and History*, 21 (1933).

Lock, R., 'The Black Death in Walsham-le-Willows', *Proceedings of the Suffolk Institute of Archaeology and History*, 37 (1992).

Lock, R., *The court rolls of Walsham-le-Willows, volume 1, 1303 to 1350*, Suffolk Records Society, 41 (1998).

Lock, R., *The court rolls of Walsham-le-Willows, volume 2, 1350 to 1396*, Suffolk Records Society, 45 (2002).

Lomas, R.A., *Northeast England in the Middle Ages* (Edinburgh, 1992).

Lomas, R.A., 'A priory and its tenants', in Britnell, ed., *Daily life in the Middle Ages.*

Lomas, T., 'South-east Durham: the late fourteenth and fifteenth centuries', in Harvey, ed., *The peasant land market in England.*

MacCulloch, D., 'Bondmen and the Tudors', in Cross, Loades and Scarisbrick, eds., *Law and government under the Tudors.*

McGribbon Smith, E., 'Court rolls as evidence for village society. Sutton-in-the-Isle in the fourteenth century', in Bailey and Rigby, eds., *England in the age of the Black Death.*

McIntosh, M.K., *Controlling misbehaviour in England, 1370–1600* (Cambridge, 1998).

Maddern, P.C., *Violence and social order. East Anglia 1422–1442* (Oxford, 1992).

Martin, J.E., *Feudalism to capitalism. Peasant and landlord in English agrarian development* (London, 1986).

Mate, M.E., 'Agrarian economy after the Black Death: the manors of Canterbury Cathedral priory 1348–91', *Economic History Review*, 37 (1984).

Mate, M.E., 'Tenant farming and tenant farmers: Kent and Sussex', in Miller, ed., *AgHEW, III.*

Mate, M.E., 'The east Sussex land market and agrarian class structure in the later Middle Ages', *Past and Present*, 139 (1993).

Mate, M.E., *Daughters, wives and widows. Women in Sussex 1350–1535* (Woodbridge, 1998).

Mate, M.E., *Women in medieval English society* (Cambridge, 1999).

Mate, M.E., *Trade and economic developments 1450–1550. The experience of Kent, Surrey and Sussex* (Woodbridge, 2006).

Miller, E., ed., *The Agrarian History of England and Wales, volume III: 1348–1500* (Cambridge, 1991).

Miller, E., 'Tenant farming and tenant farmers: the Southern Counties', in Miller, ed., *AgHEW, III.*

Miller, E., 'Tenant farming and tenant farmers: Yorkshire and Lancashire', in *AgHEW, III.*

Miller, E., and J. Hatcher, *Medieval England: rural society and economic change* (London, 1978).

Milson, S.F.C., *Historical foundations of the common law* (London, 1969).

Morris, M., *The Bigod earls of Norfolk in the thirteenth century* (Woodbridge, 2005).

Mullan, J., 'Accumulation and polarization in two bailiwicks of the Winchester bishopric estates, 1350–1410: regional similarities and contrasts', in Dodds and Britnell, eds., *Agriculture and rural society*.

Mullan, J., and R.H. Britnell, *Land and family. Trends and local variations in the peasant land market on the Winchester bishopric estates, 1263–1415* (Hatfield, 2010).

Muller, M., 'Peasant land and developments in leasing in late medieval England', in van Bavel and Schofield, eds., *Development of leasehold*.

Munro, J., 'Before and after the Black Death: money prices, and wages in fourteenth century England', in Dahlerup and Ingesman, eds., *New approaches to the history of late medieval and early modern Europe*.

Musson, A., 'New labour laws, new remedies? Legal reaction to the Black Death crisis', in Saul, ed., *Fourteenth Century England* I.

Nightingale, P., 'Monetary contraction and mercantile credit in late medieval England', *Economic History Review*, 43 (1990).

North, T., 'Legerwite in the thirteenth and fourteenth centuries', *Past and Present*, III (1986).

Orent, W., *The Plague, the mysterious past and terrifying future* (New York, 2004).

Ormrod, W.M., and P. Lindley, eds., *The Black Death in England* (Stamford, 1996).

Ormrod, W.M., 'The politics of pestilence', in Ormrod and Lindley, eds., *The Black Death in England*.

Ormrod, W.M., ed., *Fourteenth Century England*, III (Woodbridge, 2004).

Page, F.M., *The estates of Crowland abbey* (Cambridge, 1934).

Page, M., 'William Wykeham and the management of the Winchester estate, 1366–1404', in Ormrod, ed., *Fourteenth Century England*, III.

Page, T.W., 'The end of villeinage in England', *American Economic Association*, 99 (1900).

Palmer, R.C., *English law in the age of the Black Death, 1341–1381: a transformation of governance and law* (Chapel Hill, 1993).

Pearson, C.H., *English history in the fourteenth century* (London, 1876).

Pelteret, D.A.E., *Slavery in early medieval England* (Woodbridge, 1995).

Penn, S.A.C., and C. Dyer, 'Wages and earnings in late medieval England: evidence from the enforcement of the labour laws', *Economic History Review*, 43 (1990).

Pollard, A.J., *Late medieval England 1399–1509* (Harlow, 2005).

Pollock, F., and F.W. Maitland, *History of English Law*, volume II (Cambridge, 1963).

Poos, L.R., R.M. Smith and Z. Razi, 'The population history of medieval

English villages: a debate on the use of manor court rolls', in Razi and Smith, eds., *The medieval manor court*.

Postan, M., ed., *Cambridge economic history of Europe, volume I: the agrarian life of the Middle Ages* (Cambridge, 1966).

Postan, M., 'Agrarian society in its prime: part 7, England', in Postan, ed., *Cambridge economic history of Europe, volume I*.

Postan, M., *The medieval economy and society* (London, 1972).

Postan, M., and J. Hatcher, 'Population and class relations in feudal society', in Aston and Philpin, eds., *The Brenner debate*.

Powell, E., *The rising in East Anglia in 1381* (Cambridge, 1896).

Putnam, B.H., *The enforcement of the Statutes of Labourers during the first decade after the Black Death* (New York, 1908).

Raftis, J.A., *The estates of Ramsey abbey* (Toronto, 1957) .

Raftis, J.A., *Tenure and mobility. Studies in the social history of the medieval English village* (Toronto, 1964).

Raftis, J.A., ed., *Pathways to medieval peasants* (Toronto, 1981).

Raftis, J.A., 'Peasants and the collapse of the manorial economy on some Ramsey abbey estates', in Britnell and Hatcher, eds., *Progress and problems in medieval England*.

Razi, Z., *Life, marriage and death in a medieval parish. Economy, society, and demography in Halesowen 1270–1400* (Cambridge, 1980).

Razi, Z. 'The myth of the immutable English family', *Past and Present*, 140 (1993).

Razi, Z., 'Serfdom and freedom in medieval England: a reply to the revisionists', in Dyer, Coss and Wickham, eds., *Rodney Hilton's Middle Ages*.

Razi. Z., and R.M. Smith, eds., *Medieval society and the manor court* (Oxford, 1996).

Rigby, S.H., *English society in the late Middle Ages. Class, status and gender* (Basingstoke, 1995).

Rigby, S.H., 'Historical causation: is one thing more important than another?', *History*, 259 (1995).

Rigby, S.H., 'Serfdom', in *The Oxford Encyclopaedia of Economic History*, volume 4 (Oxford, 2003).

Rogers, J.E.T., *A history of agriculture and prices in England*, volume I (London, 1866).

Ross, J., *John de Vere, thirteenth earl of Oxford 1442–1513. 'The foremost man of the kingdom'* (Woodbridge, 2011).

Saul, N., ed., *Fourteenth Century England*, I (Woodbridge, 2000).

Savine, A., 'Copyhold cases in the early Chancery proceedings', *English Historical Review*, 17 (1902).

Savine, A., 'Bondmen under the Tudors', *Transactions of the Royal Historical Society*, XVII (1903).

Scammell, J., 'Freedom and marriage in England', *Economic History Review*, 27 (1974).

Schofield, P.R., 'Tenurial developments and the availability of customary land in a later medieval community', *Economic History Review*, 49 (1996).

Schofield, P.R., '*Extranei* and the market for customary land on a Westminster abbey manor', *Agricultural History Review*, 49 (2001).

Schofield, P.R., *Peasant and community in medieval England* (Basingstoke, 2002).

Schofield, P.R., 'Lordship and the peasant economy, 1250–1400: Robert Kyng and the Abbot of Bury St Edmunds', in Dyer, Coss and Wickham, eds., *Rodney Hilton's Middle Ages*.

Scott, T., ed., *The peasantries of Europe from the fourteenth to the eighteenth centuries* (London, 1998).

Searle, E., *Lordship and community. Battle abbey and its banlieu 1066–1538* (Toronto, 1974).

Searle, E., 'Freedom and marriage in medieval England: an alternative hypothesis', *Economic History Review*, 29 (1976).

Searle, E., 'Seigniorial control of women's marriage: the antecedents and function of merchet in England', *Past and Present*, 82 (1979).

Searle, E., 'A rejoinder', *Past and Present*, 99 (1983).

Simpson, A.B., *An introduction to the history of land law* (Oxford, 1961).

Smith, R.M., 'Some thoughts on hereditary and proprietary rights in land under customary law in thirteenth- and early fourteenth-century England', *Law and History Review*, 1 (1983).

Smith, R.M., ed., *Land, kinship and life-cycle* (Cambridge, 1984).

Smith, R.M., 'Some issues concerning families and their property in rural England 1250–1800', in Smith, ed., *Land, kinship and life-cycle*.

Smith, R.M., 'The English peasantry 1250–1600', in Scott, ed., *The peasantries of Europe*.

Stapleton, B., ed., *Conflict and community in southern England* (Stroud, 1992).

Statham, M., *The book of Bury St Edmunds* (Buckingham, 1988).

Stone, D., 'The productivity of customary and hired labour: evidence from Wisbech Barton in the fourteenth century', *Economic History Review*, 50 (1997).

Stone, D., *Decision-making in medieval agriculture* (Oxford, 2005).

Thomson, J.A.F., *The transformation of medieval England 1370–1529* (London, 1983).

Titow, J., 'Lost rents, vacant holdings and the contraction of peasant cultivation after the Black Death', *Agricultural History Review*, 42 (1994).

Tomkins, M., 'Park', in (no editor) *The Peasants' Revolt in Hertfordshire 1381* (Hertford, 1981).

Tompkins, M., 'Peasant society in a Midlands manor, Great Horwood 1400 to 1600' (PhD thesis, University of Leicester, 2006).

Tuck, R.A., 'Tenant farming and tenant farmers: the Northern Borders', in Miller, ed., *AgHEW, III.*

Vinogradoff, P., *Villeinage in England* (Oxford, 1892).

Virgoe, R.A., 'The murder of James Andrew: Suffolk faction in the 1430s', *Proceedings of the Suffolk Institute of Archaeology and History*, 34 (1980).

Watts, J., *Henry VI and the Politics of Kingship* (Cambridge, 1996).

Wells-Furby, B., *The Berkeley estate 1281–1417. Its economy and development*, The Bristol and Gloucestershire Archaeological Society (2012).

Whittle, J., 'Individualism and the family-land bond: A reassessment of land transfer patterns among the English peasantry c.1270–1580', *Past and Present*, 160 (1998).

Whittle, J., *The development of agrarian capitalism. Land and labour in Norfolk 1440–1580* (Oxford, 2000).

Whittle, J., 'Leasehold tenure in England c.1200–1600: its form and incidence', in van Bavel and Schofield, eds., *Development of leasehold*.

Whittle, J., and M. Yates, '*Pays reel or pays legal*: contrasting patterns of land tenure and social structure in eastern Norfolk and western Berkshire, 1450–1600', *Agricultural History Review*, 48 (2000).

Whittle, J., and S.H. Rigby, 'England: popular politics and social conflict', in Horrox and Ormrod, eds., *Social history*.

Wickham, C., ed., *Marxist history-writing for the twenty-first century* (Oxford, 2007).

Wickham, C., 'Memories of underdevelopment: what has Marxism done for medieval history, and what can it still do?', in Wickham, ed., *Marxist history-writing*.

Wood, G.A., 'Field arrangements in the west Riding of Yorkshire in the high Middle Ages' (PhD thesis, University of Leeds, 2003).

Wood, G.A., M. Purvis, and B. Harrison, 'Irregular field systems and patterns of settlement in western Yorkshire', in T. Unwin and T. Spek, eds., *European landscapes: from mountain to sea* (London, 2003).

Yates, M., *Town and countryside in western Berkshire, c.1327 to c.1600. Social and economic change* (Woodbridge, 2007).

Index

Printed and bound by CPI Group (UK) Ltd, Croydon, CR0 4YY

16/04/2025

14658569-0001